AF600588

BRIDGING EAST AND WEST

Ol'ha Kobylians'ka, Ukraine's Pioneering Modernist

YULIYA V. LADYGINA

Bridging East and West

Ol'ha Kobylians'ka, Ukraine's Pioneering Modernist

UNIVERSITY OF TORONTO PRESS
Toronto Buffalo London

Toronto Buffalo London
utorontopress.com

ISBN 978-1-4426-3077-2 (cloth)

Library and Archives Canada Cataloguing in Publication

Title: Bridging East and West : Ol'ha Kobylians'ka, Ukraine's pioneering modernist / Yuliya V. Ladygina.
Names: Ladygina, Yuliya V., author.
Description: Includes bibliographical references and index.
Identifiers: Canadiana 20190113006 | ISBN 9781442630772 (hardcover)
Subjects: LCSH: Kobylians'ka, Ol'ha, 1863–1942 – Criticism and interpretation. | LCSH: Ukrainian fiction – 20th century – History and criticism. | LCSH: Ukrainian fiction – Women authors – History and criticism.
Classification: LCC PG3948.K552 L33 2019 | DDC 891.7/932—dc23

This publication was made possible by the financial support of the Shevchenko Scientific Society, USA from the George Kusiw Fund.

University of Toronto Press acknowledges the financial assistance to its publishing program of the Canada Council for the Arts and the Ontario Arts Council, an agency of the Government of Ontario.

Canada Council for the Arts
Conseil des Arts du Canada

Funded by the Government of Canada
Financé par le gouvernement du Canada
Canada

To the memory of my father, Volodymyr Ladygin, and for the new generation of the Ladygin family: Dasia, Jimmy, and Liza

Contents

Illustrations

All illustrations are from the archives and manuscripts collection at Chernivtsi State O. Iu. Kobylians'ka Literary and Memorial House-Museum (KLMHM) and are reproduced by the museum's permission.

Acknowledgments

This book is the product of conversations with many friends and colleagues, too numerous to list. I would, however, like to thank Amelia Glaser, Steven Cassedy, William Arctander O'Brien, Marko Pavlyshyn, Halyna Hryn, Oleh Ilnytzkyj, Julie Cassiday, Richard Ratzlaff, Margaret Hogan, Andrew Moser, Adam Dahl, Derek Ettensohn, Jeffrey Thompson, Donald Rung, James Ross Macdonald, Maha Jafri, Julian Ledford, Aymeric Glacet, and several anonymous reviewers who read parts of the book in early drafts and offered helpful advice. A number of scholars provided information and suggested sources, among them Alain J.-J. Cohen, George Grabowicz, Lyubomyr Hajda, Myroslav Shkandrij, Olga Andriewsky, Olga Bertelsen, Vitalii Mykhailovs'ky, Vladyslav Grynevych, Andreas Umland, and Volodymyr Vozniuk. Several archivists and librarians shared their expertise with me and helped to locate materials. I am especially grateful to Olha Aleksic of the Harvard Ukrainian Research Institute, Alla Dyba of the T.H. Shevchenko Institute of Literature in Kyiv, and Iuliia Mykosianchyk of the Ol'ha Kobylians'ka Memorial House-Museum in Chernivtsi. I am also grateful to Oleh Panchuk, who allowed me to use his family's archival materials, much of which remain closed to scholars.

Acknowledgment is due to *East/West: Journal of Ukrainian Studies* for permission to use an earlier version of "Ol'ha Kobylians'ka's Literary Response to the First World War," to *Harvard Ukrainian Studies* for permission to use "The Early German Text of Ol'ha Kobylians'ka's First Novel *The Princess*: Transcription, Translation, Analysis," and to the Chernivtsi State O. Iu. Kobylians'ka Literary and Memorial House-Museum for their permission to use images. I also gratefully acknowledge the Office of the Dean of Graduate Studies at the University of California in San Diego for providing financial support that enabled me to conduct initial archival research in Ukraine, the

Ukrainian Research Institute of Harvard University for granting me the Jaroslaw and Nadia Mihaychuk Research Fellowship, which led to an acceleration of this project, and the Office of the Dean at Sewanee: The University of the South for a generous research grant that facilitated the project's completion.

Special thanks go to my parents, Volodymyr and Liudmyla Ladygin, my husband, James Woong Shin, and my son, Jimmy, who have always offered the strongest support and encouragement, along with a large measure of inspiration.

Abbreviations for Standard Editions

Roman and Arabic numerals refer to volume and page numbers of Maksym Komyshanchenko's historical-critical edition *Ol'ha Kobylians'ka: Tvory v piaty tomakh.* Kyiv: Derzhavne vydavnytstvo khudozhn'oi literatury, 1962–3.

I = *Ol'ha Kobylians'ka: Tvory v piaty tomakh.* Vol. 1. 1962. Edited by Maksym Komyshanchenko. Kyiv: Derzhavne vydavnytstvo khudozhn'oi literatury.
II = *Ol'ha Kobylians'ka: Tvory v piaty tomakh.* Vol. 2. 1962. Edited by Maksym Komyshanchenko. Kyiv: Derzhavne vydavnytstvo khudozhn'oi literature.
III = *Ol'ha Kobylians'ka: Tvory v piaty tomakh.* Vol. 3. 1963. Edited by Maksym Komyshanchenko. Kyiv: Derzhavne vydavnytstvo khudozhn'oi literatury.
IV = *Ol'ha Kobylians'ka: Tvory v piaty tomakh.* Vol. 4. 1963. Edited by Maksym Komyshanchenko. Kyiv: Derzhavne vydavnytstvo khudozhn'oi literatury.
V = *Ol'ha Kobylians'ka: Tvory v piaty tomakh.* Vol. 5. 1963. Edited by Maksym Komyshanchenko. Kyiv: Derzhavne vydavnytstvo khudozhn'oi literatury.

Arabic numerals refer to volume and page numbers of Oleh Babyshkin's edition *Ol'ha Kobylians'ka: Tvory v tr'okh tomakh* (Kyiv: Derzhavne vydavnytstvo khudozhn'oi literatury, 1956).

1 = *Ol'ha Kobylians'ka: Tvory v tr'okh tomakh*. Vol. 1. 1956. Edited by Oleh Babyshkin. Kyiv: Derzhavne vydavnytstvo khudozhn'oi literatury.
2 = *Ol'ha Kobylians'ka: Tvory v tr'okh tomakh*. Vol. 2. 1956. Edited by Oleh Babyshkin. Kyiv: Derzhavne vydavnytstvo khudozhn'oi literatury.
3 = *Ol'ha Kobylians'ka: Tvory v tr'okh tomakh*. Vol. 3. 1956. Edited by Oleh Babyshkin. Kyiv: Derzhavne vydavnytstvo khudozhn'oi literatury.

BRIDGING EAST AND WEST

Figure 1. Ol'ha Kobylians'ka. Chernivtsi, 1896

Introduction

At the turn of the twentieth century, Central European intellectuals, particularly those from non-dominant ethnic groups, felt sharp pressure to navigate multiple and often rival cultural, social, and political projects. Caught between the bourgeois West and the agrarian East, these intellectuals experienced every day the confrontation of progress and traditionalism, of democracy and monarchy, of religion and secularism, of multiculturalism and ethnocentrism, of capitalism and feudal economy. The case of the Ukrainian fin-de-siècle and interwar intellectuals particularly stands out because of Ukraine's exceptional geopolitical circumstances. In the nineteenth century, Ukraine, literally a borderland, was split between Austria-Hungary and Russia, and in the mid-1910s, when Europe erupted in war, the region became a main battlefield. Ukraine thus became entangled in critical historical events that were to define the course of twentieth-century history in the West. At that volatile and uncertain historical moment, Ukraine hosted tensions among diverse mass movements – monarchism, nationalism, socialism, Marxism, Bolshevism, and fascism, among others. The complex, intense relationships between individuals and this array of mass ideologies would come to define Ukrainian identity. The fact that Ukrainians were one of Europe's few ethnic groups to envision themselves as a nation but who failed to assert their national statehood in the aftermath of the First World War (Ukraine's territory was split among Russia, Poland, Czechoslovakia, and Romania) might be a logical outcome of the irresolute, disintegrated, and overly confused nature of Ukraine's intellectual and political elite at the turn of the twentieth century.

Of this generation of Ukrainian intellectuals and remarkable talents, Ol'ha Kobylians'ka (see figure 1) is an emblematic figure whose writings crystalize the contradictions of her times in their most exact form. Having completed only four years of elementary school in the

Habsburg province of Bukovyna, she became one of the leading and vitally important Ukrainian novelists of her time, famous for introducing into contemporary Ukrainian cultural debates progressive Western ideas such as social Darwinism, feminism, elitism, irrationalism, and Nietzsche's thought. Educated predominantly in German with minimal Ukrainian, Kobylians'ka succeeded as an innovative and sophisticated Ukrainian writer and was recognized as a founder of Ukrainian literary modernism. Initially grounded in the Western European culture of the turn of the century, she consciously chose to devote her life to the development of Ukrainian culture, which at the time was considered marginal, rural, and second-rate. Ironically, although it is hard to exaggerate the mass of words – scholarly and critical, panegyric and polemical, propagandistic and ideological – that has been devoted to Kobylians'ka and her work, her peculiar reception of the diverse cultural and social movements that penetrated the Ukrainian intellectual discourse at the turn of the twentieth century has been acknowledged only in a preliminary way in past criticism.

This lack of critical attention can be explained in part by the conflicted initial reception of Kobylians'ka's work, which has served to obscure the writer's contributions to the intellectual discourse of her time and to entangle her life and work in an intricate web of biographical and literary myths. In the 1890s and the 1900s, when Kobylians'ka first published her major works, the Ukrainian intellectual climate was shaped by a fervent polemic between the dominant populist model, which had developed in the nineteenth century along with Ukrainian positivist thought and the realist literature of the written popular Ukrainian language, and the emerging modernist aesthetic conviction that explicitly rejected the ideology of Ukrainian populism and its glorification of the uneducated Ukrainian peasant masses. Consequently, two opposing strands in Ukrainian literary scholarship formed the early reception of Kobylians'ka's fiction in the first decades of the twentieth century. Modernist critics, including Lesia Ukrainka, Mykola Ievshan, Luka Lutsiv, Ostap Luts'kyi, and Hnat Khotkevych, elaborated mostly on Kobylians'ka's thematic and aesthetic innovations, rightly recognizing her as a pioneer of Ukrainian intellectual prose and a psychological writer of vertiginous depth. Populist critics – particularly Nataliia Kobryns'ka, Ivan Franko, Mykhailo Hrushevs'kyi, and Serhii Iefremov – emphasized, in turn, Kobylians'ka's genuine tribute to the realist canon, either overlooking the complexity of her artistic and philosophical thought or reproaching her for excessive aestheticism and unconcealed dependence on Western culture. Eventually, the populists won the cultural debate of the Ukrainian fin de siècle and canonized

Kobylians'ka as an advocate of the Ukrainian common person and a devoted student of the culture of the Ukrainian peasantry. As a result, the complexity of Kobylians'ka's dialogue with the multiplicity of aesthetic, social, and political ideologies that sprang up in Europe at the turn of the twentieth century, and her audacious fusion of literature, philosophy, politics, and science, which she, like many other European intellectuals of her time, strove to present as a synthesized totality, have been silenced and thus never properly researched.

Despite its obvious shortcomings, the populist canon has proved to be long lasting, giving both the Western diaspora myth and the Soviet myth of Kobylians'ka their defining contours. Although several Western scholars, especially Anna-Halja Horbatsch, reanimated the populist image of Kobylians'ka with vital historical and critical discoveries that actually contested the populist canon, they remained curiously caught up in it, dwelling on Kobylians'ka's dedication to the advancement of Ukrainian culture and the all-around free development of the Ukrainian people. The post-war Ukrainian émigré scholars in the West knew exactly what their new émigré readership wanted and gave them a Kobylians'ka they could proudly call "a true Ukrainian" – a liberal and devoted patriot committed to Ukraine's aspirations for cultural and political independence. In the Soviet context, the populist canonization proved to be both enduring and beneficial. Not only did it assure the survival of Kobylians'ka's works and archival materials during the Soviet period, but it also allowed for extensive research into her life and works. The three most representative works – Oleh Babyshkin's *Ol'ha Kobylians'ka: Narys pro zhyttia i tvorchist'* (*Ol'ha Kobylians'ka: An Essay about Life and Work,* 1963), Nykyfor Tomashuk's *Ol'ha Kobylians'ka: Zhyttia i tvorchist'* (*Ol'ha Kobylians'ka: Life and Work,* 1969), and Fedir Pohrebennyk's provocative edition of Kobylians'ka's intimate diaries of the 1880s and the early 1890s, *Slova zvorushenoho sertsia* (*Words of the Troubled Heart*, 1982) – made significant contributions to the discussion of Kobylians'ka's artistic and philosophical complexity. At the same time, the three scholars shared an obvious defect: all three clung almost desperately to the use of fictionalized biographies and several highly ambiguous proclamations in support of the Soviet Union, attributed by the Soviet authorities to Kobylians'ka, to legitimize her belonging to the pantheon of Ukrainian writers of the Soviet people.

With the fall of the Soviet Union, many factual errors and critical shortcomings in Kobylians'ka's scholarship were promptly exposed, but the post-Soviet quest to reassess, or better recreate, the canon of Ukrainian literature seems to have hindered rather than promoted the thorough reassessment of Kobylians'ka's work and its long-needed contextualization in the broader European intellectual setting of her time. Although substantial progress has been made over the past twenty years in reconstructing her literary record and developing new analytical approaches and methodologies, the majority of contemporary scholars, particularly those in Ukraine, tend to manipulate textual and historical materials to adjust them to their own cultural and ideological projects. For example, the recent well overdue focus on feminist and homoerotic themes in Kobylians'ka's early fiction and renewed interest in her personal life, above all in her romantic affairs, distracted contemporary scholars from re-examining in depth the particularities of Kobylians'ka's intellectual concerns and their complex evolution in the interwar period. Post-Soviet critics also tend to limit their discussions to either selected periods in Kobylians'ka's creative career or specific themes, such as feminism, populism, modernism, social Darwinism, or Nietzscheanism, and often treat only cursorily the larger philosophical fabric of the writer's complete oeuvre and its tribute not only to fin-de-siècle but also to interwar European intellectual history.

Therefore, building on a number of recent studies on Kobylians'ka's contributions to the Ukrainian intellectual discourse of her time,[1] this book offers a new insight into Kobylians'ka's creative dialogue with contemporaneous social, political, philosophical, and cultural discourses by situating it in a broader turn-of-the-century European intellectual context. In other words, this book examines a series of philosophical conflicts and syntheses crucial to the writer's work: between a conservative view of humans constrained by nature and a more progressive belief in the possibility of creating a new human; between a deep interest in science, especially in terms of understanding human nature, and an anti-positivist exploration of the unlimited possibilities of the will; and finally between the faith and service of Christianity and the heroism of classical thought. In drawing attention to these intellectual commitments, I elaborate on the philosophical complexities and aesthetic particularities of Ukraine's pioneering modernist writer and thereby refine the discussion about the relationship between the fin-de-siècle and interwar generations of European intellectuals, women in particular, and the various aesthetic and ideological practices collected under the name of modernism.

To uncover the little-known aspects of Kobylians'ka's creative works, to gauge the depth of her intellectual thought, and to highlight the underlying structural affinities between her peculiar philosophical syntheses and diverse systems of thought and ideologies of her time, I closely examine the intersection among three main aspects of Kobylians'ka's work: aesthetics, philosophy, and ideology. For my assessment,

I combine a social and historical contextualization of Kobylians'ka's life and work with close readings of her major works, including *Liudyna* (*A Human Being*, 1894), *Tsarivna* (*The Princess*, 1896), *Zemlia* (*The Earth*, 1902), *Nioba* (*Niobe*, 1907), *Cherez kladku* (*Over the Bridge*, 1913), *Za sytuatsiiamy* (*After Situations*, 1913), *Apostol cherni* (*Apostle of the Rabble*, 1936), and a few dozen representative short stories. To that end, I use recovered original manuscripts, publications, and critical reviews together with Kobylians'ka's notes, diaries, autobiographies, and personal correspondence, written in German, Ukrainian, Russian, and Polish. Most of these biographical and literary materials are well established, but some documents related to the post-1914 period have never been published or have been long forgotten since their original publications.

While focusing on those qualities of Kobylians'ka's personality, her thinking, and her writing that are least known, poorly researched, most problematic, and most surprising, I have also sought to introduce her works to English-language readers for whom her writing might be unfamiliar. Hardly anything has been written about Kobylians'ka in English, and only a dozen of her pre-1914 short stories and one novel *U nediliu rano zillia kopala* (*On Sunday Morning She Gathered Herbs*, 1909) currently exist in English translations. Therefore, this book addresses a number of basic questions: Who was Kobylians'ka? Whom did she know? What did she read? What was the nature of her relationship with leading Ukrainian cultural and political figures? Who were her supporters, and who were her rivals? About what did she write, both as subject and as theme? How did she write? What philosophical and intellectual tenets underline her creative works? How did they evolve over time? What is their relevance in the contexts of Central European cultures and of Europe more broadly? This book, however, is neither an exhaustive biographical account nor a complete survey of Kobylians'ka's writings. To the contrary, it is focused exclusively on capturing the most distinct stages in the formation of Kobylians'ka's identity, her aesthetic taste, her social and political consciousness, and in examining how the writer, whatever else her concerns might have been, responded to and interacted with the diverse trends in cultural, social, and political discourses of her time.

The book is organized chronologically into six chapters, each concentrating on one of the major periods in Kobylians'ka's creative career. Chapter 1, "The Art of Feminist Compromise," explores Kobylians'ka's early life and her first attempts at writing and addresses several canonical myths about her development as a Ukrainian national writer. Kobylians'ka's problematic friendship with Nataliia Kobryns'ka, the leading theoretician of feminism in Ukraine, is of particular interest.

My analysis of the personal and professional rivalry between the two writers proves that, contrary to common belief, Kobryns'ka's intervention held back rather than promoted Kobylians'ka's literary career. This chapter also positions Kobylians'ka's personal conflict with Kobryns'ka as an initial instigator of Kobylians'ka's anti-socialist and anti-populist views, which were gradually solidified by her avid readings of John Stuart Mill, Friedrich Nietzsche, Darwinist theoreticians, and Russian nineteenth-century realists such as Ivan Turgenev, Fyodor Dostoevsky, Leo Tolstoy, and Anton Chekhov. Further, my reading of Kobylians'ka's first major novel, *A Human Being*, demonstrates that the writer propagated a personal intellectual evolution and recognized knowledge and individual moral self-improvement as the only ways to achieve women's liberation. At the same time, the chapter shows that Kobylians'ka criticized the socialist ideal of self-sufficient emancipationist and advocated instead a modernized yet somewhat traditional role for women within the family – as intelligent mothers, supportive spouses, and educated caregivers. The chapter wraps up with a reflection on Kobylians'ka's provocative fusion of highly unconventional ideas in terms of their intellectual and theoretical vigour with a politically conservative and even reactionary determination to rethink, reclaim, and reassert the value of tradition. The new reading of Kobylians'ka's early works and their contextualization in the broader comparative cross-cultural setting positions the writer's intellectual model as an important contribution to women's intellectual activism of late nineteenth-century Europe.

Chapter 2, "New Woman, New Myth," elaborates on Kobylians'ka's reception of Nietzsche, her vision of a New Ukrainian Woman, and her inception of what could be viewed as her alternative program for Ukraine's national liberation, which she elaborated in her 1896 novel *The Princess*. A close reading of the novel alongside Kobylians'ka's other fictional and non-fictional writings of the mid-1890s shows that *The Princess* is not only an important record of Kobylians'ka's reflections on the Ukrainian nation-building effort but also a significant landmark in Ukrainian philosophical and critical thought. The chapter's main focus is on Kobylians'ka's original fusion of Nietzsche's philosophy with Russian intellectual thought of the nineteenth century, which constitutes the premise of the writer's propagation of individual emancipation and heightened cultural awareness of national distinctiveness among the Ukrainian intellectual elite as the principal road to Ukraine's national revival. While elaborating primarily on the philosophical underpinnings of Kobylians'ka's conception of Ukraine's cultural and political regeneration, the chapter also reminds readers that feminist ambivalence towards Nietzsche is no invention of the 1970s–1990s, and that some late nineteenth-century advocates of women's rights, like Kobylians'ka, appreciated the liberating atmosphere of Nietzsche's writings and found many useful conceptual recourses in his philosophy as early as the 1890s.

Chapter 3, "The Populist Trial," addresses Kobylians'ka's confrontation with her populist compatriots in the late 1890s and early 1900s. Alongside a new reading of Kobylians'ka's "rustic" stories, I offer a fresh interpretation of her epic novel *The Earth*, comparing it to Émile Zola's text of the same title. Here I read Kobylians'ka's work as a creative response to the persistent populist request to pay more attention to peasant themes, where the writer not only exposed the populist uncritical glorification of peasants but also critiqued the dominant populist literary models.

Chapter 4, "Hidden Modernism," looks at the period from 1903 to 1913, which has often been viewed as a period of Kobylians'ka's creative decline. I contest that general thinking and discuss the writer's attempt to repackage her alternative social and political views into a compromised aesthetic form, which could be more acceptable, and thus accessible, for the populist camp. Particular focus is on Kobylians'ka's ever-growing concern about the ethnocentric understanding of nationalism among the mainstream Ukrainian intelligentsia. The chapter concludes by situating Kobylians'ka's revised theory of positive elitism in the context of other elitist ideologies of the time, such as Marxism and fascism.

In chapter 5, "War and Fiction," I examine Kobylians'ka's creative response to the First World War, which, in fact, represents a rare and little-known case of a Ukrainian woman writing about the war on the Eastern Front. Arguing against the conventional readings of Kobylians'ka's war fiction as a single artistic and ideological entity held together by its anti-war rhetoric, I prove that these works fall into several distinct cycles. The stylistic and thematic particularities of each cycle not only testify to the writer's continuous search for and experimentations with the rhetorical possibilities for expressing the unspeakable brutality of war, but they also register a gradual evolution in the writer's views on loyalty, civic duty, and national identity, alongside her simultaneous transformation from a pro-Austrian loyalist to a supporter of Ukraine's political independence. Furthermore, drawing on recent scholarship on literature of the First World War, I prove that Kobylians'ka's war stories deserve our attention not only as long-ignored curiosities from the pen of one of Ukraine's most daring and innovative writers of the time but also as valuable cultural documents that present an original perspective on the collective European experience of 1914–18.

Chapter 6, "Between the Right and the Left," examines Kobylians'ka's late texts, investigating the radical transformation of her aesthetic, social, and political views in the aftermath of the First World War. Particular attention is paid to the writer's reception of interwar fascism and its aesthetics in her 1936 novel *Apostle of the Rabble*. Drawing on recent scholarship that has indicated the intimate kinship between modernism and fascism, this chapter argues that *Apostle of the Rabble* represents an important development in Ukrainian modernism that highlights its variegated nature and points to profound contestations not only within the artistic movement but also within Ukrainian nationalism itself. The new reading of the novel places Kobylians'ka in a broader conversation with other European intellectuals of her time who engaged, directly or indirectly, with themes and images commonly found in texts by writers identified with fascism to articulate their own conception of the new movement.

While the primary focus of this study is Kobylians'ka and her intellectual heritage, its implications reach beyond the field of Ukrainian studies and as widely as the writer's own reading and writing. For comparativists, the study uncovers an alternative intellectual genealogy in turn-of-the-century European arts and letters. Rather than rehearsing various narratives about modernism as a radical response to nineteenth-century bourgeois culture in the form of Nietzscheanism, Marxism, fascism, or an aesthetic of fragmentation, this study highlights the political fissures and fusions inherent to turn-of-the-century thought. For those working in Victorian studies or comparative fascism and for those interested in Nietzsche and his influence on European intellectuals, Kobylians'ka emerges in this study as an unlikely, but no less active, interlocutor for the social and aesthetic theories that would define European debates about culture, science, and politics in the first half of the twentieth century. For feminist scholars, this study makes accessible a thorough account of a central, yet overlooked in Western criticism, woman writer who not only confronted the most significant debates of feminism in her own time, but who has gone on to be a model and a contributor within a major cultural tradition that was itself tightly woven from threads of many others, each a vibrant skein in its own right. Finally, for those interested in questions of transnationalism and intersectionality, this study's discussion of Kobylians'ka's hybrid cultural identity and philosophical program presents a relevant exemplification of cultural interchange and irreducible complexities of cultural identity.

Chapter One

The Art of Feminist Compromise

The question of why Ol'ha Kobylians'ka chose to devote her talent to Ukrainian culture is one of the most common preoccupations of criticism about her work. After all, Kobylians'ka's education was conducted predominantly in German and grounded in turn-of-the-century Western European culture, during a time when Ukrainian literature was considered marginal and second-rate. The most popular narrative about Kobylians'ka's cultural choice revolves around her accidental encounter with Nataliia Kobryns'ka, a Galician Ukrainian intellectual and the leading theoretician of the women's movement in Ukraine. According to this account, Kobryns'ka helped the young Kobylians'ka to discover her Ukrainian national identity and guided her into the realm of Ukrainian culture and literature. Kobylians'ka is partly responsible for promoting this narrative; she, in fact, introduced the story of a chance national awakening in her late autobiographies, as part of an effort to position herself as a Ukrainian national writer. In the 1921 autobiography, she intentionally exaggerated Kobryns'ka's role in the construction of her Ukrainian identity in order to downplay her own earlier reliance on German language and culture. Kobylians'ka's effort proved effective. As early as 1923, the émigré editor Vasyl' Vernyvolia was already claiming, in his introduction to a new Leipzig edition of Kobylians'ka's short story "Bytva" ("The Battle," 1896), that the author might have become a German writer had it not been for "a chance encounter with conscious Ukrainians from Galicia who opened a new world for Kobylians'ka" (Vernyvolia 1923, 4–5).[1] A few years later, the Soviet critic Pavlo Fyllypovych echoed these sentiments, emphasizing the difficult choice Kobylians'ka had to make between the thriving German culture of arts and letters and its impoverished Ukrainian counterpart (1928, 119). Most of the subsequent émigré, Soviet, and post-Soviet critics seem to accept this explanation. A close reading of Kobylians'ka's diaries and personal correspondence of the 1880s and early 1890s, however, proves that the writer's self-identification with Ukrainian culture was infinitely more complex and explosive. More importantly, it shows that Kobryns'ka's oft-referenced patronage of Kobylians'ka frequently took the form of censorship. In forms official and unofficial, in the guise of prudence, good taste, or editorial savvy, Kobryns'ka often hindered Kobylians'ka literary career, rather than promoted it.

As I will go on to show, Kobylians'ka's relationship with Kobryns'ka made the young writer suspicious of her mentor's social and political views. In particular, Kobylians'ka disagreed with Kobryns'ka's socialist conception of feminism. While she shared Kobryns'ka views on women's right to education, Kobylians'ka criticized the socialist ideal of women as self-sufficient emancipationists and educators of the people; she advocated instead for a modernized yet somewhat traditional position for women within the family context. More importantly, Kobylians'ka firmly dismissed Kobryns'ka's thesis that the emancipation of women could be achieved only as a result of the emancipation of the working class. Rejecting her mentor's class-based ideology of collective emancipation, Kobylians'ka instead advocated for individual intellectual and spiritual evolution as the only practicable path to women's liberation, framing her views with the ideas derived from reading Eugenie Marlitt, John Stuart Mill, Dmitrii Pisarev, and other Western individualist and Russian radical thinkers.

Early Life and Intellectual Influences

Kobylians'ka was neither born nor raised a Ukrainian patriot but rather grew up within a mixture of Ukrainian, Polish, and German cultures, internalizing all three as irrevocable aspects of her identity. She was born on 27 November 1863, in the small town of Gura-Humora in the Bukovyna province of what was then the Habsburg Empire.[2] She was the fourth child of Iulian Kobylians'kyi and Maria Werner Kobylians'ka, who had six other children: Kobylians'ka's older brothers, Maksymilian and Iulian, were born in 1858 and 1859, respectively; her only sister, Ievhenia, was born in 1861; and her three younger brothers, Stepan, Oleksandr, and Volodymyr, were born in 1866, 1875, and 1877, respectively (see figure 2). Iulian Kobylians'kyi was a minor administrative clerk and an imperial loyalist of Ukrainian noble decent. Like most Ukrainian intelligentsia in nineteenth-century Bukovyna, he was partially Germanized but remained in touch with his Ukrainian heritage, which was a vital part of his culture and daily life. Through the eyes of his daughter, Iulian Kobylians'kyi appears as somewhat severe and always busy at work but also as a learned man and a devoted social activist (V:239).[3] He was a prominent member of the local Ukrainian

Figure 2. The Kobylians'kyi family portrait (sitting left to right: Maksym, Ievheniia, mother, father, Ol'ha; standing left to right: Oleksandr, Iulian, Stepan, Volodymyr), Chernivtsi, 1898

community and openly opposed the pervasive Romanization in Suceava and Kimpolung (now Câmpulung), where Ukrainians were a minority. He provided free legal consultations to peasants, organized social and cultural events for the intelligentsia, ran charities, and raised money to build the first Ukrainian Greek Catholic Church of Saint Demetrius in Kimpolung, which continues to operate to this day. Kobylians'ka depicts her mother, Maria Werner Kobylians'ka, as an exceptionally kind and intelligent woman who raised seven children and took care of all the practical details and work around the house. She came from a middle-class Polonized German family. While remaining faithful to her Polish cultural heritage, she supported her husband's participation in the Ukrainian community. Once married, Kobylians'ka's mother learned Ukrainian and converted from Roman Catholicism to the Ukrainian Catholic denomination but continued to use Polish as the main language of communication with children and family.

The multicultural dynamic of Kobylians'ka's environment was both a result of her family heritage and a manifestation of a broader social trend characteristic of late nineteenth-century Bukovyna. At the time, it was the most heterogeneous of the Austro-Hungarian provinces, populated by Romanians, Ukrainians, Jews, Germans, Poles, and Hungarians. The cultural diversity of the region forced both local and imperial governments to design a working solution to the turbulent nationality question that dominated political debates in Bukovyna in the late nineteenth century. In 1910, a new Austro-Hungarian constitution and an experimental franchise law gave limited individual autonomy to the six nationalities, guaranteeing their national self-determination. This political compromise, unprecedented in the history of the Habsburg Empire, sought to boost imperial loyalty among Bukovynians. Despite numerous tensions that continued to complicate the social and political relations among different ethnic groups in the region, Bukovynians internalized deeply liberal values propagated by the 1910 constitution. As one contemporary scholar of Ukrainian nationalism observes, the political climate of the 1910s continues to resonate in present-day Bukovyna, making the Chernivtsi region the only part of Ukraine where Ukrainian nationalism peacefully coexists with minority nationalisms (Wilson 2000, 116). Living in Bukovyna, Kobylians'ka thus was subjected to the twin pressures of diverse national revivals (Ukrainian and otherwise) and assimilation to the imperial culture, where German was the dominant language of administrative and cultural exchange. Both of these tendencies influenced the formation of Kobylians'ka's identity in the early stages of her life. Although the writer grew up trilingual, speaking Ukrainian, Polish, German, and eventually acquired a good command of Romanian and Russian, her notes, manuscripts, diaries, correspondence, and autobiographies indicate that German remained her dominant language throughout her life.

Kobylians'ka was initially schooled in German and received four years of formal primary education in a public school in Kimpolung. After finishing primary school at the age of fourteen, she, like many middle-class European women of her generation, had to rely on self-education through literature because her parents did not have sufficient means to support the further education of all seven of their children. Although Kobylians'ka's five brothers attended gymnasiums and universities, she, together with her older sister, Ievhenia, read books, mostly German, from local libraries and private collections of family friends to nurture her intellectual growth. The literature available to Kobylians'ka during her teenage years was more likely to involve romances, adventures, and moralistic stories than serious philosophical works. As one of Kobylians'ka's close girlhood friends, Ol'ha Ustyianovych, suggests in her memoirs, voracious reading and literary discussions of random German classics, popular belles-lettres, and periodicals played a key role in her and Kobylians'ka's formal and sentimental education, and provided them with virtues and patterns on which they modelled their own lives (1928, 213). Ukrainian and Russian literatures did not form a part of Kobylians'ka's reading until the late 1870s.

Nineteenth-century German literature thus heavily influenced Kobylians'ka's early tastes. According to Kobylians'ka's early diaries and autobiographies, her favourite authors included Johann Wolfgang von Goethe; poet Heinrich Heine; and popular novelists Gottfried Keller and Eugenie Marlitt. These German cultural icons inspired Kobylians'ka's first, modest attempts in literature and remained important references throughout her creative career. Encouraged in her literary efforts by her brothers and older sister, the young Kobylians'ka started writing poetry in German at the age of fourteen. She wrote her early poems in a style similar to that of the late German Romantics – such as Nikolaus Lenau, Friedrich Rückert, and Ludwig Uhland – and expressed a similarly sad, melancholic, and even somewhat mystic comprehension of life (Tomashuk 1969a, 11).

Marlitt would prove to be a crucial model and influence for the young Kobylians'ka's bourgeoning feminist ideas. In 1880, at the age of seventeen, she wrote her first experimental German-language short story, "Hartenza, oder ein Bild aus einem Mädchenleben" ("Hartenza: A Sketch of a Girl's Life"), which demonstrates the strong influence of Marlitt. The story's heroine, Hartenza, is fashioned after Marlitt's characters and could be viewed as a prototype of many female protagonists in Kobylians'ka's later novels. Enticed by Marlitt's prose, Kobylians'ka wrote several letters to the German writer in which she expressed her sincere admiration and devotion. She even began translating her favourite novel by Marlitt, *Das Geheimnis der alten Mamsell* (*Old Mam'selle's Secret*, 1868), into Ukrainian and eventually incorporated many of its stylistic and thematic features – its narrative style, irony, rich description of nature, character types, plot schemes, and even core ideas – into her later works. Notably, despite Kobylians'ka's continuous reference to Marlitt's prominence in her work, scholars have sharply criticized, deliberately downplayed, or simply overlooked Kobylians'ka's tribute to the German novelist. To date, few critics have attempted to assess Marlitt's influence on Kobylians'ka's aesthetic and feminist development. Those who do comment on the topic either have taken as their point of reference the traditional reading of Marlitt's works as trivial and void of any intrinsic aesthetic value[4] or have tried, instead, to recuperate

Kobylians'ka by differentiating her from Marlitt.[5] However, more recent scholarship on Marlitt's life and work, initiated by the growing interest in feminism and popular literature in the 1980s, has re-evaluated the characterization of Marlitt as a writer more notable for her historical position than her aesthetic merits. For example, Todd Kontje, one of the recent revisionist critics of Marlitt, affirms several progressive aspects of Marlitt's popular fiction and emphasizes her important cultural work, particularly her commentary on the role of the family in a new nation at a time when the German women's movement was first beginning to organize itself. Kontje concludes that Marlitt's sudden fall from grace after 1885 had less to do with the intrinsic flaws of her work than with changing historical circumstances during which the gap she once straddled between highbrow culture and mass media swiftly became an unbridgeable chasm (1998, 199–200). Naturally, new readings of Marlitt call for new inquiries in Kobylians'ka's reception of her.

Marlitt was among the most popular and highly paid German writers in the 1860s and 1870s, but her literary reputation has been gravely compromised by a controversy regarding the alleged immorality and shallowness of her works that broke out in the German press in 1885. Although negative reviews had little effect on Marlitt's status in the eyes of her readers – Kobylians'ka among them – the bad press led to Marlitt's marginalization and discouraged literary scholars from making serious inquiries into her work during the first half of the twentieth century. It is perhaps unsurprising that early critics of Kobylians'ka have demonstrated a similarly cursory treatment of Marlitt's fiction. Mykhailo Hrushevs'kyi and Ivan Franko, key figures in Ukraine's national revival in the early twentieth century, were the first to speak about the "detrimental" influence of Marlitt's sentimental style and conformist subject matter on Kobylians'ka and to criticize Kobylians'ka's prose for that matter as somewhat reactionary. In 1898, Hrushevs'kyi, editor of the L'viv journal *Literaturno-naukovyi visnyk* (*Literature and Science Herald*), criticized Kobylians'ka's *Tsarivna* (*The Princess*, 1896) for its excessive sentimentality and its Cinderella plot (174–9, 1898]), seizing on the same two flaws that were frequently ascribed to Marlitt's fiction (Belgum 2002, 262). A few years later, in a 1905 letter to Croatian linguist Vatroslav Jagic, Franko wrote about Marlitt's style and its influence on Kobylians'ka in a similar way. Unlike those critics who have elided Marlitt's influence, Franko acknowledged the formative role that Marlitt played in shaping Kobylians'ka's writing, but, echoing Hrushevs'kyi, dismissed the aesthetic and stylistic complexities of Marlitt's work. Instead, Franko emphasized affinities between the two authors' cultural positions, interpreting Marlitt's influence in the light of ongoing public attacks on the German novelist, and characterizing her writing as sentimental and false (1976–86, 50:281). In the following decade, Franko went on to use similar commentaries to explain the lack of populist motifs in Kobylians'ka's early works. Over the past century, most scholars have followed his lead, siding with Franko's evaluations of Marlitt's works and their influence on Kobylians'ka or asserting that the latter incorporated Marlitt's sentimental style only in her early fictional works and abandoned it relatively early.[6]

Kobylians'ka's interest in Marlitt, however, was no youthful fancy. Indeed, Kobylians'ka continuously relied on Marlitt's creative formulas throughout her writing career. Like Marlitt's novels, most of Kobylians'ka's works champion freethinkers while condemning religious zealots. Likewise, both construct intelligent heroines who meet adversity with strong wills and independent minds, struggling against the prevailing traditional nineteenth-century conception of women as weak, inactive, and unthinking. In most cases, Kobylians'ka, like Marlitt, moderated radical feminism into a liberal compromise: many of her novels that begin with a firm rejection of the status quo end with qualified support for existing gender politics and social hierarchies – each heroine eventually finds her man and fulfils her destiny at home. Moreover, Kobylians'ka's novels, like those of Marlitt, are far from static Cinderella stories; rather, their heroines experience dynamic transformations as they marshal their personal abilities, determination, and moral stamina to triumph over their hostile environments. Furthermore, as Kobylians'ka suggests in her 1922 autobiography, Marlitt's "educational novels" provided her with strong female role models that played an important part in the formation of her personality (V:240).

Kobylians'ka's outspoken and self-asserting heroines, however, are not merely derivative translations of Marlitt's vision into the Ukrainian context. While using elements of Marlitt's style and plot composition, and adhering to Marlitt's treatment of feminism, Kobylians'ka's works address contemporary social and political issues that were at the centre of intellectual discussions among educated Ukrainians at the turn of the twentieth century. As is demonstrated in the later chapters of this study, the emerging and ever-changing discourse of national revival gradually became the most prominent theme of Kobylians'ka's fiction. The writer would engage with this discourse when developing her own original palingenetic visions of Ukraine's future, often grounding her imaginings in the works of European and Russian thinkers.

Before the Kobylians'kyi family moved in 1868 to Suceava, a picturesque town in southeastern Bukovyna, now a territory of Romania, Iulian Kobylians'kyi, the writer's father, was the only person who integrated Ukrainian language and culture into the family life. As Kobylians'ka noted in 1921, her father's love for his native language, culture, and people was the only reason why the Ukrainian language had survived in their house (V:241). In Suceava, Kobylians'ka entered for the first time into a broader Ukrainian community, centred around the local Ukrainian Greek Catholic Church of the Holy Resurrection. The household of the local prior, Mykola Ustyianovych, was the first truly Ukrainian house where Kobylians'ka heard the Ukrainian language outside her own home (V:229). Still, although Kobylians'ka became close friends with the prior's daughter, Ol'ha, and spent most of her time with the Ustyianovych family, her personal correspondence of this time suggests that German continued to be her main language of communication and intellectual exchange.

In 1874, the Kobylians'kyi family moved to Kimpolung, another town in southern Bukovyna, where they quickly became involved in the local Ukrainian community by organizing and hosting various charities and cultural events. In Kimpolung, Kobylians'ka took private lessons in the Ukrainian language, but stopped after only a few months of instruction, without learning properly how to read or write. In her 1921 autobiography, Kobylians'ka attributes the abrupt termination of her lessons to a lack of financial means. At the same time, her earlier remarks suggest that the skills of reading and writing in Ukrainian must have seemed superfluous at the time: there were no books or periodicals in Ukrainian available to Kobylians'ka, and no official business was conducted in the language. German literature continued to be Kobylians'ka's "only source of spiritual food" (V:232). Not until she became friends with Sofiia Okunevs'ka, the only daughter of a Ukrainian district doctor named Anatasii Okunevs'kyi, who moved to Kimpolung from Galicia in 1881, did Kobylians'ka renew her study of Ukrainian language and culture.

Captivated by the vibrant and well-rounded Sofiia Okunevs'ka and her devotion to the Ukrainian national cause, the eighteen-year-old Kobylians'ka ventured to explore her own Ukrainian identity. Okunevs'ka taught Kobylians'ka how to read and write in Ukrainian and introduced her to the major Ukrainian literary classics and key works of Ukrainian political thinkers: Taras Shevchenko, the Romantic mid-nineteenth-century poet whose literary heritage is regarded as the foundation of modern Ukrainian literature; Mykhailo Drahomanov, a prominent historian and influential political theorist who wrote the first systematic political program for the Ukrainian national movement; Ivan Franko, the literary and political giant who founded a socialist movement in Galicia; and Mykhailo Pavlyk, an important

Galician socialist and publicist. Okunevs'ka exposed Kobylians'ka to contemporary political discussions of the Ukrainian national question that brewed in Galicia in the 1870s and 1880s, a debate that differed radically from the pro-Habsburg loyalist allegations of the Ukrainian intelligentsia in Bukovyna. Kobylians'ka also credited Okunevs'ka with initiating her into the canonical works of Russian, English, and Scandinavian literatures. It is, therefore, not surprising that Okunevs'ka was the first person to read Kobylians'ka's "Hortezna." Acknowledging Kobylians'ka's insightful psychological observations, Okunevs'ka encouraged her to continue writing but suggested that she should consider writing in Ukrainian rather than German because, as she bluntly stated, "it was a crime to add where there was already plenty, while taking away from where there was so little" (IL F14, N787). Although Kobylians'ka did not immediately follow her friend's advice and continued to write in German throughout the early 1890s, her diaries indicate that she started to show more interest in Ukrainian culture and set out to define her own place in it.

Kobylians'ka's newfound appreciation of things Ukrainian, particularly literature in the Ukrainian language, was further fanned by lively social encounters at the Okunevs'kyi house. The Okunevs'kyis entertained family and friends, both young and well established, who brought new ideas, books, and debates with which Kobylians'ka actively engaged. The two most popular topics were Herbert Spencer's social theory, inspired by Charles Darwin's theory of evolution, and the role of the intelligentsia in the social reorganization of a nation. At the centre of many discussions were also the works of Russian radical writers: Vissarion Belinsky, the founder of Russian literary criticism and a passionate defender of Westernizing tendencies; Dmitrii Pisarev, a radical writer and social critic who propelled the democratic-revolutionary trend in Russia in the 1860s; Nikolai Dobroliubov, an influential literary critic who stressed the positive aspects of revolutionary life; Nikolai Chernyshevsky, the prophet of Russian populist positivism; and the major Russian nineteenth-century novelists Turgenev, Dostoevsky, and Tolstoy. These intellectual discussions produced a long-lasting effect on the young and impressionable writer.

Kobylians'ka made her first reference to Belinskii and Pisarev in a diary entry on 18 September 1884, describing her conversation about the two Russian critics with Ievhen Ozarkevych, Sofiia Okunevs'ka's cousin and Nataliia Kobryns'ka's younger brother, who promised to send her their works along with works by other Russian critics from Vienna (Pohrebennyk 1982, 58).[7] Although it is not known if Ievhen Ozarkevych ever sent those books, El'pedefor Panchuk, Kobylians'ka's personal secretary of the 1930s and the husband of her adopted daughter Olena Lukashevych, points out in his memoir that Kobylians'ka greatly admired Pisarev and often asked him to bring her his works from local libraries. According to Panchuk, Kobylians'ka loved Pisarev's "passionate character not only because he, just like she herself, admired Heinrich Heine, but also because he, just like she herself, sympathized deeply with the uneducated common people, promoted stubbornly individual rights, and fought earnestly for the emancipation of women" (Panchuk 1976, 60). Pisarev and his critical pamphlet "Pchioly" ("Bees," 1862) also come up in Kobylians'ka's first published work *Liudyna: Povist' z zhinochoho zhyttia* (*A Human Being: A Story Taken from the Lives of Women*, 1894), written in the second half of the 1880s, which suggests that at that point the writer was well acquainted with some of Pisarev's most polemical works.[8] Furthermore, Chernivtsi State O. Iu. Kobylians'ka Literary and Memorial House-Museum displays among several books from Kobylians'ka's personal library the fifth volume of Pisarev's *Polnoe sobranie sochinenii v shesti tomakh* (*Complete Works in Six Volumes*), which was published in Russian in Saint Petersburg in 1904 and includes critical articles from 1865–7 (KLMHM, N308). Two articles in this volume – Pisarev's overview of Pushkin's role in Russian culture "Pushkin i Belinskii" ("Pushkin and Belinskii") and his article "Posmotrim!" ("We Will See!" 1865), a polemic with Maksym Antonovych, a literary critic and a materialist philosopher affiliated with one of the most influential monthly journals of the time, *Sovremennik* (*The Contemporary*), about the value of Turgenev's *Fathers and Sons* – show marks of careful reading: fingerprints, stains, notes made in pencil, and bent corners. "We Will See!" is of particular interest because it presents a detailed comparative analysis of Pisarev's aesthetic and social views in regards to those of Dobroliubov and Chernyshevsky. It also makes frequent references to Pyotr Lavrov, a Russian thinker who was instrumental in shaping late nineteenth-century Russian radical thought. Although there are no known records proving that Kobylians'ka read any of Lavrov's works, Pisarev's volume demonstrates that she was well aware of their contributions to intellectual debates in late-nineteenth-century Russia as well as in turn-of-the-century Western Ukraine.[9] To Kobylians'ka's bibliography of nineteenth-century Russian radical thinkers one should also add Belinskii's *Pis'mo k N.V. Gogoliu* (*Letter to N.V. Gogol*, 1847). In this work, which became the central manifesto of Russian liberals in the 1850s and 1860s, the Russian critic denounces Gogol for supporting the church and state authorities and argues for a socially and politically committed art. Belinskii's letter figures in two lists of Kobylians'ka's personal books preserved in Chernivtsi State O. Iu. Kobylians'ka

Literary and Memorial House-Museum, one made in the 1890s and the other in 1909 (KLMHM N2009–2003, N2008–2002). Kobylians'ka's diaries, autobiographies, and personal correspondence additionally brim with references to Dostoevsky, Tolstoy, and Turgenev.[10]

As Kobylians'ka's later works demonstrate, she was particularly inspired by the Russian radical idea of the writer's exceptional role as a public figure, whose duty was to accept full moral responsibility for leading the people. At the same time, the writer also embraced Spencer's theory of social evolution by means of individual self-perfection and maximized personal liberty. The tension between Kobylians'ka's Western individualism and her recognition of a writer's social and political duty ran through her entire career and continually pushed her to revisit the essential questions of the late nineteenth century in the Russian and, by extension, Ukrainian contexts: who is to be blamed? and what is to be done? With time, Kobylians'ka tempered her somewhat positivistic vision of the world through an infusion of German Romanticism and Nietzsche's thought, finding her answers to the above-mentioned questions in the idea of an aesthetic state – a community that is morally, politically, and spiritually harmonious – led by an intellectual elite with a strong political will. (The second chapter of this book discusses this mixture of German Romanticism, nineteenth-century Russian intellectual thought, and Nietzsche's philosophy in further detail.) Notably, although aesthetic elitism was quite popular in Western Europe during the last decades of the nineteenth century, it did not make its way into the mainstream of Ukrainian intellectual discourse, which was mostly dominated by nineteenth-century Russian positivism and populism. As a result, many of Kobylians'ka's contemporaries and later Soviet theorists criticized her elitist views, if they acknowledged them at all.[11]

During the social encounters at the Okunevs'kyis' house, Kobylians'ka met Sofiia Okunevs'ka's cousin, Nataliia Kobryns'ka, the leading theoretician of the women's movement in Ukraine and the most prominent female luminary among the Ukrainian intelligentsia in 1880s Western Ukraine. Encouraged first by her father, Ivan Ozarkevych, a Greek Catholic priest who successfully combined sacerdotal and parliamentary duties, and later by her husband, Teofil Kobryns'kyi, also a priest and a devoted socialist, Kobryns'ka avidly read progressive Western literature: Henry Buckle, Ludwig Büchner, Ernst Haeckel, Charles Darwin, Ernst Renan, Ferdinand Lassalle, Karl Marx, Friedrich Engels, and John Stuart Mill, to name a few. Equally influenced by socialism and feminism, Kobryns'ka tried to balance the two and become the first woman in Europe to advocate for their synthesis. The eighteen-year-old

Kobylians'ka briefly met Kobryns'ka in the summer of 1881, when the latter accompanied the Okunevs'kyi family during their move to Kimpolung. Kobryns'ka and her enlightened ideas, particularly her enthusiastic discussion of women's role in national regeneration, instantly charmed Kobylians'ka. Their second encounter took place in 1883, after Kobryns'ka spent almost a year in Vienna, where she took some time to mourn the loss of her husband, who died in March 1882. Supported by Ukrainian activists in Vienna, Kobryns'ka returned to Ukraine committed to promoting socialism and feminism in her writing and in her efforts to organize women as a collective social force. Kobylians'ka became one of the first Ukrainian women whose life Kobryns'ka set out to change upon her return from Vienna. Over the summer of 1883, Kobryns'ka developed a curriculum and put together an extensive list of progressive European and Ukrainian texts, which included both scholastic and literary works, to broaden Kobylians'ka's education. Kobryns'ka also recognized Kobylians'ka's literary talent early on and encouraged her to write, promising help and patronage. After Kobryns'ka returned to L'viv, however, her interest in Kobylians'ka died out, and she quickly forgot her promises.

Nataliia Kobryns'ka: Mentor or Rival?

Inspired by Kobryns'ka's passion and her support, Kobylians'ka wrote several short stories that addressed issues of women's emancipation. Her "Schicksal oder Wille" ("Fate or Will," 1883) stands out the most in this cycle. It depicts an intelligent and strong-willed heroine, Iadviha, who, unlike the heroine in "Hartenza," refuses to be content with the traditional role of a housewife. Iadviha protests against petty-bourgeois limitations in women's education and becomes a medical doctor. Her protest and eventual success introduce an important social argument into Kobylians'ka's work – the question of women's right to higher education, which is absent in her first story of 1880. While narrating a success story, "Fate or Will" also addresses the issue of women's intellectual abilities through Iadviha's conversations with a male relative who opposes her pursuit of education. On several occasions, Kobylians'ka's heroine argues against the popular conservative claim of women's biological inferiority and defends women's potential to obtain an education and have a career:

> "A-ah," replied Henry with a drawl. He got up, crossed the room, stopped in front of Iadviha, and looked at her shrewdly with a sarcastic smile. "Why are women deprived of freedom and rights? Well, it's quite obvious:

> because they are not capable of using those rights properly. Besides," he continued mockingly, "women have so many duties in their own realm that a real woman – not those emancipationists – won't occupy herself with any morbid ideas."
>
> "All right," said Iadviha quietly and looked at him timidly with her flurried eyes, "and what if a woman can do something other than just her duties? What happens then? Should that potential be stifled only because it doesn't 'obviously' suit the others?" (IL F14, N181, 62–3)

This episode conveys the main premise of the story: women, as human beings, deserve the same rights to personal freedom and intellectual development as men. In her later works, Kobylians'ka expanded this thesis and argued that women's personal growth inevitably leads to the transformation of conventional families into a more democratic organization. This claim – that the transformative power of personal development would, in turn, catalyse broader social change – would come to occupy a central role in Kobylians'ka's mature feminist discourse and her views on Ukraine's cultural and political regeneration.

Kobylians'ka's next story from the Kobryns'ka cycle, "Vision" (1885), takes the form of an allegory on personal freedom (the same theme that "Hartenza" and "Fate or Will" address). The story's two main characters, Life and Love, shackled by the Power of Circumstances, struggle through "the dark night" to find Freedom. Although the main characters learn that Freedom is also a slave of Circumstances and Human Ignorance, two characters that have strong anti-government implications, their quest gives them hope for a better future. The story sums up their optimistic vision in a final allegorical proclamation that brings to mind Dobroliubov's famous article "Luch sveta v tiomnom tsarstve" ("A Ray of Light in the Realm of Darkness," 1860): "It is still far till the bright day, yet the first morning light is already here!" (IL F14, N1812, 6). Alongside several other canonical texts by Russian positivists, Dobroliubov's article was popular among Ukrainian intellectuals in the late 1870s and early 1880s; "A Ray of Light" was often evoked in discussions of the woman question because its review of the Russian dramatist Aleksandr Ostrovsky's major plays presented a strong argument in favour of improving women's position in the family. Dobroliubov exposed a world of social evil in Ostrovsky's play *Groza* (*The Thunderstorm*, 1859) and denounced the harsh domestic life and subjection of women in Moscow merchant families. He depicted the contemporary middle-class Russian family as a "realm of darkness," where ignorance and tyranny dominated daily life (1948a, 572–628). Although some critics claimed that Dobroliubov had exaggerated the conditions under which women lived, the characterization of the Russian family as a "dark kingdom" became a major social cliché for generations of Russian intelligentsia.[12] While there are no records that Kobylians'ka read Dobroliubov's works, she often used in her early texts his metaphors of a "dark kingdom" and a "ray of light," metaphors which became popular in Western Ukraine in the 1870s.[13] In "Vision," for example, she used the first metaphor to portray not only the family but also all of society as an abyss of darkness, and the second metaphor to prophesy imminent social change.

Kobryns'ka praised the progressiveness of Kobylians'ka's "Vision," but did not publish the story in her experimental almanac for women, *Pershyi vinok* (*The First Garland*, 1887). According to Kobylians'ka, Kobryns'ka was concerned that the story's bold "anti-government and anti-religious" claims made it susceptible to censorship, and thus might jeopardize the whole project (Pohrebennyk 1982, 117). Though arguably well reasoned, Kobryns'ka's rejection of Kobylians'ka's "Vision" and several other works, including her first novel *Sie Hat Geheiratet* (*She Got Married*, 1886), later known as *A Human Being* (1894), dramatically undermined the relationship between the two writers. The consequent tension between them led to radical changes in Kobylians'ka's views and corresponding alterations to the ideological framework of her later fiction. Kobylians'ka's personal letters and diaries testify that her initial fascination with Kobryns'ka, alongside her interest in feminism as it was perceived in the Ukrainian community in the 1880s and 1890s, did not last long. Kobryns'ka, who first encouraged Kobylians'ka to write and promised to help her with publication, crudely mocked Kobylians'ka's work in 1883. Without reading Kobylians'ka's first short story to the end, Kobryns'ka passed it along without proper introduction to Ostap Terlets'kyi, a historian, literary critic, and influential leader of the Ukrainian community in Vienna. Not knowing much about the young writer and not realizing that "Hartenza" was her first fictional work, Terlets'kyi called Kobylians'ka "simply an exotic flower" in Ukrainian literature – in short, a cursory phenomenon, who was out of sync with Ukrainian reality (V:609). Kobylians'ka found out about this incident by chance and was deeply disturbed by what she perceived as Kobryns'ka's duplicity.[14] On 10 November 1884, only a year after Kobryns'ka assured young Kobylians'ka of her support and patronage, Kobylians'ka wrote somewhat melodramatically of Kobryns'ka in her diary:

> Natalychka, Natalychka [Nataliia Kobryns'ka] ... you've hurt me! Why didn't you tell Terlets'kyi that it was my first work? Why didn't you even want to finish reading it? So that Terlets'kyi would denounce it, and it

> would be awkward for you to continue helping me? How thoughtful it is of you! You have long forgotten about it! But didn't you know how much my soul was rejoicing, how much I trusted you, how much hope I had when I gave you my first work ... The two of you laughed at me ... I didn't get a single word from you ... Was this the kind of criticism that should have taught me which [artistic] path to choose? (Pohrebennyk 1982, 70)

Although these words of frustration and embitterment from the twenty-one-year-old Kobylians'ka suggest youth and impulsivity, they also signal the beginning of a significant personal and professional dissociation between the two writers. Kobylians'ka's sense of betrayal heralded an important threshold in her intellectual evolution.

Gradually, Kobylians'ka's frustration with Kobryns'ka as a friend and mentor also made Kobylians'ka question Kobryns'ka's social and political views. Kobylians'ka's diaries indicate that by the mid-1880s, she began to oscillate between two extremes as to the woman question. She declared in one entry that "the woman question [did] not interest [her] anymore" and, with resentful irony, wrote elsewhere that she was appalled by "those noble defenders of women's rights." At the same time, only a few pages later, she stated that from that moment on she lived "not for [herself] but for the woman question" (Pohrebennyk 1982, 44, 112, 117). In these entries, Kobylians'ka mostly addressed her bitter words to Kobryns'ka and her feminist circle, whose activities she began to perceive in the early 1890s as inconsistent, reductionist, and superfluous (V:257). During the same period, Kobylians'ka recorded her emerging passion for broader social and political themes. By 1888, the year when she started working on her first major novel, *The Princess*, her concern with feminist issues expanded into a discussion of the general human condition and Ukraine's national revival. On 24 November 1888, she wrote that she had begun to read extensively about socialism and now recognized that "the interests of [her] people" fully coincided with her own (Pohrebennyk 1982, 174). By the early 1890s, Kobylians'ka withdrew from feminist themes and shifted her attention to the program of Ukraine's national revival. This prioritization reflected a broader shift within the Ukrainian intelligentsia at the time: a tendency to link nationalism with various other movements to which they were committed at the turn of the twentieth century.

The final split between Kobylians'ka and Kobryns'ka took place in 1886, when Kobryns'ka rejected Kobylians'ka's "Vision," "A Life Sketch from Bukovyna," and *She Got Married* from publication in *The First Garland*, which came out in 1887. The editors of the almanac, Nataliia Kobryns'ka and another Ukrainian writer, Olena Pchilka, had first worried about a possible shortage of material but were now faced with a surfeit. As editors, they had to choose from a wide range of fictional, scholastic, and critical works of predominantly modest artistic value. Surprisingly, though Kobylians'ka's early texts demonstrated a far more sophisticated handling of theme and artistry than many presented in *The First Garland*, none were included in the almanac.[15] To date, no scholarly account definitively explains their omission. Kobylians'ka's critics either reiterate Franko's apologetic remarks of the 1900s, which retrospectively describe Kobylians'ka's early works as immature, or claim that Kobylians'ka's call to individual rebellion against tradition disturbed both editors of the almanac, who adhered to dominant populist discourse. Neither of these critical narratives offers much detail or evidence in support of its claims.

A more convincing explanation can be found in Kobylians'ka's own speculation about Kobryns'ka's sense of professional rivalry. As Kobylians'ka inferred, Kobryns'ka found *She Got Married* similar to her own short story "Zadlia kusnyka khliba" ("For a Crust of Bread," 1884). In response, Kobryns'ka suggested changes that would, ostensibly, allow *She Got Married* to harmonize better with her own piece, scheduled to appear in the same volume (Pohrebennyk 1982, 125).[16] Kobylians'ka interpreted Kobryns'ka's offer as an attempt to simplify and distort the integrity of her work. On 2 June 1886, she recorded her outrage in her diary:

> Zosia [Sofiia Okunevs'ka] told me that my story would be accepted for publication with some changes because it is similar to the story that Kobryns'ka wrote. I was shaken by rage, and Zosia got scared. She tried to calm me down and said that the changes would be minor. I *don't want* them to accept my story out of pity ... Natal'tsia [Nataliia Kobryns'ka] herself asked me to write it for the almanac ... God, why haven't I broken all relations with the Ozarkevych family already? I cannot stand all of them now! (Pohrebennyk 1982, 124)

The emotionally charged passage conveys the two forces that would drive Kobylians'ka's creative work in the early 1890s: her irritation with Kobryns'ka and her professional pride. Kobylians'ka rejected Kobryns'ka's offer, and, as a result, her story was not included in *The First Garland*. After this incident, Kobylians'ka remained courteous with Kobryns'ka only as a social formality (Pohrebennyk 1982, 125).

Disillusioned in Kobryns'ka as a mentor, Kobylians'ka gradually came to see some differences between her and Kobryns'ka's views on the woman question. While visiting Kobryns'ka in August 1889, she observed that her ideals differed from those of Kobryns'ka and her circle.

At Kobryns'ka's house, Kobylians'ka wrote, no one appreciated the "passionate love, poetry, and power" of her beliefs; she felt "like a stranger" there and had to keep her views "hidden deep in [her] heart" (Pohrebennyk 1982, 186). While Kobylians'ka and Kobryns'ka both agreed on the importance of higher education for women and argued that, as human beings, women deserved the same rights as men, they chose different ideologies to frame their feminist views. Kobryns'ka, who collaborated closely with Franko and Pavlyk, the leading Ukrainian radicals of the time, adhered to the socialist view of the woman question, according to which emancipation of women could be achieved only in a socially progressive state and only as a result of the emancipation of the working class.[17] Kobylians'ka, who was disconnected from the social and political developments in Galicia and who followed the individualistic philosophy of German Romanticism, rejected socialism, identifying it in the mid-1890s with terrorism, degeneration, and chaos.[18] Inspired by John Stuart Mill, Friendrich Nietzsche, Darwinist theoreticians, and nineteenth-century Russian realist writers such as Turgenev, Dostoevsky, Tolstoy, and Chekhov, Kobylians'ka questioned the socialist notion of equality and promoted instead personal intellectual evolution, recognizing knowledge and individual spiritual self-improvement as the only plausible path to women's liberation.

Kobylians'ka was especially critical of the socialist ideas of "going to the people" and "free love." According to Kobylians'ka's diaries and literary writings, these emancipationist doctrines were premature for a nineteenth-century Ukrainian context in which the majority of women lacked a formal education and continued to depend on male relatives or husbands. Under these circumstances, Kobylians'ka argued, a feminism grounded in socialist practices of "going to the people" and "free love" would be both extremist and counterproductive; socialist feminism, she claimed, would only exacerbate the social injustice that women suffered (V:333). Kobylians'ka articulated her frustration with the fashionable emancipationist tendencies of her time in her letter to Mykhailo Pavlyk of 11 October 1891:

> [Our women's] movement is artificial, and until we have more intelligent women, until they understand correctly the theory behind the woman question, as English, American, and German women do, it will remain so. For now, knowledge is ... our only weapon ... First, our women have to understand their human rights. They must know what they want. They must feel it because until they do, individual efforts can do little. At best, they can bring only transient achievements. (V:257)

In this excerpt, Kobylians'ka accused the newly emerging Ukrainian women's movement of doctrinarism and an ignorance of the realities that Ukrainian middle-class women experienced. In the same letter, she rejected feminist extremism and re-emphasized spiritual and intellectual self-development as the key goals that women should pursue in their fight against social injustice.

Concerns about feminist doctrinairism additionally permeate a public address that Kobylians'ka delivered at the first congress of the Society of Ruthenian Women in Bukovyna in Chernivtsi in October 1894. Kobylians'ka opened her speech with a critique of the popular understanding of feminism among Ukrainian women and firmly spoke against radical gestures, such as the rejection of marriage and the provocative adoption of male attire and manners, which, according to her, did little to promote women's rights to education and work (V:151–2). Kobylians'ka pointed out further that real progress would more likely be achieved though education and changes to daily and domestic life. She explicitly objected to the view that "women exist only to become mothers and wives" and used a Darwinian argument to emphasize that women, as human beings, deserved the same rights for personal development and self-fulfilment as men (V:153). At the same time, she assessed women's position in Ukrainian society with a bracing pragmatism, arguing that women should not lose sight of their calling in the home and framing conscientious motherhood as one of the most significant functions that women could perform in Ukrainian society at the time. In her conclusions, Kobylians'ka asserted that, contrary to popular belief, women's personal advancement would not ruin families but would help transform them into a more democratic organization, where women would function as supportive and loving companions to men and capable caregivers to children, raising them as "firm, determined, and pure characters" (V:155–6). Although rather modest, Kobylians'ka's speech at the First Women's Congress is her most complete public statement on feminism. While clearly drawing on the progressive legacy of the European women's movements of her time, Kobylians'ka eventually moderated radical feminism into something more palatable to the mainstream Ukrainian audience, accounting equally for the potential positive and negative effects of women's emancipation.

Stepan Smal'-Stots'kyi, a renowned Bukovynian linguist and literary critic who, as co-editor of the newspaper *Bukovyna*, had played an important role in popularizing Kobylians'ka's fiction in the 1890s, offered one of the best but least-known assessments of Kobylians'ka's departure from the radical feminists of her time. In a 1927 critical review that commemorated the fortieth anniversary of Kobylians'ka's creative career, Smal'-Stots'kyi observed that Kobylians'ka's political ideal for women fundamentally differed from the audacious emancipationist model championed by the mainstream feminists of her time. Smal'-Stots'kyi claimed that Kobylians'ka celebrated a kind wife and good mother who would contribute to the development of national history not with her sex but with her refined and exemplary personality. To support his claim, Smal'-Stots'kyi presented a detailed analysis of Kobylians'ka's two major texts, *The Princess* and *The Earth*, and quoted from one of her letters, where she elaborated on her understanding of the role women could play in the development of Ukrainian nationhood:

> To create our own state ... we need women – not dolls, but heroines. We need heroines in running a household and in raising children. We need heroines who, if needed, can replace fathers; heroines who, when left by their husbands, could remain on the pedestal of purity and high morals, and who would pursue only one goal – not themselves and their demanding I, but their children. (1928, 279)

Smal'-Stots'kyi's evaluation confirms that Kobylians'ka's criticism of feminist extremism, along with her belief that women could better themselves and their societies without compromising their commitment to love and family, was a firm conviction that she maintained throughout her creative career. Kobylians'ka's views on feminism are thus neither radical nor conservative. Rather, they are both: radical in their intellectual and theoretical approach, but conservative in their resolution to forge a new traditional conscience. In this regard, Kobylians'ka continued a specific European tradition that strove not to destroy but to rethink, reclaim, and reassert the value of tradition itself, something to which she was exposed first through Marlitt and Keller, and later through Turgenev, Dostoevsky, Tolstoy, and Chekhov.

Kobylians'ka's diaries and personal correspondence of the 1880s and early 1890s thus demonstrate that the writer engaged actively in discussions of feminism during the early years of her literary career, but ultimately withdrew in the 1890s from women's societies and feminist discourse, turning her interest instead to broader cultural, social, and political issues, such as Ukraine's national revival. Only her early works from the 1880s, written while she was close to the Okunevs'kyi-Ozarkevych family, exclusively address the woman question and engage creatively with the rhetoric of prevailing feminist discourses of the time. The most representative example in this body of works is Kobylians'ka's first published novel, *A Human Being* (1894), which acutely reveals the intrinsic nature of Kobylians'ka's particular brand of radical conservative feminism.

The Alternative Feminism *of A Human Being*

On 10 November 1884, after reading Kobryns'ka's story "Shums'ka," later known as "Dukh chasu" ("The Spirit of the Time," 1883), Kobylians'ka commented on Kobryns'ka's writing in her diary:

> Natal'tsia's new story came out, and it's rather good. But she doesn't write so that I cannot surpass her. I was furious when I read that scribing! She is all over the place ... But what do I care about [her]? I would rather read other books. What I really want is to write a novel. I hate those Ozarkevyches with all my heart. I really wish I had nothing to do with them. I cannot even express how sick I am with them. And she [Kobryns'ka] is the worst. Anyway, I can manage without their support. (Pohrebennyk 1982, 70)

While criticizing Kobryns'ka's story and even dismissing the writer's talents, Kobylians'ka's clearly retained a competitive attitude towards her erstwhile mentor: as she herself put it, she pledged to study contemporary literature and philosophy so that her own future creative writings could outshine Kobryns'ka's work. Within a year, Kobylians'ka began writing *She Got Married*, later known as *A Human Being*, addressing the same subject and using characters and motifs similar to those found in Kobryns'ka's "The Spirit of the Time" and "For a Crust of Bread": the inevitable change in the social position of women and the antagonistic reaction such a change might cause in a provincial setting. In the 1960s, Nykyfor Tomashuk was the first to point out parallels between Kobryns'ka's and Kobylians'ka's stories. He, however, concluded that despite similar characters and storylines, Kobylians'ka's text fundamentally surpassed Kobryns'ka's in stylistic complexity. According to the critic, while Kobryns'ka constructed linear, moralistic narratives with schematic, two-dimensional characters, Kobylians'ka examined the psychology of her protagonist through a sophisticated narrative style that centred the perception of the heroine, Olena Liaufler (1969a, 99).

Several other stylistic features of Kobylians'ka's first novel that contrast even more sharply with Kobryns'ka's stories have come to define Kobylians'ka's fiction as innovative and modernist. Influenced by Turgenev and Dostoevsky, who revolutionized techniques for perceiving and representing the inner life in fiction, Kobylians'ka used dialogue and dialogic internal monologues to provide entry into Olena's intense internal struggle. The use of dialogue also allowed Kobylians'ka to individualize the speech of secondary and even episodic characters, thereby creating a multiplicity of impassioned human voices that convey not only the characters' personalities but also their world views with force and palpability. Another important formal feature, which Kobylians'ka would deliberately use to depict the invisible, internal dynamics of her characters in her subsequent writings, is the mixture of genres. In *She Got Married*, the main story is undercut with elements of personal letters, confessions, philosophical contemplations, flashback memories, and dream narratives. This stylistic intricacy, itself inseparable from the novel's complex philosophical material, would become the signature innovation that Tomashuk saw as elevating Kobylians'ka's style and ideas over Kobryns'ka's. It is thus not surprising that Kobryns'ka was alarmed while reviewing *She Got Married* for *The First Garland* and eventually rejected Kobylians'ka's novel for publication.

Although Kobryns'ka's motives for keeping Kobylians'ka's works from publication in *The First Garland* might seem obvious, some scholars claim that it was Franko who turned down Kobylians'ka's work (Makovei 1963, Tomashuk 1963, 268; Pavlychko 2002, 217). Little factual evidence supports this theory, however. The only known record of Franko's commentary on *She Got Married* appears in his article "Manifest Molodoi muzy" ("Manifesto of the Young Muse," 1907), which he wrote twenty years after the publication of *The First Garland*. In his essay, Franko briefly mentions that he found Kobylians'ka's early work inappropriate for publication in *The First Garland* because of its "sweet and sentimental Marlitt style" (1976–86, 37:413). The specific target of his criticism remains ambiguous. As we know, Kobylians'ka submitted three stories for *The First Garland* – "Vision," "A Life Sketch from Bukovyna," and *She Got Married* – but Franko's statement does not specify the exact title of the text he reviewed. Furthermore, "Manifesto of the Young Muse" was Franko's apologetic response to public attacks by Ostap Luts'kyi, a young and flamboyant member of the modernist circle, the Young Muse, who blamed Franko for trying "to destroy young Kobylians'ka as a writer" (qtd. in Tomashuk 1963, 247). Forced to explain himself, Franko likely referenced his earlier critical reviews of Kobylians'ka's first published works, in which he had condemned her so-called sentimental Marlitt style (1976–86, 41:156, 526), to justify retrospectively the rejection of *She Got Married* from *The First Garland*.[19] Surprisingly, in the same apologetic statement, Franko praised Kobylians'ka's *A Human Being* (the final published version of *She Got Married*) as well as her later story "The Battle," professing amazement at the scope of Kobylians'ka's talent (1976–86, 37:413). Oleh Babyshkin, a prominent Soviet researcher of Kobylians'ka's life and work, was the first to suggest that, had Franko known the original edition of *A Human Being*, he would have used the fact that Kobylians'ka was rewriting the final version of her first novel under his constructive guidance as an important argument against Luts'kyi's accusations (1963, 42). Although he highlighted several occasions when his word had been instrumental in bringing Kobylians'ka honours and monetary awards, Franko, however, did not seize the opportunity to defend himself from the allegations more broadly. At the same time, while there is neither evidence for Franko's role in the evaluation of *She Got Married* nor any plausible tension between Kobylians'ka and Franko, Kobylians'ka extensively commented in her diaries and correspondence on Kobryns'ka's discontent with Kobylians'ka's artistic challenge to her "The Spirit of the Time" and "For a Crust of Bread." It is thus possible to assume that Kobryns'ka, who handled most of the editorial work herself and personally copied all the materials for *The First Garland* before presenting them to Franko for his final review, was responsible for the rejection of Kobylians'ka's novel.[20] The same Kobryns'ka who mocked and misrepresented Kobylians'ka's first work to Terlets'kyi in 1883 most likely withheld *She Got Married* from Franko in 1886.

Disheartened with the arrogance of Ukrainian editors, Kobylians'ka appealed to German critics, "the foreigners [who] would tell [her] whether her work was of any value" (V:180). After a few minor corrections, Kobylians'ka sent her work to Fedor Mamroth, editor of a popular Vienna journal, *An der schönen blauen Donau* (*By the Beautiful Blue Danube*). Although the text was rejected on the grounds that it was "too long and philosophically too complex for the mainstream readers of the journal" (V:608), Mamroth wrote a warm letter to Kobylians'ka in which he praised her novel for its "extremely interesting theme, outstanding episodes, common sense, and original thoughts" (qtd. in Makovei 1963, 47). The Austrian critic encouraged Kobylians'ka to continue writing and advised her "under no circumstances to let the quill out of her hands" (V:608). Buoyed by Mamroth's words, Kobylians'ka made further corrections, translated her text into Ukrainian, changed its title to *A Human Being*, and sent it in 1888 to the Galician socialist journal *Pravda* (*Truth*). This publication attempt also failed; as the journal's editor put it, "the author ... [did] not know the Ukrainian language" (qtd. in Makovei 1963, 47). Nonetheless, Kobylians'ka did not give up. In 1894, after substantial revisions of the Ukrainian prose of the text, the novel debuted in the Ukrainian journal *Zoria* (*The Morning Star*) under the title *A Human Being: A Story Taken from the Lives of Women*. Curiously,

Kobylians'ka dedicated the new version of her text to Kobryns'ka, arguably to underscore the literary and polemical challenge she presented to her well-established former mentor.

The instantaneous success of *A Human Being* not only proved Kobryns'ka wrong in her evaluations of Kobylians'ka's artistic potential but also challenged the superficiality of Kobryns'ka's feminist discourse. *A Human Being* proposed an alternative perspective on feminism, which Kobylians'ka framed not in terms of popular socialism but in terms of Western individualist philosophy. While working on the novel, Kobylians'ka studied philosophical works that supported women's right to professional education and predicted that the emancipation of women would double the mass of intellectual potential available for the higher service of humanity. Most tellingly, *The Enfranchisement of Women* (1851), by Harriet Taylor and John Stuart Mill, and *The Mission of Our Century: A Study of the Woman Question* (1878), by Irma von Troll-Borostyani, shaped Kobylians'ka's feminist convictions in the mid-1880s. Kobylians'ka's writings of the time, both fictional and non-fictional, show that she was especially interested in Darwinian explanations of women's natural potential. Her reading thus inspired her to engage with Darwin's theory of evolution, as well as theories that adapted Darwin for a social context, such as the German naturalist Ernst Haeckel's determinism and British philosopher and sociologist Herbert Spencer's synthetic philosophy. Two documents preserved in Kobylians'ka's archives demonstrate the young writer's meticulous research. The first work, a nineteen-page conspectus in German, "Etwas über die darwinistische Theorie" ("Notes on Darwin's Theory"), investigates the evolutionary principles shared by Jean-Baptiste Lamarck, Darwin, and Haeckel, all of whom identified natural forces, but not rational thought or spiritual belief, as the major agency fuelling human endeavour (IL F14, N1017). The second document is a fourteen-page outline of Serhii Podolyns'kyi's article "Hromadivstvo i teoriia Darvina" ("Socialism and Darwin's Theory," 1881), published in the Ukrainian periodical *Hromada* (*Community*). Podolyns'kyi's article examines a Marxist reading of Darwinism that characterizes natural selection's emphasis on the survival of the fittest as one of the main underpinnings of a capitalist morality that legitimizes and is legitimized by man's selfish struggle for self-preservation. Alongside the Marxists' use of Darwin's evolutionary theory to critique capitalism, the second document also analyses the socialist justification of solidarity as more beneficial for human progress than the selfish individualism propagated by Haeckel (KLMHM N1992–1992). By fusing the key arguments delineated in these two documents with a personal reading of the woman question, Kobylians'ka arrived at an original vision of feminism. She presented this vision in the symbolically titled *A Human Being: A Story Taken from the Lives of Women*, in which the heroine rejects grand liberal doctrines rooted in determinism and chooses a more conservative path to achieve personal liberation.[21]

A Human Being features a middle-class girl, Olena Liaufler, who grows up in a small provincial town in the well-off family of His Majesty's Forest Counsellor Mr Epaminondas Liaufler. The inquisitive Olena reads widely; through books, she comes to be moulded by the progressive ideas of her time. After the Liaufler family declares bankruptcy, however, Olena's parents ask her to put her liberal fancies aside and marry the wealthy Mr K to save the family from poverty. Olena despises Mr K's self-absorbed and brutish personality and rejects his proposal, refusing to sacrifice her soul to meet the physical needs of her family. After six years of hard work on an isolated ranch in a remote village, however, Olena outgrows the idealist rhetoric of her youth and marries the wealthy Mr Fel's, an attractive local forester, who secures a decent living for her and her family.

Until recently, critical literature on Kobylians'ka has treated her first novel exclusively as a feminist narrative that advocates a woman's right to financial independence. Osyp Makovei, Kobylians'ka's first editor and a close friend, was the first to point out the story's polemical claim that women should define themselves through work and develop their own views about their role in a society (1963, 44). Marxist scholars also acknowledged Kobylians'ka's tribute to the woman question but often appropriated her social commentary for their ideological needs, reading Kobylians'ka's heroine as a typical victim of the age. For example, the Romanian Marxist scholar Magdalena Laslo characterized *A Human Being* as Kobylians'ka's most successful elaboration of the woman question. According to Laslo, the novel achieved this critique by consciously imbedding the issue of women's emancipation in the concrete social and economic conditions of bourgeois society and exposing them as the driving cause of discrimination against women (331). Post-Soviet feminist readings of *A Human Being*, in turn, have brought to light the previously silenced aspects of the novel – its Darwinism, female sexuality, and human psychology – and celebrated Olena Liaufler as the first "anti-Marusia" type in Ukrainian literature. That is to say, the first female character depicted as a body and not an icon, and therefore the antithesis of the heroine in Hryhorii Kvitka-Osnovianenko's classical story "Marusia" ("Marusia," 1834) (Hundorova 2002, 96–7; Pavlychko 2002, 128–9). Despite these valuable observations, however, recent feminist readings remain limiting because they overlook the textuality of Kobylians'ka's novel. Like most modernist works, *A Human Being* challenges the reader not to seek a meaning but to help create it.

Most post-Soviet critics tend to overemphasize the novel's ending, where the heroine bursts into tears moments before her wedding. As a result, they have read *A Human Being* as a narrative of failure and a betrayal of feminist ideals, disregarding the evolutionary implications of Olena's delayed self-discovery. Though post-Soviet scholars acknowledge the theme of Olena's budding sexuality, they put it in opposition to the heroine's beliefs. In most recent critical accounts, Olena's sexual drives and mental aspirations are antagonistic and fatally irreconcilable; accordingly, the ending cannot help but fail to resolve or synthesize the heroine's desires.[22] However, a close reading of *A Human Being*, contextualized within the complete oeuvre of Kobylians'ka's writings, points in a different direction. In light of Kobylians'ka's specific feminist ideas, Olena's story emerges as a painful but successful negotiation between the heroine's instinctual and spiritual ambitions.

On the structural level, *A Human Being* is a hybrid text organized around two main themes: testing (*Prüfung*) and development (*Bildung*). Its heroine, initially an idealist and eccentric, undergoes several trials, the last of which facilitates a dynamic transformation of her views and frames her as a thinking individual capable of deriving knowledge from her own life experiences. The combination of these two novelistic modes was a challenging novelty within the Ukrainian literary tradition but a popular model in other European contexts, especially in the German and Russian literatures that influenced the young Kobylians'ka.[23] By merging *Prüfung* and *Bildung* Kobylians'ka managed to accommodate two polemical programs: to offer a feminist critique of conservative anxiety about the progressive ideal of a new modern woman and to expose what she viewed as the naive and shallow nature of dominant feminist discourse in the Ukraine of her time. The first part of the novel thus deals with the dependent position of women in a family, which Kobylians'ka attributes to a lack of education for women. The second part, during which the heroine undergoes life-changing trials that trigger her intellectual growth, denounces Ukrainian feminists for their extremism and argues against the premature implementation of their doctrines in a traditional society. As *A Human Being* imagines it, a hasty, ideologically extreme socialist feminism would lead to personal tragedies, rather than to a reconfiguration of the unjust social order and universal salvation.

The novel uses clear, formal markers to introduce each argument by starting each of the two parts with a related German-language epigraph. The first part opens with a quotation from an unspecified source:

> Das Reich der Lüge ist aufrecht, wie es noch niemals gewesen. Die Wahrheit selbst wagt sich, nur in gleißenden Fetzen vermummt, aus ihrem Winkel hervor. (I:45)
>
> [As never before, falsehood triumphs everywhere. Truth dares to creep out of its corner only when it is wrapped in brightly alluring rags.] (Franko trans., 163)

This epigraph makes a subtle, but strong, claim – falsehood reigns everywhere – that suggests by means of its authoritative tone to look for a degree of deception in everything, that is, not only in the beliefs of the antagonistic characters but also in the heroine's thoughts and judgments, whose emptiness and delusion gradually become evident as the story progresses. The second part, which complicates the pathos of mainstream Ukrainian feminist rhetoric of Kobylians'ka's time, opens with a quotation from *Allzeit voran* (*Ever Forward*, 1872) by Friedrich Spielhagen, a popular nineteenth-century German novelist who, like Eugenie Marlitt, fell from literary eminence in the late 1880s:

> Es Lebt in mir die Liebe zur Freiheit, der feste Entschluß, mich nicht knechten lassen zu wollen, es sei von wem es sei; nimmer mein Haupt zu beugen, wo meine Seele es nicht cann; mein Leben zu leben, wie Ich es verstehe, den Weg zu gehen, den Ich mir vorgezeichnet, und mich durch nichts von diesem Wege abbringen zu lassen; durch keine Schmeichelein, durch keine Drohung, mag [der Mensch] denn führen, wohin er [der Mensch] will. (I:70)
>
> [Within me, lives a love for freedom and a strong determination not to let anyone enslave me, never to bend my head where my soul cannot do the same, to live my life as I understand it, and to follow only that path that I myself have chosen, no matter how difficult it might be. May he [a human being] disregard all the flattery and threats and go where he [a human being] wants.]

Alluding to nineteenth-century individualism, this citation positions individual freedom of choice as central in the second part of the text. More importantly, it highlights the significance of a harmonious equilibrium between human cognition, symbolically represented by the

German "das Haupt" (head), and an internal emotional world, conveyed by the German "die Seele" (soul or psyche). The delicate balance between the rational and the sensual underlies Kobylians'ka's main argument against what she perceived as detrimental feminist extremism, through which women become possessed by ideas that overdetermine and distort their consciousness and their lives. A close look at *A Human Being* further proves that Kobylians'ka rejected the fundamental premises of the dominant Ukrainian feminist discourse of her time and expressed utter contempt for the emerging Ukrainian intelligentsia and their taste for the radical, grand, and dramatic.

As the first epigraph suggests, the story opens by exposing the heroine's social environment as "das Reich der Lüge" – literally, "the realm or kingdom of lies." This metaphor alludes to Dobroliubov's concept of the "dark kingdom" that Kobylians'ka had previously used to decry the harsh domestic life and subjection of women in middle-class provincial families. In *A Human Being*, however, Kobylians'ka describes the Liauflers not as a hopelessly ignorant and brutish abyss, as she had done when representing families in her earlier stories "Fate or Will" and "A Life Sketch from Bukovyna," but as an ordinary middle-class family. In her novelistic treatment, the Liauflers are not necessarily evil; they are, however, deluded and misguided by the limitations of their provincial setting, in which progressive social developments often clash with traditional values. Kobylians'ka conveyed the impoverished social reality of the periphery by creating a range of lively characters with distinct, often ironic, voices that delineate their personalities and outlooks. This polyphony satirizes the dominant, traditional understanding of the role of women in a family and injects claims in support of women's rights for education and self-expression.

Mrs Liaufler, Olena's mother, who epitomizes conservative views on womanhood, is the liveliest character in the opening scene. She shares many personality traits with Mrs Shums'ka, the main heroine in Kobryns'ka's story "The Spirit of the Time." Like Kobryns'ka's heroine, Mrs Liaufler resents her daughter's talk about women's right to education and social mobility, reveals similarly apocalyptic visions of women's emancipation, and associates any deviation from conventional morality with extreme libertinism, promiscuity, and the dissolution of the traditional family. Like Mrs Shums'ka, Olena's mother intuitively fears her daughter's enthusiasm for liberal ideas. She characterizes Olena's ambitions as a demented obsession inflicted by "a wicked and a dangerous demon [who] has gained control over her daughter's soul ... and carted [her] off ... to the land of idiocy and lunacy" (I:48; Franko trans., 163). Yet, contrary to Mrs Shums'ka, who furiously rips up her daughter's books and protests against her granddaughter's wish to become a teacher, Mrs Liaufler avoids forcing her authority on her daughter and recognizes Olena's freedom of choice. Through the shared image of a conservative mother, then, Kobylians'ka's text responds to Kobryns'ka's, while also sketching an alternative: Mrs Liaufler is far from a mirror replica of Kobryns'ka's protagonist. By subordinating Mrs Liaufler to the status of a secondary character and making her outdated, foolish beliefs a foil for Olena's progressive views, Kobylians'ka takes aim at the conservatives whom she considered pathetically incapable of keeping up with new social phenomena. Rather than joining in their lament for the doomed destinies of unfortunate provincial girls, Kobylians'ka introduced a new type of female character in Ukrainian literature, an intelligent heroine who meets adversity with a strong will and an independent mind.

Kobylians'ka presented her twenty-year-old heroine as a loving and respectful daughter but also a spirited and rebellious individual, whose liberal views clash with traditional conceptions of womanhood. Olena expresses her progressive understanding of the woman question with special clarity in her conversations with Stefan Liievych, a medical student from the University of Vienna. At first, Liievych appears to be the most cultured and educated character, an ostensible "apostle of truth" who enlightens Olena about "the blessedness of heaven" (I:50; Franko trans., 164), but is eventually revealed to be little more than a mediocrity and a poseur. During their first conversation, Liievych brings up the subject of the New Woman and makes sharp comments on the limited education of upper-middle-class women in Ukraine:

> Speaking about emancipation of women, that struggle was won a long time ago in Switzerland and other progressive countries. It is so shameful that women in our country are so backward. Not only do they not worry about gaining equality with men, they consider it an idle fancy. Having buried themselves within four walls, they make no effort to read any sensible information about this matter in order to rid themselves of their outdated, foolish, and quite ridiculous beliefs. And it's pointless to talk [to them] about attaining a solid education, or understanding natural science and materialistic philosophy. Having familiarized themselves only superficially with discrete branches of knowledge and isolated facts about world history, they consider themselves adequately armed to meet the challenges of life. And in the difficult position that they occupy in society, they hope to mount a struggle for their existence with just this smattering of knowledge ... It fills me with despair ... when I think about the comatose

> state of our women and how little they care about their independence! (I:50; Franko trans., 165)

While Olena agrees with Liievych's observations about the generally poor state of women's education in Ukraine, she finds herself at odds with his hostility towards Ukrainian women, whom he considers responsible for their ignorance and passivity and, consequently, for their own subjection. She objects by pointing out that, it is not because of their inherently flawed nature that Ukrainian women seem less progressive than European ones, but rather because of limitations in their education and upbringing. Eventually, both young people agree that if women want any positive change in their current social position, they should be more proactive in preparing themselves for the future. Their discussion ends with a resolution reminiscent of Kobylians'ka's belief in individual self-improvement as a means to personal liberation: the two characters agree that knowledge must be "the main weapon" in women's fight against social injustices. The novel's arguments in support of women's education and self-development, together with its open critique of women's apathy and ignorance have come to define what one critic has long acknowledged as "Kobylians'ka's particular brand of feminism" (Bohachevsky-Chomiak 1988, 106). This dual emphasis – on the transformative power of education and the dangers of passivity – has consistently informed all Kobylians'ka's works related to questions of women's social and political agency.

Olena's second conversation with Liievych is also ripe with philosophical reflections that reference Darwinian theories. While the novel approaches evolutionary frameworks with ambivalence, rejecting some formulations but endorsing others, its general goal is to promote respect for women's individuality in a broader humanistic sense. In the beginning of their conversation, Olena and Liievych reveal that they are secretly engaged but cannot get married until Liievych finishes his studies abroad. While saying goodbye, Liievych shares his concerns about Olena's fidelity, which he grounds in a determinist outlook that demonstrates a deeper scepticism about human agency. He points out that Olena is simply "a human being" – moreover, a female human being – who is conditioned by biological and biographical factors: in short, she has no agency over her own life. Appalled by her fiancé's selfishness and lack of confidence in her character, Olena rebuts his statements by arguing, on the contrary, that humans are driven by their volition and free will. Olena's rhetoric indicates that she is a fully formed person with strong liberal ideals, grounded not only in the progressive natural and social theories of her time but also in prosaic experiences and virtues. More importantly, the conversation articulates a glaring difference between her and Liievych's world views, which in turn allegorizes a debate in Ukrainian culture. The conversation, that is, symbolically juxtaposes the dominant tradition of the Ukrainian intelligentsia, who often adopted one or the other grand, totalizing system to explain society and propose wide-reaching solutions for human suffering, with the counter-tradition of thinkers who rejected on principle the possibility of such revolutionary, capacious salves.

While foreshadowing the heroine's dramatic disillusionment in her first fiancé, Olena's confrontation with Liievych also sets in motion a series of formidable trials of her character and ideals that eventually help her to define what it means to be human for herself. These trials begin with the bankruptcy of her family, when her desperate parents implore her to marry a well-off court adjunct, Mr K, to save the family from ruin. Olena refuses by arguing that her personality is incompatible with his and that their marriage would lead to a more profound ruin than financial instability. She describes Mr K as a cold, calculating, and brutish person who lives only for his own enjoyment and "whose 'I' constitutes the only world he knows" (I:74; Franko trans., 188). Olena exposes his tyrannical nature and calls him an indulgent, myopic, promiscuous "egoist" who uses women only to quench his lust:

> He is an egoist, a proud man, and, as he once bragged ... there is nothing in the world that can still amaze him – he has enjoyed it all, tasted it all, and no woman has the power to hold his interest for any length of time because, as he says, he knows everything about them ahead of time. He knows that all he has to do is to lift a finger and he could have ten of them at the same time. The difficult social issues of life, for example, do not concern him in the least because, as he says, there are enough students, philistines, and other insane people to look after that. (I:74; Franko trans., 188)

Olena's observations about Mr K characterize her as a wise and insightful woman capable of grasping Mr K's circumscribed views and foreseeing the inevitable enslavement and spiritual degeneration she would experience in a marriage with him. Neither parents nor friends can dissuade her. The heroine emerges victorious from her first trial, which suggests that her wit, will, and determination are sufficient to combat social pressures.

Olena's second trial, however, comes as a direct result of her refusal to marry Mr K. Financially ruined, her family moves to a remote farm where they can barely meet their material needs. The grievous village life, hard labour, and intellectual deprivation stifle Olena, who quickly realizes that "there is no greater punishment for an agile young spirit, someone who is clever, energetic, and possesses an overly refined mind, than such a lifestyle" (I:82). Daily toil, she fears, might erode her spirit, degrading her until she is apathetic to all but her physical survival. The heroine, however, does not give in to her frustration. Instead, she develops different strategies, one after another, to overcome poverty, proving to be an excellent farm manager and a responsible head of the family. Olena's efficiency, resourcefulness, and financial savvy have little to do with the literary prose she had once admired as a young girl; moreover, they have no ideology but are part of her more general habits of caring for everyone. Her appreciation for daily work and simple acts of kindness also set her apart from the mainstream intelligentsia of her time, who cultivated a taste for high drama, great sacrifice, and passionate romance, and regarded prosaic virtues as unimportant if not harmful. Despite its hardships, Olena's manifestly non-intelligentsia lifestyle presents her as a competent and resilient person capable of managing her emotions and dealing with financial scrutiny, a fit survivalist.

While the first two trials test Olena's determination and commitment (*Prüfung*), the third and final one triggers Olena's maturation (*Bildung*). The heroine's irrational passion for an attractive but modestly educated forester, Mr Fel's, whom she eventually marries, facilitates a painful process of self-discovery that demonstrates that she can learn not only from books and daily experiences but also from persistent self-exploration. Post-Soviet critics have discussed Olena's exploration of her sexuality in length. They recognize Kobylians'ka's heroine as the first woman in Ukrainian literature to talk about her erotic feelings but often read her sexuality as a "biological trap," which secures the survival of the species but does not ennoble a woman's soul (Pavlyshyn 2008, 67; Tomashuk 1969a, 99). Surprisingly, while using psychoanalytical theory to explain Olena's emotional breakdown in the moments before her wedding, post-Soviet critics ignore the revitalizing nature of sexual satisfaction celebrated by the psychoanalysts and other thinkers who influenced Kobylians'ka's intellectual growth. Although there is no evidence that Kobylians'ka read about Sigmund Freud's research on hysteria and female sexuality, published less than a year after *A Human Being*, her diaries suggest that she had been introduced to new developments in psychology and psychiatry through her friend Sofiia Okunevs'ka, who studied medicine in Zurich and Vienna in the late 1880s and early 1890, and who eventually became the first female gynaecologist in the Habsburg Empire.[24] Kobylians'ka's diaries and correspondence also testify that the young writer was well acquainted with the works of nineteenth-century Russian radical thinkers, Pisarev in particular, who recognized sexual satisfaction as a defining precondition for the harmonious development of the human mind and connected sexual deprivation with spiritual degeneration.[25] In fact, Kobylians'ka used Pisarev's discussion of bodily pleasures to frame Olena's understanding of sexuality and its liberating effects.

Minutes before she encounters Mr Fel's for the first time, Olena watches an anthill and recalls Pisarev's renowned pamphlet "Pchioly" ("Bees," 1862), in which Russia's materialist philosopher criticized mid-century Russia through a satirical investigation of the division of labour in a beehive:

> All her attention was on an anthill that rose in a small hillock in front of her. She thought about the division of labor among those insects and suddenly recalled an article by Pisarev, entitled "Bees." She had read it quite a long time ago. What a blazing exasperation she had felt after reading that work. How many fiery thoughts had risen in her soul against the "drones" ... the insects moved so swiftly, rushing about at a steady pace, without ceasing, without tiring. A strict order prevailed here, and every ant had its designated job. Did the life that teemed in the world of these tiny creatures awake any thoughts or memories in her mind? (I:82; Franko trans., 197)

In this passage, Olena evokes Pisarev's critique of the social order that divides its members into exploiters and exploited, as well as his critique of the various members of the bee colony: promiscuous queen bees, lustrous drones, and foolish, indoctrinated worker bees ("plebeian-castrates") (1958, 122). Although Olena admires to some degree the "strict order" that defines the world of the ants, she also echoes Pisarev's criticism of the worker bees, whom the Russian critic considered responsible for their own subjugation. In "Bees," Pisarev denounces the worker bees' self-sacrifice and communal commitment as "destructive stupidity" (1958, 119, 128). He insists that grand communal ideas undermine individual aspirations; such philosophies condemn their followers to debilitating drudgery in the eternal darkness of despotic, traditional societies. As Pisarev puts it, only through individual experiences and self-discovery can people understand the real meaning of what is important in life, without which no progressive change is possible. In line with his naturalistic framework, Pisarev also characterizes bodily pleasures and sexual experiences as the most potent stimuli for augmenting an individual's views. Accordingly, for Pisarev, the doomed state of the worker bees, and by extension that of all the downtrodden, derives from the repression of their sexuality. Pisarev's main criticism, however, was targeted not at the working class but at self-proclaimed liberal thinkers – those pseudo-intellectuals or doctrinairians who derived their knowledge from books and not from real-life experiences. As Pisarev observes, these propagators of lofty dogmas perceive life only as "a rhetorical figure deprived of flesh and blood," and, therefore, generate only barren, idealistic visions that have no relevance to the truths of individual happiness (1958, 115–16). In Olena's first encounter with Pisarev's work, these very ideas trigger a "blazing exasperation" in her soul and "awaken new thoughts" minutes before her first encounter with Mr Fel's (I:82).

Notably, although 1880s Ukrainian intellectuals widely discussed Pisarev's "Bees," Kobylians'ka was the first to use it in a fictional text, embedding her own criticism of feminist doctrinairianism in a broader critique of idealism, liberalism, and positivism.

Kobylians'ka's allusion to Pisarev casts Olena's decision to pursue farm life as a doomed existence brought about by the heroine's perverted, idealistic notions of heroic action, duty, and dramatic self-sacrifice. In this light, Mr Fel's, whose first appearance immediately follows the reference to Pisarev's "Bees," plays the role of Pisarev's provocateur – a figure who brings confusion into Olena's world and thus stimulates the revision of her earlier idealism. In their first scene together, Mr Fel's rescues Olena in a carriage wreck, a symbolic encounter that highlights the larger role he is to play in the heroine's life. Initially, however, Olena recognizes neither the liberating promise of the passion ignited by Mr Fel's nor his noble nature. Fearing her newly discovered sensuality, she subjects herself to psychological turmoil before finally admitting to herself that she is physically attracted to Mr Fel's. Kobylians'ka depicts Olena's agony through a series of intense, self-deprecating speeches, which capture a certain duality, a lack of wholeness characteristic of all living human beings, and a mixture of strength and weakness. Initially, Olena acts as if she has been bewitched by Mr Fel's: "blood rushes to her face, her heart begins to pound ... a strange fire burns in her eyes, and her nostrils quiver" and she is seized by strange feelings that confuse but also please her (I:84; Franko trans., 198). The stronger her erotic desire grows, the more frightened she becomes, experiencing the awakening of sexual desire as a threat not only to her virginity but also to her chaste, idealistic beliefs. By focussing on Mr Fel's's lack of scholarly erudition, Olena tries to undermine his sexual appeal and thus to regain her composure, but she quickly recognizes that her defensiveness against the natural callings of her body contradicts her own beliefs. Her revelation brings to light the discrepancy between her personal desires and those noble but naive ideals that had fascinated her from a young age. Eventually, Olena resolves her conflict in a marriage that the text casts as financially and biologically sound and intellectually motivated. The resolution of the novel thus affirms rather than undermines the decision that Olena had developed out of the conditions of her life and that she had considered in all aspects in the solitude of her village.

Although Olena fails to put into words her unconscious motives, her genuine attraction, its escalation, and its eventual liberating consequences are gradually revealed in a series of conversations, flashback memories, and dream sequences. Olena's uncertainty about her true feelings is first suggested in a confrontation with her younger sister, Iryna, who sees only pragmatic considerations behind Olena's pursuit of Mr Fel's, or what she calls a disgraceful husband hunt (*lovy*). Consequently, Iryna perceives her sister's decision to marry Mr Fel's as self-negation and spiritual death. Her rhetoric resonates with Olena's own doubts, and she succeeds in making her older sister feel "like a dog that has been punished for some wrongdoing" (I:92; Franko trans., 204). Olena, however, remains resolute in her decision to marry and rebuts Iryna's accusations with convincing arguments. First, Olena indicates that no ideological principle would lead her to refuse Mr Fel's's proposal; she does not, that is, oppose marriage as an institution. Furthermore, while acknowledging that Mr Fel's is not as refined and educated as she is, Olena argues that, unlike Mr K, he is a good man of not only remarkable physical strength but also exceptional kindness and decency. More importantly, Olena points out that Mr Fel's is an eager reader and shows sincere interest in her views. Her remarks imply that Mr Fel's would be a compliant and enthusiastic student and that Olena could eventually raise his erudition to a desirable level. Here the heroine's argument resonates with Kobylians'ka's belief in the potential of intelligent women to transform families into a more democratic organization by being supportive and loving companions to the men around them, whether fathers, husbands, brothers, or sons. Although Olena's married life is left to the reader's imagination, some of Kobylians'ka's later heroines who succeed in educating a new generation of intelligent men – such as Mania Obryns'ka in the 1909 novel *Cherez kladku* (*Over the Bridge*) – suggest that Olena's character hypothesizes a feminist reversal of Chernyshevsky's call for men to support women's access to education. Kobylians'ka had personal experience with such a role: she

Figure 3. Osyp Makovei, Chernivtsi, 1898

raised her youngest brother, and later, her niece and her niece's two sons. Perhaps even more importantly, she had taken pains to refine the aesthetic taste of her first editor Osyp Makovei, with whom she had fallen passionately in love in the late 1890s (see figure 3). These biographical details underscore Kobylians'ka's belief in the power of intelligent women to reform and educate the less privileged men and women around them.[26] In her concluding speculation, Olena claims that Mr Fel's's love for her "will not leave her untouched [because] when love comes from kind individuals it has the power to elicit reciprocal feelings" (I:93; Franko trans., 205). This faith in the transformative power of her sincere attraction to Mr Fel's suggests a happy future for the well-matched couple.

The intricate dream sequence that opens the final chapter of Olena's self-discovery further promises that the marriage will be a desirable and rewarding union. After her argument with Iryna, "frenzied ideas and fantastic images ... race like mad, one after another," in Olena's head. Tossing and turning in bed, "as though she is engulfed by flames," Olena thinks about Mr Fel's. When she finally falls asleep, she dreams of a strong man who resembles Mr Fel's and who eases her anxiety and helps her embrace the truth about her feelings:

> It seemed to her that huge, roaring waves were rushing towards her and were breaking over her head. They raged and blustered violently, and from their midst emerged a voice so loud, powerful, and derisive, that the earth shuddered and strange tremors coursed through her body. Her eye soared over the waves illuminated by a reddish golden glow. The voice increased in intensity until it plumbed the depth of her soul. Her heart was pounding – it was close to breaking. She wanted to yell, to shout a reply, but the sea suddenly ... became peaceful and smooth. And over its golden surface walked a man, tall, bold, and with radiant brow; he came right up to her and ... smiled. And they were not at all surprised that they had not seen each other for so long. They delighted in one another and argued, and all the while the sea roared its ancient familiar song – a song about love. And the sun flamed in the western sky with a crimson radiance. (I:101–2; Franko trans., 214)

In Freudian terms, the violent and derisive roar of the sea represents an external threat, possibly financial instability and social pressures. Olena's angst and inability to protect herself against the menacing voice of the sea could represent, on the one hand, her inability to convince Iryna of the honesty of her intentions and, on the other, her fear of the unknown, be it financial ruin, social disgrace, or her budding sexuality. A strong man who tames the sea and walks on its waters to rescue Olena recalls Mr Fel's and confirms Olena's sincere belief in his ability to break through personal limitations, overcome obstacles, and achieve success. The couple's delight in one another, along with the soothing song of the pacified sea, "an ancient song of love," and a spectacular backdrop of the sunlit sky, amplifies the positive image of the strong man and the heroine's confidence in him. Olena's dream acquires a particular significance if we reverse the key phrase in the epigraph to the second part of the story, presented as Olena's life motto, and read German "Seele" as "psyche." The outcome – "wo meine Seele beugt, da kann mein Haupt auch" (where my psyche bows [submits], my head [reason] can do the same) – frames Olena's decision to marry Mr Fel's as a reconciliation of her natural desires and her determination to live according to her own will and inclination. In this light, Olena's dream emphasizes the irrational dimensions of the human mind: those same forces that, throughout Kobylians'ka's novel, shape human lives as strongly as material conditions. The dream thus offers a critique of the determinist conception of human behaviour that Kobryns'ka had presented in "For a Crust of Bread."

The ending of *A Human Being*, where Mr Fel's emerges as Olena's rescuer for the third time, solidifies the life-affirming message of Olena's dream. Previous criticism has read the closing scene of the novel, where the heroine breaks into tears minutes before her wedding, as a hysterical breakdown triggered by the unbearable discrepancy between Olena's individualistic aspirations and the presumably sad reality of a marriage of convenience.[27] A set of telling textual details that immediately precedes Olena's tears, however, suggests an alternative reading that points to the success of Olena's journey. For instance, the heroine loses her composure after rereading the last letter she receives from the deceased Stephan Liievych, her first fiancé, who unexpectedly dies of typhus in Vienna at the beginning of the story. The text of the letter, which only "seems to be concise" (zdaiet'sia korotkoho zmistu), provides insight into Liievych's character. This moment also recalls the famous death scene of Ivan Turgenev's *Ottsy i deti* (*Fathers and Sons*, 1861), which Kobylians'ka viewed as "an extremely intelligent book that opened [her] eyes on many things" (Pohrebennyk 1982, 68). Like Liievych, Turgenev's hero Ievgenii Bazarov is a medical student with progressive views who also dies from typhus. Bazarov addresses his last conscious words to the woman he loves. According to Pisarev, whose works Olena greatly admires, Bazarov is a radically new hero, "a man of vigor and action," whose integrity and strength of character is expressed with exceptional clarity in his death (1955, 44–5). As Pisarev put it, "to die like Bazarov" – that is to die gracefully embracing the inevitable – "is the same as to perform a great act of bravery" (1955, 45–6). By extension, Pisarev would be unlikely to consider Liievych's final moments a model for emulation. The most glaring difference between Liievych's and Bazarov's last conscious moments lies in their attitudes towards death and their concern for loved ones. Bazarov, for his part, accepts his lot and does not indulge in miraculous fantasies of recovery, stating that a doctor cannot deny obvious symptoms (Turgenev 2009, 153). Liievych, in contrast, collapses in sentimental denial, complains about his physical pain, and longs for Olena's nursing services:

> I would very much like to have you here with me and to feel your hand on my forehead, my little darling ... Now when my head is hurting so terribly, you would do anything in your power to ease my pain. I am convinced that you would do everything differently from us doctors, and I am sure it all would go away sooner. (I:105; Franko trans., 217)

In contrast to Bazarov's speech, Liievych's words categorize him, to borrow Pisarev's terms, as "a ranter and a dilettante" (1955, 45). The thirty-year-old Olena, a mature woman who has undergone intense intellectual self-examination, can overlook neither the pathetic tone of Liievych's letter, nor its glaring contrast to her naïve, youthful admiration of a man she once believed to be a "truly whole person" whose erudition cast an unflattering shadow over Mr Fel's. With "a bitter smile," Olena tears up the letter along with all other correspondence she received from Liievych "into tiny pieces," an action which emphasizes her decision to separate from the deceased. She is distressed and feels overwhelmed with a strange feeling when Mr Fel's arrives: "A hitherto unknown, stubborn, and wild feeling gripped her – it was only a feeling. She hated. She hated from the depth of her soul. She would kill, would curse, would crush ... But would it be him? She was the one to blame! She and she alone ... and what could be her justification? That she is a human being?" (I:105). In the rhetorical question about the object of her hatred, Olena evokes a male figure, but, given the content of Liievych's last letter, the identity of her target remains obscure. Which man Olena has in mind, Mr Fel's or Liievych, illuminates what exactly she is trying to justify: her marriage or her illusions about her first fiancé. The ambiguity of the object of Olena's hatred is further complicated by the symbolic implications of the closing scene. When Mr Fel's enters the room, Olena reaches out to him with both of her hands, "as if asking for rescue" (nemov by prosyla riatunku; I:106). Mr Fel's takes her hands, raises her from the ground, and shelters her in his embrace, echoing the moment when he saved Olena from falling out of the jolted carriage, as well as the behaviour of the man in Olena's erotic dream. The symbolic links between the three intimate scenes imply not hatred but Olena's sincere attraction and desire to be dependent on Mr Fel's. Although Mr Fel's completely misreads the nature of Olena's tears, the discussed textual evidence suggests that Olena's marriage is hardly a treacherous exchange of her soul for material stability that nullifies her earlier liberal convictions, but a union in which she is most likely to flourish, both physically and spiritually.

A closer look at *A Human Being* thus shows that Olena's decision to marry Mr Fel's is well in line with her Darwinian and individualistic views that recognize the importance of sexual satisfaction in a healthy mental life. Olena is not a victim of the social order but an insightful, resolute, and resilient person capable of distinguishing between reality and dogmatic abstractions, whose goal is to create an environment where she can pursue her intellectual aspirations. She is clearly a new type of heroine that subverts traditional Ukrainian literary models, who, according to Kobylians'ka, only know how to "sign in the moonlight" (zitkha[ty] do misiachen'ka), while awaiting a perfect suitor who could secure their proper position in society (V:332). At the same time, Olena's practicality and egocentrism challenge the self-sacrificing and doctrinarian nature of the emerging radical heroine promoted by Franko and Kobryns'ka: the village teacher or postal worker who devotes her life to grand populist ideas of "saving the people." Indeed, Kobylians'ka's new type of emancipated heroine advocates an alternative venue for personal liberation, permitting a liberal compromise, which I propose to read not as a betrayal of feminist views but as an expression of sound judgment and healthy pragmatism.

Conclusion

When contextualized within Ukrainian debates of the 1880s about Social Darwinism and feminism, Kobylians'ka's diaries, personal correspondence, and early writings bring to light several inaccuracies in popular myths about Kobylians'ka's formation as a Ukrainian national writer. First, the new inquiry firmly asserts that the writer's self-identification with Ukrainian culture was not a miraculous revelation inspired by a chance encounter with Ukrainian patriots from Galicia, but rather an intricate, gradual process that took root in the writer's childhood during interactions with her father and several other Ukrainian families. The new approach to Kobylians'ka's archival materials also challenges the canonical narrative about her reception of the feminist program as it was envisioned by Kobryns'ka and problematizes the common consensus on the latter's role in the promotion of Kobylians'ka's literary career. Rather than a straightforward mutual admiration, the relationship between the two women was rife with personal conflicts that would shape Kobylians'ka's anti-socialist and anti-populist sentiments. The new reading of Kobylians'ka's tribute to Eugenie Marlitt, along with her allusions to Turgenev and nineteenth-century Russian radical thinkers, also indicates a telling trend in Kobylians'ka's early writings and an interesting continuum in nineteenth-century literature. Foremost, Kobylians'ka's reading material suggests that what radical critics often dismissed as overly sentimental in fin-de-siècle literature might be more appropriately positioned as part of the genealogy of the late nineteenth-century realist novel. The connections with nineteenth-century realist fiction are especially evident in Kobyalins'ka's peculiar feminism of "conscientious motherhood." Protesting against the patriarchal subjection of women, Kobylians'ka moulded her radical ideas into a liberal compromise by combining elements of progressive and conservative currents of thought. Kobylians'ka's new model is clever, daring, and elegant, and to either condemn her fiction as merely reactionary or to celebrate its emancipatory moments while ignoring its more problematic aspects, such as her support of traditional gender roles in family, would be to obscure the careful balancing act that keeps it poised between either extreme. Placed in historical perspective, Kobylians'ka's early writings thus exemplify the internal tensions of the late nineteenth-century literary tradition that seeks both to disseminate a new middle-class morality, and to protest against the restrictive implications of that morality for women.

Chapter Two

New Woman, New Myth

One of the defining moments in Ol'ha Kobylians'ka's writing career took place in the early 1890s when she moved together with her parents and two younger brothers to Chernivtsi, the capital of the Austrian province of Bukovyna. At the time, it was one of the most vibrant cultural and political centres in the Austrian Empire, and it offered many opportunities for personal development and self-realization to the up-and-coming writer. As Kobylians'ka wrote in her 1927 autobiography, in Chernivtsi she "entered the Ukrainian community, was introduced to Ukrainian literature and periodicals, and interacted with educated Ukrainians, their wives, and Ukrainian youth – in short, [she] entered 'the heart' of Ukrainian Bukovyna" (V:223). Within a couple of years of the move, Kobylians'ka joined several philanthropic organizations, began to participate in local Ukrainian literary circles, established contact with leading publishing institutions in Chernivtsi and L'viv, and developed personal relations with many prominent Ukrainian cultural and social activists, such as Ievheniia Iaroshyns'ka, Mykhailo Pavlyk, Stepan Smal'-Stots'kyi, Vasyl' Lukych, and Osyp Makovei, who played an important role in popularizing her works among Ukrainian readers.

The scope and intensity of artistic and intellectual growth that Kobylians'ka underwent in the first years after her move to Chernivtsi are evident in the complex aesthetic and philosophical fabric of her major fictional work of the period, her second novel, *Tsarivna* (*The Princess*, 1896). Initially, in 1888, Kobylians'ka conceived her new novel – a semi-biographical story of a downtrodden heroine who works her way to personal freedom – as a sequel to *A Human Being* and a follow-up on her earlier discussion of individual volition and critical thinking as the main driving forces of all human endeavours. However, in the early 1890s, two cultural discoveries – the intellectual discussions of the Ukrainian national revival and Nietzsche's philosophical thought – altered Kobylians'ka's original plan and placed the reconstruction of the Ukrainian national myth as the novel's central concern.

At the time when Kobylians'ka arrived at Chernivtsi, Ukrainian populists – mostly students, secular intelligentsia, and young priests, who established a variety of civic, educational, and economic associations across Galicia and Bukovyna in the 1870s and 1880s – dominated the discussion of Ukraine's potential political future. Their ideology was structured around a belief in the values of the Ukrainian peasant community, which, as they perceived it, was characterized by a love of freedom and democracy. The 1890 establishment of the Radical Party and the 1895 publication of Iulian Bachyns'kyi's *Ukraina irredenta*, which espoused the political independence of Ukraine,[1] solidified the influence of the populist movement on the intellectual discussions in Western Ukraine of the mid-1890s. While accepting wholeheartedly the narrative of Ukraine's right to political self-determination and the call for intellectuals to be in the vanguard of cultural and political progress, Kobylians'ka questioned the populists' idealization of the common man as the main driving force of Ukraine's national liberation. Influenced by Russian radicalism through Vissarion Belinsky, Ivan Turgenev, Dmitrii Pisarev, and other Russian thinkers of the nineteenth century, Kobylians'ka saw a typical Ukrainian, similar to a typical Russian as decried in the works of Russian radicals, as a passive and inert being with an inherent slave morality. In this regard, Nietzsche's criticism of the men of his day, particularly their "herd morality" that values the individual only insofar as she or he serves the group, resonated with Kobylians'ka's emerging contempt for populist treatment of the Ukrainian peasantry, whom she saw at the time at best as merely "great raw material for the future" (V:239). Similarly, Nietzsche's appeal to cultivate a new way of thinking that prioritized individual creativity, imagination, intuition, and feelings, along with his call to pursue a new way of life that celebrated continuous individual self-perfection, spoke directly to Kobylians'ka's conception of a cultural revolution as the only way to rescue Ukraine from old myths, old values, and old human types, which, as suggested in her novel *The Princess*, she perceived as unfit for the future.

Kobylians'ka's contemporaries, however, paid little heed to the philosophical dimensions of *The Princess* and often criticized its tribute to Nietzsche, whose individualism was viewed at the time as either irrelevant or reactionary, and even detrimental to Ukraine's national struggle. Early Soviet critics were even more condemnatory of Kobylians'ka's Nietzschean themes and placed *The Princess* at the margins of the Ukrainian canon.[2] As a result, for the past hundred years, *The Princess* has been viewed, with a few exceptions offered by post-Soviet critics, as Kobylians'ka's secondary text and a mere sample of her sentimental domestic fiction. *The Princess*, however, is not only a beautifully written psychological novel but also a significant landmark in the development of Ukrainian philosophical and critical thought. Not only does it introduce Nietzsche into a Ukrainian cultural context for the first time and make one of the first attempts in European literature to use Nietzsche's ideas to shape an image of the New Woman whose actions challenge the conventional bourgeois order of the day, it also proposes a radically new myth of Ukraine's national liberation. The premise of Kobylians'ka's new national myth constitutes an intricate philosophical fusion of Nietzsche's concepts of the "higher people" and the overman, which the German philosopher developed in *Thus Spoke Zarathustra*,[3] and the foundational populist dictum about the cultivated man's duty to society first formulated by Pyotr Lavrov in his *Istoricheskie pis'ma* (*Historical Letters*, 1870).[4] Drawing on these two philosophical traditions, Kobylians'ka projected individual emancipation and heightened cultural awareness of national distinctiveness among the intellectual elite as the principal road to the development of Ukrainian high culture and, consequently, to Ukraine's collective liberation.

Ol'ha Kobylians'ka's Nietzsche

Nietzsche's influence on European culture of the turn of the twentieth century was profound and widespread. His brilliant style, compelling images, and audacious criticism of Western society touched deep cultural chords, reverberating with, reinforcing, and reactivating ideas already present in the emerging modernist culture. Nietzsche's command to "break the old tables of values" (1978, 23 and 196–215) was particularly attractive to those dissatisfied with positivism, rationalism, and utilitarianism and gave them a new justification for their rebellion against modern culture and morality, which was already underway in the last decades of the nineteenth century. His association of myth with aesthetic creativity and his assertion that myth is essential to the health of a culture, that "only a horizon defined by myths completes and unifies a whole cultural movement" and provides the state's unwritten laws (1967, 135) spoke directly to modernists on the right and left, inspiring them to search for a new ruling idea by which to live. While Nietzsche's admirers celebrated him as the apostle of a new culture, a new art, a new beauty, and a new kind of human being – courageous, creative, and free – his detractors regarded him as a demonic figure, a prophet of immorality, and a symptom of cultural degeneration.[5] The complex and often controversial response to Nietzsche's philosophy is mostly rooted in the fact that Nietzsche did not offer a coherent philosophical system but rather presented his ideas in a highly metaphorical style, open to multiple interpretations. It is not surprising, therefore, that his intricate images and aphorisms were often detached from the original texts and grafted onto a wide variety of artistic, literary, and political programs. Consequently, at the turn of the twentieth century, the common perception of Nietzsche and his views was shaped mostly by secondary interpretations and artistic adaptations featuring "Nietzschean" protagonists, usually in exaggerated or vulgarized form. In this context, Kobylians'ka's first-hand knowledge of Nietzsche's major works clearly stands out: while many of her contemporaries, particularly in Eastern Europe, read Nietzsche in translations that varied in accuracy and completeness, she read in the original German his *Untimely Meditations* (1876), *The Dawn* (1881), *Thus Spoke Zarathustra: A Book for Everyone and No One* (1883–92), *Twilight of the Idols, or, How to Philosophize with the Hammer* (1888), and several other unidentified works.

Kobylians'ka discovered Nietzsche at the time when Ukrainian society was undergoing an all-pervasive cultural, political, and social crisis that would eventually explode with the outbreak of the First World War. Nietzsche's general myth of the remote historical future as the locus of creativity and value, together with his specific myth of the overman as the creator of cultural values in the future, which the German philosopher developed in his *Thus Spoke Zarathustra*, gave Kobylians'ka a conceptual framework for cultural and political reflections that fuelled her opposition to populism. Not only did Nietzsche's ideas make her question the dominant populist program that framed the peasantry as the wellspring of Ukraine's national liberation, called the intelligentsia "to identify with the folk," and propagated a "going to the people" ideology (Franko 1976–86, 45:148), but they also inspired her to furnish a new Ukrainian national myth and a new Ukrainian ideal hero – an intellectual leader devoted to the prosperous future of her or his nation who is also not shy to challenge the pessimism, passivity, and resignation of her or his own people. Although the fusion of Nietzsche and nationalism might appear startling because Nietzsche's individualism seems to contradict nationalist ideologies that subjugate the individual to the collective, some scholars of Nietzsche's influence in Eastern Europe point out that "the regressive-progressive influence of Nietzsche's thinking (use of the past to discredit the present and point to new models for the future) deepened the nationalities' search for their own cultural roots and ultimately impacted on the national independence movements" in Eastern Europe in the first decades of the twentieth century (Rosenthal 1994, 23).

More surprising, however, is Kobylians'ka's adaptation of Nietzsche's ideas to her feminist agenda. At the time when her contemporaries publically accused Nietzsche of being a "hater of women" ("Frauenhasser"), "despiser of women" ("Frauenverächter"), and "enemy of women" ("Frauenfeind"),[6] Kobylians'ka recognized the potential that Nietzsche's ideas could have for shaping the new woman of the twentieth century. Accordingly, she casted her image of a new Ukrainian ideal hero as the New Woman whose actions not only challenge the conventional bourgeois order of the day but also problematize the popular radical socialist concept of the new emancipated woman and her claim to "free love." Considering that Kobylians'ka was developing her interpretations of Nietzsche in the early 1890s – almost a decade before Nietzsche's thought had garnered considerable acceptance and manifested itself thematically in the works of other European writers, artists, and philosophers – Kobylians'ka thus could be viewed as one of the first European intellectuals to read Nietzsche as a liberator of the downtrodden social groups. Kobylians'ka was also one of the first to conjoin in her cultural and political views personal and national emancipation, which she saw as complementary, not conflicting.

Most likely, Kobylians'ka first read Nietzsche around 1892, the time when she integrated several Nietzschean motifs in the final edition of her first novel, *A Human Being*. The writer's reference to Nietzsche's famous dictum on women and a whip from *Thus Spoke Zarathustra* – "You go to women? Do not forget the whip!" (1978, 67) – stands out the most. It comes up in a conversation that takes place between Olena Liaufler's father and his friend, a local physician, who recommends that Mr Liaufler keep a whip handy and not be shy "de-ne-de tsviakhaty batizhkom" (to strike with a whip here and there) in dealings with women, and his daughter in particular (I:59).[7] In the same year, Kobylians'ka also quoted directly from *Thus Spoke Zarathustra* in the early version of her humorous short story "Vin i vona" ("He and She," 1895), which was originally titled with another famous dictum from *Thus Spoke Zarathustra* – "Der Mensch ist Etwas, das überwunden werden soll" ("Man Is Something That Shall Be Overcome").[8] In Kobylians'ka's personal correspondence, her first reference to Nietzsche also appeared in 1892. In a letter written on 5 July, her friend Sofiia Okunevs'ka asked Kobylians'ka how she liked Nietzsche, implying that the writer must have read some of his works by then (IL F14, N811). From this point on, Kobylians'ka frequently discussed Nietzsche in her letters to Okunevs'ka, Osyp Makovei, Avhusta Kokhanovs'ka, Khrystyna Alchevs'ka, and other correspondents. While her friends often remained ambiguous about Nietzsche and his audacious claims, Kobylians'ka articulated vivid interest in and genuine fascination with "the great prophet" and his views. According to her diaries, in addition to Nietzsche's several original works, Kobylians'ka also studied George Brandes's *Menschen und Werke: Essays* (*People and Works: Essays*, 1894) and Hugo Kaatz's *Die Weltanschauung Friedrich Nietzsches* (*The Worldview of Friedrich Nietzsche*, 1892–3), both of which were among the first critical attempts to map out Nietzsche's philosophy and played an important role in introducing Nietzsche to a broader audience.[9] Kobylians'ka's notes on Nietzsche also prove that, as opposed to the majority of the so-called Nietzscheans who derived their cursory knowledge of Nietzsche from secondary sources and often based their readings on exaggerated or vulgarized interpretations of Nietzsche, she studied his works thoroughly and critically. Therefore, it makes sense to look in Kobylians'ka's writings not only for direct quotations, allusions, and parallels in imagery and vocabulary but also for a well-rounded, coherent position vis-à-vis, or even polemics with, Nietzsche's ideas.

Past critics have long recognized Nietzsche's influence on Kobylians'ka. Osyp Makovei, Kobylians'ka's close friend and editor, was the first to acknowledge Nietzsche's "positive influence" on her world view. As Makovei stated in his 1896 introduction to the first publication of *The Princess*, Nietzsche taught Kobylians'ka "to look at the world from a more elevated perspective, drew her attention to style ... and, despite his whimsy and brutality towards women, taught her to be strong and courageous" (1954, 45). Makovei's positive assessment, however, is one of the few enthusiastic commentaries on Kobylians'ka's interest in Nietzsche that came from her contemporaries. From the late 1890s onward, many leading Ukrainian intellectuals criticized Kobylians'ka's tribute to Nietzsche, whose affirmation of a positive noble hero was explicitly hostile to their populist ideology. Nataliia Kobryns'ka, Kobylians'ka's quasi-mentor, went so far as to warn the young writer against Nietzsche. "Don't waste your time on Nothing [Nietzsche]," she wrote to Kobylians'ka in 1894, "the world calls him a criminal ... the arrogance of that man is terrible, and where there is such arrogance, there is barely any grain of true understanding" (IL F14, N756). Several other prominent contemporaries – Ahatanhel Kryms'kyi and Lesia Ukrainka – also endowed Nietzsche with derogatory epithets and decried him as an "insane" and "scandalous" propagator of "frivolous lifestyle" (1963, 38; 1963a, 70). The most contentious attack, however, came from Serhii Iefremov, a pro-socialist political activist and literary critic, who condemned Kobylians'ka's interest in the fashionable philosopher and his dictum "anything is permitted to the higher people" (1993, 78–80). In his article "V poiskakh novoi krasoty" ("In Search of the New Beauty," 1902), Iefremov labelled Kobylians'ka as an elitist who was bent on inscribing perverted foreign substances into the Ukrainian context after reading too much Nietzsche, and denied her the title of a Ukrainian author altogether (1993, 119–21). One of the main explanations for contemporaries' criticism of Kobylians'ka's interest in Nietzsche is the lack of proper exposure that Ukrainian intellectuals had to the German philosopher in the 1890s. The first phase of Nietzsche's reception in Ukraine was mostly shaped either through secondary sources or transmuted adaptations by Polish and Russian pseudo-Nietzscheans, who linked their decadent beliefs with exaggerated and often vulgarized interpretations or even cheap imitations of Nietzsche.[10] As a result, not only Ukrainian populist critics of the 1890s but also the leading figures of Ukrainian modernism of the 1910s – Mykola Voronyi, Ostap Luts'kyi, Mykola Ievshan, Mykyta Sribliansʼkyi, and Andrii Tovkachevs'kyi – had only cursory and often corrupted knowledge of Nietzsche's philosophy and read him either as a reactionary anti-socialist or as a scandalous nihilist (Pavlychko 1999, 132). It is not surprising, therefore, that Kobylians'ka's contemporaries could not appreciate the full scope of her peculiar reading of Nietzsche and her complex adaptations of Nietzsche's views on friendship, marriage, self-overcoming, redemption, and prudence for her own philosophical system.

Luka Lutsiv, a prolific émigré scholar of Ukrainian literature, made the first critical attempt to analyse Nietzsche's influence on Kobylians'ka more thoroughly. In his 1928 study "O. Kobylians'ka i F. Nitsshe" ("O. Kobylians'ka and F. Nietzsche"), he drew attention to biographical similarities between the German philosopher and Kobylians'ka: he emphasized that both writers were influenced by Greek mythology, German Romanticism, and Darwin's theory of evolution. He also offered the first comprehensive survey of Nietzschean motifs in Kobylians'ka's fiction – the eternal recurrence, great noon, overman, and "higher people" to name a few. Lutsiv, however, claimed that Kobylians'ka simply borrowed Nietzschean motifs and concepts without understanding their complex meaning (Lutsiv [1975], 176). Throughout the twentieth century, Lutsiv's approach of judging Kobylians'ka's reception of Nietzsche dominated Kobylians'ka scholarship.[11]

Only recently, critics have made significant progress in approaching Kobylians'ka's Nietzsche anew. Some have elaborated on Nietzsche's ideas of Apollonian and Dionysian creative impulses in Kobylians'ka's program of cultural regeneration,[12] and others have expanded the list of Nietzsche's motifs that Kobylians'ka employed in her fiction and read her reception of Nietzsche as a dialogue in which she worked out her own understanding of Nietzsche's ideas by polemicizing with the German philosopher.[13] Building on recent scholarship that has elaborated in length on the undeniable presence of Nietzsche in Kobylians'ka's works, the following reading of Kobylians'ka's first novel *The Princess* elaborates on how the writer used Nietzsche in her broader discussion of personal and national liberation and in her elitist vision of Ukraine's political future – a topic that has been established by post-Soviet scholars in a preliminary way.[14] The novel's contextualization in the broader European intellectual discourse of the 1890s, along with some new archival evidence, proves that Kobylians'ka's reception of Nietzsche was more nuanced and original than previously acknowledged.

The Princess: Philosophical Reflections in Artistic Form

The main story of *The Princess* revolves around a simple and rather conventional plot that resonates with many stories within nineteenth-century domestic fiction. Its heroine, Natalka Verkovychivna, is a destitute orphan of petit-bourgeois origin who suffers from family despotism in the house of her greedy and unscrupulous aunt. Throughout the story, the heroine patiently and diligently outwits her oppressive aunt and other malicious characters and overcomes many emotional and social barriers to achieve professional accomplishment and happiness in a well-matched marriage. Kobylians'ka wrote the first version of *The Princess* between 1887 and 1889 in German, but she could not publish it in its original language. After a few unsuccessful publication attempts in German-language periodicals, Kobylians'ka translated her novel into Ukrainian,[15] but it took many editions, corrections, and several title changes before *The Princess* was serialized and then came out as a complete publication in the Chernivtsi-based Ukrainian paper *Bukovyna* in 1896.[16]

Only the first twenty pages of the German manuscript have survived (see figure 4), but they contribute much to our understanding of Kobylians'ka's literary development as a writer. Namely, they provide insight into the differences between Kobylians'ka's modes of address to her initially intended German-speaking audience and her eventual Ukrainian readership. The most obvious difference between the two versions of the text is that the Ukrainian text offers more refined dialogues and expands and nuances descriptions of nature, which enhance the psychological portraits of the main characters. However, it is the discursive and culturally defined changes between the two variants of *The Princess* that most tellingly show Kobylians'ka's transformation as a writer. One of the major conceptual differences between the two texts appears in the opening paragraph, which starts with a statement, "I was born on November 29," positioning a particular historical individual as the subject. In the original German text, the gender of the first-person narrator is undefined and is specified only in the second paragraph, where the narrator points out that the foregoing ruminations comprise "the philosophical effusions of a young girl" (KLMHM N1681–1681, 1). In the Ukrainian language, the gender of the subject is reflected in the verb, which makes gendering inevitable in the opening paragraph of the Ukrainian text. This grammatical specificity annuls the original conceptual set-up, which in the German manuscript introduces the protagonist as a human being first and a woman second (I:109). Furthermore, in the second paragraph of the Ukrainian text, the German sentence "Is the mental life of a person, and that of a female in particular, really such a nothing that one should pay it less attention than they pay the organism itself?" (KLMHM N1681, 1) is abridged to "Is the spiritual life of a woman less interesting than her organism?" (I:109). The differences between the two sentences suggest that the foregrounding of the protagonist's gender in the Ukrainian version is not only grammatically determined but also premeditated by Kobylians'ka. Whereas in the German text Kobylians'ka emphasized the mental and emotional life of a person, a human being, and thus set out to examine a human psyche by using a female character, in the Ukrainian version she prioritized the psychology of a woman, thus foregrounding a feminist agenda. Kobylians'ka's emphasis on the feminist theme in the Ukrainian text could be viewed as a strategic move to suit the contemporaneous demands of Ukrainian readers, who were rapidly developing a taste for domestic fiction and literature on feminist themes after the 1887 publication of *The First Garland*, the first literary almanac written by and for women. Most likely, this decision was dictated by Osyp Makovei, Kobylians'ka's editor of the time. Given that by the early 1890s Kobylians'ka had withdrawn from Kobryns'ka and criticized her feminist activities as inconsistent, reductionist, and superfluous,[17] the introduction of the feminist theme and its subsequent development in the Ukrainian text could be also read as a continuation of Kobylians'ka's challenge to Kobryns'ka's socialist vision of feminism, a challenge that was introduced in *A Human Being*. In any case, both considerations would have been irrelevant in the early German version intended for a German-speaking audience.

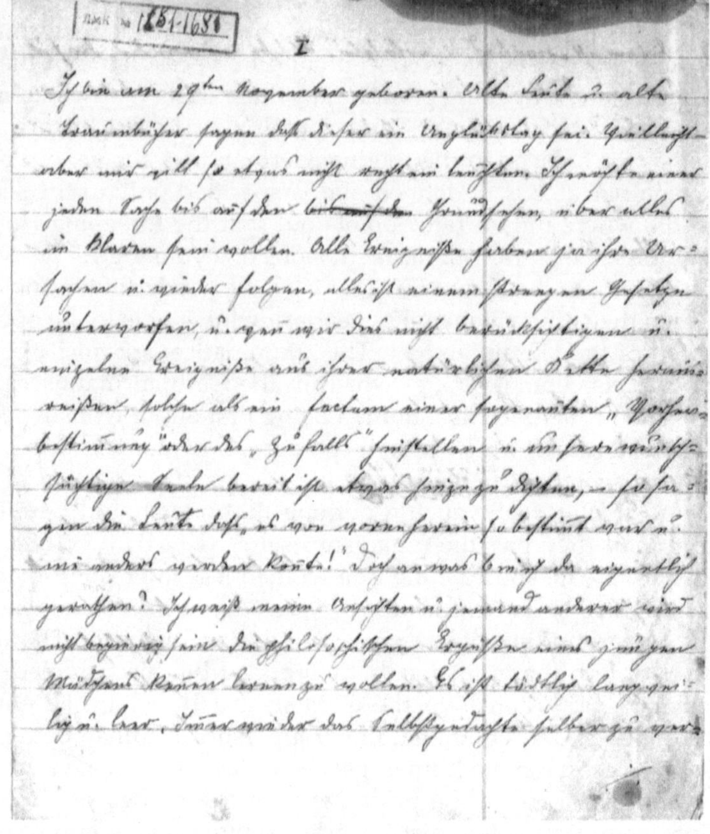

Figure 4. *Tsarivna*, German-language handwritten manuscript, page 1, ca. 1894

Another difference between the original German-language and the final Ukrainian-language versions of *The Princess* that demonstrates Kobylians'ka's awareness of the two different social and cultural markets is the ethnic identification of one of the main antagonists in the story. While the first twenty pages of the German text offer no ethnic definition to any of the characters, the Ukrainian text promptly introduces the narrator's aunt as "a Polonized German," a telling character description: in the sociocultural context of nineteenth-century Western Ukraine, Germans were often associated with the cultural other, either exemplary or ominous, while Poles and Polonization were linked to violence, treason, and immorality. As Kobylians'ka's later works show, she was well aware of the ethnocentric and xenophobic tendencies among her Ukrainian readers and often used definitions of non-Ukrainian ethnicities to enhance her description of negative character traits.[18] Considering modern notions of the arbitrary, provisional, and imagined nature of nations, Kobylians'ka's ethnic determinism is in itself problematic,[19] but the absence of any derogatory ethnic reference in Kobylians'ka's early German text, alongside Kobylians'ka's persistent effort to articulate for her Ukrainian readership detrimental consequences of ethnocentrism and xenophobia (discussed in the following chapters), suggests that the introduction of ethnic definitions in the Ukrainian text was dictated by the Ukrainian social and cultural contexts of the time. Clearly, Kobylians'ka's originally intended German-speaking audience would not be able to register these culturally defined nuances.

While stylistic and discursive differences between the German and Ukrainian versions of *The Princess* prove that Kobylians'ka was thoroughly taken with a cultural translation of her work, its original critical reviews show that, despite all modifications, the novel's complex programmatic subject matter remained, for the most part, inaccessible or irrelevant to Ukrainian readers. While celebrating the aesthetic quality of the work – its lavish descriptions of nature and astute psychological portraits – Kobylians'ka's compatriots, as noted before, had little appreciation for her dialogue with Nietzsche and often viewed *The Princess* as a mere sample of well-written yet sentimental domestic fiction. Kobylians'ka's personal letters of the late 1890s show that the young writer found such reviews unwarranted and that she was not shy to express her dissatisfaction with what she characterized as the "old-fashioned" and "circumscribed" aesthetic taste of her Ukrainian critics (V:330). When Mykhailo Hrushevs'kyi read *The Princess* as a Cinderella story, in which the heroine was only slightly modernized by her reading of Nietzsche (Hrushevs'kyi 1898), Kobylians'ka was deeply hurt, as can be judged from her letter to Osyp Makovei of 16 March 1898:

> How could he write something so old-fashioned? He transformed Natalka, who was a thinking individual from the very beginning, into some kind of a Cinderella, who suffers under her evil stepmother and stepsisters and waits for a prince. He says she is modernized because she reads Nietzsche! It seems that that *panok* [little mister] doesn't read anything besides Ukrainian literature because he seems not to know that there are already different types of women, who strive for much more than just a marriage! He assumes too much authority and rights ... while everything

he writes is mediocre ... He doesn't see anything but the plot ... If he were better informed ... he wouldn't write such non-sense! (V:330–1)

In the same letter, Kobylians'ka also offered an extended commentary on the symbolic connotations of her main characters and underscored that the plot was of no importance in her novel, and that she used it only to mould her philosophical system and social critique into a form that would be most accessible to her prospective Ukrainian readers. At the end of the letter to Makovei, she claimed that her work was an important threshold in the history of Ukrainian literature, that it was "not for entertainment, but for contemplation," and that "the more one reads it, the more he or she understands its essence" (V:330).

Apparently, Kobylians'ka's polemic had little effect on her addressee, Osyp Makovei, because in his own review of *The Princess*, he argued for the novel's absolute social and biological determinism. He compared it to Gabriele Reuter's naturalist novel *Aus guter Familie* (*From a Good Family*, 1895) and Anna Radius Zuccari's moralistic novel *Teresa* (*Theresa*, 1886), both of which feature a life struggle of subjugated, middle-class young women. As her letter written to Makovei on 13 January 1899 suggests, Kobylians'ka was less than pleased with his reading of her "thinking" and wilful Natalka as some kind of "Goethe's Werther in a skirt" (Makovei 1963, 53) and a mirror image of Reuter's and Zuccari's hysterical heroines:

I read your review ... and was unpleasantly surprised by your stereotypical views about women and your belief that they would rather rush into *any kind* of marriage than live without a husband. I think there are only two reasons that can force women to act that way: daily bread and excessive sensuality. A woman, who has an income and values herself, and who cannot marry the one she really loves, *would never run after a man*. You say ... that all three – Natalka, Agatha, and Theresa [Reuter's and Zuccari's heroines, respectively] – drive themselves to hysteria in their pursuit of marriage; by doing so, you basically endorse Laura Marholm's words that "a man constitutes the sole meaning of a woman's life." I would like to ask you where do you see Natalka's *excessive sensuality and hysteria*? Perhaps, when she is completely devastated because her work is sent back? Or maybe you see it in her longing for a better and more refined life ... Your Marholm's standards are very low. I don't know why you are relying on them when you judge women ... According to you, every unwedded woman is excessively sensual and hysterical. *I implore you to revise your conclusions and emphasize first of all not Natalka's love to Marko and Oriadyn, but that what you mention briefly later on – the fact that "she is a thinking*

> *individual"* ... The most brilliant women and men alike fall in love. Goethe, like [Sofiia] Kovalevs'ka, George Sand, and many others, couldn't live without love, but you wouldn't say that love constituted the sole meaning of their lives ... [In your view], an unwedded woman is a hostage of her sensuality ... With claims like this, you have distanced yourself from me. Now, every man can point a finger at me or at any [unmarried] girl of my age and say: she is *hysterical* herself; she is at *that age* ... Perhaps you didn't mean to present me in such unfavorable light, but you are actually the first who did this. Neither Kryms'kyi nor Hrushevs'kyi did so. (V:385–6)

In her polemic, Kobylians'ka accentuated Natalka's self-confidence, strength, and professional ambition and rearticulated her earlier arguments that position her heroine as an "antithesis" of Reuter's and Zuccari's characters (Panchuk 1970, 137) by pointing out that Natalka has more far-reaching goals than marriage and sexual satisfaction.

It seems, however, that despite Kobylians'ka's consistent attempts to draw critical attention to the broader social and political issues in her work, Makovei, alongside the rest of the prominent Ukrainian critics of the time, disregarded the philosophical and ideological complexity encoded in elements of the novel's structure, particularly in the configuration of relationships between characters. Paradoxically, Russian censors were perhaps the only group among Kobylians'ka's contemporaries to sense the subversive, pro-Ukrainian message of her second novel, when they banned it from publication in Saint Petersburg in 1898.[20] The original critical reviews of *The Princess* that canonized it as a story of unaccomplished feminist ambition proved long lasting. Even today, the notions of frustrated aspirations and lack of agency continue to shape critical readings of Kobylians'ka's second novel. In the 1960s, when Soviet Ukraine experienced an ideological thaw, Nykyfor Tomashuk problematized the early readings of *The Princess* but hobbled his discussion by claiming that, while Kobylians'ka's heroine expressed many progressive views at the beginning of the story, she eventually abandoned all of them for the sake of marriage (1969a, 52). Later critics, post-Soviet ones among them, also read Natalka's story as, if not a defeat, then not quite a success story. While justly recognizing *The Princess* as "the first and most consistently feminist [text] in Ukrainian literature" (Bohachevsky-Chomiak 1988, 105), and making many important observations about its allusions to Nietzsche, they often see it as a failure either to create an overman (Hundorova 2002, 120) or to overcome unexpected life circumstances and "vypadok" (chance), which, according to one critic, Kobylians'ka believed to play a decisive role in all human endeavours (Pavlyshyn 2008, 129–42).

Martha Bohachevsky-Chomiak gives *The Princess* and its programmatic vision the most credit when she compares Kobylians'ka's work to Chernyshevsky's renowned novel *Chto delat'?* (*What Is to Be Done?* 1863). She, however, limits her discussion by equating Kobylians'ka's heroine with Chernyshevsky's Vera Pavlovna, the embodiment of the radical socialist understanding of the New Women (Bohachevsky-Chomiak 1988, 109). While Kobylians'ka's work, like Chernyshevsky's text, might be structured around the issue of the reorganization of relations between the sexes, and might also offer a daring program of action, even a cursory look at the two texts proves that Kobylians'ka's heroine is fundamentally different from Vera Pavlovna. As opposed to Chernyshevsky's heroine, who is preoccupied primarily with either her passions or utopian socialist visions, Natalka understands that only independent "cognitive work" and continuous self-improvement and self-overcoming fills human existence with meaning and leads to autonomy, both personal and collective (I:227). Bohachevsky-Chomiak's commentary about conceptual and symbolic affinities between Chernyshevsky's and Kobylians'ka's texts, however, is not entirely unjustified and merits consideration.

The New Woman: Kobylians'ka's Version

A brief analysis of the most glaring differences between *What Is to Be Done?* and *The Princess* not only provides helpful insight into the discussion of Kobylians'ka's links to Chernyshevsky and Russian radicalism more broadly defined[21] but also elaborates on how Kobylians'ka adopted Nietzsche in her understanding of the woman question and the question of Ukraine's national regeneration. The main distinction between the two texts is rooted in their attitudes towards the role of women in family and society. Chernyshevsky's novel depicts "new people" (novye liudi) who were motivated by rational egoism – a belief that the interests of the educated rational individual and society coincide – and practised gender equality. Its heroine, Vera Pavlovna, pursues an independent life by organizing a successful sewing cooperative, which eventually demonstrates that people can live and work together harmoniously for mutual benefit. In the broadest sense, Chernyshevsky's novel became "a Bible for all advanced Russian women with aspirations towards independence," whether they thought and acted as organized feminists or as revolutionaries (Stites 1978, 89). It reinforced their ideas on education, economic independence, and the moral imperative of helping not only women but also all "the people" to struggle for their rights and liberation. It also propagated "free love," a socialist doctrine of personal emancipation and sexual freedom, by advancing a broader program of relations between the sexes, an understanding of erotic love, a tenet of generations of revolutionaries that would define their unspoken allegiances from then on. According to Mykhailo Pavlyk, an important Galician socialist and publicist of the late nineteenth century, Chernyshevsky's novel was one of the most popular texts in Western Ukraine and exerted a colossal influence on the Ukrainian radical intelligentsia before the turn of the century (qtd. in Bohachevsky-Chomiak 1988, 109). As the main feminist themes of *The Princess* suggest, Kobylians'ka's reception of the key ideas embedded in *What Is to Be Done?* was more critical than that of Chernyshevsky's admirers.

While Kobylians'ka might have shared Chernyshevsky's criticism of the patriarchal order and might have sided with his argument in support of women's education, she challenged the Russian critic's designs for personal and collective liberation. She did so by questioning the utopian nature of Chernyshevsky's positivist program and its lack of connectedness with the real conditions of life. Kobylians'ka was especially critical of the fanatical idealism and lack of personal agency characteristic of Chernyshevsky's heroine and demanded far more than short-term success and temporary sexual satisfaction for her Natalka. Although Chernyshevsky's Vera Pavlovna is able to lead an active and engaging life, her actions are circumscribed by the dominant order, and she remains immature and dependent on her male companions throughout the novel. Despite the fact that Vera Pavlovna achieves financial independence and a comfortable social status, at the end of the story, as she acknowledges herself, she is not completely free and only hopes that "in a few years [she] will be able to stand on [her] own feet" (Chernyshevsky 1985, 348). When in the next sentence the narrator observes that "there is no real happiness without total independence," and that women rarely experience this type of happiness, his words underscore the fact that, despite a long and exhausting struggle for autonomy, Vera Pavlovna fails to become utterly free and ultimately happy (Chernyshevsky 1985, 348). As opposed to Chernyshevsky's heroine, whose limited success turns out to be no more than a chance gift from her self-sacrificing husband, Kobylians'ka's heroine uses personal resources to overcome external and internal obstacles. Choosing as her life motto Nietzsche's imperative "to be her own goal," which the German philosopher introduced in his *Human, All Too Human* (1879) and further developed in *The Gay Science* (1882), and other works,[22] Natalka becomes a "great power in herself," a Nietzschean "higher person" who is capable of not only supporting her husband and raising her future children but also of fighting "for the highest goals that reach beyond her everyday happiness," namely, the liberation of her people (I:227).

The second conceptual difference between Kobylians'ka and Chernyshevsky lies in their approach to the institution of marriage. Although in both works marriage is not a final destination but a means for two people to move beyond the traditional limits placed on men and women through domesticity, they differ in their discussions of alternative nuptial arrangements. While Chernyshevsky called on his audience to use marriage as an escape strategy, Kobylians'ka pointed out that such often rushed and premature decisions impaired individual freedom to almost the same degree as forced marriages did. She developed her argument by expounding on her earlier idea of individual self-improvement as a way to women's liberation, which she introduced in *A Human Being* and reinforced in *The Princess* with Nietzsche's critique of marriage and traditional womanhood from *Thus Spoke Zarathustra*. Although many of Kobylians'ka's commentators dwell on Nietzsche's overall negative characterizations of traditional woman in the "On Little Old and Young Women" passage in *Thus Spoke Zarathustra* (1978, 65–7), which they viewed as irredeemably misogynistic,[23] Kobylians'ka paid more attention to the "On Child and Marriage" passage of the book. She appreciated its nuanced distinction between ignoble and noble men and women and openly embraced Nietzsche's generic classification of all marriages into two types: one that reduces both partners and is no more than "the filth of the soul in pair" and the other that promises to produce something higher than mere self-reproduction to create "the creator," the ultimate overman (1978, 69–70).

Similar to Nietzsche's discussion, Kobylians'ka's reflection on an ideal marriage – a union of free and self-sufficient individuals – opens with an exposition of the potential destructiveness of ill-matched marriages of convenience. *The Princess* brims with portrayals of dysfunctional families, but the union of Natalka's uncle and aunt is the most telling example. In one of her quasi-rational speeches intended to mock Natalka's dreams about "tender feelings," Natalka's aunt confesses that although her own marriage might be peaceful, it lacks intimacy and mutual understanding:

> Aren't you ashamed to say that to my and your uncle's faces? ... Well, that's right. How can someone who feeds on the poison of romantic novels say anything else ... I don't understand what this love is. When I got married, I didn't have the slightest symptom of that poetic sickness. I ran my household properly, raised kids with God's help, and took care of my husband ... But to dream about love ... I ought to be ashamed of it. It's sheer fantasy.

> If I hadn't married your uncle, I'd have married someone else. He'd be an honest, quiet, and shy lad, and I'd be the same maiden. At your age, I was already raising Muniechko and taking care of the household, but you ... you talk about love! Well, as you make your bed, so you must lie on it. You are old enough to understand what is good and what is evil. (I:122)

Natalka's aunt despises love as "a poetic sickness" that inevitably leads to hardship and projects marriage as a dutiful means of procreation and reaffirmation of the status quo. Although the ridiculousness of the aunt's rhetoric is self-evident, the story exposes it further by elaborating on a series of loveless marriages and their calamitous consequences that drive young people to ruin. The hapless marriage of Natalka's younger cousin Lienochka stands out the most in this regard. Encouraged by her mother, Lienochka enters into an ill-matched but rationally sound wedlock with the elderly Professor Lorden. Once the initial excitement settles, Lienochka's marriage turns out to be a disastrous bond – the very kind that Nietzsche describes in his *Thus Spoke Zarathustra* as "the filth of the soul in pair" (1978, 70). "There was rarely a day," Natalka's uncle observes at the end of the novel, "that went without screaming and squabbling" in Lienochka's married life (I:397), and she eventually regrets her rushed decision and destroyed youth. *The Princess* suggests a similar disastrous outcome for Oriadyn, Natalka's first love, who also ignores his feelings and yields to the prevailing philistine order by marrying the only daughter of his wealthy Polish supervisor. As suggested through the story of Oriadyn's parents, a Ukrainian nineteen-year-old maiden of noble descent and an impoverished Gypsy musician, Kobylians'ka did not give much credit to the radical idea of free love either. The unrestrained passion and self-indulgence of Oriadyn's parents not only lead them to physical death but also subject their illegitimate offspring to social disdain and financial hardship.

Natalka's personal life choices further highlight the potential danger of not only the marriage of convenience but also the concept of "free love." When Natalka cancels her forced engagement with Professor Lorden and rejects Oriadyn's proposal to run away to a remote village and enjoy their "free love," she ironically proves that her aunt was right to consider her "old enough to understand what is good and what is evil" (I:122). In both cases, Natalka justifies her decision by admitting that she is not ready, either spiritually or intellectually, and must achieve personal and financial freedom on her own before she can join someone, be it in wedlock or outside it. When several years later she marries Doctor Marko, who shares her philosophy of life and highly refined aesthetic sensibility, no external or internal pressures interfere with Natalka's decision. She does it out of her own free will.

The story of Natalka's intimate life shows that Kobylians'ka's alternative vision of marriage greatly resonates with Nietzsche's belief that only "the self-conqueror, the commander of [one's] senses, the master of [one's] virtues," can create a productive marriage in which the two partners would not merely reproduce but produce "something higher," "a living monument to [their] victory and liberation" (1978, 69, 211). Kobylians'ka's vision thus does not challenge directly the basic principles of religion, morality, or civil order. Yet her unconventional understanding of marriage grounded in equal partnership, alongside her desire to rethink, reclaim, and reassert the traditional role of women in family and society, clearly makes her conservatism more radical than the doctrinaire revolutionarism of many of her compatriots who propagated "radical egoism" and "free love." Natalka's personal story thus could be viewed as another elegant fusion of conservative and revolutionary currents of thought characteristic of Kobylians'ka's early fiction but now reinforced with Nietzsche's philosophy.

A New Ukrainian Heroine as a New National Myth

The conceptual links between Kobylians'ka and Chernyshevsky are not exhausted by the writers' interest in the reorganization of relations between the sexes. Like Chernyshevsky, Kobylians'ka utilized the life story of her heroine to articulate an alternative program for restructuring all social and political relations. Following the nineteenth-century Ukrainian literary tradition, Kobylians'ka used her heroine to represent Ukraine and its social and political dynamics. From the mid-nineteenth century onward, Ukrainian writers commonly used images of violated, docile, or self-sacrificing women to symbolize their oppressed nation. In the Ukrainian cultural context, this tradition derived from folk songs and was canonized in Taras Shevchenko's poetry, where Ukraine was often represented through images of orphans, lovelorn girls, mermaids, or simply poor folks who suffered at the hand of the rich. These heroines were usually unable to have normal human relationships and often died, which, as some scholars argue, symbolized Ukraine's political impotence (Grabowicz 1982, 61).[24] In the last decade of the nineteenth century, progressive Ukrainian writers somewhat modified these heroines and adjusted their symbolic implication to the new dynamics in Ukraine's social and political sectors. Like Chernyshevsky's Vera Pavlovna, the new Ukrainian heroines often demonstrated strong intellectual concerns, a need for political involvement, and powerful emotional and sexual desires, but were eventually driven to madness, sickness, or alienation by the same social order they dared to challenge.

According to one recent critic, the modified Ukrainian heroines signified the arrival of a new spirit and a new hope for change on the one hand, but highlighted the inability of their societies to embrace new progressive ideas on the other (Shkandrij 2001, 198).[25]

Compared to these heroines, Kobylians'ka's Natalka is a radically new character type: not only does she recasts her historical moment but she also reconfigures the traditional models of national martyrdom by offering a new, victorious myth of Ukraine's cultural and political liberation. While assigning to her heroine a distinct social and political mission that echoed many Russian radical slogans of the late nineteenth century, Kobylians'ka, however, chose as a role model for her heroine not Vera Pavlovna, the icon of Russian radicalism, but Nietzsche's concepts of "higher people" and the overman. In the opening section of *Thus Spoke Zarathustra*, in "Zarathustra's Prologue," Nietzsche called on his contemporaries to account for their failings and pursue a new way of life. He presented this new way of living as an epochal transition from mere human beings to virtually a new species, an overman (1978, 12–14). While framing the overman as a historical goal, Nietzsche also presented him as a personal and quite ambiguous new kind of ideal for each individual, predicated on self-overcoming – a perpetual aspiration to be more than one is and a continuous transcendence of a present state. "Man is something that must be overcome" (1978, 12, 199, 287), as Nietzsche insisted, and only "higher people" – those who are "brave," "open-hearted," "selfish," autonomous, possessed of great will, able to reject conventional virtues, able to endure great suffering, but also able to laugh, to dance, and to assert new values – are capable of achieving it (1978, 268–96). Tellingly, Nietzsche envisioned the process of self-overcoming as an individual experience and did not offer his readers any specific prescriptions on how to pursue it. As some commentators observe, this is precisely the reason why *Thus Spoke Zarathustra* can be simultaneously a book for all, that is for anyone who is responsive to Nietzsche's call to self-overcoming, and for none (Pippin xxiv). Kobylians'ka's creative works and some archival materials suggest that she, as opposed to many of her contemporaries, read Nietzsche's overman as a philosophical metaphor that conveys an ultimate attitude to life that places regeneration and new beginnings as its highest values.

The writer's brief comment on her reception of the overman, which she penned on a visiting card of her brother, for example, unequivocally suggests that she had a deep appreciation for Nietzsche's figurative language and his affinity for symbolism: "One should never forget that Nietzsche as a man of the future wanted in *Zarathustra* a character *who is not from our world*, and to whom, therefore, no one can actually relate in any intrinsic way" (qtd. in the original German in Pavlyshyn 2008, 92).[26] Accordingly, Kobylians'ka designed her novel as a story of the heroine's gradual maturation and intellectual transformation. Like Nietzsche's overman who undergoes three successive metamorphoses of his mind – the camel, the lion, and the child stages (1978, 25–8) – Natalka also endures three stages of spiritual and intellectual self-discovery. In Kobylians'aks novel, these stages are identified through Natalka's carefully chosen symbolic nicknames: Lorelei, Princess, and Lotus Blossom. The Lorelei stage deals primarily with Natalka's struggle against the pettiness, vulgarity, and pervasive materialism of her philistine environment. It culminates with her relative financial freedom and a complete separation from her malicious family. The Princess stage focuses on Natalka's emotional life and overcoming of the self. The heroine completes this stage by getting her passion for Oriadyn and her budding interest in Doctor Marko under control and by learning how to defend her own views and assert her own will. The final stage of Lotus Blossom elaborates on Natalka's personal and professional achievements. This stage is embedded in Nietzsche's metaphor of "the great noon," which Nietzsche associated with the philosophical conception of emerging from error into truth. In Nietzsche's works, "the great noon" could be seen as both a general metaphor for human enlightenment and a specific moment in which that enlightenment occurs. *Thus Spoke Zarathustra* positions it as a transitional moment that signifies the beginning of a new life. "And it is the great noon," Zarathustra claims, "when man stands in the middle of his way between beast and overman and celebrates his way to the evening as his highest hope: for it is the way to a new morning" (1978, 78–9). Notably, if we consider Natalka's interest in Ukraine's national life and her persistent identification with the Ukrainian people, "the great noon" that she enjoys at the end of the story could symbolize not only a beginning of her new life but also a new hope for Ukraine's national regeneration.

The framework of the three-stage metamorphosis organizes Kobylians'ka's novel as a cyclical progression of Natalka's psychological development, which presents the heroine's story through her emotional experiences: love, hatred, anxiety, sensuality, and instincts. In this light, the novel's understanding of personal history seems to approximate Nietzsche's idea of genealogy, which the German philosopher introduced in his *On the Genealogy of Morality* (1887). This concept has been recognized as Nietzsche's "perspectivist historical method," which dispels the dominant myth of totality and views human existence as a myriad of countless lost events without a point of reference, making them open to reinterpretation (Foucault 1977, 140, 154–5). In one of her commentaries on *The Princess* that criticizes the traditional approach to evaluating human lives centred around basic biographical facts and chronologies (birth, marriage, education, etc.), Kobylians'ka pointed out with irony that her Natalka "didn't have any history because she didn't have any facts" (I:377). Similar criticism permeates the opening paragraphs of *The Princess*, where the heroine rails against deterministic attempts to explain her future by her past. In her introductory diary entry, Natalka juxtaposes her "I" to collective authority and law, ironically represented by "old folks" and "books on dream interpretations" (sonnyky). Her statement, "I was born on November 29. The old people and books on dream interpretations say that this day is the day of doomed destiny" (I:109), comprises a sardonic commentary on the popular, deterministic beliefs in peoples' origins and their capacity to account for their characters or determine adequately their lives. Her subsequent contemplations on determinist dogmas, such as "everything is predetermined from the beginning and cannot be otherwise" (I:109), amplify her criticism of the totalizing nature of the collective "we" that sacrifices individual interests to the execution of what it assumes to be the law of history or the law of nature. The tension between an individual and a collective reaches its pinnacle when Natalka describes herself as an object of social abuse in the hostile family of her uncle and reflects on the detrimental effects of her oppressive environment. The mirror scene, which the heroine cursorily mentions in her entry, is also designed to illustrate an ironic point. When the heroine catches a glimpse at her reflection in the mirror, all she can see is what has been mediated through language by her abusive relatives – a grotesque image with eyes "too big," face "too pale," and hair "too red" (I:110). The next flashback memory, of her deceased grandmother who used to admire Natalka's beauty, however, forces the heroine to question the projected image of herself and triggers her decision to become, despite all odds, "very, very, very happy" (I:111). While it is possible to argue that harsh material conditions facilitate Natalka's defiance, her somewhat chaotic and emotionally charged writing accentuates the spontaneity of her decision and frames her imagination, innate sensitivity, and strong will as the main driving forces that allow her to overcome her anger and desire to blame others for her miserable state and envision a new life not only for herself but for her downtrodden people.

Notably, Natalka's initial tendency to hold others responsible for her subjugation, alongside her utmost hatred towards her aunt and her cousins, brings to mind the very slavish attitude that Nietzsche calls *ressentiment* – the key concept that underlines Nietzsche's discussion of slave morality, first introduced in his *On the Genealogy of Morality* and later developed in *The Case of Wagner* (1888). Nietzsche describes *ressentiment* as a form of reactiveness associated with a bad conscience, hatred, and a displacement of blame for one's own failure or inferiority onto an external agent, an imaginary enemy. The weaker someone is, Nietzsche asserts, the weaker is his ability to suppress this reaction, and, vice versa, the more a person is active, strong willed, and dynamic, the less place and time is left for contemplating all that is done to him or her, and his or her reactions become less compulsive. According to Nietzsche, "the slave revolt in morality begins when *ressentiment* itself becomes creative and gives birth to values: the *ressentiment* of beings denied the true reaction, that of the deed, who recover their losses only through an imaginary revenge. Whereas all noble morality grows out from a triumphant yes – saying to oneself, from the outset slave morality says 'no' to an 'outside,' to a 'different,' to a 'not-self'; and *this* 'no' is its creative deed" (1998, 19).[27] Initially deprived of any agency to stand up for herself, Natalka – like Nietzsche's human being of *ressentiment* who "looks obliquely at things," seeks "hiding places, secret passages and back doors," and "knows all about being silent, not forgetting, waiting, belittling ... [and] humbling oneself" (1998, 20) – is overwhelmed with hostile feelings and resentment as the first pages of her diary suggest. Only continuous education and ruthless self-examination gradually allow her to overcome her anger and become what Nietzsche defines as "a full human being" (1998, 29) – an active, self-asserting being who has chosen herself to be her own goal and from whom, to continues with Nietzsche's words, "a chosen people shall grow" (1978, 77).

While describing Natalka as a concrete historical subject with firm individualistic views and a strong will, the opening scene also establishes clear symbolic links between the story of Natalka's life and the history of Ukraine's political marginality. The image of an abused orphan that introduces Natalka to the reader is a conventional trope of Ukraine's cultural and political subjugation in nineteenth-century Ukrainian literature. Another popular image that the novel uses to evoke the symbolic link between the heroine and the Ukrainian people is the image of a mermaid, a preternatural being restricted to a limited space, time, and function who cannot lead a normal life. In the first flashback sequence, Natalka's grandmother calls her "rusalon'ka" (a mermaid) (I:110). Early descriptions of Natalka also highlight her abnormal looks. For example, while admonishing her husband for suggesting that their niece is pretty, Natalka's aunt describes the heroine as some kind of horrid and bewildering creature:

> Pretty? Ha! For once, have a closer look at her beauty, at her long red braids that cannot be done in any fashionable way, at her chalk-pale face,

> and at her inhuman green eyes, and tell me then, if she is pretty. Don't look at her red lips – it is a sick redness. There is not a drop of blood in her face ... In a word, she is a horrid creature!" (I:113)

A few pages later, Natalka's cousin Lienochka compares the heroine's "golden-red hair" and "sea-greenish eyes" to those of Lorelei, an enchanting siren-like mermaid from German folklore popularized by Heinrich Heine (I:125). In Heine's interpretation, Lorelei sits on a cliff above the Rhine and unwittingly distracts shipmen with her beauty and song, causing them to crash on the rocks. From this point on, Lorelei serves as a leading leitmotif of the first part of Natalka's story, which deals with the drudgery of her prescribed life.

Notably, although Natalka, like Kobylians'ka, admires Heine's poetry, she does not accept Lienochka's projected identification. As suggested by the dream that Natalka sees shortly after Lienochka compares her to Lorelei, she rejects the German folkloric mermaid as her alter ego. In her dream, Natalka encounters Heine's Lorelei and is initially mesmerized by her beauty and her enigmatic "half dull, half indifferent" gaze (I:126). In an attempt to become closer to the mermaid, she starts singing the first stanza of Heine's "Die Lorelei" ("The Lorelei," 1824), but the mermaid stops singing and throws her harp into the sea. Lorelei's abortive gesture brings Natalka out of her stupor, and she embarks to chase the harp that the waves swiftly carry away. The dream ends with Natalka's utmost excitement about her maritime adventure and an ebullient vision of the magical "land of the noon" (poludennyi krai), which promises the heroine a new, prosperous future (I:126). The utopian connotations of the dream, alongside its allusions to Nietzsche's metaphors of "seafaring," "laughing waves," and "the great noon" that feature prominently in *Thus Spoke Zarathustra*,[28] frame Natalka as an antithesis of Heine's heroine: whereas Lorelei remains a "hopelessly" static character doomed to never-ending misery and solitude, Natalka proves to be an active being who skilfully navigates the raging sea, which traditionally represents a hostile environment and life's unpredictability, to a safer and more prosperous place. In this light, the symbolic juxtaposition of Lorelei and Natalka indicates that Kobylians'ka used traditional tropology not only to link Natalka's story to the history of Ukraine's political subjugation but also to subvert the dominant myth of Ukraine's martyrdom through the story of Natalka's victorious liberation and personal achievement.

In addition to conventional imagery and its symbolic implications, the novel also presents explicit claims that frame Natalka and her life story as representations of Ukraine and its potential political future.

In one of the most memorable examples, the heroine openly identifies with the Ukrainian people:

> I have been thinking recently that there are people like nations; that is, that the characters of some people are often identical to the characters of individual nations ... For example, you can expect with confidence that some people will act in one way or the other, and that they can accomplish something immensely impressive and significant. There are also people of unique beauty that remain always fresh and unblemished with the pettiness of daily life. There are also nations like that. And on the contrary, there are exceptionally gifted people, who, nevertheless, are entirely overwhelmed with sorrow. They want to achieve so much, but they rarely get anywhere. They are doomed to suffer and grieve ... I despise their song of eternal suffering as much as I despise the subservient and sickly-anxious expression on the pale face of our people. We have become weak because our remorse over the past and the sound of that forlorn melody ... have lulled our power to impotence. Isn't it true? Ah ... It's true. And I am a daughter of Ukrainian people too. (I:215)

While exposing the inert nature of Ukraine's national movement, this passage also imagines a nation as a single individual and suggests that Natalka's development mirrors what is, or should be, occurring in the nation's psychology. Similar logic underpins Natalka's later statements, when the heroine explicitly associates her own mode of thinking with a more hopeful political future for her people:

> We are a dormant, lazy, but positive force, which is used to endurance as much as a prisoner is used to his shackles. But when this force is shaken and bewildered with its own blood, it will destroy the oppressive hand once and for all. If even one hundredth of my people feel the way I feel, we will never perish! I am consumed with the elemental nature of my people ... and when one feels this way one doesn't perish! (I:257)

Encoded in this passage is a view of a nation as an organic entity with innate vitality, and a strong belief in Ukraine's potential for national regeneration. In the final pages of *The Princess*, when Natalka prophesies that the Ukrainian people would achieve the same success as she enjoys in her personal life, the heroine once again draws parallels between her own accomplishments and Ukraine's political struggles, her personal "great noon" and Ukraine's political future:

> It is impossible that the hour of the great noon won't strike for her and her people; that all their strength won't suffice to illuminate their unique and

> unblemished beauty and their potential for independent existence. It is impossible! Their great noon must arrive! Yes, their great noon will arrive despite all malicious and hostile circumstances that have been haunting her and her people for a very long time. There is still power in the world ... There is still love ... She feels how it overwhelms her and ... doubles her strength so that she can fight her own battle and the battle of her people. (I:387)

The narrative emphasis on the "independent existence" of the Ukrainian people connects Natalka's personal liberation to Ukraine's cultural and political independence and suggests that the heroine's story of self-discovery, intellectual growth, professional accomplishment, and personal happiness could be read as a daring program of action.

The novel's vision on Ukraine's political future is further elaborated in a series of polemical conversations between Natalka and Oriadyn, a man with whom the heroine is passionately in love and whom she first identifies as an exceptional "son of her people." Early in the novel, Oriadyn is enthralled with questions of Ukraine's national liberation and plans to devote his life to "the most adverse problems" of his people (I:159). Although at this point he "cannot yet decide in which direction to go first" (I:159), he shows a vivid interest in socialist revolutionary theories. At first, Natalka is attracted to his radical idealism and admires him as a representative of one of the most progressive political movements of the time, which was officially institutionalized in Galicia as the Ukrainian Radical Party (URP) in 1890. As she puts it, "he was a Social Democrat and an ardent admirer of Marx ... He believed that salvation would come from socialism ... [and that] the reign of the socialist dogmas will stimulate real progress" (I:146–7). Enthused with Oriadyn's passion, Natalka eagerly learns about socialism but quickly discovers discrepancies in Oriadyn's socialist views. First, she begins to question the totalizing nature of the socialist program, which disregards differences in cognition, education, age, gender, and ethnicity. Then she gradually grows suspicious about the Marxist abolition of bourgeois property and social redistribution, which contradicts her idiosyncratic views. She becomes particularly apprehensive of Oriadyn's determinist claims. In one of their later conversations, Oriadyn projects the change of material conditions and not the transformation of the human mind as the main precondition for social progress. "We must look for the preconditions of social change," he claims, "not in human heads, not in the growing understanding of the 'eternal' truth or untruth and justice, but simply in the change of the modes of production and exchange; not in religion and philosophy, but only in the economy of the specific age" (I:147). Although Oriadyn insists that socialism is "neither a disease nor a delusion artificially created by individual minds, but a natural movement," his dogmatic rhetoric makes Natalka suspect that a socialist system might turn into "a more brutal and reckless power than the current [imperial] regime" – a note she makes in one of her diary records that captures her intuitive fear about the innate elemental nature of socialism and the chaos that it might cause in the future (1:155). Curiously, in Komyshanchenko's 1962 edition of *The Princess*, the original Ukrainian adjective "h**ru**bsha" (more brutal) is deliberately substituted with "h**ly**bsha" (more profound), which cunningly transforms Natalka's angst about socialism into its veneration (I:146). This textual alteration is a telling example of the manipulative nature of Soviet criticism, which often forged original documents and data either to prove a socialist dogma or to protect a writer from marginalization and critical oblivion. It seems that the latter is the case with Komyshanchenko's 1962 edition of *The Princess*.

Natalka's relatives also share her anxiety about socialism. When her uncle identifies Oriadyn as a radical socialist, he juxtaposes him with the traditionally conservative Ukrainian society and even projects him as the dangerous and evil other:

> They [radical socialists] are mischievous entrepreneurs. They have no beliefs and no character. They can neither commit to a stable course of actions nor can they follow any legal regulations. They are spiritual mutants, who were created by false teaching ... They claim the role of reformists, but all they do is pursue other people's property. They have no fear of death because they have no God. (I:149–50)

By speculating about how long Oriadyn would stay committed to "caring for the people" (I:151), Natalka's uncle further suggests the doctrinaire nature of Oriadyn's beliefs. His speculations turn out to be well grounded as it becomes obvious when the young man starts treating everyone as no more than a "chess piece," and "orchestrates" them "on his chessboard at will" in the pursuit of personal interests later in the story (I:310).[29] Professor Lorden, Natalka's first fiancé and Lienochka's eventual husband, amplifies the uncle's graphic imagery of imposters and spiritual mutants by pointing out that "proletarians" like Oriadyn "multiply awfully fast" and contaminate their environment "like the plague." Coincidentally, Professor Lorden gives progressive socialists the same name that the Bolshevik terror, the so-called red plague, would acquire in the 1920s (I:150). Although Natalka does not completely agree with her uncle's and Professor Lorden's evaluations of Oriadyn, she eventually rejects socialism as an alternative road to Ukrainian's liberation and conceives her own program of social and political progress that draws on Nietzsche's concept of the overman and selected elements of nineteenth-century Russian radicalism.

Contemplating Oriadyn's earlier statement about the power of the "self-made" intelligentsia that "generates progress" (I:146), Natalka conceives of a group of highly educated and aesthetically refined intellectuals, Nietzschean "higher people," as Ukraine's leadership group of "national awakeners." By this time, Oriadyn gives up on his youthful idealism because of financial hardship – he is no longer "the fanaticized fool as [he] once used to be," as he puts it (I:376) – and only mocks Natalka's eagerness for social activism. He resorts to Darwinian theories to argue that the Ukrainian people have no "internal impulse" to turn their destiny around, and that only a foreign initiative can foster any substantial social and political changes for Ukraine (I:216). The heroine objects with characteristic acuteness: "Oh, no! [It is so sad that] we use this type of arguments to justify our ... [social and political indifference]. I think quite the opposite that despite all odds there are people of exceptional character, who make more powerful influence on their environments than the material circumstances, but these people could not abide by any existing laws" (I:216–17). Natalka defines her understanding of "exceptional characters" through Nietzsche's metaphor of "higher people," who, as implied, could facilitate the spiritual rebirth of the whole nation through personal example and thereby could eventually lead their people to a better social and political order. Oriadyn replies sarcastically that it is utterly naive to believe that a few people could generate any substantial social or political change. While pointing out that an individual without a collective is no more than "a torn-off member that dies in solitude," Oriadyn supports his argument with a convoluted passage from Nietzsche that underscores the supremacy of primitive, materialistic drives in human nature: "We are the mob hodgepodge that wants to live with one day and master human destiny" (I:235–6). Here Oriadyn misquotes Nietzsche's call on the "higher people" to overcome the mob from *Thus Spoke Zarathustra*:

> What is womanish, what derives from the servile, and especially the mob hodgepodge: *that* would not become master of all human destiny. Oh nausea! Nausea! Nausea! *That* asks and asks and never grows weary: "How is man to be preserved best, longest, and most agreeably?" With that – they are the masters of today. Overcome these masters of today, O, my brothers – these small people, they are the overman's greatest danger! (1978, 287)

While Nietzsche's passage clearly celebrates the "higher people" and their ability to transcend the present cultural crisis, Oriadyn picks only on Nietzsche's cultural pessimism. In this regard, Oriadyn's selective reading of Nietzsche is a telling example of a blatant misrepresentation of Nietzsche's ideas, which in the 1890s dominated Nietzsche's reception in Europe, and which Kobylians'ka decried in her work. Frustrated with Oriadyn's superficial readings of Nietzsche, Natalka counters with another line from the same passage from *Thus Spoke Zarathustra* that highlights the German philosopher's calls on the higher individuals "to overcome the mob hodgepodge" (I:236). When Oriadyn inquires mockingly on how to find these Nietzschean "higher people" among Ukrainians, Natalka urges him first to become a cultivated person himself and then to teach less privileged Ukrainians how to follow in his steps (I:236). In her appeal, Natalka underscores individual spiritual emancipation and the heightened cultural awareness of the Ukrainian elite as the principal road to Ukraine's collective liberation.

Natalka's vision of the new Ukrainian elite thus shares many philosophical affinities with Nietzsche's concept of the "higher people" and their social mission. In the passage "On the Bestowing Virtue" at the end of the first book of *Thus Spoke Zarathustra*, Nietzsche elaborated on two important themes that problematize his alleged character as an antisocial thinker – generosity and gift-giving virtue. While rejecting pity and Christian love of one's neighbour, Nietzsche recognized "gift-giving," that is, sharing one's wisdom with others out of the autonomous overflow of power on the part of the giver, not in response to any need of the recipient, as one of the most defining virtues of the "higher people" (1978, 58). Elsewhere, Nietzsche described this noble sentiment of giving out of an internal sense of exceeding wealth in the following way: "The feeling of fullness, the power that seeks to overflow, the happiness of high tension, the consciousness of wealth that would give and bestow: the noble human being, too, helps the unfortunate but not, or almost not, from pity, but prompted more by an urge begotten by excess of power" (2003a, 195–6). Elaborating further on the idea of gift-giving in "On the Bestowing Virtue," Nietzsche also suggested that the ultimate mission of the "higher people," in the pursuit of personal self-realization, is to advance the fulfilment of his or her community as a whole, or, as Nietzsche put it, to inspire others to evolve and thus grow into "a chosen people." This collective transformation, Nietzsche believed, would eventually bring to life the overman, Nietzsche's ultimate goal for humanity (2003a). Along with the image of a "physician" who, as Nietzsche suggested in the preface to *The Gay Science*, might be able in the future to cure humanity of its suffering, Zarathustra's link of the "higher people" to a broader communal goal in "On the Bestowing Virtue" is a rare instance of Nietzsche's contemplation of a social agenda. Considering Nietzsche's more frequent and elaborate critique of communal instincts, particularly the human desire for self-preservation, as represented, according to Nietzsche, by foundational principles of Christian morality and the modern state (1998, 35–66), it is not surprising that Nietzsche's contemporaries often overlooked the social dimension of Nietzsche's "higher people" and the overman. Like Nietzsche, Kobylians'ka's heroine also envisions Ukraine's new national leaders as the progenitors of communal progress who would conceive, develop, and disseminate among the oppressed masses critical ideas that would potentially promulgate social and political reform.

Natalka's vision of the new Ukrainian elite, however, does not completely coincide with Nietzsche's concept of the "higher people" and the overman. Unlike Nietzsche, Natalka assigns a clearly defined and relatively short-term social mission to her Ukrainian "higher people." Her explicit emphasis on the elites' pivotal role in the social and political enlightenment of the masses particularly stands out, recalling Pyotr Lavrov's theories of the cultivated man and his duty to society. In his *Historical Letters* of 1870, Lavrov defined the key ethical principles of populism, the value foundation on which Russia's economic and political regeneration was to be based. At the core of his argument was the concept of a debt (*dolg*) – a debt to "the people" (*narod*) incurred by the privileged minority. Lavrov asserted that educated men and women owed their enlightenment to the suffering of the less privileged, whose toil created the material conditions for their success, and that they had to repay this moral debt. His idea of moral debt implies action directed to others, not to self-interest but to the material transformation of the social order. In contrast to Chernyshevsky, who insisted that only people who act out of purely egoistic motives could move society forward (1985, 114–15), Lavrov observed that the interests of an individual were identical with the interests of society and argued that genuine "self-perfection" is impossible without social betterment.[30] Western Ukrainians were first introduced to Pyotr Lavrov's works through Mykhailo Drahomanov, a prominent political theorist and an important public figure in Kyiv who maintained correspondence with Lavrov for years, and later through Ivan Franko's 1872 German-language translation of Lavrov's selected works. Ol'ha Kobylians'ka's allusions to Lavrov, as well as her in-depth studies of Pisarev's cultural criticism, including his reflections on Lavrov's contributions to nineteenth-century Russian radical thought, suggest that although her knowledge of Lavrov's thought might not have been shaped by close reading of his original works, she was well acquainted with his contributions to the Russian radical thought of the late nineteenth century.[31]

While not completely embracing Lavrov's concept of "debt," Kobylians'ka's heroine conceives her "higher people" as the only social group that have both the vision and the opportunity to move their society forward. In doing so, she sides with Lavrov's belief in critically thinking individuals and their potential to change the course of history and promote progress. Like Lavrov, Natalka also treats her cultivated minority as an open, not a closed, elite. It is particularly evident in her commitment to add to the ranks of her "higher people" through the educative force of her own work, which she hopes will facilitate an opportunity for self-improvement for all Ukrainians, regardless of their social background. This fusion of Nietzsche's individualistic concept of the "higher people" with the foundational populist principle of the intellectual's moral debt to "the people" testifies to Kobylians'ka's deep understanding of Nietzsche's call to self-overcoming and its potential to generate major social transformations. While Kobylians'ka's vision might be an adaptation and a daring modification of Nietzsche's concept, it is, nevertheless, one of the most informed interpretations of the time. More importantly, it clearly stands in sharp opposition to the pervasive misrepresentations of Nietzsche's thought among her contemporaries, to the so-called Nietzscheanism – a "surrogate religion" that propagated selfishness, hedonism, immorality, promiscuity, ruthlessness, and oppression of the weak, alongside Nietzsche's ideals of individualism and iconoclasm (Rosenthal 1986, 7–8).

Natalka's understanding of the "higher people" and their social role is best conveyed through the evolution of her relationships with the men she loves, Oriadyn and Doctor Marko. At the beginning of the story, Natalka describes Oriadyn as an ideal candidate for Ukraine's first "higher man." Only gradually does she realize that he is no more than a poseur, Nietzsche's "last man," one who seeks security, comfort, and happiness (1978, 17), or, to continue with Lavrov's rhetoric, a true "apostle of stagnation" who for personal material gain gives up his idealistic quest to diminish the toil of the less privileged and attempts to persuade Natalka to do the same (1967, 138). The heroine first registers the change in Oriadyn's commitment to Ukraine's national liberation when, upon his return from a prolonged trip, he articulates his "reluctance" (*zneokhochenist'*) to work for the betterment of others (I:233). While later analysing their conversation, Natalka turns to Nietzsche's "Maxims and Arrows," N38 and N41, from his *Twilights of the Idles* (2003b, 37) to reassess her and Oriadyn's roles in Ukraine's political future:

> The German "prophet" Nietzsche asks somewhere in one of his works:
>
> *On your value*: Are you genuine? Or are you only an actor? A signifier? Or that which is signified itself? – In the end, you are no more than an imitation of an actor.

> *On your relations with others*: Do you want to accompany? Or to go on forward? Or to go off alone? You must know what you want and that you want ... When I think of Oriadyn, these words inadvertently come to my mind. (I:243–4)

Natalka thus senses Oriadyn's pretentious nature, but despite her intuition, she continues to believe in his potential to become a Nietzschean leader of her people. She becomes more critical only after her friend Oksana shares her own suspicions. After attending Oriadyn's lecture on the state of the national economy, Oksana blatantly calls him a vulgarized conservative:

> Oriadyn's lecture was overly conservative ... Why was he speaking almost ironically when he spoke about socialism ... Ah, Natalka, if you only knew how disgusted I am with people who don't believe in anything, who know everything, have everything, can accomplish everything in no time! They are like that substance [that] loses its properties and turns into complete ooze because it sits still for too long. People like that aren't the strongest individuals, Natalka. (1:285)

From this point on, Natalka begins to realize and acknowledge that, although Oriadyn is talented and insightful, he does not act on his beliefs, always measures his private interests against the interests of the people, and wastes his energy on trivial pursuits. In fact, Natalka's later descriptions of Oriadyn bring to mind those educated but passive and self-centred Ukrainians whom Kobylians'ka decried in her diary entry of 13 January 1888:

> There are many kind and wise people, whose charity is well known and whose education, social status, and power could do so much ... But they think differently because they mastered better than others dry knowledge, facts, numbers, and paragraphs, and, as a result, feel steady on their feet. But when someone, whom they raised poorly, suffers because he cannot see the right way any longer ... then those wise and kind judge him, preach harsh morals to him, give him something to eat and something to wear, and kindly show him to the door ... as if saying, it's a great big world out there, go look for your daily bread elsewhere. (Pohrebennyk 1982, 157)

Only at the end of the story, when Natalka becomes utterly free from her passion for Oriadyn, is she able to acknowledge that he was no more than "an illusion" (I:371).

While Oriadyn fails to live up to Natalka's expectations, Doctor Marko, a Croatian stepson of her benefactor and her husband-to-be, displays in the unity of his private and public behaviour and in his wholehearted dedication to the progress of his nation the very integration of mind, conscience, and heart that Natalka associates with the "higher people." Although Doctor Marko's character is ambiguous and from the first glance he has barely anything "heroic" about him (I:263), Natalka acknowledges his erudition, warm-hearted nature, and refined aesthetic sensibility. She soon discerns in his character the two main qualities that she assigns to her ideal intellectual leader. On the one hand, she admires Doctor Marko as an "arystokrat dukhu" (aristocrat of spirit) and a Nietzschean "seafarer" who travels the world in pursuit of knowledge and self-discovery. But on the other hand, she celebrates his humility and dedication to his people. The latter frames Doctor Marko as Lavrov's "invisible hero of humanity" who might not have performed "a single striking deed" but who "sustains in the society the tradition of human dignity and the consciousness of what is best" (Lavrov 1967, 142–5). Doctor Marko's self-description is a clear allusion to Lavrov:

> Periodicals won't write about me because I am neither a politician nor a writer. Essentially, I don't enjoy any fame, and I never cared much about getting publicity and a so-called name. I only try to be sincere and help those who come to me with trust. All I want to be is ... a worthy son of my country ... I don't care much about anything else, and that is why I belong to those, about whom people do not "hear" much. (I:279)

It is this personal dignity, the unquestioned rejection of the private pursuits of ordinary man, and active idealism with a concrete project and a true goal in mind that attract Natalka to Doctor Marko and transform her own character.

The story also uses two of Nietzsche's metaphors to accentuate Doctor Marko's formative role in Natalka's cognitive and spiritual evolution: the narrative of the ultimate healing and the image of the seashells. In his speech "On the Virtues," Zarathustra deprives his followers of what he calls "their toys," the ideals of their immaturity: "reward, retribution, punishment, and revenge in justice" (1978, 96). He then promises that the new wave from the sea of knowledge will shower them with "the new colourful shells," the new ideas that will comfort and guide them in the future (1978, 96). Similarly, Doctor Marko presents Natalka upon his return from an extended voyage around the world with a collection of colourful seashells that he picks for her on the distant shores of India. By analogy with Nietzsche's work, Doctor Marko's gift represents Natalka's new values that replace those of conventional goodness and humility. In this regard, Doctor Marko resembles Nietzsche's ultimate healer, who cures his patient, Natalka in this case, with the ultimate gift of personal example and overabundant wisdom (German "die Gift") rather than with the drugs (German "das Gift"). Curiously, in the first book of *Thus Spoke Zarathustra*, where Nietzsche differentiated between Christian pity and the gift-giving virtue of the "higher people," the German philosopher plays with the same essential ambiguity of the word "gift" rooted in the German language to decry Christian prescriptive truisms. Like the Greek word "pharmakon" (poison or cure), the German word "Gift" simultaneously carries both positive and negative significations. In its feminine form, "die Gift" signifies "gift" or "present" (from the German verb "geben," meaning "to give"). In its neutral form, "das Gift" signifies "poison." Nietzsche carefully avoided the feminine form in *Thus Spoke Zarathustra*: instead of using "die Gift" to describe the "gift" that Zarathustra brings to humanity, he used derivatives of the word "Geschenk." Nietzsche, however, used "das Gift" and its derivatives to designate "poison" in several key passages, "Vom Biß der Natter" ("On the Adder's Bite," [1930] 71–3) is the most notorious example.[32] The symbolic connotations of Doctor Marko's professional vocation and his gift of the seashells thus position him not so much as someone who rescues Natalka from financial insecurity and social marginalization by giving her what she needs, but rather as someone who facilitates her transition to "the great noon," that is, the third childlike stage of her self-overcoming.

One of the most important changes in Natalka's world view that Doctor Marko initiates is her revision of her somewhat xenophobic, anti-Polish sentiments. Growing up in Western Ukraine, Natalka internalizes the prevailing Ukrainian attitudes towards Poles, whom she blames for Ukraine's political marginalization and whom she consequently hates with "innate hatred" (vrodzhena nenavyst') (I:250):

> Poles as a nation tyrannized and persecuted Ukrainian people for centuries. They crushed and flogged Ukrainians, drained their strength, sucked their blood; humiliated and scorned them ... They forced their domination and kept Ukrainians from light and elevation. [Poles constitute] a nation that grew and developed through filth and slyness, while [Ukrainian] people ... Oh, God, where is the truth? (I:337–8)[33]

Alarmed by Natalka's "almost one-sided attitudes" (I:292), Doctor Marko urges her to be "civil" towards other nations: "Everyone has its own unique 'I'. Our ancestors might define us in one way or the other, but it is wrong to hold an individual responsible for the collective or, vice versa, to blame the collective for the actions of one person. This is the reason why I treat others with kindness" (I:269). Doctor Marko points out that blind hatred is "a proof of intellectual deficiency" and alludes to Nietzsche's concept of *ressentiment* to remind Natalka that "higher people" know no hatred or envy (I:269).[34] Thereby he encourages Natalka to re-evaluate her attitude towards Poland through a thorough study of Polish literature and culture. More importantly, he draws Natalka's attention to the notion of personal responsibility and points out that Ukrainians might be held accountable for their misery as much as Poles, if not more. In his defence of Polish people, Doctor Marko suggests that instead of complaining, Ukrainians should prove through their work and intellectual achievement that they deserve to be treated with respect.[35]

Doctor Marko's advice on cultural re-evaluation becomes a trigger for another life-changing transformation: it helps Natalka to learn how to channel her hatred into creative projects and how to shape her novel into a valuable cultural text that promises to contribute to the betterment of Ukrainian culture. Shortly before her first encounter with Oriadyn, Natalka conceives a liberating idea, and, like many intellectuals of her time, Kobylians'ka included, chooses literature as her form of social activism.[36] Oriadyn is the first to recognize the outstanding quality of Natalka's work and to support her early experimentations with writing. He insists that Natalka should make writing her "duty" (I:145), and she does so. Although the heroine shares her frustration every time her work is publicly mocked or rejected for publication, there is barely any information about its plot or subject matter. Only once, Natalka mentions in passing that her novel addresses the woman question (I:123–4). Later in the novel, she points out that it describes her most intimate feelings and thoughts, that it captures "all her bare soul" (I:380). This is, perhaps, the main reason why she takes it personally when publishers reject her work. Doctor Marko's help with the publication of Natalka's writing solidifies his crucial role in her cognitive and professional growth because, if it were not for him, Natalka's work might not have been published and she might have not written her subsequent texts, which promise to have "positive ramifications" for the future of her people (I:396).

Despite Doctor Marko's central role in Natalka's life, past critics paid little attention to his character and its symbolic implications. At best, they commented on his ethnic identity and read Natalka's marriage to a Croatian as Kobylians'ka's desire to infiltrate foreign matter into the Ukrainian cultural paradigm, and thus to disrupt the cultivation of national consciousness.[37] The question of why Doctor Marko is a Croatian and not a Ukrainian is indeed compelling. Nikolai Dobroliubov's review of a similarly controversial issue in Russian literature – Ivan Turgenev's Bulgarian hero Insarov in *Nakanune* (*On the Eve*, 1860) – can be helpful in elaborating on the symbolic meaning of Doctor Marko's ethnic background. In his 1860 polemical review "Kogda zhe priidet nastoiashchii den'?" ("When Will the Real Day Come?"), Dobroliubov claimed that Turgenev's Bulgarian character could be easily substituted by "a Serb, a Czech, an Italian, or a Hungarian, but not ... a Russian" (1948b, 415) because Russian intellectuals, he observed, were virtually superfluous in Russia's social and political life of the late 1850s. At the time, "Russian life [was] so well arranged," he noted sarcastically, "that everything in it induce[d] [only] calm and peaceful slumber" (1948b, 420). Kobylians'ka's descriptions of Natalka's environment have a lot in common with Turgenev's rural Russia and frame Doctor Marko as similar to Insarov – as a yardstick against which to measure the Ukrainians in *The Princess*. Kobylians'ka's assessment of her compatriots and Ukraine's political future, however, is not as gloomy as that of Turgenev or Dobroliubov regarding their respective circumstances. While Russian critics had little hope for Insarov's kind of heroism in Russia,[38] Kobylians'ka presented Doctor Marko as a powerful external impulse and an exemplary model for emulation, a "high person," who helps release Natalka's latent energies for personal liberation and for an idealistic fight for the cultural, social, and potentially political progress of her people, a tenet that became an inspiration for generations of Ukrainian women and men from then on.[39]

Conclusion

Following closely the debates of the early 1890s on feminism, socialism, populism, Marxism, Russian radicalism, Nietzsche's philosophy, and questions of Ukraine's national regeneration, Kobylians'ka used her second novel, *The Princess*, to articulate her own views on the most discussed questions of her time. In developing her arguments, she relied on a variety of philosophical and literary materials as well as on real-life attempts at their realization that were practised in Western Ukraine in the 1880s and 1890s. This intricate mixture of different sources, with their different semantic potentials, produced an original combination of elegant style, impressive philosophical rigour, and remarkable clarity of persuasion, turning *The Princess* into an important contribution to European modernist literature and intellectual thought.

The Princess thus demonstrates that Kobylians'ka was not only a talented artist, an insightful psychologist, and a savvy student of philosophy, but also an aspiring political theorist and a brilliant mythographer. She used imaginative writing to provide her readers with a new model of the imagined future and with new rules and precedents for moral action. Kobylians'ka's use of Nietzsche's ideas to shape an image of the New Ukrainian Woman whose actions challenged the conventional patriarchal order is perhaps one of the first attempts in European literature to apply Nietzsche to a feminist agenda. While providing Ukrainian women with a new self-asserting role model that promoted women's rights to better themselves and their communities without compromising their own human dignity and their cherished beliefs in the sanctity of love and family, Kobylians'ka's new heroine also reconfigured the traditional Ukrainian models of national martyrdom by offering a new, victorious myth of Ukraine's liberation. Kobylians'ka framed her new national myth by fusing Nietzsche's ideas of the "higher people" and "the great noon" with the principal populist doctrine of the intellectual's duty to "the people," asserting thereby new national imperatives: social development and emancipation of women; modernization of high culture; and cultivation of a highly educated national elite with a strong will to facilitate cultural and political changes. By foregrounding the regulatory and emancipatory functions of high art in her program, Kobylians'ka implicitly suggested that high culture could define, sustain, and direct Ukraine's nation-building effort, providing it with what Ernest Gellner, one of the leading theoreticians of nationalism, has described as "cognitive centralization and codification."[40] In this light, Kobylians'ka's idea of a Ukrainian national project is clearly elitist but in a positive way, which recalls the "nobly chivalrous model" (shliakhets'ko-lytsars'ka model') that Oksana Zabuzhko, a contemporary Ukrainian writer and cultural critic, delineates in her interpretation of Lesia Ukrainka's cultural heritage (Zabuzhko 2007, 291–342), and which many contemporary Ukrainian intellectuals consider crucial in Ukraine's ongoing state-building project.[41]

Kobylians'ka's later fictional and non-fictional writings show that although she toned down her references to Nietzsche and radically changed her approach to challenging the deeply ingrained ideals, rituals, ceremonies, and artistic forms of the Ukrainian populists in the decade preceding the First World War, Nietzsche's aestheticism, intellectualism, and individualism remained permanent in her world view.

Chapter Three

The Populist Trial

Shortly after formulating her elitist conception of Ukraine's political future in *The Princess,* Kobylians'ka turned to the analysis of the Ukrainian common man and his potential for political agency that was going to preoccupy her in the ensuing decade. This did not signify any change in Kobylians'ka's interests or outlook but was the logical outgrowth of the position taken in her earlier works. If her thesis on "cultural revolution" was to be made cogent to a broader Ukrainian audience and the expectation of future national regeneration to be based on it, she needed to show that Ukrainian peasants, whom the Ukrainian populists idealized as the main driving force of Ukraine's national liberation, were unfit for political struggle by virtue of the inner dynamics of their cultural and social development. Kobylians'ka first attempted this analysis in a series of short stories, which she wrote concurrently with her work on *The Human Being* and *The Princess*. The two works from this series are particularly relevant for a discussion of Kobylians'ka's early anti-populist representations of the people (*narod*): "Pryroda" ("Nature," 1887–97) and "Nekul'turna" ("Uncultured," 1896). It is, however, Kobylians'ka's third novel *Zemlia* (*The Earth*, 1902) that constitutes the most poignant and most complete record of her anti-populist discourse.

The original reception of Kobylians'ka's rustic fiction was complicated by the fact that the notion of "the people" (*narod*) had strong political connotations in late nineteenth-century Ukraine. Following the Russian populists (*narodniki*), Ukrainian intellectuals of the mid-nineteenth century recognized "the people," that is, the peasantry, who made up the overwhelming majority of Ukraine's vast population, as the makers of history, and dedicated themselves to their welfare. By the 1880s, populism was established as a dominant intellectual current in Ukraine. While Russian populists focused on social action and created revolutionary organizations such as *Zemlia i volia* (*Land and Freedom*, 1876) and *Narodnaia volia* (*The People's Will*, 1979), Ukrainian populists prioritized national enlightenment and bridged their social doctrines with a strong nationalistic concern for the emancipation of the people from foreign domination. According to Ghita Ionescu, an American scholar of populism and its national characteristics in Eastern Europe, in the late nineteenth century this version of populism, or rather "peasantism," was prominent in many countries of Eastern Europe, where it evolved as a reaction to both Russian populism (*narodnichestvo*) and Western socialism (1969, 99). Lacking political organization and subjected to surveillance of all social and cultural activities by the authorities, particularly within the Russian Empire, Ukrainian intellectuals gradually resorted to propagating their views in literature and other cultural productions. By the end of the nineteenth century, the populist notion that literature ought to serve the people and raise their level of culture and education, as well as political and economic awareness, was firmly instilled in the minds of Ukrainian intellectuals (Čyževs'kyj 1997, 588–618; Pavlychko 2009, 39–49; Zabuzhko 2007, 291–320). Ivan Nechui-Levyts'kyi, Panas Myrnyi, and Borys Hrinchenko were the most prominent Ukrainian populist writers, whose work reflected the prevailing attitude of the time in its most precise form and set up the dominant fictional model, the realist model, which propagated an espousal of the peasant language and the peasant way of life in Ukrainian turn-of-the-century culture.

In this context, any deviation from the dominant populist discourse was often regarded as an act of national betrayal. It is not surprising then that populist critics, who initially greeted Kobylians'ka's works that focused on the life of the intelligentsia with scorn and pointed out their perceived non-Ukrainianness with respect to language, themes, ideology, and psychology,[1] celebrated her rustic fiction, particularly her 1902 peasant novel, *The Earth*.[2] Some populist critics, however, found their modernist aesthetics and less than flattering depictions of the Bukovynian peasants problematic. Serhii Iefremov's critical review "In Search of the New Beauty," which came out within a month after the original publication of *The Earth*, was perhaps the strongest populist attack on Kobylians'ka. The main issue of Iefremov's critique of *The Earth* was its modernism with its aestheticism, mysticism, intellectualism, and individualism, in which the populist critic saw a threat to the national movement's cohesiveness. Kobylians'ka's letter to Osyp Makovei written on 15 December 1902 indicates that while Kobylians'ka was more or less accustomed to critical attacks on her modernist aesthetics, she was deeply frustrated with Iefremov's hostility and his conspicuous misinterpretations of her peasant characters and their rhetorical significance:

> I read Iefremov calmly ... I can tell that he doesn't critique me objectively but tries to mock me, or at least to undermine me in the eyes of my so-called admirers.... He dwells entirely in vain on my sentence "I won't kiss the mob on the lips" and doesn't see that I never slander that "mob" in any of my works, not even in the shortest of my pieces: neither in "The Peasant," "At St. John's Monastery," "Uncultured," "In the Fields," nor in *The Earth*, "Time," "Humility," etc. ... If he cannot understand or doesn't want to see this, there is nothing more I can say! (V:520)

At the time, Kobylians'ka felt compelled to soften her critical observations about the common Ukrainian man and make it clear that in her works she criticized not the common Ukrainian man, but the populist concept of "the people." In her 1922 autobiography, she expressed the same idea with even more directness:

> The two years that I spent in [the village of] Dymka gave me the opportunity to have a closer look at the peasant life, which I knew very well beforehand because I used to stop by the peasant huts every time I was in the mountains ... I used to love the people and I love them even to this very moment. I look at them with the same eyes that I look at trees, flowers, or at the rest of the living nature. Their lack of refinement and aestheticism, either in language, behaviour, or habits, is the only thing that upsets me about them, but essentially they harbour a lot of richness, freshness, and depth. What splendid material for the future they are! (V:239)

As a neo-Romantic devoted to the cause of Ukraine's liberation, Kobylians'ka, like many of her Ukrainian contemporaries, valourized the innocence, power, and natural beauty of folk culture. As a Westernizing intellectual and an admirer of Nietzsche, she, however, was critical of the coarse aspects of that culture. In fact, this sentiment permeates all of Kobylians'ka's works about Ukrainian peasants. To be precise, while acknowledging the vitality of the Ukrainian folk culture, Kobylians'ka's rustic fiction foregrounds the peasants' lack of education and of a broader understanding of cultural, social, and political relations, which, if underestimated, could lead to violent conflict and thereby brutalize the national movement. In this way, Kobylians'ka deconstructed and reconstructed images of peasants inherited in Ukrainian literature, challenging the deeply ingrained ideals and popular practices of the Ukrainian populists and thus further supporting her belief in the development of high culture as a main precondition of Ukraine's liberation.

Peasant Themes in Ol'ha Kobylians'ka's Early Fiction

There are three distinct chronological cycles in Kobylians'ka's depictions of peasants in the 1890s. Each cycle has its idiosyncratic formal structure and reflects a particular stage in Kobylians'ka's evolving aesthetic, philosophical, social, and political views, which appear with more detail in her longer works of each period: *A Human Being* (1887–94), *The Princess* (1896), and *The Earth* (1902), respectively. The first cycle, coinciding with the writing of *A Human Being*, foregrounds sharp criticism of the Ukrainian pseudo-intellectualism and pseudo-liberalism of the time. The most telling example of a short story from this period is "Nature" (1887–97). In this story, Kobylians'ka juxtaposed her first fictional peasant character with an educated, middle-class heroine to emphasize the alienation of the Ukrainian progressive intelligentsia from "the people" onto whom they projected their hopes and dreams about Ukraine's national regeneration. Kobylians'ka placed dialogue at the centre of her early stories to illuminate the dramatic differences in culture and world views between the two types of her characters – namely, peasants and intellectuals – through their communion with each other. The second cycle of Kobylians'ka's depictions of the peasantry emerged at the time when the writer was working on *The Princess*, whose philosophical framework draws simultaneously on Nietzsche's concept of the overman and populist doctrine of the intellectual's moral debt to "the people." In her two major stories of this period, "Chas" ("Time," 1895) and "Uncultured" (1996), Kobylians'ka continued to contrast intellectual and peasant characters but attempted to work out a new model for their interaction by using extensive dialogical confessions that brought out the inner thoughts of the peasant characters with characteristic rigour. In this cycle, Kobylians'ka's educated characters no longer judge the superstitious views, naiveté, and lack of agency of their peasant conversationalists but make an effort "to see and understand [the peasant] soul," as one critic put it (Turnerova 1963, 299). The third cycle of Kobylians'ka's peasant stories encompasses her late-1890s stories such as "Na poliakh" ("In the Fields," 1898) and "Pid holym nebom" ("Under the Open Sky," 1900), which lack any sharp juxtapositions but use formal structures to convey critical messages. Rather than relying on the direct authorial commentaries and convenient projections of the educated characters, Kobylians'ka animated her new peasant characters, creating vibrant polyphonic narratives. This mode proved most effective in demystifying and demythologizing the critical understandings sacred to the populist contingent: the idealized nature of the village community and the natural person, the Ukrainian villager.

Kobylians'ka's short story "Nature" is the most representative work of the first cycle that equally exposes both "the simple peasant" and "the delusional intellectual" mind. Written in 1887 but first published in 1895 in German and only in 1897 in Ukrainian, the story features a sexual encounter between an educated, upper-middle-class maiden and a young peasant, a well-off Hutsul.[3] Kobylians'ka's frank depiction of what is perceived as socially deviant behaviour, as well as its symbolic implications, problematizes any simplistic notions of national solidarity. Past critics, however, have avoided discussing the central event of "Nature," an encounter that starts with a playful dialogue but ends in sexual violence. Kobylians'ka's contemporaries focused either on the descriptions of nature or on the intricate psychological portraits of the main characters, which, according to these critics, revealed Kobylians'ka's talent as a psychological writer of great depth for the first time (Alchevs'ka 1963, 155–6; Franko 1963, 86; Makovei 1963, 61–3). Soviet critics also either avoided commenting on the rape scene (Komyshanchenko 1962, 17) or only briefly addressed the class preference of the heroine (Babyshkin 1956, 26; Tomashuk 1969a, 67–8 and 72). Only in the 1990s did Ukrainian feminist critics begin to draw attention to the sexual exchange between the two characters and to talk about eroticism, gender relations, and female sexuality in Kobylians'ka's early work (Hundorova 2002, 34–5 and 42; Pavlychko 2009, 87). While acknowledging that the heroes' sexual encounter is an instance of rape, feminist critics, however, read it exclusively as a social phenomenon, overlooking the fact that representations of rape have been long used in literature as a rhetorical device for a range of different sociocultural, political, and economic issues and conflicts (Sielke 2002, 5). A close look at "Nature" suggests that the rape narrative frames the story as a stylized tragicomedy of illusions and failures, which underscores the social and political impotence of the Ukrainian intelligentsia and complicates the populist consensus on ethnic solidarity and national identity.

"Nature" opens with a detailed description of the unnamed heroine, a twenty-year-old unmarried daughter of a local lawyer, presented as "a Ruthenian from top to bottom" (I:401). In her description of the heroine's Ukrainianness, which is mainly reflected in her laziness and "melancholy sadness ... reminiscent of hapless [Ukrainian] people" (I:401), Kobylians'ka projects ethnicity as a natural, biological, inborn category. The writer also comments on the heroine's class and education by presenting her as well read but naive and oblivious to the real world, from which she has been carefully sheltered like an "exotic plant from a greenhouse" (I:401). The heroine's sheltered existence is further linked to her wild imagination, intense sensitivity, and almost sickly irrational longing for the unknown, which shape a character reminiscent not of the victorious type of the New Woman but of the very same type of pseudo-intellectual whom Kobylians'ka decried in *A Human Being*. Put differently, we can read the heroine, who literally is forced to be a lover of a peasant, as a tragicomic embodiment of the Ukrainian populist intelligentsia, the so-called *khlopomany* (peasant lovers), who while seeing "the people" predominantly from the outside, idealized them, exalted their virtues, and set out to build an ideal society based on their traditions.[4]

The character of the young Hutsul is introduced through the heroine's perspective. One recent critic evaluates his description as Orientalist and reads it as an expression of Kobylians'ka's uncritical predisposition to Ukrainian peasants (Pavlyshyn 2008, 71–2). The evolution of the heroine's discourse and its unfortunate consequences, however, also suggest that Kobylians'ka might have used Orientalist rhetoric with its excessive romanticizing strategically in order to expose the cultural distance between the Ukrainian populist intelligentsia and "the people." There are indeed a great many unsubstantiated assumptions as to Slavic phenotypes in the heroine's initial descriptions of the young Hutsul:

> He had pure Slavic features ... tall, flexible, well built, as all his compatriots. He had an exceptionally beautiful face: it was gloomy and thoughtful, tender around the lips, and Slavic in its top part – that is, slightly too wide – but it didn't take away from his good looks. His hair was traditionally cut over the eyebrows and covered the forehead. His clothes complemented his beautiful body. (I:404)

The extended description of the Hutsul's appearance suggests that the heroine has little understanding of the young lad's inner life and moral values but sees him only from the outside. Her earlier attempt to paint a portrait of the good-looking peasant leads to the same conclusion. Her later unconcealed mockery of the Hutsul's views about "destiny," "God's will," and the "unlucky hour" also emphasize her cultural alienation from the young Hutsul (I:410). The heroine, however, switches to a different discourse reminiscent of the 1880s *khlopomany* dogma of ethnic solidarity once she registers a strong sexual attraction to the young man. The new rhetoric allows her to view the object of her desire as an equal in spite of, and through, the cultural differences. "I am the same as you, I am also a Ukrainian" (I:411), the heroine replies when the young man comments on her fluency in the Ukrainian language. The heroine's self-identification seems unexpected and almost forced to her conversationalist, but, driven by his budding physical attraction, he also accepts the new discourse and proceeds to treat the heroine as he would an equal, which is to say that he rapes her on the spot.

The highly aestheticized description of the rape scene and a surprisingly brief description of the heroine in its aftermath suggest that Kobylians'ka had little interest in depicting accurately the true, dehumanizing social experience of sexual violence, but rather used the rape narrative as a literary motif to address broader social and political issues. By foregrounding the brutal consequences of the heroine's excessive romanticizing and naive understanding of equality, the story offers a pungent answer to one of the central questions of the late nineteenth-century intellectuals' debates about whether the Ukrainian intellectuals and peasants had enough in common to identify as members of the same ethnic group and pursue a mutual cause of national liberation. The story's reconfiguration of rape most effectively articulates the spiritual weakness and political incompetence of the Ukrainian intelligentsia, which, as implied, was utterly incapable not only of fighting for the well-being of the whole nation but also of securing its own survival at the turn of the twentieth century. The story's depiction of the Hustul's behaviour during and after the rape scene also deconstructs the idealized image of the Ukrainian common man. While recognizing his great power, the story makes it explicit that he remains wild, uncontrollable, potentially self-destructive, but, most importantly, completely indifferent to any national identification. The Hutsul's psychological breakdown in the aftermath of the rape, together with his tragic but highly satirical revelation at the end of the story, unmasks his ignorance, superstitious beliefs, and lack of any understanding of the laws and civil code, offering a sharp critique of "the raw peasant mind" that finds its only consolation in either religion or witchcraft. The story of the rape and its effect on both characters thus suggest that, although Kobylians'ka's recognized the need for a cultural revolution in the village, she believed that an ill-conceived "going to the people" was not the right way to achieve it. As the story implies, and as Kobylians'ka argued elsewhere, fanatical and often self-sacrificing projects of the Ukrainian intelligentsia contributed neither to educating the underprivileged nor to forging any ethnic solidarity. On the contrary, such behaviour only promoted class antagonism and exacerbated cultural stagnation. Kobylians'ka's use of rape in "Nature," therefore, goes far beyond challenging the conservative consensus on gender and sexuality. It explicitly critiques the ill-conceived populist practices of "going to the people" and undermines the ideologically inspired presumption that Ukrainian peasants are noble creatures – one of the key narratives that dominated liberal thought in late nineteenth-century Ukraine – as utopian and disconnected from real-life conditions. More broadly, "Nature" refutes a naturalist conception of ethnic solidarity that defines ethnicity as a natural category and claims that people who share the same ethnicity naturally wish to share the same political unit. While acknowledging that people of the same ethnicity often share many biological and cultural traits, Kobylians'ka's story highlights the contingency of ethnic solidarity that requires far more than nature alone.

After "Nature," Kobylians'ka returned to the peasant theme only in 1895, when she published two short stories, "Time" and "Bank rustykal'nyi" ("Rustic Bank"), which feature peasants as central characters. One Soviet critic claims that Kobylians'ka wrote both stories, alongside her 1896 short story "Uncultured," in the same manner as "Nature" and used similar principles in depicting peasants, whom, as the critic observes, she continued to juxtapose with educated, middle-class heroines (Tomashuk 1969a, 67–8). During the Soviet period, this reading was never questioned, most likely because of the limitations placed on literary criticism by the Soviet regime under which even the slightest suggestion of Kobylians'ka's anti-populism could have led to her official denunciation. After the collapse of the Soviet Union, while rereading Kobylians'ka's major works anew, Western and post-Soviet Ukrainian scholars also paid little attention to Soviet interpretations of Kobylians'ka's rustic stories. A close look at "Time" and "Rustic Bank," however, shows that in the mid-1890s, Kobylians'ka altered the overall tone of her depictions of peasants and their interactions with the intelligentsia. From derogatory and condemnatory she changed them to kind and sympathetic. Accordingly, she no longer presented her new peasant characters as coarse and primitive others but depicted them as complex beings who, despite their lack of formal education, led vigorously independent mental and moral lives, often of considerable subtlety.

In both stories, Kobylians'ka continued to use dialogue as a structural device, but it was no longer the threshold to action, as in "Nature," but the action itself. In "Time," for example, peasants' dialogic confessions not only expose their prejudices and thereby juxtapose them to the educated heroine's views but also objectively externalize the complexity of their mental lives. The intricate voice combinations of the dialogic confessions help the story to convey the subtle influence of the educated heroine on the peasant mind in a much more productive way than the direct authorial commentaries in Kobylians'ka's earlier works. In contrast to the heroine in "Nature," the educated heroine in "Time" no longer lectures or mocks her peasant interlocutors with clichéd arguments; rather, she encourages and guides them to contemplate on their own ideas, thereby stimulating their cognitive transformation. In her philosophical discussion with an old Hutsul woman on personal agency and free will, the educated heroine deliberately guides her own words to penetrate the old woman's speech:

> The old Hutsul woman slowly turned her face in my direction.
> "Did you say something?"
> "No, I was just thinking."
> "What good is in thinking? No one has ever thought of everything."
> "Why is that, dear?"
> "To think or not to think does not make any difference because no one has ever thought up how to avoid the most terrible evil of all."
> "What kind of terrible evil?"
> "What kind? Well ... It's still far away from you. You're still as young as a dove. But for me ... Well, death is the most terrible evil of all."
> "Death ... that is true, thinking cannot turn it away."
> "So you see.... You do see ... And what does everything else matter?"
> "Death is something bound to happen ... but it's not the most terrible evil of all."
> "Not the most terrible evil! It never turns out well for anyone ... But then, that's how it must be because it's God's will."
> "How is that, dear?"
> "I just said – God wills so ..."
> "Wills what?"
> "How things are."
> "Well, a human being can will too ..."
> The old woman sadly shook her head. (I:472–3)

On the formal level, we can read this conversation as the old woman's internal dialogue because there are barely any markers that separate her utterances from the words of her upper-middle-class conversationalist. The formal markers, or better the lack thereof, show how the rhetoric of the educated heroine permeates the old woman's words and makes her aware of competitive views on the inevitability of death, the existence of human will, and, by implication, the positive ramifications of thinking, which, as further suggested, helps individuals to assert their own voices. Mikhail Bakhtin's concept of the intentional authorial dialogization of characters' utterances is especially helpful in gauging Kobylians'ka's creative use of the dialogical nature of speech in this scene. As Bakhtin pointed out in one of his most complete statements on his philosophy of language, his 1934–6 essay "Discourse in the Novel," someone else's persuasive ideological discourse is of decisive significance in the evolution of an individual consciousness:

> Consciousness awakens to independent ideological life precisely in a world of alien discourses surrounding it, and from which it cannot initially separate itself; the process of distinguishing between one's own and another's discourse, between one's own and another's thought, is activated rather late in the development. When thought begins to work in an independent, experimenting and discriminating way, what first occurs is a separation between internally persuasive discourse and authoritarian enforced discourse, along with a rejection of those categories of discourse that do not matter to us, that do not touch us. (2008, 345)

In this light, Kobylians'ka choice of the dialogic potential of speech over direct statements provides an interesting insight into the writer's interpretation of the populist program of "going to the people," which calls on the educated Ukrainians not simply to go and propagate liberating ideas to the people, but to engage in the complexity of the peasant world in a more sophisticated way.

Another novelty in Kobylians'ka's depiction of peasants that first appeared in "Time" is the writer's unremitting enthusiasm about the potential regeneration of peasant consciousness. While juxtaposing two peasant characters with clashing views, the old Hutsul woman and her daughter Illinka, the story projects the possibility of the cultural and moral transformation of the peasant mind. Throughout the story, the educated heroine draws the readers' attention to a sharp visual contrast between the old mother, with her "dull and drowsy gaze," and the daughter, whose unusual grace and physical strength recall those of a "tigress." At the end of the story, the middle-class heroine initiates a dialogue between the two peasant women that elucidates their differences and eventually forces the old woman to acknowledge that her daughter "has already a mind of her own" (I:473–4). If we consider that Kobylians'ka wrote "Time" around the same time that she discovered Nietzsche and his concept of the overman, we could read the two peasant heroines as symbolic representations of the first two Nietzschean stages in the evolution of the peasant consciousness. In this light, the old woman could be seen as a beast of labour, Nietzsche's camel, who possesses a sense of duty in bearing what she is ordered to bear, while Illinka-the-tigress could be read as Nietzsche's lion who desires to create her own freedom. The third and final Nietzschean transformation of the peasants' consciousness is projected as inevitable and fast approaching in the final lines of the story, where the educated heroine admires Illinka's singing:

> While Illinka's song rang through the forest as a call to happiness and joy ... I thought of her powerful, clear voice as of an event ... The ravines reverberated with its echo. It seemed that her courageous and compelling voice rebounded from one cliff to another and resonated ever farther and farther, ever higher and higher ... It seemed that her call was flying somewhere very far away, into a mysterious distance. (I:475)

This statement is perhaps the only utterly enthusiastic recognition and reinforcement of the possible cultural and moral evolution of the peasants in Kobylians'ka's oeuvre. Considering that chronologically "Time" overlaps with the brief period in the writer's creative career when she was first introduced to the liberationist national ethos by Ivan Franko, Mykhailo Pavlyk, Ievhenia Iaroshyns'ka, Stepan Smal'-Stots'kyi, Vasyl' Lukych, and Osyp Makovei, it is fair to suggest that the writer might have been fascinated not as much with the populist enthusiastic celebration of peasants' spiritual, cultural, and political potential but with vibrant personalities of these prominent Ukrainian intellectuals who shared populist convictions among Western Ukrainians in the 1870s, 1880s, and 1890s.

By 1896, a year after she wrote "Time," Kobylians'ka had already tempered her enthusiasm about the potential transformation of peasants' world views by introducing elements of scepticism and doubt in her next rustic story, "Uncultured." As Kobylians'ka stated in a letter to Makovei on 17 December 1898, the main objective of "Uncultured," which depicts another unusual Hutsul woman, is "to portray the beauty of an uncultured being with all her inborn happiness and irrepressible, blissful ignorance" (IL F14, N166). The title of the story suggests that despite the prominent tones of admiration, Kobylians'ka juxtaposed her peasant heroine Paraska with culture, education, and, by extension, social progress. A brief commentary on Paraska's character by the omnipresent narrator highlights this tension in the beginning of the story, making Kobylians'ka's favourable representation of the "uncultured" peasant heroine highly ambiguous: "[Paraska's] lively dark eyes radiate joy. Her every movement, every fluctuation of her voice expresses the vigour of her untrammeled life, her humour, and ... her childlike naiveté" (II:333). Although this description starts with an affirming assessment of Paraska's optimism, it ends in an abrupt reference to the heroine's naiveté and blissful ignorance, which dialectically undercut all the preceding positive qualities. The contradictory nature of the introductory description sets up the overall tone of the story, which continually oscillates between humorous presentation and grief-inspiring subject matter, seamlessly intertwining genuine admiration with sharp criticism.

Paraska's own stories, which she shares with her educated conversationalist, convey the duality of her nature. Despite their half-joking manner of narration, Paraska's tales gradually make it obvious that the heroine's life is filled with nothing but hard work, suffering, and violence. While adorning her stories with a veneer of idyllic bliss, witty pranks, and self-aggrandizement, all the Hutsul woman can tell about her youth is that she "worked and served, laboured for others because she had the strength" (II:332). Shockingly, her most exciting memory is an instance of attempted rape. Here Kobylians'ka once again uses the trope of sexual violence to make a social commentary, alluding to her earlier use of rape rhetoric and its symbolic implications in "Nature." Paraska's story, however, is quite different from the one narrated in "Nature." As opposed to the educated, upper-middle-class heroine in the earlier story who could do nothing but beg her rapist for mercy, Paraska puts up a fierce fight and forces her attacker, a fellow Hutsul shepherd with whom she used to work as a seasonal labourer, to back off. Not only does she yell out curses and threats, but she also bites, scratches, kicks, and punches the shepherd, making him abide by her will:

> He rushed at me like a madman and instantly tore the shirt on my chest.
>
> "We will see," he snuffled, "who will croak like a chicken," and he pushed me to the ground. Then I ... God forbid!
>
> "Hey! Hey! Hey!" I screamed and began to fight with him. I was fighting to the death! He was strong, bewildered, tried to push me down, but I resisted ...

"You will croak! You will!" He groaned. He grabbed me by the throat and tried to throw me to the ground.

"You will croak!" I said and bit him on his hand so hard that he screamed from pain. He screamed, and I jumped up to my feet and rushed at him!

And he rushed at me ... He was so furious. He wanted to kill me, but I didn't wait and punched him right in the face! I wasn't scared any longer.

"Do you see my fist? Do you see it," I blustered, "and do you see the teeth? I will maul you, bastard! I will eat you alive! I will rip you apart! Hey! Hey! Hey!" I came up close to him and looked at him. I was enraged! He stood there silently and bareheaded because his hat had fallen to the ground. He was pale as death.

"Bandit!" I said and swung my both fists at him, "Do you really think I am of this kind? Damn you!" I spat and walked away.

Then he picked his hat from the ground and went back to the mountains. (II:335)

The abrupt reversal in the perpetrator's behaviour produces a strong rhetorical effect inversely proportional to the effects generated by the conventional rape narratives: rather than distancing the victim and the violator, as happens in "Nature," it asserts their sameness and mutual recognition. Paraska manages to avoid being raped because she, as opposed to the violated heroine in "Nature," truly has what it takes to communicate her will to the assaulting Hutsul peasant and she speaks the precise sociocultural language that he understands: she bites, scratches, kicks, punches, and curses. As an intertextual reference, Paraska's story thus revisits Kobylians'ka's earlier criticism of the cultural alienation between the Ukrainian intelligentsia and "the people" from a different standpoint that underscores that, although at one time the Ukrainian peasantry and intelligentsia might have had the same ethnic roots, they operated within the matrix of two distinct and often antagonistic cultures.

The story of the attempted rape, alongside Paraska's other two tales, also brings out the dramatic difference between populist stereotypes of an idyllic village and the grim reality hidden beneath it. Paraska's second story about her loveless marriage, for example, draws attention to a certain inconsistency in the heroine's behaviour: the same heroine who fiercely resists the attractive shepherd agrees passively to marry an old widower she does not fancy. Like the young Hutsul in "Nature," Paraska explains all her misfortunes as "a predetermination by fates" (II:340), which reveals her fatalist beliefs that delimit her otherwise rational mind and rebellious spirit. If we consider Kobylians'ka's advocacy of cultural enlightenment, free will, and personal agency, it is hard to overlook here the writer's irony about Paraska's superstitions, which problematizes and thereby demythologizes populist discourse on the ideal values of the Ukrainian village community.

Kobylians'ka's criticism reaches its crescendo in Paraska's last story about her night wandering through the woods in search of the "devil's mill" (moara dracului). This allegorical narrative, like the story of the Hutsul's bewildered wandering through the woods in "Nature," could be easily read as a representation of the relentlessly dark and dreadful existence of the Ukrainian peasantry. The story clearly implies that despite their many positive qualities, Ukrainian peasants often become victims of their own doomed views and superstitious beliefs. Therefore, although Kobylians'ka emphasized for the populist critics that her story depicts "the beauty of the uncultured being," the story's graphic images bring out a critical disposition towards the "twisted peasant mind," and those who naively propagate it as a defining force in the Ukrainian national revival.

Lesia Ukrainka (see figure 5) was the first to acknowledge the subversive aspects in "Uncultured" and to celebrate its groundbreaking aesthetic and ideological significance. In a letter written to Kobylians'ka on 18–30 January 1900, she defined "Uncultured" as one of the most innovative works in Ukrainian literature of the time:

> You might not believe me, but we [Ukrainian intellectuals of Eastern Ukraine] desire the green Bukovyna more than any Parisian play, especially after reading your "Uncultured." What a magnificent story is this "Uncultured." I cannot even tell you what a fantastic impression it made on me. What character types, what descriptions of nature it has! There are no descriptions of nature in our literature that can surpass yours, and I'm ready to admire you just for that because I love descriptions of nature in literature and I always missed them in our [Ukrainian] fiction. Speaking about Paraska, I didn't expect from an Austrian Ukrainian the sincerity and bravery with which you depicted her character and her life story. While reading, I continually exclaimed to myself, "Bravo, Miss Olga! Long live art! Long live freedom!" Your fellow, properly raised countrymen must have given you a good scolding for your "Uncultured" because they are not used to a woman, even if she is a writer, daring to write "something peculiar like that." Please do not think that I, too, find "something peculiar like that" in your "Uncultured." There is nothing excessively coarse in it. Even its most powerful passages are like the fortissimo of a good pianist, which can never be too coarse. (1963b, 75)

Figure 5. Ol'ha Kobylians'ka and Lesia Ukrainka, Chernivtsi, 1901

In this fragment, Ukrainka acknowledged that Kobylians'ka's representation of the peasant woman as an irrational, impulsive, and superstitious natural being was an unprecedented act of daring that challenged the mainstream populist canon and positioned Kobylians'ka as a radical modernizer of Ukrainian literature. In the early 1900s, similar commentaries and recognition came from other prominent Ukrainian modernists such as Vasyl' Stefanyk and Makhailo Kotsiubyns'kyi, who developed comparable approaches to depicting peasants in which they fused their admiration for the Hutsuls' authentic spirit with a sharp anti-populist criticism of the Hutsuls' superstitious beliefs, lack of formal education, and sociopolitical crudeness.[5]

The third mode in Kobylians'ka's representations of peasants emerged in the 1898 short story "In the Fields." The story is one of the first fictional adaptations of the tragic homicide, a presumable fratricide, which took place in a well-off peasant family that Kobylians'ka knew personally, and that she later featured as the central event in her 1902 novel *The Earth*. "In the Fields," however, does not mention the homicide but rather concentrates on the prior history of the family, which conveys the agony of the old parents whose oldest son is recruited into the Austrian military. The main plot revolves around a comic story of how the old peasant couple entrusts a local Jew, Ben'iamin, with a large sum of money to pay off officials and keep their son home but ends up losing both the money and the son. The narrative is structured as a dialogue, but in contrast to the earlier stories, there are no educated middle-class characters to provide the ideological framework for the text. The story focuses exclusively on the interaction between peasant characters, exposing their outlook on life through their communications with each other. On the one hand, their conversations present the old couple as honest, caring, and hard-working people. On the other hand, however, they portray the two characters as ignorant proprietors who cannot function outside their natural environment, the village. Thereby, Kobylians'ka once again undercuts her positive description of peasants with her ironic exposure of their fatalistic beliefs and limited personal agency. The story ends with an allegorical passage that reiterates Kobylians'ka's earlier call "to bring a ray of light into the darkness" of the Ukrainian village:

> A lonely voice penetrated the sombre mass of mist that enveloped the gnawing anguish, which grew increasingly thicker and ran its heavy waves as far as the eye could see, making all colours fade. Unnoticed, it sang the only tune: *Give me light! Give me light!* (III:323)

This ending might be pulling the story into a different, formal direction, but it nevertheless complements Kobylians'ka's overall critique of the peasants' incompetence by arguing for the urgent need for enlightenment.

Vasyl' Stefanyk was one of the first to recognize and praise Kobylians'ka's innovative approach to portraying peasants. He also was among the first to point out the overly soft and timid nature of social and political criticism in Kobylians'ka's new story. After reading "In the Fields," he wrote to Kobylians'ka on 16 December 1898:

> I read your story "In the Fields." It is good because it is written in the precise tone of that blue mist that covers out fields ... But you bury all the sharp edges that could hurt people in your heart. You bend all the simple lines that escape harmony with your delicate hands. I see a poet in its every line. From your every work, you look at me with sad kindness, as if you were Virgin Mary, whose heart is pierced with swords but whose face radiates love to all. (2007, 221)

In the same letter, Stefanyk urged Kobylians'ka to be more audacious in her descriptions and offered as an example his brief account of a brutal murder, which took place in his neighbourhood village and which he later adapted into a short story, "Novyna" ("The News," 1899). Kobylians'ka's grievous depictions of the Bukovynian village in her 1902 novel *The Earth* suggest that she took seriously Stefanyk's advice to bring out the "sharp edges" of Ukrainian peasantry. In its lyrical power, its narrative conviction, its epic and mythical grandeur, and its immediate social implication, Kobylians'ka's rustic novel *The Earth* is unprecedented in Ukrainian literature.

The Earth

Kobylians'ka finished *The Earth* in April 1901 and published it in the L'viv literary monthly *Literary and Scientific Herald* in 1902. Within several months, the novel came out as a separate edition. Its story is roughly based on true events that took place in the fall of 1894 in a Bukovynian village, Dymka, where the older of two sons in a well-off peasant family named Zhyzhyian was shot dead under mysterious circumstances. The immediate family and the whole village suspected the younger son, but the official investigation pronounced him not guilty. Kobylians'ka, who lived in Dymka for several years in the late 1880s and then regularly visited her family estate there for the rest of her life, knew the Zhyzhyian family very well.[6] She was deeply moved by the incident and decided to write about it. As she pointed out in her letter to Osyp Makovei written on 11 July 1902, she spent several years collecting materials and working out different aspects of the story before she began to write her novel in 1898 (V:509). Incidentally, it was the same year when several influential populist critics suggested that she ought to pay more attention to the plight of the Ukrainian common man (see figure 6).[7] This curious congruence sets up a sociocultural framework that allows us to view *The Earth* as Kobylians'ka's response to the populist requests. While addressing the sombre and unremitting hardships of Ukrainian peasants, Kobylians'ka's rustic novel does not glorify their suffering, as populist critics might have expected. Instead, it complicates the ongoing discussion of "the simple peasant mind" by featuring it as, if not necessarily "simple," then "too self-centred" and "raw" to be fit for any political struggle.[8]

The majority of Kobylians'ka's contemporary critics, as well as Soviet critics of the 1930s, disregarded the strong anti-populist rhetoric

Figure 6. Ol'ha Kobylians'ka at the celebration of Ivan Franko's twenty-fifth anniversary of his literary career (sitting left to right: M. Pavlyk, I. Iaroshyns'ka, N. Kobryns'ka, O. Kobylians'ka, D. Lepkyi, A. Chaikivs'kyi, K. Pan'kivs'kyi; middle row left to right: I. Kopach, V. Hnatiuk, O. Makovei, M. Hrushevs'kyi, I. Franko, O. Kolessa, B. Lepkyi; top row left to right: I. Petrushevych, F. Kolessa, O. Kyshakevych, I. Trush, D. Luk'ianovych, V. Ivasiuk), L'viv, 1898. This photograph is a copy of the image printed in *Ol'ha Kobylians'ka: Al'manakh u pam'iatku ii sorokolitnioi pys'mennyts'koi diial'nosti, 1887–1927*, Chernivtsi, 1928, p. 137

in *The Earth* and seized instead the opportunity to appropriate its peasant themes for their own ideological agendas. With a few exceptions, over the last hundred years, critics have viewed *The Earth* as the writer's brush with populism. Accordingly, they regarded Kobylians'ka as "a defender of the Ukrainian common man, a devoted student of the culture of the Ukrainian peasantry, and a storyteller for whom the plight of the poor and the neglected was a central concern" (Tarnawsky 2001, v). Paradoxically, despite its obvious shortcomings, Kobylians'ka's canonization as a populist writer proved to be beneficial. Not only did it assure the survival of Kobylians'ka's works and archival materials during the Soviet period, but it also allowed for prolific research into her life and works.[9] The initial enthusiastic reviews of *The Earth* by populist critics, particularly those by Franko, allowed Soviet critics to frame the novel as a psychological study of the Ukrainian peasantry grounded in their social reality, which, presumably, decried the detrimental nature of private ownership.[10] Only in the 1990s, after the collapse of the Soviet Union, were Ukrainian literary scholars able to address Kobylians'ka's anti-populism openly. Most of them, however, inherited the main critical framework from previous scholarship and continued to read Kobylians'ka's novel as a story of fratricide, focusing either on the psychological or on the sociological grounds that led to the murderous crime. The first post-Soviet account that offers a truly new conceptual approach to Kobylians'ka's *The Earth* is Marko Pavlyshyn's recent reading of the novel's fratricide as a speculation that allowed Kobylians'ka to raise broader philosophical issues, such as questions about the role of causality in human affairs (2008, 143–69). Using Pavlyshyn's argument as a starting point, the following analysis demonstrates that in addition to questioning turn-of-the-century determinist theories of human behaviour, Kobylians'ka's depictions of the peasant mind with all its fatalistic, irrational, and superstitious views challenged populist glorifications of peasants and presented rural life in a manner that undermined the traditional view of the Ukrainian village as a noble and wholesome environment.

On the level of the plot, *The Earth* is a story of a mysterious murder in a well-off peasant family, depicting the family's dramatic disintegration, which takes place over the timespan of some ten years. The story evolves against the majestic backdrop of country life, which captures every aspect of the countryside and offers a panoramic view of the Ukrainian village populated with diverse characters from different social strata: rich landlords, well-to-do farmers, struggling sharecroppers, tenant farmers, smallholders scratching out a laborious living, seasonal migrant workers, household servants, demobilized soldiers, public officials, travelling musicians, soothsayers, village teachers, provincial clergy, and tavern keepers. But for all the vigour with which populist critics promote Kobylians'ka as the champion of ethnographic village studies and chronicler of the daily life of the common people, neither her descriptions of village life nor her portrayals of peasants have any traces of naive glorification. On the contrary, just as Stefanyk requested in his 1898 letter, they are so grim as to recall the overly sombre colours of Émile Zola's peasant novel *La Terre* (*The Earth*, 1887). Although there are barely any critical or scholarly references to Kobylians'ka's reception of Zola and his naturalism, the similarities between Zola's and Kobylians'ka's texts leave no doubt that the Ukrainian writer, who on several occasions admitted reading Zola "out of literary duty" (I:216), not only was familiar with one of the foremost novels among Zola's Rougon-Macquart series but also used many of its thematic, structural, and even symbolic elements in her own work. Kobylians'ka's tribute to Zola is particularly palpable in her depictions of peasants, who, like Zola's heroes, are featured, almost without exception, as tough, harsh, ungrateful, concerned solely with their short-term interests, superstitious, barely Christian (perhaps deists), childish, deceitful, stoical, mean, and greedy. Accordingly, violence, instinct, sexual passion, and incest rule in the village of Kobylians'ka's creation, where all human relations, like those in Zola's work, are deformed by corrupted social norms that verge on bestial savagery.

The point of departure in Kobylians'ka's novel, as in Zola's, is elegantly simple: the elderly peasant couple, Ivonika and Mariika Fedorchuk, who have worked hard all their lives to accumulate land but have grown too feeble to continue to look after it properly, hope that their two sons, Mykhailo and Sava, will take care of their land and expand it by hard work and successful marriages. Their younger son, Sava, refuses to obey and starts courting his landless and good-for-nothing cousin Rakhira. Their relationship generates tension among all members of the family. Shortly thereafter, the older son, Mykhailo, who initially condemns Sava's pursuit of Rakhira, also falls in love with a poor girl, Anna, whom the parents would likewise not be willing to accept. Fearing parental disapproval, Mykhailo postpones telling his parents about Anna and tries to exploit their argument with Sava for his own benefit. Consequently, Mariika and Ivonika unjustly demonize rebellious Sava while equally unjustly idealizing Mykhailo. Things become particularly complicated when the parents threaten to leave Sava without an inheritance, which instigates a violent conflict between the two brothers. Outraged by the perceived parental unfairness and blinded by uncontrollable lust for his cousin and the land he believes he is about to lose, Sava publicly swears to make his relatives pay dearly for their injustice. A few days later, Mykhailo is found murdered in a neighbouring forest. Although the story does not disclose the real murderer, the readers, alongside the whole village, Anna, Ivonika, and Mariika, are led to believe that Sava is responsible for the crime. As in the real story of the Zhyzhyian family, the official investigation does not find any evidence that can incriminate Sava and pronounces him not guilty. The end of the story deals with Anna. Within a few months after Mykhailo's funeral, she gives birth to twins he fathered, but the two boys die shortly after because Mariika refuses to recognize them as grandchildren and Anna has neither the means nor the physical strength to care for the infants. A few years later, after recovering from the tragic events connected to Mykhailo's death, Anna marries an older peasant, Petro, and gives birth to another boy, whom she decides to break free from the oppressive dependence on the land by giving him an education. Ironically, it is Ivonika and Mariika who help Anna accomplish her goal in repentance for their earlier harsh treatment of Mykhailo's bride and his newborn twin sons.

The dramatic story of the Fedorchuks' decline is intertwined with monumental descriptions of nature and various aspects of country life, which intensify the inner emotional and cognitive life of the characters. The novel's emphasis on the relationship among nature, location, and people recalls the very composition of Zola's novel. As in Zola's work, the action in Kobylians'ka's novel is dominated by the seasonal cycle of nature, marked by a succession of agricultural activities involved in the task of cultivating the earth, starting with a spring and ending with a fall sowing and, in between, all the manifold seasonal activities of plowing, haymaking, reaping, cattle-raising, and beekeeping. The seasonal village activities are further measured against the human cycle of birth, marriage, and death, with the accompanying country events of markets, fairs, weddings, religious wakes, and funerals, which allegorically project village life as a cyclic, and thus stagnant, natural existence.

Furthermore, all events in Kobylians'ka's novel, like those in Zola's work, take place against the essential backdrop of the weather, with its devastating hailstorms and murderous summer heat, pallid springs and gorgeous Indian summers, chill autumn rains and furious winter blizzards. Like Zola, Kobylians'ka used lavish descriptions of nature to dramatize the different emotional states of her peasant characters, portraying them as natural, not sociocultural, beings. Kobylians'ka's chronology of the seasons, however, is different from that in Zola's novel. Kobylians'ka's *The Earth* starts not with an autumn harvest sequence but with a spring cultivation of the land, and ends not with Zola's joyful spring sowing but with a description of the wintertime stagnation of all agricultural activities that coincides with the emotional devastation of the old Fedorchuks. By reversing Zola's chronological order of the seasonal sequence, Kobylians'ka altered its symbolic meaning, thereby rejecting Zola's optimistic celebration of natural regeneration, which the French novelist prophesied at the end of his text.

Kobylians'ka's treatment of the earth also differs from Zola's. As suggested by the identical titles of the two novels, the earth plays an important role in both works as the central character that dominates all other characters, who are inextricably linked to it through their daily toil. In the final analysis, all the tragic events in both texts are triggered by the characters' uncontrollable desire to possess land, which is painted consistently in terms of human relationships because, as both works suggest, it is more valuable than people for the peasants. But whereas Zola pictured the earth predominantly in bright colours, associating it either with a desirable woman or with a nourishing mother, Kobylians'ka projected it as a cruel oppressor or a trap that keeps those bound to it away from civilized cultural and urban centres and drains all their vital powers and human dignity. The difference between the two texts' representations of the earth could be inferred from the reflections of Fouan, the unfortunate patriarch of the declining peasant family in Zola's *The Earth* (quotation 1); Hourdequin, the owner of the largest and the most mechanized farm in the village of Zola's creation (quotation 2); and Ivonika Fedorchuk, the richest peasant landowner in Kobylians'ka's novel (quotation 3):

> (1) [Fouan] had adored his land like a woman, who kills you and for whom one murders. [He had] no love for wife or children, nothing human: just the land! (1980, 38)
>
> (2) Ah! This earth, how he [Hourdequin] had come to love her! And with a passion beyond the sharp greed of the peasant, with a sentimental, almost intellectual passion, for he felt it to be the common mother, who had given him life, substance, and to whom he would return. (1980, 451)
>
> (3) Ivonika loved [the earth]. He knew it in all its seasons and in all its moods as well as he knew himself. It reminded him of a human being and demanded a sacrifice ... and it frightened him more than the darken[ed] sky that prophesies a storm. [At times] it was truly malicious ... It took nourishment away from everything that grew and lived on it and forced it all to faint, fade, and ... petrify. (II:30)

These three passages convey the overall attitudes of the two writers towards the cultivation of land and its effect on those who are linked to it. While criticizing the peasantry, whose moral filth does not match the goodness of the earth in his novel, Zola frames the countryside as a more natural and thus a healthier environment than the city throughout the Rougon-Macquart novels.[11] Kobylians'ka, in contrast, depicts a Ukrainian village that resembles Dobroliubov's dark kingdom by juxtaposing its monotonous and stupefying lifestyle with the invigorating dynamic of urban centres.[12] Kobylians'ka's radical deviation from Zola's point of view suggests that she used only those formal aspects of Zola's work that helped her either to create a panoramic view of peasant life or to highlight the fundamental relationship between peasants and nature. As to an ideological framework, Kobylians'ka pursued a completely different goal and contrasted nature with culture to prioritize the latter, and thus promote her elitist vision of cultural revolution as a means for Ukraine's liberation.

Indeed, Kobylians'ka's novel is far from being a blatant remake of Zola's masterpiece. Another fundamental difference between the two texts lies in Kobylians'ka's rejection of the determinist explanations of human behaviour that dominate Zola's fiction and that some populist and Soviet critics tried to ascribe to her text. Kobylians'ka criticized Zola and other naturalist writers for placing too much emphasis on the objectified descriptions of the external world, particularly on its coarser and more repulsive aspects and thereby completely ignoring the internal life of their characters (V:317). She believed that people's will and their deeper, unconscious desires are far more important in shaping actions, accounting for such human behaviour as violence, than heredity or social environment.[13] This is precisely what the epigraph to Kobylians'ka's *The Earth* highlights: "We are surrounded by many abysses that destiny has dug out for us, but the deepest of them all is ... in our hearts" (II:7).[14] Therefore, while recognizing Zola's literary genius and adapting many formal aspects of his peasant novel, particularly his rich descriptions of nature and seasonal village life, Kobylians'ka altered her own narrative by focusing primarily on the psychological portraits of her characters. As a result, she created not only a striking account of the unremitting hardship of the Bukovynian peasantry but also a study of the interior lives of her villagers, which proved to be iconoclastic in the context of the Ukrainian fin-de-siècle populist ideology.

Kobylians'ka conveyed the inner life of her characters by animating her peasant heroes and skilfully manipulating the narrative mode in her novel. She presented the main story of *The Earth* through a variety of third-person subjective perspectives that switch from one character's viewpoint to another's. On the one hand, this approach allows for the in-depth analysis of the protagonists' personalities, but on the other hand, it presents all events exclusively as perceived or as understood by the characters, which makes it virtually impossible to discover the truth about Mykhailo's murder. This structural composition that prioritizes the inner personality of each character over the main factual event brings Kobylians'ka's work close to Fyodor Dostoevsky's polyphonic fiction, particularly his last work, *The Brothers Karamazov* (1880), where the Russian writer used the pretext of a mysterious murder to explore and expose the conflicted psyches of his heroes. Like Dostoevsky, Kobylians'ka used dialogue and dialogic internal monologues to reveal the private thoughts and emotions of her characters. The use of dialogue, in turn, allowed Kobylians'ka to individualize the speech of all characters, even secondary and episodic ones, which created a multiplicity of human voices that reflect not only personalities but also the characters' outlook on life. It is precisely these Dostoevskian insights into human thinking that make Kobylians'ka's projected countryside far more grief inspiring than that depicted in Zola's *The Earth*.

Kobylians'ka's *The Earth* introduces all its principal characters in the opening wedding scene. Despite a degree of fascination with the picturesque Bukovynian peasants, the scene conveys a sincere concern with their circumscribed world views, which are opposed in principle to the ideas of education and progress. The dynamic tension between a peasant mode of thinking and progress is captured through a description of a wedding dance, where the readers are both captivated and repelled by the sweat, bodily dirt, and dust; the red, glistening faces of the dancers; their violent gestures; and the unbridled, animalistic emotion that controls and motivates their every movement and action. The graphic dance scene is immediately juxtaposed with a sad conversation between Ivonika and his well-to-do neighbour, Dokiia. Both characters lament over an unrealized hope to unite their children, and thereby their property, in marriage. While expressing love and sincere concern about the well-being of their children, both Ivonika and Dokiia reveal a distorted understanding of happiness, measured exclusively in acres of land. Both characters make it clear that their decisions, which ruin the future of their children, are rooted in prejudices and superstitions, but neither of them admits personal responsibility for their families' misfortunes. Like the Hutsul characters in Kobylians'ka's earlier rustic stories, they justify all calamities by attributing them to evil spirits, bad fortune, and God's will. It is hard to overlook the explicit irony in Ivonika's and Dokiia's conversation, which conveys Kobylians'ka's doubt in the peasants' potential to secure the future of the Ukrainian nation. Ivonika's direct self-identification with Bukovynian peasantry and his broad statements about the peasants' lack of social and political agency articulate Kobylians'ka's irony with equivalent deliberation:

> And what about us [peasants]? No matter what we say, no one looks at us. There is nothing we can do. We can bow to the lords, kiss their hands on both sides, but if we say something, it remains "plebian." No one would listen to us ... [because] as soon as the lord raises his voice ... we ... we get scared right away ... and back off. I know from my own experience that it cannot be otherwise. (II:27)

Although this passage avoids direct statements, it uses Ivonika's own voice to expose his "plebian" morality with its fatalistic conception of the world. Ivonika's closing remarks also suggest that he and the rest of the peasant community, with whom the old man identifies by using the collective pronoun "we," re-project their conformist, "plebeian" views onto their children and thereby deprive future generations of Bukovynian peasants of free will and individual agency. Pavlyshyn rightly detects Nietzsche's motifs of the "herd" and "herd morality" in Kobylians'ka's representation of Ivonika's world view here and elsewhere in the text (2008, 162–4).

Later in the novel, it becomes obvious that Kobylians'ka placed the detrimental influence of the parents' circumscribed world views on the younger generation of peasants at the centre of her work. As it turns out, all the younger characters – Mykhailo, Sava, Anna, Rakhira, and Parasynka – fail because of their inherited lack of self-confidence and personal agency. While Dokiia's daughter, the sixteen-year-old Parasynka, immediately enters the story as a "silent instrument of someone else's will" (II:20), the other characters' lack of agency becomes evident only with time. Mykhailo's weaknesses come to light once he joins the military and leaves his natural environment, the village. The fast-paced rhythm of urban life and the demanding and often brutal reality of military service make Mykhailo aware of his helplessness, which leads to psychological distress and an identity crisis:

> Weeks passed by since Mykhailo left his land, but he couldn't get used to the regimented military life. It was so hard to perform everything that was expected of him! It was brutal, despotic, and so different from his work on his land, to which he gave all his youthful energy in the past ... The austerity that reigned everywhere and crushed everything around here flared at him every minute like a sharp, shiny knife ... [The hardship of his new life often made him] cry like a child. Some of his comrades used to laugh at him. They used to say that everything always seems depressing at first, but eventually people get used to it all. He couldn't get used to the military. He was ruining himself here. He couldn't keep together all that he saw clearly there, in the fields. His steps were hesitant and awkward

> because he couldn't dare to walk with his usual pace. His movements were slow and timid because they weren't his usual movements. The clothes he was wearing took away his confidence. And where was he supposed to derive it from? His confidence and belief in his personal worth left him the moment he left his land. (II:106)

While exposing the brutality of the imperial army, this passage simultaneously reveals Mykhailo's fatal flaw, his hopeless inability to function outside his village. The story elaborates on Mykhailo's internal anguish through his later monologues and conversations with Ivonika. The most powerful of them is perhaps Mykhailo's appeal for Ivonika's help when the young peasant struggles to define his place in this new social context. The father-son conversation proves that Mykhailo's reflections on "what it means to be a peasant" are filled with other peoples' words projected on him either by his father, his superiors, or his fellow soldiers. Like Natalka Verkovychivna in Kobylians'ka's 1896 novel *The Princess*, Mykhailo refuses to identify with the pathetic image of an insignificant creature that his family and acquaintances force upon him – in Mykhailo's case, it is a "cursed dog" (II:121). Despite the explosive potential of his defiance, however, his contemplations do not provoke any decisive actions. As opposed to Kobylians'ka's educated Nietzschean heroine in *The Princess*, Mykhailo accepts his father's views on the social status quo, which solidifies his sense of personal ineptitude and insignificance.

Mykhailo's and Ivonika's father-son conversation is a turning point in the novel, after which Mykhailo continually fails to assert himself, triggering a chain of tragic events that claim his and his children's lives. By the end of the novel, both Mykhailo and Ivonika emerge as self-negating heroes or, better yet, anti-heroes: both conform to the unfavourable, existing state of affairs, which, as Ivonika puts it, is "bigger than them" and which "neither of them can change" (II:121). More importantly, both prioritize memory and the prevailing social norms, valuing endurance and mediocrity but not the independent will and protest, which, as Kobylians'ka's previous novel *The Princess* foregrounds, constitute the main preconditions for personal liberation and consequent social change. Mykhailo's and Ivonika's world view thus shows strong affinity with a set of qualities that Nietzsche defined in his treatise *On the Genealogy of Morality* as "slave morality." In the first essay of his *Genealogy*, Nietzsche argued that there are two basic types of morality: "master morality" and "slave morality." In *The Gay Science* and *Thus Spoke Zarathustra*, Nietzsche also described this fundamental division between the moralities of the "herd" and that of "high people."[15] He identified "master morality" as a "yea-saying" attitude where "good" and "bad" are equivalent to "noble" and "despicable," respectively. Most of all, Nietzsche celebrated masters' ability to create and assert their own values. As to the "slave morality," he described it as a "nay-saying" attitude or "herd morality," which places the highest value on that which is useful or beneficial to the weak or powerless, projecting humility and endurance as the highest virtues of humankind. Nietzsche argued that *ressentiment*, a form of reactiveness associated with a displacement of blame for one's own inferiority onto an imaginary enemy, an evil master, is the only value-creative agency of the slaves.[16] Highlighting the fact that the "herd" seeks to impose its values universally, Nietzsche claimed that the coexistence of these two types of moral outlooks is impossible (1998, 19). Taking into consideration Kobylians'ka's appreciation of Nietzsche and his philosophy, it is hard to view Mykhailo's and Ivonika's conformity to the status quo in a positive light.

The only character in *The Earth* that shows any promise for transcending the oppressive morality of traditional peasant society and for generating change is Ivonika's youngest son, Sava. He is first introduced from Ivonika's perspective as a rebellious character who refuses to live by the wisdom of his parents:

> Sava is not like Mykhailo! But he is my son too ... He is a different branch. He is growing and leaning somewhere ... but it's not towards the good and not towards us ... Dancing is the only thing on his mind. If he only could, he would spend all his time wandering with his rifle through the fields and the woods ... He doesn't care if the animals have water or not as long as he is not thirsty. He doesn't care what the weather is like and if it's good or bad for the earth and the crops, or if it might kill the bees as long as his private matters are in order and he has enough honey to mix with his moonshine and he can drink it secretively with God knows whom ... Yes, it's true that he is still young. He is only nineteen. But when Mykhailo was seventeen, he was my right hand and helped me as much as he does now. At his age, I was working for others and lowered my head to people and God. Anyway, I hope that when he grows older, he grows smarter as well. I say smarter because he is already very smart ... incredibly smart! So young, but can outsmart all sorts of trickery. (II:23–4)

Ivonika's description frames Sava as Nietzsche's life-asserting dancer, an eternal wanderer, an inventive trickster, and a skilled hunter. It also suggests that the young lad is perceived as evil only because his priorities are different from those of his kin. Some of the later portrayals that focus on Sava's lack of respect for his parents, elders, prevailing social values, and Christian morality further accentuate his indignation at the patriarchal order and traditional way of life and project him as a strong-willed person who dares to construct his own life and assert his own wisdom. His recalcitrant nature, alongside some other positive characteristics – cleverness, courage, firmness, decisiveness, and self-confidence – place Sava's image in sharp contrast with that of Mykhailo. At the critical moment of the story, when Mykhailo's weakness of character comes to light, Ivonika underscores his sons' differences by acknowledging that Sava is more mature, resourceful, and resilient than his older brother:

> [Mykhailo] was like a child. Sava wasn't like that ... If Sava joined the military, he'd endure all its challenges and hardship firmly and stubbornly. Sava wouldn't wave his fists in vain, and he wouldn't have as much trouble as [Mykhailo] does. He wouldn't be scared of them either. Sava is made of iron. His body might seem slender and delicate, but it is made of iron. (II:124–5)

This passage celebrates Sava's ultimate expression of stubbornness, iron will, and self-affirmation that Mykhailo lacks. Sava's incestuous relationship with his landless cousin Rakhira amplifies the contrast between the two brothers even more. Despite parental disapproval, he makes up his mind to marry the poor girl, demonstrating the courage, faithfulness, and commitment that Mykhailo lacks in his relationship with Anna.

Sava's potential to break free from the traditional "peasant mentality," however, is undermined by his unbridled passion. The object of Sava's affection, Rakhira, turns out to be a mendacious and ambitious girl who "does not hesitate to employ any means, even the basest acts, to satisfy her own desires" (II:191). It does not take her much effort to make Sava interested in taking over Ivonika's land and in achieving a favourable social status. By indulging Sava's every wish, she drains the inherent nobility of his soul and fills it with her spite instead, turning him into the wild and uncontrollable beast who has much in common with the main character in Kobylians'ka short story "Nature":

> Perhaps, no other girl in the world could love the way [Rakhira] did! He was a different person in her arms. She drank all his strength and energy with her full red lips. She drank them every time her eyes looked at him. And that gaze that either laughed at him or showered him with sparks made him soft and took all his power and will away. Her laughter ... took

> all his thoughts away ... and her words always had a way to match his state of mind. (II:34)

Rakhira thus subdues Sava's will and becomes an insurmountable obstacle that impedes his personal growth. As Kobylians'ka's notes to the unfinished second part of *The Earth* demonstrate, Sava's dramatic failure to master his passions for Rakhira gradually transmutes him into the same self-negating and self-destructive anti-hero as the rest of the peasant characters in *The Earth*.[17]

As the story progresses, the "softened" and stupefied Sava quickly absorbs Rakhira's lust for land and falls prey to the same corrupted views shared by his father, Mykhailo, and the rest of the village community, which Sava had initially rejected. His dialogues with Rakhira capture the deliberate penetration of the girl's rhetoric into Sava's consciousness, illuminating how his dreams and desires slowly merge with Rakhira's ambitions, and how he gradually transforms into an obedient tool of Rakhira's will. The best example of Rakhira's mental manipulations comes up in one of their conversations, during which Rakhira methodically and cold-bloodedly guides Sava to conceive Mykhailo's murder:

> It all had to happen the way she imagined it, the way she thought it up, and the way she wanted it. It couldn't be otherwise ... He had to get the land from his relatives, and the rest didn't matter to her ...
>
> "What are you waiting for, Sava? Are you waiting for Mykhailo to come back from military service?"
>
> "I'll have to go to the military too ... They didn't take me last time, but they might take me next time!"
>
> "You too? But didn't they already take Mykhailo?"
>
> "Yes, it's true, but I have to serve too ..."
>
> She was silent for a moment and then said, "If you had another brother, would he also have to go to the military?"
>
> "Of course!"
>
> "Would you have to go then?"
>
> "Do you really think I wouldn't? All the more so!"
>
> "How so?"
>
> "Because one of us would still stay with the old parents! Do you understand?"
>
> "How do you know? Who told you that," she asked.
>
> "I know that! I know that from the father! Everyone knows that."
>
> She was silent and deep in thought. In a moment or two, she said, "And what happens when there is only one son in a family?"

> "Then he could be exempt from military service. Then they can say, 'The old parents are weak, and he must stay at home to take care of them and their household.'"
>
> She stopped asking questions ... and began to bite her nails. After some time, she started again:
>
> "When Mykhailo comes back, you would have to go. After you came back, he would get married and your father would give him the best land ... but you have the same right to it as he does ... the same or, perhaps, even more!"
>
> Both got quiet and sat so for some time ... The rooster crowed. It was midnight. [Sava] woke up from his thoughts ... His eye started to wander and finally rested on a bottle of moonshine. He got up.
>
> "Is there anything left?" he asked ...
>
> He opened the bottle and ... drank everything to the last drop ...
>
> "You have nothing to worry about," he said, and a cruel smile distorted his tender, childlike features. (II:191–2)

In this conversation, Rakhira is clearly in control. By avoiding any direct requests and asking only a series of provocative questions, she makes Sava realize his disadvantageous situation and lures him to contemplate the benefits of being the only son in the family. On a formal level, Sava's and Rakhira's dialogue is structured in the same way as the conversation between the old Hutsul woman and the unnamed educated heroine in Kobylians'ka's 1895 short story "Time." As in the earlier story, there are barely any formal markers that separate the utterances of the two conversationalists, and thus Sava's and Rakhira's exchange could be easily read as the hero's internal dialogue with an internalized image of the girl who embodies his basest desires. In the 1902 novel, Kobylians'ka, however, used the dialogical potential of Sava's speech to pursue a different ideological goal from that in "Time." While in the 1895 story Kobylians'ka exploited the formal structures of the Hutsul's conversation with an educated lady to suggest the possibility of influencing "the raw peasant mind" in a positive way, in *The Earth* she applied the same technique to illustrate how easily the peasant mind could be manipulated and subjected to a self-destructive cause.

Rakhira is not the only character who uses Sava's "otherness" and defiant habits for personal gain. At the end of the novel, the whole village community uses the pretext of Sava's incongruity and perceived "evilness" to brand him as a murderer and to create a convenient explanation of Mykhailo's violent death. Guided by the darkness of their hearts and by corrupted materialist beliefs that accept lust for land as a valid motive for a crime, first Sava's parents and later the rest of their village blame the young lad for the murder. The accusation only aggravates the communal tragedy and subjects the only rebellious character to spiritual paralysis and social disdain. Although there is no factual proof of Sava's guilt,[18] Ivonika openly states at Mykhailo's funeral that "he, unlike judges, has no need for proofs" to know who is to blame for Mykhailo's death because "his own heart named the murderer" (II:231). His wife, Mariika, also arrives at the same conclusion and "intuitively feels that her son is a murderer, a fratricide" (II:230). As the unfinished second part of the novel suggests, the parental verdict proves to be more powerful and more detrimental than the official resolution of the local court, and the only nonconformist and self-asserting hero eventually turns into a social outcast and spiritual cripple. Sava's dramatic failure to master his own passions and to assert his will demonstrates how easily the celebrated rebellious spirit of the natural people, the Ukrainian villagers, alongside their innate thirst for freedom, could be undermined by the inhibiting horizons of their immediate environment. Sava's story is, perhaps, Kobylians'ka's most powerful assertion of her sharp anti-populist critique of the circumscribed cultural, social, and political agency of the Ukrainian peasantry.

In the final analysis, the downfall of the Fedorchuk family could be traced to the main common cause of all tragic events in the novel: not the private property or the inherent vice and impiety but the peasants' doomed world views and culture. Kobylians'ka's critique of the uneducated peasant mind, which, as she saw it, was unfit for Ukraine's future, its cultural and political development, is a logical continuation of her earlier celebration of intellectualism and high culture. The connection between Kobylians'ka's earlier elitism and her demythologization of the Ukrainian village is particularly evident in the optimistic ending of *The Earth*. After taking its characters and, by extension, its readers through a series of sordid confessions that expose the complex but crude world view of the Ukrainian villagers, *The Earth* elaborates in its closing chapter on Anna's hopes for the future of her son. The heroine makes it clear that she wants to "tear [her son] away from the land" (vidirvaty vid zemli) and to "turn him into a real human being" by giving him an education because, as the authoritative voice in the closing sentence of the novel highlights, only as an educated person of culture can a peasant productively employ his inherent "heroic nature and deep prophetic instincts" to contribute to Ukraine's cultural, social, and political struggle (II:297–8). As opposed to Ukrainian populists, who celebrated the inborn virtues of the peasant mind, and to Zola, who believed in the natural regeneration of a peasant mentality, Kobylians'ka argued that pure nature could stimulate neither cultural nor social nor political progress. Instead, she called public attention to an urgent need for a fair re-evaluation of the current social and political aptitude of the Ukrainian peasantry and those doctrines that viewed the common man as a repository of culture and primary maker of history. By suggesting the possibility of a rigorous transformation of peasant consciousness, *The Earth* thus rearticulates Kobylians'ka's earlier call to develop high culture.

Conclusion

As a close look at Kobylians'ka's representation of peasants and its evolution throughout the 1890s demonstrates, the writer in no way degraded "the people" but portrayed them exactly as she saw them: genuine in their world view but uneducated and thus limited by their customs and beliefs. By revisiting the best examples of nineteenth-century realist fiction and by bridging it with other popular aesthetic and philosophical frameworks of her time, such as psychologism, irrationalism, and mysticism, Kobylians'ka succeeded in crafting a new artistic model that challenged the underlying doctrinairianism of the Ukrainian fin-de-siècle populist ideology. Instead of focusing on the material conditions and ethnographic peculiarities of everyday village life, which was a common practice in the nineteenth-century Ukrainian realist tradition, and which several patronizing populist critics requested of her, she analysed the emotional and cognitive lives of her peasant characters. By placing dialogue at the centre of her works, by individualizing her characters' speech, and by exploiting its dialogical potential, she externalized and extended the inner personal dimension of her peasant characters, which articulated their "raw mind" with unprecedented directness. As early as in "Nature," "Time," and "Uncultured," Kobylians'ka outlined the peasant mind as chaotic, self-destructive, and thus unfit for any social or political struggle. Her 1902 novel *The Earth* only solidified this view by using formal markers to project the structure of the bewildered peasant mind not only on an allegorical plane but also in a formal and direct manner. Therefore, Kobylians'ka was the first Ukrainian writer who deftly demonstrated that the noble nature of the common Ukrainian man and the romantic purity of interpersonal relations and family harmony in the Ukrainian village celebrated by the populists was a utopian myth that could not serve as a beacon of Ukraine's cultural and political regeneration.

Chapter Four

Hidden Modernism

The publication of Ol'ha Kobylians'ka's third novel, *The Earth*, became an important cultural event in Ukrainian literary circles. It not only stimulated a discussion of Kobylians'ka's significance in contemporary Ukrainian literature but also intensified the ongoing debate about the role of literature in the nation-building process. While Ukrainian intellectuals of the pro-Western camp enthusiastically welcomed Kobylians'ka's new work, some Ukrainian populists criticized her rejection of the dominant populist fictional model. Serhii Iefremov was among the first to sense the subversive, anti-populist rhetoric in *The Earth*. As mentioned in the previous chapter, in his article "In Search of a New Beauty," he attacked Kobylians'ka's stylistic innovations, accusing her of aestheticism, mysticism, intellectualism, decadence, and excessive Nietzscheanism – all of which he saw as incompatible with a populist program and thus unfit, and even "sinful," for a Ukrainian milieu. As he put it, Kobylians'ka's literary style was "a harmful and antisocial literary trend prone to corrupting immature minds" (1993, 120). Iefremov's review was clearly not a critical study of Kobylians'ka's novel and its ideological messages but a part of his broader, ongoing polemic with modernism and its cult of individualism, in which he saw a threat to the cohesion of the Ukrainian national movement.

Kobylians'ka and her supporters were aware of the underlying argument in Iefremov's article but nevertheless were compelled to refute his accusations. Within a few weeks of the publication of Iefremov's article, many prominent Ukrainian intellectuals – Ivan Franko, Lesia Ukrainka, Hnat Khotkevych, Mykhailo Kotsiubyns'kyi, and Vasyl' Stefanyk, to name a few – wrote open letters to *Kievskaia starina* (*Kyivan Past*), the literary monthly that published Iefremov's article, and other popular journals to rebut Iefremov's interpretation of Kobylians'ka and her contributions to Ukrainian literature. Many also wrote directly to Kobylians'ka to express their admiration and support. Mykhailo Kosach, Lesia Ukrainka's older brother, who was also a writer and social activist of a pro-Western socialist orientation, was among the first to assure Kobylians'ka that she was not alone in her struggle with the provincial mentality of the mainstream Eastern Ukrainian intellectuals. He condemned Iefremov's attack as "an unjust assault" (nespravedlyva napast'), "filth" (merzota), a "lie" (brekhnia), and "piggery" (svynstvo), and urged Kobylians'ka not to take it seriously with peculiar eloquence: "I must say, it is difficult to take offence at a pig because it snorts and does not sing. All you have to do is ... to show it the way from the company of good people back to its pen" (1963, 88–9). Hnat Khotkevych, a prominent Ukrainian writer whom Iefremov also criticized in his belligerent article, made similar statements first in a personal letter to Kobylians'ka and later in his article "Klika pry chasopysi 'Kievskaia starina' i ii vidnoshennia do Ol'hy Kobylians'koi" ("A Clique at *Kyivan Past* and Its Treatment of O. Kobylians'ka," December 1902):

> As long as [Iefremov's] "Notes to the Reader" treated Symbolists as a general phenomenon, I could only wonder how it was possible that something so ignorant could be published in a periodical. When Sier'ozha Iefremov unleashed all his scorn on me and yakked about my "misanthropy," I could handle it just fine. But when this mister went so far as to "criticize," in the provincial sense of this word, as esteemed an artist as Kobylians'ka, it was too much ... What kind of approach is that? What sort of citation aims at the mockery of the *Moscow Herald* readers? What kind of tone is that? In principal, what right does some Sier'ozha have to treat the works of a writer, who is well respected far beyond Ukraine, with such brutal insolence? [His "criticism"] is a pure mockery. It is a ludicrous survey of the worst expressions and mistakes ... You can call it anything but a critical review. Hiding behind the backs of some hard-hearted "patriots," this mister dares to use the patronizing tone of a teacher, or even a mentor, with a prominent writer. His article is brimming with pedagogical idioms, such as "let us see if she accomplished her objective," "she completed her task satisfactorily" (that is, earning a C or a C+), "to approach her work with a yardstick," or even better, "to plunge into the depth of her talent ..." What is this? No one has ever used this kind of rhetoric with the worst enemies of Ukraine, let alone its best people. (1963a, 91)

Despite its somewhat melodramatic tone, Khotkevych's passage captures well the widespread indignation that Iefremov's derisive criticism spawned among Kobylians'ka's supporters.

Lesia Ukrainka's open letter to *Kyivan Past* was one of the most compelling responses to Iefremov in defence of Kobylians'ka. Unfortunately, it was never published and eventually lost, though Ukrainka recorded in her private correspondence that it was well circulated and widely discussed among Ukrainian intellectuals in January and February 1903. In a letter written to Kobylians'ka on 27 February 1903, Ukrainka claimed that her critique forced Iefremov to seek indirect reconciliation with Kobylians'ka. She mentioned that Iefremov sent her three apologetic letters in which he assured her that he had no intention to disavow Kobylians'ka as a writer, or to question her significance in Ukrainian literature, but wanted only to share his concerns about Kobylians'ka's literary style and its possible ramifications as to the ideological tasks of contemporary Ukrainian literature. Despite the overall triumphant tone, Ukrainka ended her letter with an alarming remark, where she admitted that Iefremov's article was only the beginning of Kobylians'ka's confrontation with the populist camp in Eastern Ukraine and called on Kobylians'ka "not to give up the fight, and not to renounce her neo-Romantic course" (qtd. in Kosach-Kryvyniuk 1970, 671).

Ukrainka's hidden fears about Kobylians'ka's reaction to critical attacks from the populist camp turned out to be well founded. Although Kobylians'ka claimed that she had read Iefremov's article "very calmly" and with a clear understanding that his review was not, in any case, "an objective critique" (V:520), her letters to Makovei over the winter of 1902–3 testify to a profound distress, if not despair. As Kobylians'ka suggested in one of those letters, Iefremov made her question both the artistic merits of her works and their relevance to the Ukrainian national cause. She was especially concerned about Iefremov's accusations of anti-patriotic activities, and she immediately set out to prove to Makovei and, by extension, the broader Ukrainian audience that she was "not a complete deviant after all" (V:524). In her 1903 autobiography, she began her quest to assert herself as a writer committed to the Ukrainian national movement with a public dismissal of her early modernist style as an immature delusion and an outline of her new aesthetic and ideological goals firmly embedded in populist discourse. Her next step was a thorough revision of her literary style. In the ensuing decade, Kobylians'ka made every effort, at least rhetorically, to separate herself from Nietzscheanism, naturalism, decadence, and symbolism, which some critics read as an act of her concession to populism. Kobylians'ka's writings of the 1903–13 period, however, show that her anti-populist views, particularly her belief in the power of an educated elite to generate political change and lead Ukraine's nation-building effort, grew even stronger despite her growing concerns about the rapid disintegration of Ukrainian political forces in the 1910s. A close look at Kobylians'ka's 1905 short story "Dumy staryka" ("The Thoughts of an Old Man") and her three major novels of this period – *Nioba* (*Niobe*, 1905), *Cherez kladku* (*Over the Bridge*, 1912), and *Za sytuatsiiamy* (*After Situations*, 1913) – proves that Kobylians'ka altered her literary style not to conform to the old platitudes of populist realism but to embed her elitist vision of Ukraine's national liberation in the long-familiar, comprehensible literary forms that would be more accessible to the broader readership and thus would appease populist critics. As will be demonstrated in this chapter, this stylistic revision did not mean stooping to the level of lowbrow boulevard literature, but it did mean engaging with the public's taste. A number of telling conceptual affinities between Kobylians'ka's 1903–13 vision of Ukraine's political future and other elitist ideologies of the time – Marxism and proto-fascism are the most telling examples here – along with some new forms of expression that Kobylians'ka developed during this period further prove that the desire to modernize Ukrainian culture and use her art as a platform for disseminating her social and political views remained firm in Kobylians'ka's pre–First World War rethinking and reframing of her art.[1]

1903 Autobiography: A Life Record or a Strategic Projection?

The first autobiography Kobylians'ka wrote was contained in an 1898 letter to František Řehoř, a Czech ethnographer who popularized her works among Czech readers in the late 1890s. In this account, Kobylians'ka listed her latest publications, briefly commented on her education, and discussed her literary interests, sharply distinguishing herself from Zolaists (*zolisty*) and other representatives of the so-called crude realism (V:317). Kobylians'ka wrapped up her letter to Řehoř by suggesting that he should contact Osyp Makovei for further information and critical reviews of her work. Her second autobiography, which she wrote in 1903, is significantly longer and more nuanced. Its opening paragraph outlines its structure with distinctive precision:

> It is always hard for a writer to tell his audience about himself. First and foremost, he wonders what would his audience want to know, and what would be an interesting story to tell. Generally, the writer starts with a description of his birth, his parents, his education, the beginning of his

> literary career, and his literary influences. At the end, he generally provides statements on his aesthetic preferences and on the innovative aspects of his works. (V:213)

While enumerating the generic themes of a typical autobiography, this passage introduces two important points that Kobylians'ka omitted from her 1898 autobiography, namely, the aesthetic movement that defined her work and what she perceived as her major contribution to the Ukrainian intellectual discussions of her time. Curiously, both issues directly address the two central lines of Iefremov's criticism in the *Kyivan Past*. Several other factual inconsistencies between the first and second autobiographies, alongside a dramatic change in style, rhetoric, and ideological framework, suggest that Kobylians'ka wrote her second autobiography to refute Iefremov's unflattering labels and to project an alternative self-image, which underpins the writer's profound concern with her literary reputation and public status in 1903.

The most obvious difference between the two autobiographies lies in the amount of biographical data that Kobylians'ka presented in each text. While in 1898 Kobylians'ka barely offered any facts about the early stages of her life, she dwelled at length in her 1903 autobiography on her limited access to knowledge. She claimed in the latter text that when she first started experimenting with literature, she was only "an unconscious, immature, and wild romantic" who had a limited understanding of "what the word literature really meant," and used to write "without any external initiative, any proper intellectual community, or artistic guidance, which could have nurtured her young soul" (V:214). She explained her lack of formal education, or what she metaphorically called "an array of colours without any system or order" (V:215), as the main reason for the limited populist ideological content in her early writings. Although Kobylians'ka's account of her early life might present the true story, it does not quite fit the time frame she suggests in the 1903 autobiography. By describing her short story "Pid holym nebom" ("Under an Open Sky," 1898) as one of her early works (V:216), the writer implied that some of her best pieces of the early period – *The Princess*, "Nature," "The Battle," "Uncultured," and "Valse mélancolique"[2] – were also immature and insignificant in terms of aesthetic, philosophical, or ideological content. If we consider the well-known record of Kobylians'ka's meticulous studies of European and Russian philosophers in the 1890s and the rich scholarship on the aesthetic complexity of her 1890s works, it might be fair to suggest that in the 1903 piece, the writer deliberately misrepresented her biographical facts, constructing yet another mythical narrative that proved instrumental in her canonization as a populist writer and in the eventual survival of her literary heritage during the Soviet period.

Kobylians'ka's manipulation of facts becomes even more evident when we compare the lists of selected publications that she chose to discuss in each of the two early autobiographies. In the 1898 version, Kobylians'ka commented in length on her 1896 novel *The Princess* and on her most representative short stories of the period, which she claimed as her favourites, if not her best works. In 1903, Kobylians'ka, surprisingly, mentioned neither *The Princess* nor "Valse mélancolique," the most innovative of her stories, which some scholars list among the founding works of Ukrainian modernism. Instead, she elaborated on "Uncultured" and *The Earth*, emphasizing their peasant subject matter, and thus promoting them as populist texts. While talking about her future works, Kobylians'ka also prioritized themes related to the populist canon. Her commentary on Petko Todorov, a Bulgarian writer known for his treatment of folk themes in literature, is particularly telling:

> Recently, I became very interested in Petko Y. Todorov, a Bulgarian writer. His novels, or better their themes, drew my attention to folk legends and fairytales ... His new, thoroughly original, and extremely valuable views on literature and art influenced me so strongly that I want to abandon my previous modernist course, and follow instead his path, which seems to me the only artistic possibility for capturing the true essence of the folk art, poetry, and character. (V:217)

Kobylians'ka's projection of folklore and the people as the primary object of her future artistic contemplation, alongside her denunciation of modernist aesthetics as unfit to transmit the complexity of the true character of the people, speaks loudly of what might seem to be her public conformity to a populist aesthetics. Her attempt to rebrand her original interest in modernism as an immature delusion, and to shift public attention to her works that fit better into the populist canon, also suggests that at this stage in her literary career she wanted to be seen not as a modernizer of Ukrainian literature but rather as a national writer, a writer of the people, with whom she openly identified at the end of the 1903 autobiography: "[My fiction] reflects the eternal sorrow of an oppressed people, the sorrow, which has passed into our blood and cannot emancipate itself from pain. Perhaps, some might see it as a defect, but it characterizes me in the same way as it characterizes my people" (V:217). The fact that Kobylians'ka was eventually canonized as a committed defender of the Ukrainian common man and a devoted student of the culture of the Ukrainian peasantry shows that her attempt to appease populist critics was successful. Her first post-Iefremov fictional work, "The Thoughts of an Old Man," however, proves that the degree of her devotion to the peasant culture, as well as the degree to which she abandoned modernist aesthetics in her post-1902 fiction, was minimal.

"The Thoughts of an Old Man"

Kobylians'ka finished her 1903 short story "The Thoughts of an Old Man" within three months of promising Makovei to prove with her next written work that she deserved to be called a devoted Ukrainian patriot. Curiously, she wrote it while working on her second autobiography, where she openly conformed to populist aesthetics. Naturally, we might expect "The Thoughts of an Old Man" to be as pompous and compliant as her letter to Makovei or her 1903 autobiography, but a close reading of the story presents a much more complex dynamic, indicating that Kobylians'ka's public conformity to populist rhetoric was less a sincere conversion than a strategic move.

Past critics have pointed out that "The Thoughts of an Old Man" is written in the form of a testament with clear intertextual references to the Bible and Taras Shevchenko's canonical poem "Iak umru, to pokhovaite" ("When I Die, Bury Me," 1845), which is commonly known as "Zapovit" ("A Testament") (Tomashuk 1969a, 130; Krupa 2004; Pavlyshyn 2008, 207–10). Indeed, Kobylians'ka adapted many compositional and stylistic features from 1 Corinthians and even quoted its section on Christian love (1 Cor. 13:4–13).[3] The plot of the story resembles, in turn, that of Shevchenko's poem, where a dying old man shares his age-old wisdom with his family and, by extension, with his people. The story's patriotic rhetoric that equates family with nation and places historical memory and preservation of traditions among the primary preconditions of national progress also resonates with that of Shevchenko's poem.[4] The old man's ultimate advice to his children captures the story's patriotic massage best: "Do not lose from your sight the golden thread that links you to your ancestors, and, in that way, to your people ... because otherwise the history of your future might also disappear (III:384, 385, 387). It is hardly a surprise, then, that Kobylians'ka's intertextual allusions to canonical texts, alongside her religious and patriotic pathos, convinced her contemporaries and one recent scholar that the ideological message in "The Thoughts of an Old Man" is as much in sync with mainstream populist narratives as its compositional organization.[5]

In his recent analysis of Nietzschean themes in "The Thoughts of an Old Man," Pavlyshyn, however, problematizes pro-populist interpretations of Kobylians'ka's story. Although the critic spends little time on the ideological aspects, he points out that Kobylians'ka not only alludes to, but also quotes from, Nietzsche's *Thus Spoke Zarathustra* in "The Thoughts of an Old Man," while elaborating on marriage and its sociocultural significance in the Ukrainian society of her time. The two stories that the old man tells about his two children, Pavlyshyn argues, resemble the two different marriage scenarios that Nietzsche outlined in *Thus Spoke Zarathustra*. Pavlyshyn detects the first type – a union of a worthy man with a "beast" that inevitably leads to the moral and spiritual degradation of the worthy man – in the sad story of the old man's son. Indeed, in the beginning of the story the reader learns that the young fellow used to be a talented musician and had prospects of becoming a "reformer of [Ukrainian] folk music" and of "making other nations recognize the richness of [Ukrainian] melodies," but he ruined his life by marrying a beautiful woman of little intelligence, whom the old man scornfully likens to an apocalyptic beast with "seven heads, seven mouths, and seven eyes" (III:381). The harmonious marriage of the old man's daughter, Pavlyshyn points out, represents, on the other hand, the so-called Nietzschean ideal, a marriage of two self-conquerors of equal intellectual and moral might who are capable of creating remarkable children.[6] Pavlyshyn argues that Kobylians'ka projected this type of marriage as a desirable scenario for her personal relationship with Makovei, which did not come true because Makovei rejected Kobylians'ka's proposal of intimacy.[7] Although Pavlyshyn's reading of the marriage of the old man's daughter's as ideal is problematized by the story's criticism of its antisocial nature, it demonstrates that Kobylians'ka continued to draw her creative ideas from Nietzsche's works, thus advancing and not rebuking her earlier fictional models.

Kobylians'ka's criticism of Nietzsche's ideal marriage and its antisocial nature, suggested in the marriage of the old man's daughter, links "The Thoughts of an Old Man" to the writer's earlier philosophical and literary models even more. As the second half of the short story highlights, despite the harmony and intellectual vigour that reign in the family of his daughter, the old man is deeply concerned with her and her children's excessive preoccupation with themselves. The old man's concern is rooted in his conviction that the true happiness of an individual is defined not only by "the laws of nature" and "the laws of human soul" but also by "the laws of society" (III:384). Accordingly, the old man declares, self-perfection should not be a goal in itself but only a step forward towards a more far-reaching goal – the pursuit of a broader communal, or even better, national ideal. The old man's message is embedded in his reference to the Great Commandment of loving one's neighbour. "Children," he forewarns his offspring and the reader at the end of the story, "You are so preoccupied with yourselves that you have forgotten the words of God: 'Love your neighbour as you love yourself.' You love your neighbours only through your own personality. But your personality obscures the wider horizon that Jesus opened with his love ... [and that's why] your future ... as I see it, is covered in mist" (III:385). As this passage suggests, the story treats individual self-perfection as a transitional stage and emphasizes broader social and political goals of community building. Notably, the implied philosophical fusion of Nietzsche's individualism with a distinct social program reiterates Kobylians'ka's earlier propagation of a Ukrainian intellectual elite as the main driving force of Ukrainian national regeneration and underscores the story's continuation of, rather than deviation from, the philosophical and ideological framework that Kobylians'ka developed in her works of the 1890s. The critical tension between the conventional composition and concealed elitist ideology in "The Thoughts of an Old Man" indicates that Kobylians'ka responded to populist demands by somewhat simplifying the aesthetic composition of her work only to repackage her elitist views into a more acceptable literary form.

All Kobylians'ka's major post-1903 novels exhibit similar tendencies. Not only do they maintain anti-populist ideological agendas, particularly a celebration of individualism and an elitist vision of Ukraine's nation-building effort, but they also gradually nuance it under the pressure of the ever-changing social and political climate in Europe in the first decades of the twentieth century.

Niobe

Kobylians'ka began writing her first post-Iefremov novel, *Niobe*, over the summer of 1904 in Bad Nauheim, a world-famous resort town in Germany where she spent a few months recovering from a temporary paralysis that she had suffered in October 1903. She completed the novel in Chernivtsi in October 1904 and published it in 1905 in issues 89 and 90 of *Kyivan Past*, the same monthly periodical that published Iefremov's critical article, "In Search of a New Beauty," in 1902. According to one biographer, *Niobe*, alongside some personal statements that Kobylians'ka made in her letters to friends and family over the summer and fall of 1904, shows that her trip to Germany not only improved her health but also boosted her creativity and confidence in her work (Vozniuk 2006, 110–11). Although Kobylians'ka's contemporaries mostly treated *Niobe* as a literary text of little artistic or ideological significance, and, as a result, Soviet and post-Soviet critics discussed it only cursorily, the novel testifies to a distinctive development in Kobylians'ka's view on questions of Ukraine's national liberation that merits consideration. While shifting her critical attention back to the intelligentsia, Kobylians'ka, however, did not simply revive an ideal type of Ukrainian intellectual from her earlier works. Rather, she focused on the mainstream Ukrainian intelligentsia, whose image she painted with the same grievous colours she had used for the peasant characters in *The Earth*, presenting Ukrainian middle-class society at its hypocritical worst.

Niobe has a simple plot but an intricate compositional structure. As in many of her earlier works, Kobylians'ka avoided complex scenarios and positioned dialogue as the main action in the novel. One Soviet scholar argued that the novel's unconventional and rather loose narrative structure, with no real resolution, alongside its polemical nature and the highly politicized subject matter of all its dialogues, positions *Niobe* as "a novel of ideas." Consequently, the Soviet scholar treated dialogue in *Niobe* as purely a dramatic form, a mere exposition, and a pedagogical device that Kobylians'ka used to confront and reduce different opinions to a single ideological common denominator (Tomashuk 1969a, 130). Placing a strong emphasis on dialectics, Soviet critics, however, overlooked the innovative qualities of Kobylians'ka's dialogue, which, as observed earlier, she notoriously employed to bring out the inner irrational man of her heroes, and to capture the multiple and varied voices of public discussions. Arguably, all dialogues in *Niobe* deal with the intense emotional and cognitive life of the main characters, which suggests that Kobylians'ka used dialogue not to orchestrate tendentious discussions, but rather to highlight the irrevocable multiplicity and dialogic nature of voices that permeated cultural, social, and political discussions in the Ukrainian middle-class circles of her time. The novel, of course, is not lacking in either social or political commentaries, but they appear only through the complex, symbolic implications of the main characters and their interactions.

Niobe has two parts, each depicting a conversation between Anna Iakhnovych, a seventy-year-old widow of a deceased Eastern Catholic priest and a mother of twelve, and her two oldest surviving children, Ostap and Zonia. The first part has fourteen chapters, where Anna and Ostap lead a conventional, face-to-face dialogue by taking turns to relate their personal stories and narrate the life dramas of other members of their family. The second part, during which Anna and her blind grandson engage in an original trio with Zonia's confessional diary, could be seen as a one-act play. Although all monologues, soliloquies, and dialogues in *Niobe* are dialogic in nature, they dwell predominantly on the interiority and individuality of the characters, simultaneously bringing out their corrupted outlooks on life and highlighting their alienation from one another. Notably, while focusing on the inner lives of her characters, Kobylians'ka minimized the use of dreams and descriptions of nature, which she often used in her earlier works to enhance the psychological portraits of her earlier character, and which Iefremov strongly criticized for their symbolism and mysticism and stylistic non-Ukrainianess (1993, 74, 83, 92–3, 96–7, and 101). There is only one dream sequence and one description of a murky autumn night in *Niobe* that help to bring out Anna's superstitious beliefs and to intensify the dramatic setting of her struggle with her drunken son, Andriusha. We can surely read this stylistic adjustment as a precaution similar to one that Kobylians'ka took in "The Thoughts of an Old Man" to reduce the chance of populist attacks on her modernist aesthetics.

Although Kobylians'ka significantly simplified the plot structure of her 1905 novel, she used an elaborate network of intertextual references to frame it. As the title implies, Kobylians'ka equated the story of Anna Iakhnovych and her children, who end up either dead or spiritually crippled, with the fate of the classical heroine Niobe and her fourteen unfortunate children, first recorded in Homer's *Iliad*. Kobylians'ka's allusion to the classic story, particularly the parallel in Anna's and Niobe's grieving for their lost children, is obvious. Less transparent but in no way less significant is *Niobe*'s link to the foundational work of modern Ukrainian literature, Ivan Kotliarevs'kyi's *Eneida* (*Eneida*, 1798), a travesty of Virgil's *Aeneid*, in which Kotliarevs'kyi transformed the Trojan heroes into Ukrainian Cossacks. On the one hand, we can interpret Kobylians'ka's indirect allusion to Kotliarevs'kyi as another protective measure similar to the Shevchenko reference in "The Thoughts of an Old Man," which Kobylians'ka used to minimize populists' attacks on her tributes to modern European literature. But on the other hand, it suggests a genre reference to *Eneida*'s parodic nature. In *Niobe*, elements of parody permeate the caricatured transformation of the arrogant and narrow-minded ancient heroine into a Ukrainian, upper-middle-class matron.

The conceptual parallel between Kobylians'ka's and Kotliarevs'kyi's texts merits particular attention because its symbolic implications help us to gauge Kobylians'ka's criticism of the mainstream Ukrainian populist intelligentsia and its inability to form values and aesthetic morals through which Ukrainian people could articulate their social, cultural, and political unity. Kobylians'ka's indirect allusions to Nataliia Kobryns'ka's 1884 story "The Spirit of the Time" and its tragicomic protagonist Mrs Shums'ka underscores similar parodic connotations. Like Kobryns'ka's heroine, Anna Iakhnovych dearly loves her children but is too rigid to understand the "new-age views" of her offspring (III:61). Like Mrs Shums'ka, Anna knows "only one church, one path, one goal." She knows "only 'this way' or 'no way'" (III:10) and often neglects or intentionally suppresses the individual aspirations of her children. Consequently, as her son Ostap sadly observes, Anna creates only "spiritual cripples" and "beasts" out of her naturally "beautiful, smart, and intelligent" children (III:63). In this respect, we can also compare Anna's failure as a parent to Ivonika Fedorchuk's inability to prepare his two sons for independent life in *The Earth*. This dynamic network of intertextual references thus projects ignorant parenting and dogmatic reinforcement of traditional, hypocritical conventionalities, alongside their detrimental consequences for children and, by extension, the future of the whole community, as the main themes in the first part of *Niobe*.

While addressing issues of parenting and motherhood, Kobylians'ka refrained from tendentious authorial claims and allowed her characters, Anna and Ostap, to voice the major issues in question. In their exchanges, Anna and Ostap evoke many of Kobylians'ka's earlier theories on the role of women in public spaces and re-project conscientious motherhood as one of the most significant social functions women could perform in any society. Ostap also introduces a new argument that calls attention to the glaring lack of accomplished women in Ukrainian politics and culture, and elaborates on the new challenges, objectives, and duties that Ukrainian women face in modern times:

> [Women] have responsibilities not only to themselves and their families, but also to their nations. Look at the women from other nations. Do you remember what their social status used to be? Look where they are now. For example, have a look at their contributions to art, science, literature, and all other fields, which men used to dominate, so to say, in the past. Or would you rather see our strong and capable women, I would even say extremely capable women, always following one path? Our time and our circumstances also require that we nurture different types of women. In addition to good housewives and good mothers, to whom I give primacy everywhere and at all times, we also need intelligent workers in society. We need women artists and other outstanding women, so to say. The development of our culture and progress itself demand it. (III:62)

Ostap's far-reaching insight strongly resonates with Kobylians'ka's rhetoric in her 1903 correspondence with Makovei, where she defended her own status as a public figure. Within the novel, Ostap's reflection, however, remains only a desirable ideal that none of the female characters are able to achieve. Although Anna's daughters Maria, Lidia, and Olena are naturally strong and extremely capable, Anna and her husband shelter them from high culture and social and political debates, raising them instead to be "good housewives" (III:62). Only Zonia, who is brought up differently by her childless aunt and uncle, strives for and approximates to Ostap's projected ideal but finds herself unable to assert her voice in her oppressive, patriarchal social environment.

Kobylians'ka opened her parodic portrayal of Anna's flawed parenting in the first chapter, where the heroine frames Christianity as the main source of her moral virtues. In the epigraph to *Niobe*, Kobylians'ka quotes from 1 Corinthians 13, placing a great deal of merit on Christian love. However, from the novel's third paragraph onward, it becomes increasingly evident that Anna's understanding of Christianity is corrupted, and that her love for children does not correlate to the Christian ideal presented in Paul's first epistle to the Corinthians. While conveying Anna's anxiety about her move to a big city, the story underscores her hostility towards the non-Eastern Catholic Christian congregations through her commentary on the city's cultural and religious diversity:

> [After the move,] Anna was always irritated and in a bad mood. She tried to distinguish the tolling of the bell of her church in the mixture of tolling bells, but it was all in vain. Alongside the bell ringing that she recognized as "hers," she heard the bells of an Orthodox church, a Protestant church, and a Catholic church. She felt as if something uninvited was forcing itself on her, sucking from her soul the last drops of peace and comfort that she needed so badly. (III:9–10)

Shortly, the story links Anna's anxiety about different religious denominations to her proclivity for xenophobia and ethnocentrism, which she demonstrates fully when she protests Ostap's and Zonia's decisions to marry non-Ukrainians. Both cases reinforce Anna's distorted understanding of Christianity and illuminate her inability to love and respect not only her neighbours but also her own children.

The destructive influence of Anna's religious fanaticism on her children and its far-reaching symbolic implications become especially evident in the second chapter of the novel when Ostap announces his decision to marry a Jewish woman, "a Jewess" (zhydivku), as Anna calls her, whom she "could never love or even respect as her daughter-in-law" (III:10). As in the previous example, there are no direct authorial claims. In his response to Anna's objection and minutes before leaving his parental house for good, Ostap makes all the logical connections himself, decrying the moral hypocrisy of his parents:

> I am leaving ... but before I do so, I give back all your "religious" upbringing and spiritual virtues, with which you prepared me for life. Your hearts are filled with fanaticism, primitive feelings, and parental egoism. You do not care either about truth or about the human qualities of the woman, who is going to share her life with me. All you care about is blind and age-old hatred, which has no place in my heart ... In this matter, I cannot have anything in common with you and do not need any wisdom from you anymore. I am a mature person, and I am well prepared for life ... As to my religious beliefs, I am an atheist and, like many people before me, I think that religion is a splendid illusion that was designed to control people – nothing more. (III:14)

It does not take much to pick up elements of Karl Marx's 1843 critique of religion in Ostap's comments on the utilitarian nature of religion, which indict the whole system of Anna's values, including her parenting principles, as flawed and inherently oppressive.[8] Later in the scene, Ostap eloquently ties his parents' hypocritical views to the pitiable state of the Ukrainian intelligentsia. When he incidentally learns that his younger brother does not go to school any longer only because he does not show enough progress to be able to enter a seminary later on – in other words, to utilize his cognitive abilities for material profit – he transposes Anna's utilitarian understanding of education to the national level. "As long as Ukrainians want only to preach [popyty]," Ostap declares, "they will have no power to do anything else but preaching. They should not complain then that their destiny is filled with mournful church music!" (III:15). This remark introduces the broader issue of the Ukrainian intelligentsia and its inability to lead the Ukrainian nation in its complex struggle for self-determination because, as the novel implies, they lack motivation, dedication, and proper training. Kobylians'ka revisited this theme anew in her inter-war novel *Apostol cherni* (*Apostle of the Rabble*, 1936), in which she first sent her main protagonist to get an education in the leading European universities, then placed her new leader-type character in a seminary, and then enlisted him in the military to prepare him fully for Ukraine's political struggles of the 1920s and 1930s.

Starting with Ostap's declaration, *Niobe* consistently underscores parallels between the Iakhnovych family and the Ukrainian people, projecting all its characters as symbolic, if not typical, representations of the mainstream Ukrainian intelligentsia of the time. We can surely read Anna's character as an embodiment of the Ukrainian conservative populist intelligentsia, and her children as representatives of a new generation of Ukrainian intelligentsia. Anna's oldest son, Ostap, the first to enter the story, is initially introduced as an intelligent and compassionate radical who shows promise for transcending the provincial morality of the Ukrainian conservative intelligentsia. His lack of will and consideration, however, promptly undermines his youthful idealism and resolute nature. As Ostap acknowledges, his decision to break with the traditional order is instigated not by rational convictions but by pure passion. Consequently, like some other rebellious but immature heroes in Kobylians'ka's earlier works – Sava in *The Earth* and the old man's son in "The Thoughts of an Old Man" – Ostap fails to negotiate between his instinctual and civic ambitions and becomes a victim of his own illusions and fanaticism. Despite his enthusiasm, love, and commitment, his marriage turns out to be a Nietzschean disaster because it was premature and ill-conceived. As a result, his life also turns out to be a failure. Ostap's blind son, who is "ill-conceived" outside of wedlock, is a quintessential representation of the hero's meagre personal achievements. Naturally, Anna explains Ostap's misfortunes as a logical consequence of his rebellion against tradition and parental will. Ostap, however, sees the root of his ruin elsewhere and claims that if only he and his siblings "were guided by stronger hands in their childhood" (III:37), and if only those hands "forged each of them individually, until the sparks showered from them, as from the hot iron" (III:63), "they could have had a chance to become human beings" (III:37). Ostap's vivid artisan metaphors reiterate Kobylians'ka's emphasis on early childhood education and its decisive role in the formation of exemplary individuals with strong social and political wills. Accordingly, Ostap's allegorical argument identifies parenting as an intricate and laborious process, which, as Ostap observes, Anna, together with many other Ukrainian parents, fails to recognize and, as a result, ends up annihilating the human being in her offspring.

While outwardly exposing the prosperous bourgeois establishment as merely a disguise for inward disintegration and moral decline, the life stories of Ostap's siblings who abide by the parental will offer an even stronger attack on bourgeois conventionalities of marriage, the family, religion, and the great hunger for respectability. Whereas Ostap is only "crippled" by his disappointment and despair at his brutal reality, most of his younger siblings mutate in their provincial setting into a type that the novel designates as "bestial" – that is, they lack the cultural and civic consciousness that Kobylians'ka associated with the notion of a human being in her earlier works. The story of the uneducated drunkard Andriusha is a telling case in point and is crucial to understanding the whole unravelling, parodic effect of *Niobe*. As a young lad, Andriusha ventures into the world armed only with a few dogmatic concepts of good and evil – "this way or no way" (III:10) – but learns quickly that everything he used to believe in is a sham when the girl he fancies rejects him because of his meagre social prospects. Unable to cope with humiliation, despair, and ever-growing frustration with human selfishness and lust for material gain, Andriusha takes to the bottle to alleviate his pain and escape the drabness of his everyday existence. The intensity of Andriusha's traumatic realization of personal impotency and social worthlessness is transmitted in his half-conscious drunken confession, which takes place on the night of his father's death. Tormented by the conflicted feelings of duty, guilt, and hatred, Andriusha bursts into a horrendous vocalization of his long-repressed feelings after Anna questions him about the funeral money that he spent in a tavern:

> "Be quiet, you old monster ... Why do you always have to torment my heart? It seems that only that that concerns you is important and nothing else! Be quiet, I tell you ... Otherwise ... God knows ... I'll kill you, as a ..." Andriusha ... covered his ears and went on yelling, "I didn't deliver anything, no money or anything else because I had to leave it all in a tavern. I gave Lidka only a few pieces of ragged underclothes, so she can dress up [father] for the coffin tomorrow because that is where he is heading now. Now you know what you wanted to know. If your curiosity, you old monster, is truly so great that you are willing to torment me, know this once and for all! Don't you think I cursed you when I was leaving the tavern empty-handed earlier today? You and that old cripple, who calls himself my father! I cursed you both for giving me life! May God forgive you because I cannot do it. I can't because I have nothing left in my heart; I have nothing but hellish pain. This is the life that I owe you. Oh, I cannot wait to see at last how you lay speechless and motionless on your deathbed! Only then I would be free to go to that basin and drink enough water to stay on its bottom till Judgment Day ... It would be the end to all of this. But because of you, I must sustain this dog's life. I must make sure that you don't have to go from door to door and beg for a crust of bread because all your other sophisticated children could care less about you. They prefer to care for themselves rather than for their elderly! Get away from me! Get away!" (III:52)

Andriusha's drunken speech conveys his psychological struggle, which pictures him as torn between the values of society and the values that stem from within his own nature: rootedness and commitment to family, on the one hand, and restlessness and egocentric self-affirmation, on the other. His bitter commentary about his siblings provides another telling insight into the complex internal dynamic of the Iakhnovych family, projected as a dysfunctional and self-negating unit. Both aspects of Andriusha's confession carry strong symbolic implications that allude to Kobylians'ka's critical view of the Ukrainian intelligentsia and its cultural, social, and political impotence, which becomes increasingly dark in the remainder of the novel. Particularly striking here is Kobylians'ka's allegorical criticism of the dominant populist positivism and its rejection of human volition and innate striving for freedom, justice, and progress. As implied in Andriusha's personal story and the stories of his siblings, fanatical celebration of materialism and traditional values often drives young and naturally talented people to ruin and self-destruction.

The second part of *Niobe* focuses on Anna's distant daughter Zonia, who grows up at the house of Anna's childless sister and her husband, also an Eastern Catholic priest. Apparently, Zonia's caregivers have a fundamentally different and much more far-reaching approach to raising children than Anna and her husband do. Although Zonia's step-parents value practical skills and the ability to run a household as much as Anna, they prioritize education and the cultivation of aesthetic taste while raising Zonia. As opposed to Zonia's biological parents, Zonia's uncle believes that "a woman without more subtle taste is like a harp without strings," and points out that aesthetic "taste is honed not only by science and knowledge, but also by art and beauty" (III:79). Accordingly, he teaches Zonia foreign languages and introduces her to Western European literature and art. He also cultivates Zonia's civic consciousness and emphasizes the special role the intelligentsia plays in the cultural, social, and political development of a nation. While analysing her uncle's social and political beliefs, Zonia calls him "a sincere lover of people" (shchyryi narodoliubets') whose views, however, differ fundamentally from those of the so-called populist *khlopomany* (peasant lovers) activists. As Zonia observes, her uncle equally criticizes those who dissociate themselves from the people completely and those who become so "intimate" with the people "that hugging and kissing are the only elements that are missing" in their intercourse (III:79). According to the uncle's logic, neither group contributes to the social and political development of the Ukrainian nation. Naturally, in sharp contrast to her siblings and the mainstream Ukrainian intelligentsia their characters represent, Zonia grows up to be an educated person with a refined aesthetic taste, and her strong sense of civic duty and patriotic commitment promise to have positive social ramifications.

Zonia's education and unconventional outlook on life bring her close to the other iconoclastic heroines in Kobylians'ka's early fiction, such as Olena Liaufler and Natalka Verkovychivna. In *Niobe*, Kobylians'ka, however, does not focus on the heroine's character transformation or on her triumph over conservative social norms, but rather dwells on Zonia's conflict with her narrow-minded surroundings, represented by her mother and her fiancé, Oleksa, who is studying to become an Eastern Catholic priest. Kobylians'ka used an unusual formal composition to dramatize the lack of understanding between the young heroine and her social environment. She structured the second part of the novel as a one-act play with some elements of a Greek tragedy, where Anna and Zonia function as main characters, and Anna's blind grandson operates as a chorus that observes the heroines' interactions and periodically comments on them. The exchange between Anna and Zonia, however, is orchestrated not as a traditional face-to-face dialogue but as a complex interplay of two dialogic soliloquies. In an original duo that Anna leads with Zonia's diary, which the younger heroine wrote purposefully for her mother, both women share their intimate feelings and private thoughts while addressing each other but can neither hear nor respond to each other because they are separated in time and space. While their displaced communication better facilitates self-expression, it denies both heroines the opportunity to achieve any understanding or compromise, which only highlights the glaring differences in their views.

Anna's response to Zonia's aesthetic aspirations and anti-populist views is particularly revealing of Kobylians'ka's emphasis on the contrast and collision, rather than on the synthesis, of the heroines' individual views. Zonia opens her diary with a statement on the innate crudeness and "lack of any aesthetic refinement" (neestetychnist') of the Ukrainian peasants, which make it impossible for her to relate to the populist projects of "going to the people" (III:80). She continues by juxtaposing her liberal cultural ideals with the mainstream preoccupation with the folk and their culture, and declares herself to be, in contrast, "a woman of high culture" who has yet to discover her social and political mission. It is hard not to recognize in this self-description Kobylians'ka's ideal type of an intellectual, a poet of a new humanism whose aesthetic teaching, as well as personal example, could bring about change in society.

Anna is less than enthusiastic about Zonia's longing for spirituality, beauty, and sophistication. She counters her daughter's rhetoric with a telling statement on the sociocultural potential of the Ukrainian peasantry. Her statement deserves to be quoted at length because it is one of the most majestic and artistic descriptions of "the people" in Kobylians'ka's oeuvre, which most likely is also the main reason why first the populist and later the Soviet critics received *Niobe* favourably:

> My dear child, I don't know how to answer you. I'm an ordinary woman and don't have much (well, any) education. The Holy Scripture is my only knowledge. If only your educated father were alive and you opened your heart to him, he would certainly tell you these words: "Go into the world, my beautiful and gentle child. Test your strength and your mind on others and find out who you really are. When you figure it out, you will understand what kind of person you ought to be. You awakened a longing for your own 'I,' in your heart, and it torments you. You might waste all the precious time of your youth on dreams and phantasmagoric questions, but beware! The best dreams and the deepest longing don't contribute even a hair to the development of the human spirit ..." You are honest and obedient, as a Christian woman ought to be, and it comforts me. May God keep you that way. I don't quite understand what you mean by the typical "style" of a Ukrainian woman, but as long as you keep to simplicity, that pure and unpretentious simplicity, and have a pure heart, your style will shine through on its own ... As to the people, honour them! Think! When you go into the forest, you cannot find there the same order as in a well-kept and carefully planned garden. But what you can find there instead is such power and richness, such unconscious poetry and unique beauty that no one can even dream of in a well-kept garden ... The same is with our people, my dear child! Our wild and uncultured people, our neglected and often despised people ... Honour the people! (II:81–2)

Anna's idealization of peasants is brimming with the same enthusiasm and fascination that permeate Kobylians'ka's early peasant stories of the mid-1890s. Since Zonia cannot respond to Anna's statement, it is fair to suggest that Kobylians'ka included Anna's soliloquy not only to generate a dialectical discussion between the two heroines but also to present the populist view in all its lyrical beauty and might, and thereby to emphasize the diversity of social and political discourses that circulated in Ukraine in the first years of the twentieth century.

Zonia's and Anna's exchange reveals a degree of criticism. It is targeted not as much at their particular views but at the nature of their interaction, which signals the rupture in the authentic mother-daughter relationship. A series of brief but passionate comments from Anna's blind grandson further intensify the dramatic irony of Anna's and Zonia's inability to communicate. In one of his remarks, the blind fifteen-year-old ironically points out that his soul, "the soul of the blind man," is not "as blind" to Zonia's suffering and emotional turmoil "as the souls of those who surround her" (III:346). Indeed, Anna's grandson is paradoxically the only person who, despite, or perhaps because of, his physical disability, understands the reasons that led to the disintegration of the Iakhnovych family and, by implication, of the Ukrainian intelligentsia.

Zonia's confrontation with her fiancé, Oleksa, further highlights the ideological tension that, as projected earlier in the novel, defined the cultural, social, and political situation in Ukraine of the time. The heroine conveys her personal drama by recording in her diary a sequence of face-to-face dialogues with her fiancé. Her introduction suggests that she initially idealized Oleksa as an exceptional individual and an exemplary representative of the Ukrainian nation. She particularly admired his commitment to the well-being of the common people and even likened him to a saint and apostle who has "advice and a lesson for everyone" and finds "a special word tuned to the individual needs and life circumstances of everyone who approaches him" (III:85). Surprisingly, although Zonia is herself a faithful patriot, she does not share Oleksa's enthusiasm about "going to the people." While sympathizing with the suffering of the masses, she is unable to "fraternize" (bratatysia) with peasants because she is deeply appalled by their crudeness. Gradually, it becomes evident that Zonia's understanding of patriotism and civic duty profoundly differs from that of Oleksa. She values the devotion of many Ukrainian intellectuals to the populist project of enlightening the masses and their self-sacrifice but believes that the cultivation of a Ukrainian elite and high culture is as important, if not more, to Ukraine's nation-building effort. Her views highlight the critical dichotomy between the two related but fundamentally different notions, "the people" and "a nation."[9] Oleksa, in turn, sees Zonia's elitism and her veneration of European culture as a threat to, if not a betrayal of, the Ukrainian national movement. Their contradictory views perpetually trigger debates, which bring to mind Kobylians'ka's own conflict with the populist camp, particularly her 1902 confrontation with Iefremov.

From early on, Oleksa criticizes what he sees as Zonia's social passivity and tries to convince her in a classical populist manner that the prime duty of every educated Ukrainian is to bring "the light and the culture" to the people (III:85–6). Zonia objects and claims that although she admires the eagerness of many young educated Ukrainians who want to make a difference in their society, she finds their enthusiasm premature, irrational, and insufficient for any critical change. The heroine shares her concern with the general tendency to "take everything to the loud marketplace and either praise or denounce it," and declares that sheer excitement and self-aggrandizement would give neither culture nor a better future for the Ukrainian people would neither enhance the culture of the Ukrainain people nor provide for them a better future. Instead, she highlights the need for critical thinking and a broader cultural context. She insists that the educated classes must first and foremost perfect their national culture, develop new aesthetic standards, and create a new system of values through which the Ukrainian people can define, sustain, and direct their nation-building effort. She sees high culture as a force that can serve a consolidating, regulatory, and indeed emancipatory function in society. That is why she castigates the ill-conceived and often fanatical actions of the mainstream Ukrainian populist intelligentsia and calls on them to follow the lead of highly developed European nations, such as Germany, and to take note of their emphasis on high culture and the ideal of an aesthetic state. The heroine's argument recalls Kobylians'ka's mid-1890s views on the role of aesthetic education in the formation of exemplary citizens and the role of high culture in the nation-building process. In the early 1900s, most Ukrainian modernists held similar views and argued that their politically fragmented nation required a strong tradition of high art (a coherent, normative culture) in order to forge a unified consciousness. This is also precisely the view that Iefremov strove to dispute in his 1902 article, fearing that the cultural elitism and excessive aestheticism of modernist writers could hinder the cohesiveness of the nation-building effort in Ukraine.

Zonia's conflict with Oleksa escalates when a German professor of art comes to spend a summer in their neighbourhood. The character of the German artist has no name and no personality. It is a collective image, which Zonia views as "an exemplary representative of his nation" but that Oleksa, together with Zonia's mother and aunt, vilifies as an "alien" (chuzhynets') who poses an imminent threat. The German professor becomes a catalyst in Zonia's critical reassessment of Oleksa's character and his rigid views, and instigates the heroine's breakup with her fiancé. From early on, Zonia recognizes in the German professor an ideal of a cultivated person whose refined beliefs and aesthetic taste create a striking contrast to Oleksa's excessive rationality and lack of aesthetic sophistication – his so-called "hoof of prose," as Zonia metaphorically designates her fiancé's materialistic views. Oleksa also admits the cultural superiority of the German artist, but, in contrast to Zonia, he develops a sincere hatred of his rival, which brings out his deep sense of self-doubt and inferiority complex – an astute commentary on the Ukrainian conservative populist intelligentsia.

Driven by jealousy and envy, Oleksa gradually moves from critical attacks on Zonia to a broad criticism of the general fascination with everything non-Ukrainian among the Ukrainian intelligentsia. Remarkably, Oleksa's rhetoric, as well as his logic, reiterates almost literally Iefremov's critique of the strong pro-Western orientation in Ukrainian modernist culture. This curious detail, alongside the fact that Iefremov himself was a seminary graduate and a devoted populist, gives us room to assume that Oleksa might be a parodic caricature of Iefremov, and his argument with Zonia might be a direct reference to Kobylians'ka's own conflict with the populist critic. The following excerpt from one of Oleksa's belligerent monologues provides a convincing piece of evidence:

> The foreign culture often influenced and blinded our souls so much that we couldn't see our own, even when it was much better and greater. We often renounced our most characteristic colours *for the sake of the foreign*, and, as if hypnotized, joined the rival's camp ... We often do it unconsciously only because we have a strong tendency to adapt to something different and because we have little courage, or rather we have little strength and persistence, to *proper cultural existence* as *a small nation* ... Yes ... *we have a strand of treason in us* ... How many of us have deserted and continue deserting to the rival's camp only because the *grand foreign* [culture] seemed to us greater and better than ours? *We* have this tendency ... But go! Go away all of you, false and "shaky"! Go away and leave us alone! It's not the *number* that constitutes the strengths and power, but only *the conscious will and intelligentsia*! (III:110–11)

Oleksa's xenophobic declaration evokes Kobylians'ka's concern about the populists' unjustified aggression against internal opposition, and particularly about the populists' proto-totalitarian campaign to purge Ukrainian culture from everything that does not fit into their understanding of Ukrainianness. The melodramatic tone of the speech, together with Oleksa's excessive bewilderment, has a strong parodic undertone. Kobylians'ka pushed her criticism even further by italicizing, and thus bringing to attention, several key phrases. The first emphasis is on "for the sake of the foreign," which questions the implied binary opposition between foreign and native, indirectly suggesting that alternative options – translation, adaptation, and mutual enrichment – are also possible in the intercultural exchange. The second visual highlight targets Oleksa's emphasis on the subjugated cultural, social, and political position of the Ukrainian people as "a small nation," which he urges his audience to accept as Ukraine's manifest destiny. This attitude fundamentally differs from Zonia's and indeed Kobylians'ka's ideal of the future flowering and world recognition of the Ukrainian nation, and thus accuses the mainstream populist Ukrainian intelligentsia, Iefremov in particular, of a narrow-minded political vision. The last visual emphasis is on "conscious political will and strong intelligentsia," which, paradoxically, the hero projects as the key preconditions for Ukraine's national regeneration. Oleksa's statement evokes the very premise of Kobylians'ka's elitist program of national liberation, but within the context of his speech, its far-reaching perspective is undermined because he – an indoctrinated, bigoted, and hot-headed character – parades himself as an ideal intellectual leader. This semantic oxymoron calls attention to the apparent contradiction between the grand ideal and the ill-conceived practical implementation of the populist emancipatory program. More importantly, it demonstrates that Kobylians'ka once again used a complex network of formal and symbolic markers to expose the intrinsically ruinous egocentric and ethnocentric understanding of patriotism, which at the time defined the general view of her populist critics, and to question their self-proclaimed authority on Ukraine's nation-building effort.

Niobe thus is far more complex than past critics have admitted: although it is not quite a "novel of ideas," it embeds a shrewd ideological message in a subtle psychological study of the mainstream Ukrainian intelligentsia. Through dialogue, the novel creates gripping psychological portraits that expose the confused world views of the Ukrainian populist intelligentsia, particularly their materialism, utilitarian understanding of culture, premature political enthusiasm, and pronounced tendencies towards xenophobia and ethnocentrism. Open criticism of the populist heterophobia was a new development in Kobylians'ka's anti-populist rhetoric and can be seen as a reaction to Iefremov's 1902 attacks on pro-Western motives in her earlier works and in the emerging Ukrainian modernist culture in general. In addition to the direct criticism of populist dogmatism, the novel also argues in support of an alternative route for the Ukrainian nation-building effort, reiterating Kobylians'ka's earlier elitist views. Although *Niobe* does not directly denounce the populist "going to the people" program, it emphasizes that "going to the people" by itself cannot generate any significant cultural, social, or political change in Ukraine, and thereby reiterates Kobylians'ka earlier belief that Ukraine's political liberation could be achieved only through the development of Ukrainian high culture. The idea of a cultural revolution proposed in *Niobe*, defined by an intimate fusion of politics and art, becomes even more prominent in Kobylians'ka's two other post-Iefremov novels on the Ukrainian intelligentsia.

Over the Bridge

Spanning more than 300 pages, *Over the Bridge* (1912) comprises Kobylians'ka's longest work, which many critics find too long and too slow (Vernyvolia 1923, 15; Tomashuk 1969a, 167; Babyshkin 1956, 51; Hundorova 2002, 164). Kobylians'ka, however, valued *Over the Bridge* as her favourite novel because of its rich biographical data and insightful reflections on the contemporary Ukrainian intelligentsia (V:241). As she pointed out, she collected the materials presented in the novel, both biographical and critical, over a fifteen-year period, which amplifies the historical and conceptual significance of her work:

> Speaking about the story *Over the Bridge*, from the time I completed *The Princess*, I was entertaining the idea of writing a similar story but with one major difference: [in the new work,] the spirit of its heroes should be more elevated, and their thoughts should go farther and deeper than those of the heroes in the first novel. I collected materials gradually to prepare myself, so to speak, for this work. (V:241)

These lines confirm that, in some respects, in *Over the Bridge* Kobylians'ka continued to develop her earlier views, which she first introduced in 1896 – namely, her elitist vision of an ideal intellectual hero that draws on Nietzsche's concept of the overman and nineteenth-century Russian theories of the intellectual's duty to society.

Kobylians'ka made her first attempt to write *Over the Bridge* in 1901. According to her correspondence with Makovei, she originally wanted to model the novel's main male character after him, and thus to project her intimate friend as the embodiment of her new intellectual ideal. Kobylians'ka's request for personal information from Makovei, which she sent to him on 12 August 1901, is particularly telling in this regard:

> I would like to write a novel, and I have being making notes for some time now ... I need some biographical information about the time when you were a young boy, and when you were in your mid-20s. I can pick up from there on my own. Give me whatever notes you like, but make sure they capture well your character in the early years of your life. I really need it. I implore you not to refuse my request. I have a brilliant idea, so help

> me to put it on paper. Be for once so kind ... I will let you read the novel, and if you don't approve it, I won't publish it. But if you like it, I will dedicate my work to you. Please, do not think I'm going to write another "Valse mélancolique" or something of that kind ... The work I'm planning to write will be completely new. It will be something I've never written before. I think you will really enjoy it ... The only thing I'm afraid of is that you might withdraw and won't write to me! Oh God, I wish you could trust me. I would really like to bring ... [you] on stage. I will present ... [you] in such garments that no one will ever recognize [you] ... White lilies will bloom for him ... You will send me your notes on the year-by-year description of ... [your] life, won't you? Please write to me as a reward for all the letters I wrote and all the sorrows I had, and everything will be fine. At least, we will leave a novel after us. No one will know. This is how the literati deal with their wounds. This is what the poets do. (V:487–8)

Curiously, this fragment is a part of one of the most intimate letters Kobylians'ka wrote to Makovei, over the summer of 1901, in which she declared her love and proposed to live with him without being officially married. According to Kobylians'ka's personal correspondence, Makovei ignored all of Kobylians'ka's letters that she wrote in June and July 1901 and resolutely rejected her offer of intimacy in a face-to-face encounter that took place sometime between July 27 and 5 August 1901.[10] After realizing that she would not be able to have any romantic relationship with Makovei in the future, Kobylians'ka made a bold proposition to feature him in her new novel on the life of the Ukrainian intelligentsia in an attempt to rescue their friendship and literary collaboration. In a letter that she sent to Makovei a couple of weeks after her passionate confession, Kobylians'ka reiterated her request in a more reserved manner and shared her plans for the future novel in a businesslike tone:

> I asked you for notes, and you promised but didn't send them to me. I really need a work that will keep my soul and my head occupied. I started writing a long novel, but I cannot write much without your notes. Please do not think that I am going to write a trivial piece. It will be about the life of the intelligentsia, and it will be as serious a work as *The Earth* ... They say it is impossible to write a novel about the life of the Ukrainian intelligentsia. Oh, it is quite possible! One must only open one's eyes and become more sensitive to people and their feelings ... I would like to discern some consequences from your life and your character and, of course, from those of other people. I worked out a plan that deals with a broad context ... I have matured a lot since the time when I wrote *The Princess*

> and other stories about [the] intelligentsia. I am not afraid to work on serious subjects anymore. It seems to me that in the past I wasn't progressive enough and didn't have my eyes opened wide enough ... But now, I want to write about it ... Send me whatever notes you have. (V:489–91)

In both letters, Kobylians'ka elaborated extensively on the complexity of Makovei's personality and his unusual ability to synthesize two fundamentally different identities – one of a cynical materialist and another of a refined poet. This combination of character traits projects an intimate fusion of the material and the poetic, or, better yet, the rational and irrational aspects of life as the main mission for her ideal intellectual type. Makovei, however, did not approve of Kobylians'ka's idea "to bring him on stage" and to use their relationship as a framework for a novel (V:489). He insisted that any public disclosure of their personal story would inevitably ruin their friendship. But, as their consequent correspondence suggests, Kobylians'ka had no intention of yielding to Makovei and was forced to postpone the writing of her panoramic, semi-biographical novel only by a series of unexpected tragic events – notably the 1902 confrontation with Iefremov and her 1903 stroke and temporary paralysis.

Kobylians'ka returned to the idea of writing a semi-biographical novel about the Ukrainian intelligentsia only in 1909. As she highlighted in her 1922 autobiography, she did not feel ready for the project at the time, but the premature death of her youngest brother, Volodymyr, inspired her to commemorate his life and work in her fiction (V:241). Kobylians'ka finished *Over the Bridge* in less than two years. From January to December 1912, the novel was published in the L'viv monthly *Literature and Science Herald* and came out as a separate edition in 1913. In February 1912, after the publication of the first sections of the novel in the *Herald*, Kobylians'ka sent an angry letter to the journal's editorial board in which she complained about the numerous typographical errors in the printed text of her work. While demanding a more thorough treatment for her novel, Kobylians'ka emphasized that *Over the Bridge* was a special work because she wrote it "with a true belief that it was [her] last fictional work" (V:614). This remark further supports Kobylians'ka's claim that *Over the Bridge* is a product of her long-term reflections, which allowed her to sum up her thoughts on the two central questions that preoccupied her throughout the 1890s and the 1910s – Ukraine's national liberation and the role of the Ukrainian intelligentsia in it.

Contrary to the 1901 plan, Kobylians'ka used her youngest brother, Volodymyr, as a model for the main character of the novel, Nestor

Obryns'kyi, who embodies the writer's ideal of a cultivated intellectual with a strong political will. She also modelled many secondary characters after her other relatives and close friends, which enhanced the authenticity and thus the realism of the depicted story. Curiously, despite Makovei's earlier objection, Kobylians'ka included a character designed after him – a well-off thirty-five-year-old government worker, Bohdan Oles', who functions as the novel's narrator. She also used elements of her personal story of her intimate relationship with Makovei to frame the novel as the story of Bohdan's courtship with Mania Obryns'ka, Nestor's older sister. Kobylians'ka structured her novel as a memoir written for therapeutic reasons by Bohdan, who tries to recreate, reassess, and come to terms with the traumatic events that took place over a fifteen-year period between his first encounter with his wife-to-be, Mania Obryns'ka, and their eventual marriage. Bohdan's narrative takes the form of a quest aimed at understanding the self in relation to his family, friends, and broader community. As a result, his assessments of others and their outlooks on life often become more important than the record of his own internal world. The outline of Bohdan's motives evokes parallels with Kobylians'ka's incentive to write a semi-biographical novel about the Ukrainian intelligentsia and her attempt to renegotiate the relationship between "private" and "public," and thereby to derive from her personal experiences a broader theoretical assessment of the social and political agency of the contemporary Ukrainian intelligentsia.

In her initial response to *Over the Bridge*, Lesia Ukrainka underscored the verisimilitude of the novel's characters, events, and attitudes:

> Someone dark haired [a description Lesia Ukrainka used for Kobylians'ka] must have lost a lot of health with her *Over the Bridge*. It must have been very painful to bring out all those memories ... I recognize the saint Anna [Kobylians'ka's mother] and your brother Volodymyr ... I recognize so much that I cannot be objective about this novel. I cannot critique it. I see it as a chunk of life that one must yet come to terms with. One cannot critique such things. (1963e, 162)

Notably, while acknowledging the influence of the autobiographical materials on her reception of *Over the Bridge*, Ukrainka, like many later critics, also observed that the authenticity of the material does not in any way undercut the novel's aesthetic and philosophical composition.

Most past critics consider Bohdan Oles' as the key hero of the novel.[11] The opening sentence of the novel, however, states that the main focus of Bohdan's memoir is not on him but on men and women he used to know, suggesting that Bohdan's courtship with Mania Obryns'ka might be only a background for Kobylians'ka's critical reflections. Mykhailo Mochul's'kyi, one of the novel's first critics, who wrote an introduction to the 1913 edition, was the first and one of the few to acknowledge the utilitarian function of Bohdan's character and his personal story:

> Kobylians'ka once wrote in her story "Vin i vona" ("He and She"), "Women have bizarre taste – womanish taste. The only thing they care about is whether the main characters would get married or not. For them, it is the most important issue." This is why the writer developed a love story for those who see the marriage of the main characters as the most important moment in a novel, and presented the more sophisticated audience with a gift of ideas and portraits of [the] human soul. (1963, 164–5)

Mochul's'kyi did not elaborate any further, either on Kobylians'ka's social and political ideas or on the aesthetic value of her psychological portraits. Neither did later scholars of Kobylians'ka and her work. Even the most extensive monographs barely provide any analysis of *Over the Bridge*, focusing mostly on the so-called salon-like (Chopyk 1998, 95) or romance-like (Hundorova 2002, 160) narrative of Bohdan's love story. Consequently, past critics comment predominantly on Kobylians'ka's failure to achieve her own goal, that is, to create refined characters whose spirit would "be more elevated" and whose thoughts would "go farther and deeper" than those of the heroes in *The Princess* (Vernyvolia 1923, 15; Babyshkin 1956, 51; Tomashuk 1969a, 167; Hundorova 2002, 164).

In fact it is neither Bohdan Oles', who resembles Osyp Makovei, nor Mania Obryns'ka, who has a lot in common with Kobylians'ka, but rather Nestor Obryns'kyi, a character modelled after Kobylians'ka's deceased brother, and his interactions with others that constitute the nexus of Kobylians'ka's critical reflections. First of all, the novel closely follows only Nestor's personal growth from early childhood until well into his mature years. According to Kobylians'ka's 1901 letters to Makovei, this is precisely the formula she planned to use to capture the complex cognitive and spiritual formation of the intellectual protagonist in her work on the Ukrainian intelligentsia (V:489–91). Second, although Nestor plays only a marginal role in Bohdan's love story, he indirectly brings Bohdan, a conservative materialist, and Mania, a committed idealist, together, symbolically bridging the same two major aspects of life, the rational and irrational, which Kobylians'ka had positioned earlier as the main mission for the novel's ideal intellectual hero. Nestor is also the only character who initiates philosophical discussions and reflects critically on questions of patriotism, social and political activism, and the role of the intellectual elite in Ukraine's national revival. Therefore, it merits examining Nestor's cognitive, emotional, and everyday life in order to gauge Kobylians'ka's mature thoughts on the role of the Ukrainian intelligentsia in Ukraine's social and political development.

If we were to describe Nestor's character in a few sentences, our results would be almost identical to the portrait that one post-Soviet biographer of Kobylians'ka paints of her brother Volodymyr:

> As a boy, he was very inquisitive and was fascinated with nature. He collected insects. Later on, he learned how to play the cello and was very good at it. He was fond of folklore. He was exceptionally gifted, dedicated, and perhaps even a little too punctual and scrupulous. He was a "straight-A" student, top student in a public school, then in a gymnasium, and later at Chernivtsi University, where he received a degree in law in 1901. In 1903, he earned a doctoral degree in law and started his internship in the Chernivtsi Court. He always lived with his parents and his sister ... He devoted all his energy first to studies and later to work, but neglected his health and doctors' advice ... In 1908, he was diagnosed with tuberculosis and died soon thereafter. (Vozniuk 2006, 119–20)

A series of anecdotes that introduce the thirteen-year-old Nestor in the first part of the novel complete a picture that foregrounds his distinctive character – punctuality, inquisitiveness, dedication, altruism, but, most importantly, independence. Early on, Nestor's favourite phrase – "On my own!" – becomes his life motto and underpins all of his mature beliefs and actions.

In the second part of the novel, which tells the story of Nestor as a young scholar, his pronounced individualism and self-reliance permeate his political views, especially his take on political activism. Nestor's conversation with Bohdan, which takes place during their incidental encounter after a ten-year separation, is particularly revealing in this regard. When Bohdan asks Nestor whether he belongs to any academic circles, Nestor sarcastically notes that one has to be a "politician" and belong to a "party," that is, to forgo one's freedom and individuality to be a member of any student organization (IV:107). As Nestor explains, this is something he is not willing to do. He elaborates further that although he would gladly give his life for the Ukrainian people and their progress, he believes that at this time his life does not have enough value, and that he must "develop his own culture according to his individual potential and at the highest level of its understanding" (IV:107) before he can start any serious political work. He goes on to juxtapose his beliefs with the views of the mainstream Ukrainian intelligentsia, including those of Bohdan, and to criticize their naive idealism. Earlier in the novel, this type of intelligentsia is described with characteristic irony as "an intelligent plebe, who has not fully shed the plebeian skin, and whose deeds and progress, as a result, remain hampered, disenfranchised, and insular; who has no broader vistas, but a glimpse into the tearful traditional past and a narrow perspective into the future" (IV:62).[12] Nestor's main criticism focuses mostly on the premature social and political activism of contemporary intelligentsia. He sums up his argument by claiming that contemporary politicians purposely manipulate young people and often trick them into commitments that lead to their personal ruin, and that "a lot of [Ukrainian] absurdity and sorrow should be ascribed to the [spiritual] impoverishment through politics" (IV:107). Accordingly, Nestor continues, one should "stand above parties" and assert one's individuality and independence of thought to make any significant social or political changes in Ukraine (IV:107). With his argument, Nestor thus problematizes the dominant political discourses, which brings to mind Kobylians'ka's earlier critique of populism, its dogmatism, and its detrimental consequences for young, enthusiastic minds.

Over the Bridge develops its social and political critique further by attacking not only political parties and their doctrinaire ideologies but also the Ukrainian intelligentsia and its cultural, social, and political apathy. Nestor's accusation of his fellow academics of abandoning their function as an intellectual elite by what he calls "coming down into the marketplace" in his second conversation with Bohdan is particularly representative:

> [Our intelligentsia] talks eagerly and with enthusiasm ... But I don't like being around them. Even more so, I don't like going to the so-called gatherings or reading papers and periodicals ... You see, every time I pick up a periodical, especially the daily kind, I get an impression that I enter a restaurant, where everyone talks about his own thing. As I see it, periodicals destroy our ability to think for ourselves ... and [our intelligentsia], or at least its majority, are no better than periodicals. Their every thought seems overheated and experienced only superficially. Everything they do, write, or say seems rushed and done without any balance or internal strength. It all seems to be done not for the sake of work and its quality, but exclusively for self-satisfaction, in a businesslike manner. I believe every individual life could be an artistic creation, but nowadays it's no more than a business. We don't see any value in work itself, but only in what

> we can get for it. The greatest art of our life is to get the greatest possible compensation for the smallest possible contribution. That is why our lives turn into an eternal race, an eternal hunt. At the same time, life isn't rid of beauty. But I wonder, do they see it? When? Even in those brief moments when they are on their own, even then they cannot see it. They are always chasing after something better and wait for something newer. (IV:119–20)

Nestor clearly embeds his critique of Ukrainian intellectuals and their inability to think critically – that is, their purely mechanistic belonging to the class of intellectuals – in Marx's theory of alienation. Following Marx's line of argumentation, Nestor points out that capitalism reduces the labour of the intellectual to a commercial commodity that can be traded in the competitive labour market, stripping off its original, constructive socio-economic quality that typically plays an active part in the collective effort for personal survival and the betterment of society.[13] In his reflections on how to overcome this intellectual alienation and the devaluation of Ukrainian academia, Nestor, however, does not follow Marx – there is no call for political revolution and abolition of bourgeois property. Instead he offers a Nietzschean vision, suggesting that only a highly educated intellectual elite can lead Ukrainian people towards a better life by separating the good and beautiful from contemporary materialism:

> We all yell everywhere we go, "Work for the people," but all our "laborious accomplishments" are meant not for the whole people, but exclusively for "the peasants." I ask, shouldn't we go beyond the work for the peasants in our struggle? Shouldn't we distinguish ourselves, I mean intelligentsia, in a separate stratum, which would require its own work, science, art, and other cultural achievements? We have done, or at least are trying to do, something for the peasants. But what about our intelligentsia? So far, we have done nothing for our intelligentsia. I dream about having many accomplished intellectuals, as many as possible. I dream about a truly national cultural elite. But, frankly speaking, we don't understand its true value because of the peasants. And that is one of the major reasons of our characteristic misery. I wonder ... what could be a better ideal for a human than another human, one refined hard-working human among thousands of noble figures? Meanwhile, what is the real nature of a contemporary Ukrainian? Have we discovered it yet? A Ukrainian doesn't know it. He hasn't learned even the scope of his own strength through the work of its intelligentsia ... He hasn't figured out the grand calling of his people. Broadly speaking, we are a people who haven't discovered themselves yet. So how can a Ukrainian organize the mass of people, I mean the whole

> people, *as long as he doesn't organize himself* first as an individual, then as a mass, and finally – as a nation? Granted, we rejected God, but we did it only because other, more progressive nations rejected Him. But whereas those other nations replaced God with science, art, and an opportunity to discover themselves, their own power, and culture, whereas other nations search for a new morality and new values for their people, we barely stand at the lowest level of their past cultural development. Or, perhaps, it's not true? What did we give to our peasants to stimulate the noble impulses in their soul or mind? Did we give them science or culture? Oh, well ... I have so much to say on the subject. (IV:121–2)

This passage juxtaposes Nestor's vision of the intellectual elite with mainstream populist understandings of the intelligentsia and its social and political role in Ukrainian society and captures a fundamental distinction between the two strands of thought. Nestor suggests that the mainstream Ukrainian populist theorists treat elites in a utilitarian way by viewing them as merely the servants of their peasant-oriented ideology. He, in turn, argues that national intellectual leaders must remain undefiled by popular mass movements and must cultivate their own ideology, aesthetic values, and moral standards, which, he believes, would eventually direct the whole nation to a better future. To a world ruled by materialism and bourgeois complacency, Nestor contrasts a world ruled by beauty and aesthetic principle. To the image of "the indoctrinated servant of the people," he suggests an image of the "poet-seer" who is, in a very Nietzschean way, beyond the good and evil of the marketplace and thus can transcend present-day cultural, social, and political stagnation. At the same time, Nestor links his Nietzschean model to a clear political mission: just like Natalka Verkovychivna in Kobylians'ka's *The Princess* and the old man in "The Thoughts of an Old Man," Nestor projects individual self-perfection as a politically valuable direction that has the potential to lead the whole nation to better things.

In the 1960s, one Soviet critic recognized Nestor and his social and political ideas as "a new phenomenon in Ukrainian prose and a fresh product of the Ukrainian social and political life of the time" (Dziuba 1986, 27). Owing to the constraints imposed by Soviet ideology, this critic had no choice but to frame in the best Marxist tradition "the intellectual's duty to the working class" as Kobylians'ka's central ideological directive in *Over the Bridge*, thereby marginalizing her emphasis on consolidation and regeneration of an intellectual elite as simply a minor, transient step in this process (Dziuba 1986, 25). A close reading of the novel, however, suggests the opposite. Nestor, who gradually becomes the embodiment of his own intellectual ideal, proves with his last breath, in the best Bazarov tradition, that continual self-perfection and hard work "for the sake of work and its quality" bring more far-reaching results than any passionate oration in the middle of the marketplace.[14] In his last days, while fatally ill with tuberculosis, Nestor continues working and divides his time equally between writing his magnum opus and helping Ukrainian peasants to settle their matters in court. In the somewhat utopian ending of the novel, his dedication and work ethic earn admiration among his friends and acquaintances. More importantly, they inspire those who love him to rethink their own attitudes towards life and their role in society. In his death, Nestor becomes a Nietzschean herald of a new age whose personal example sets in motion the unification of the Ukrainian intelligentsia, which is tellingly represented through the marriage between Bohdan Oles', an intelligent plebe, and Mania Obryns'ka, an intellectual aristocrat.

Recent critics seem to be scornful about the happy-ending resolution of *Over the Bridge*. Tamara Hundorova, for example, reads Bohdan's and Mania's marriage as a "pseudo-synthesis" where the intelligent plebe forces the intellectual aristocrat to renounce her modernist views and emancipationist aspirations (2002, 177). Accordingly, Hundorova, alongside some other scholars, interprets the novel's emphasis on traditional family values as a sign of Kobylians'ka's reconciliation with and conformity to populism (2002, 178; Chopyk 1998, 89–90). Dwelling on the presumably implied gender inversion of the main characters in *Over the Bridge*, Hundorova also explains the ostensible shift in Kobylians'ka's social and political views through the writer's own identity crisis and reads the novel as a "hysterical text" that requires a psychoanalytical interpretation (2002, 170). Considering Kobylians'ka's decade-long effort to make her fiction more accessible to mainstream Ukrainian readers, we should not, however, discard the possibility that the writer used a conventional gendering formula, where a man is associated with authority, to conceal her elitist argument rather than conform to populist conservatism. In 1912, the writer's views, however, remained tuned to her earlier propagation of a modernized yet somewhat traditional role for women within the family. Like some other heroines in Kobylians'ka's earlier intellectual novels whom she often modelled after canonical characters created by Jane Austen, Charlotte Brontë, George Sand, and Eugenie Marlitt – Olena Liaufler and Natalka Verkovychivna are the best examples here – Mania Obryns'ka starts as an ambitious idealist who longs for a radically new life, but gradually undergoes a profound rethinking regarding the value of tradition and eventually arrives at a conclusion that resonates with one of Kobylians'ka's major moral and aesthetic principles: "Real life and experience, but, foremost, 'modernity' itself, taught me to preserve those 'old-fashioned' traditions that remain pleasant and dear to our hearts despite their old-fashioned nature" (IV:339). These lines appear at the end of the novel to frame Kobylians'ka's sociocultural message: while decrying the mainstream populist intelligentsia, particularly their conservatism and peasant-oriented ideals, the novel also criticizes the so-called radical modernists – that is, pseudo-Nietzschean nihilists, decadents, symbolists, and futurists – who reject tradition altogether. In *Over the Bridge*, Kobylians'ka thus reasserted herself as a radical conservative by propagating, on the one hand, innovative elitist ideas but opposing, on the other hand, major left-oriented radical movements, which at the time many of her compatriots perceived as progressive. Kobylians'ka's criticism of the contemporary Ukrainian intelligentsia reached its apogee in her next novel, *After Situations* (1913).

After Situations

Kobylians'ka wrote *After Situations* in a relatively short period, and it came out within a year of the original publication of *Over the Bridge* in the pro-modernist literary monthly *Ukrains'ka khata* (*Ukrainian Hut*) in 1913–14. The novel features the story of a love triangle involving a gifted pianist, Aglaia-Felicitas Fedorenko; a university professor of art history, Ivan Chornai; and his Germanized younger brother, Iohanes Shvarts. All three characters belong to the educated upper middle class, and could be read as representatives of the new pro-Western generation of Western Ukrainian urban intelligentsia who continually challenged social norms. As often is the case in Kobylians'ka's writings, a series of dialogues among the main characters constitute the main action of the novel. While placing dialogue in the centre, Kobylians'ka, however, did not focus solely on bringing out the inner person of her characters, as she often did in earlier works, but rather foregrounded social and political discussions that highlight a clear link between the characters' self-consciousness and their world views. The result is an intricate fusion of personal life with the life of ideas, that is, of heroes' personalities and their lofty ideological thinking. This approach allowed Kobylians'ka to transmit the novel's ideological subject matter in a way that preserved its capacity to generate meaning yet simultaneously maintained a critical distance, neither confirming nor repudiating it.

Many critics have recognized questions of nationality, nationhood, and patriotism as the most discussed concerns in *After Situations*, but they have said surprisingly little about the novel's national discourse and its complexity. Concentrating exclusively on Aglaia's personal struggle for self-assertion, past critics have read the novel's discussion of the national question at best as Kobylians'ka's "means for structuring the novel's main argument" (Pavlyshyn 2008, 238) – a critical reflection on creative individuals' fatal inability to succeed in conservative bourgeois society (Izotov 1928, 89–91; Babyshkin 1963, 166; Pavlyshyn 2008, 238; Tomashuk 1969a, 167). This reading equates Aglaia with Kobylians'ka's other emancipationist heroines and frames feminism as the central theme in *After Situations*. A close analysis of the novel alongside its contextualization in Kobylians'ka's complete oeuvre, however, demonstrates that the story of Aglaia-Felicitas Fedorenko – unlike those of Olena Liaufler in *A Human Being*, Natalka Verkovychivna in *The Princess*, or Mania Obryns'ka in *Over the Bridge* – is not a story of "becoming" but a story of "being." Neither a cognitive nor a spiritual transformation takes place in *After Situations*, and Aglaia's tale serves mostly to frame Kobylians'ka's reflections on questions of patriotism and Ukraine's national revival. Atypical for Kobylians'ka's intellectual prose, the absence of any positive, let alone heroic or messianic, characters provides curious insight into the complexity and subversiveness of its ideological implications. Although Aglaia, Professor Chornai, and Shvarts demonstrate many character features that Kobylians'ka deliberately ascribed to her ideal intellectual heroes – refined education, aesthetic sophistication, rebellious nature, and strong will – all three lack a sincere commitment to a broader social agenda, which Kobylians'ka projected in all her preceding intellectual prose as the most essential quality of an intellectual leader. Preoccupied with personal gains and pleasures, all three characters continually chase after new experiences or, as the title of the novel tellingly suggests, after new "situations," but end up trapped by tragic consequences because of their lack of consideration for others. By the end of the story, Aglaia, Professor Chornai, and Shvarts emerge as pathetic and self-negating anti-heroes who represent the new generation of pro-modernist, but often pseudo-progressive, Ukrainian intelligentsia.

After Situations is divided into three parts, each deconstructing the initially positive image of one of the three main characters. The first part focuses on Aglaia-Felicitas Fedorenko. The heroine's name, literally the first words of the novel, immediately stand out, calling attention to its oxymoronic nature, suggesting a certain contradiction or paradox in Aglaia's character. Aglaia-Felicitas is a combination of two mythical names: in Greek mythology Aglaia is associated with the youngest of the Three Graces, also known as the goddess of beauty, splendour, glory, magnificence, and adornment; Felicitas is known as the goddess of good luck and fortune in Roman mythology. The name symbolically forecasts a successful and happy life for the heroine, which both Professor Chornai and his brother, Shvarts, point out on several occasions throughout the novel. The heroine's peasant last name, Fedorenko, however, substantially undercuts the optimistic symbolism of her hyphenated first name. If we compare it to its regional variation, Fedorchuk, which Kobylians'ka used for the main peasant characters in *The Earth*, a degree of implied mediocrity, narrow-mindedness, and even fatalism becomes obvious. The paradoxical aura around the heroine builds up when Aglaia's talent for music is juxtaposed with the poor quality of her "cheap" (pidlyi) instrument, primitive education, and chaotic upbringing. The opening section of the novel dwells extensively on the dynamics of the Fedorenko family. While projecting Aglaia's mother as a self-centred materialist who "does as little as possible for her children, concentrating instead on increasing the estate" (V:7), the work describes Aglaia's father as a self-absorbed loner who "was interested in his [children] as little as in sparrows under his roof" (V:8). Considering Kobylians'ka's views on the importance of early childhood education, which she developed in the 1890s, it is easy to predict the life story of a naturally talented heroine who grows up "in a house of wild chaos, conflicting views, continuous quarrels, bargaining, illnesses, pretence, ignorance ... and so on" (V:12). Aglaia's sad story brings to mind some other tales from Kobylians'ka's earlier works – those of the young Iakhnovyches in *Niobe* and the two Fedorchuk brothers in *The Earth*, who were also initially strong, smart, and inquisitive children but grew up, because of parental negligence, into wild, impulsive, and often easily manipulated people. Lacking any guidance as a child, Aglaia gradually turns into a confused, imbalanced, and self-negating character. Even in music, despite all her talent and exceptional taste, she becomes neither a creator nor a reformer but only a performer of someone else's music, that is, an executor of someone else's vision and will. The allegory of "playing to someone else's tune" symbolically emphasizes Aglaia's submissive character, which juxtaposes rather than equates her with Kobylians'ka's previous self-asserting heroines.

A story of Aglaia's temporary conversion to Russophilism, a movement popular at the turn of the twentieth century in Western Ukraine that espoused pan-Slavic ideas and sought the protection of the Russian tsar, further illuminates the heroine's narrow-mindedness.[15] Early on in the novel, Aglaia is described as an ethnic Ukrainian with some Romanian or Armenian heritage. At first, she seems to care little about national identity or any other social or political matters, and instead devotes most of her time to fashion and music. Her attitude gradually changes when she falls in love with Andrii, a student of philosophy who introduces her to several popular social discussions and movements, one of which is Russophilism. Without giving much thought to Andrii's reasoning, Aglaia eagerly adopts his position and becomes overnight a passionate advocate of Russophilism. Later in the story, when Professor Chornai asks Aglaia to explain her ideological position, she is unable to produce any coherent narrative and instinctively bursts into generalizations to fend off Professor Chornai's implied criticism: "[I] simply don't want to belong to that inert, uncultured, coarse mass, which has recently started calling itself Ukrainian, which cries, begs, argues, and curses using simple vulgar words, which cannot raise its head when needed and cannot make any heroic sacrifices. In a word, I don't want to belong to a mass that most likely, would remain forever a petty bourgeois" (V:23). Although Aglaia's speech is powerful, it is not an argument but only an opinion, which points to the irrational nature of the heroine's conviction and her identity crisis. Professor Chornai challenges Aglaia's views further with two simple questions – by what right does she, an ethnic Ukrainian who speaks perfect Ukrainian, call herself a Russian? and has she ever visited Russia to speak so authoritatively about its so-called healthy element and potential for progress? At this point, the young girl is so confused that the best she can do is to run away from Professor Chornai and thus escape his questioning. Aglaia's inability to defend her ideological position suggests that her Russophilism is grounded not in critical reflections but rather, as implied further in the novel, in her erotic memories of Andrii, who dies from tuberculosis shortly after their engagement. Consequently, when with time a new and much stronger feeling takes over Aglaia's imagination, she has no difficulties adjusting her views to those of her new passion, Professor Chornai, and transforms, again almost overnight, into an avid defender of Ukrainian language and culture. Curiously, Aglaia acknowledges the importance of the erotic element in her decision making when she later shares the story of the evolution of her world view with Shvarts. As the heroine admits, she "returned to the path that she once abandoned" because of Andrii "under the influence of a handsome and educated man," Professor Chornai (V:91). Aglaia's confession reveals her uncritical and superficial mode of thinking.

The novel's discussion of Russophile ideology becomes particularly interesting if we consider that Kobylians'ka's father, Iulian

Kobylians'kyi, was a traditionalist Russophile (Vozniuk 2006, 125–6), and that the writer, although she respected her father's views, never shared his political outlook. In *After Situations*, Kobylians'ka links Russophilism with the character of Aglaia's deceased fiancé, Andrii, and makes it an expression of his intellectual persona. In a few brief scenes that address Russophilism as an ideology, Kobylians'ka avoids any direct commentary on its political objectives but articulates its social and political significance in the Western Ukrainian context of her time by ascribing Russophile views to several characters. For example, Professor Chornai had advocated Russophile ideology in his student years and changed his views only after meticulous studies and numerous trips to Russia. Shvarts had also been involved in a Russophile cause but deviated from it after rediscovering his innate Ukrainianness. Although Professor Chornai's and Shvarts's Russophile views are never presented in the text, the reference to their transformation conveys an important sociohistorical development: while highlighting the widespread popularity of Russophilism among Western Ukrainian intellectuals at the turn of the century, the novel registers its reassessment and gradual decline in the 1910s. Further in the story, while exposing Aglaia's Russophile views, Kobylians'ka preserves their capacity to signify as an idea and aims her criticism not so much at Aglaia's views but at their superficial, immature, and inconsistent nature. Pavlyshyn suggests that the pathos of the heroine's belatedly discovered Ukrainophile pronouncements encourages the reader to identify with Aglaia "in her 'Ukrainian' moments and to read her fascination with the Russian myth as a symptom of the weakness of colonized Ukrainian culture" (2008, 239–40). The critic, however, does not acknowledge that pathos is a recurrent rhetorical device, which Kobylians'ka repetitively used to individualize Aglaia's speech and thereby to expose the emotional, rather than cognitive, triggers in her reasoning. In this light, we can easily read Aglaia's flamboyant presentation of her Ukrainophile statements not as markers of Kobylians'ka's affirmation of Ukrainophilism but rather as indicators of the superfluous nature of the heroine's views, which she is likely to abandon as soon as she falls for a person with different social and political convictions.

Similarly, Kobylians'ka maintained her critical distance while addressing Ukrainophilism and concealed her ideological commentary in the symbolic connotations of Professor Chornai's character that represents the Ukrainophile strata of Ukrainian society in the novel. Professor Chornai is first introduced as an exceptional character defined by three equally important factors: social status, class, and nationality. As Aglaia tellingly puts it, he is "a professor, a great lord, and a Ukrainian"

(V:32). As a professor and "a man of scholarship and work" (V:39), he teaches art history at a prestigious Austrian university, undertakes research trips, and is universally respected among his colleagues. As a well-off aristocrat, he enjoys a degree of financial freedom that allows him to engage periodically in minor philanthropic projects, such as soliciting jobs for his students and sponsoring their education. And as a Ukrainian and a sincere patriot, he is committed to the proliferation of the Ukrainian language and culture. While reflecting on the tight interconnectedness of these major aspects of Professor Chornai's personality, Aglaia gradually grows to idealize him as an exemplary representative of the Ukrainian nation and an ideal role model. Naturally, she projects his ideological views, Ukrainophilism, in a favourable light. It would, however, be erroneous to read either Aglaia's first impression or Professor Chornai's Ukrainophile rhetoric as Kobylians'ka glorification of Ukrainophilism because both eventually prove precarious and ill-conceived.

Professor Chornai's grand character, alongside his Ukrainophile pathos, is first challenged in a brief episode with one of his female students, most likely an ethnic Ukrainian, who is mocked by her whole class because she mispronounces some German words. Surprisingly, instead of standing up for the helpless and utterly embarrassed student, Professor Chornai simply interrupts his lecture and leaves the auditorium. While his gesture implies discontent, it simultaneously exposes fear of potential tension and complications that could jeopardize his academic reputation. The second challenge comes from Professor Chornai's prodigal brother, Iohanes Shvarts, who probes the degree of Professor Chornai's commitment to the Ukrainian cause even further. In one of the first conversations with Aglaia, Shvarts contests the respectful social status of his brother by a general attack on academia:

> I know too well that five-eighths of all official scholars are liars, two eighths are fools, one sixteenth are cynics, and the rest, as I say, have their throats plugged. I despise them and would gladly break all their bones ... because knowledge without the ability to act on it is a barren nonsense. Those scholars know well why we should write "u" and not "y," but they don't understand the difference between a *beast* ... and a *human being*. They fear that which they don't have and don't know. They fear imagination. (V:70)

Shvarts's sardonic commentary is an exaggeration but it brings up several valid points about the limited agency of Ukrainian scholars in Austrian academia and in the broader imperial context. When Aglaia mentions Professor Chornai, Shvarts ironically points out that, although his brother might have excelled academically, his voice, like the voices of many Ukrainian intellectuals, is silenced and thus has little influence on Ukrainian social and political dynamics. There is an obvious connection here with Nestor Obryns'kyi's criticism in *Over the Bridge*: whereas Nestor decries the loud orations of his academic colleagues, Shvarts highlights their lack of agency, implying the same ineffectiveness of the mainstream, educated Ukrainian elite.

Later in the story, during the first face-to-face confrontation with Professor Chornai, Shvarts makes similar remarks and accuses his brother of conservatism, cowardice, and lack of compassion. He supports his argument with a story from the distant past when Professor Chornai refused to help Shvarts, who was wrongfully accused of treason, because Professor Chornai feared that it might damage his good reputation, or as Kobylians'ka put it, that it might "leave a black stain" (V:124). Shvarts wraps up his argument with a prophetic speculation that sooner or later, the same fear of public disdain might push Professor Chornai to turn his back on Aglaia because his conservatism can never recognize or accept, let alone support and defend, the eccentric nature of the young girl. Indeed, at the end of the story, when Professor Chornai finds Aglaia trapped and compromised by his brother, he resolutely dissociates himself from her to protect his good name, just as he did in the similarly precarious situations with his student and younger brother. This dramatic deglorification of Professor Chornai suggests Kobylians'ka's criticism of the Ukrainophile activists, who advocated pro-Ukrainian sentiments but remained apolitical and conformist to the imperial status quo. It is noteworthy that Kobylians'ka neither asserted nor repudiated Ukrainophilism as an idea but rather exposed its main traits, both positive and negative, in an artistic way by embedding them in the character of Professor Chornai and his actions.

Iohanes Shvarts, the third key character in the story, also undergoes a similar deglorification. He is first presented as an ardent advocate of Nietzscheanism – a popular pro-modernist ideology that, according to one critic, grew into "a surrogate religion" which spread in Eastern Europe in the 1910s (Rosenthal 1986, 7) and which suggests a degree of ambivalence in the young man's character. Nietzscheanism was roughly rooted in Nietzsche's thought, particularly in what was perceived as the nihilistic aspects of his philosophy, and mandated a specific set of values and attitudes.[16] These values included individualism, heroism, courage, adventurousness, willingness to struggle, pride, sensuality, self-expression, self-affirmation, affirmation of life, defiance of death, iconoclasm, and contempt for the mob, for bourgeois society, for tradition, and for custom. The second part of the novel positions most of these qualities as the defining character features of Shvarts, projecting him as a somewhat Nietzschean hero – a man of many trades, sophisticated taste, polymath knowledge, strong will, and a self-assertive character. Several brief stories about his rebellious youth and unjust expulsion from his family, church, and native country, alongside his sincere and passionate longing for his lost Ukrainian identity, incite Aglaia and, by extension, the reader to sympathize with the young man and even admire his strong personality. His bold Nietzschean criticism of the Ukrainian people and their political apathy, which resonates with Kobylians'ka's own views, also elicits praise: "If a people [*narod*] wants to become great, powerful, and free, its ideal must be not an obedient plebe [*muzhyk*], but an impatient warrior, who would be prepared to work more with a sword than with a plow" (V:92–3). The third part of the story, however, quickly undermines the initial positive impression by revealing the "demonic" nature[17] of Shvarts's Nietzscheanism and by showing how his vulgar interpretations of Nietzsche translate the German philosopher's most celebrated values into selfishness, hedonism, oppression of the weak, and lust for power. An episodic story of Shvarts's mistress, who has no name and thus no personality of her own within the story, is one of the most powerful expressions of his ruthlessness, immorality, promiscuity, and worship of power for its own sake. As it turns out, Shvarts seduces and then kidnaps a young girl. Once he quenches his lust, he exploits her in his experimental hypnotism shows and makes money from her public humiliation. When the tormented girl finally dies from psychological traumas, the young man only comments coldly, "it is for her own best" (V:89). The story of Shvarts's mistress is a turning point after which *After Situations* focuses predominantly on Shvarts's obsessive preoccupation with his skills to use and manipulate people through deception and, if necessary, force for his own benefit. His advances on Aglaia present a telling example. Fascinated with Aglaia's talent for music, Shvarts devises a plan to seduce her and hopes to take her to California, where he can profit from her musical performances. Although his plan falls apart, it instigates a major scandal that culminates in a dramatic denouncement of all three characters. Professor Chornai turns out to be a conformist coward, Aglaia, a pathetic fool, and Shvarts, an immoral, self-centred tyrant. Since Kobylians'ka positioned Shvarts as an artistic representation of Nietzscheanism by fusing the movement's core values with the character's mode of thinking and acting, her implied criticism of the popular pro-modernist, pseudo-Nietzschean movement and its antisocial, and oftentimes openly militant, ideology, becomes obvious. This, however, does not undermine Kobylians'ka's lifelong appreciation of Nietzsche and his thought.

The tragic ending of the novel, Aglaia's death and Professor Chornai's despair, makes *After Situations* an even darker text than Kobylians'ka's first dystopian novel, *The Earth*, which deals with the demystification of the Ukrainian peasantry. Whereas *The Earth* leaves the reader with a hope for regeneration of the Ukrainian village, *After Situations* imposes a profoundly pessimistic portrayal of the Ukrainian intelligentsia and its circumscribed political potential on the eve of some of the most tragic events in Ukraine's history – events that would take place during the First World War and immediately thereafter. The novel's main point is best articulated through the symbolic implication of Professor Chornai's eventual realization that all of them – he, Aglaia, and his younger brother – are equally responsible for the dramatic ruin of their lives because they all were "active but blindfolded and divided among themselves" (navpomatsky aktyvni, khoch i vidokremleni v sumi mizh soboiu) (V:146). While acknowledging some agency and the will of the three characters, who represent the new generation of the pro-modernist Ukrainian intelligentsia, Professor Chornai's realization also exposes their lack of broader, community-oriented ideals and compassion for others. Although *After Situations* ends on a pessimistic note, it is neither a decadent nor a nihilistic text. On the contrary, in the context of Kobylians'ka's generally optimistic, if not utopian, intellectual prose, the 1913 novel stands out as a powerful and thought-provoking dystopian work that calls on the educated Ukrainian public to distinguish between self-centred patriotic pathos and broader cultural, social, and political goals aimed at Ukraine's national liberation.

Conclusion

Although Kobylians'ka made visible formal and stylistic changes in her post-Iefremov prose, she remained firm in her elitist views on Ukraine's national revival and continued to challenge the dominant populist discourse in the pre-war decade. One of the most pronounced points of conflict between Kobylians'ka's ideas and the populist visions of Ukraine's political future lay in the political role that Kobylians'ka ascribed to an intellectual leader. Whereas Ukrainian populists, in typical Marxist fashion, contained elites as an educated minority destined to serve the interests of the underprivileged masses, that is, as part of the ideological superstructure, Kobylians'ka placed the intellectual elite at the centre of her thought and envisioned a class of highly educated and cultured leaders who would determine not only their own ideology but also the course of Ukrainian politics and society. As early as in *The Princess* (1896), but even more so in *Niobe* (1905), *Over the Bridge* (1912), and *After Situations* (1913), Kobylians'ka grafted selected elements of Nietzsche's overman to her vision of an ideal intellectual leader, which the pro-Western Ukrainian modernists welcomed with enthusiasm but which the populist camp received with disdain. Kobylians'ka's model, however, was not the elite of executive power that was popular among many members of the European radical modernist intelligentsia (Mosse 1988, 298–305) but an intellectual aesthetic elite. While emphasizing the significance of high culture and aesthetic education in the formation of any nation, Kobylians'ka also deviated from the popular modernist motto of art for art's sake and reassigned a concrete program of national regeneration to her post-Iefremov and pre-war intellectual hero.

Naturally, Kobylians'ka's adoption of the populist myth of national rebirth opened some points for her reconciliation with populists. At the same time, her synthesis of proto-Nietzschean elitist thought with the national revival agenda brought her a vision for Ukraine's national liberation close to the radical strand of thought that would become far more familiar as radical nationalism rose in the 1920s and 1930s. Besides embracing the most obvious similarities of radical nationalist ideologies – the call for national spiritual renewal and the propagation of a strong charismatic leader – Kobylians'ka, like many radical nationalist thinkers of the day, firmly rejected all forms of rationalism. Already in the early 1890s, she saw the most distinctive human faculty not in reason, as her populist compatriots used to believe, but in instinctual forces and in the capacity to be inspired to heroic action and self-sacrifice through the power of belief, myth, and symbol, such as the family, the nation, the leader, or the regeneration of culture. Kobylians'ka's anti-rationalism was closely connected to her anti-conservatism – another feature of post-war radical nationalism. Although Kobylians'ka supported many traditional beliefs, particularly those related to the family, she never sought to turn the clock back and continually stressed a forward-looking movement. Her criticism of crowds and the old-fashioned provincial intelligentsia that clung tenaciously to conservative ideals was particularly harsh in the pre-Iefremov period. Between 1903 and 1913, Kobylians'ka was forced to disguise her anti-rational and anti-conservative sentiments and embed them in the symbolic implications of her characters – Anna Iakhnovych, Bohdan Oles', and Professor Chornai. Kobylians'ka's firm repudiation of ethnocentrism, xenophobia, and any other type of heterophobia was probably the major conceptual aspect that set her views apart from the popular radical nationalist ideologies of the time and that eventually complicated her relations with the Ukrainian radical nationalists in the 1920s. In the post-war fiction, which will be examined in the last chapter of this study, Kobylians'ka's elitist views became more nuanced and pronounced. The same is true about her use of the proto-religious language of spirit, belief, sacrifice, and hedonism.

Chapter Five

War and Fiction

An entangled series of conspiracies, treaties, and alliances that involved both major and minor European states led to the escalation of global conflict in the response to the assassination of Archduke Franz Ferdinand of Austria, heir to the Austro-Hungarian throne, who was murdered by a Serbian nationalist, Gavrilo Princip, in Sarajevo on 28 July 1914. Within days, the armies of Europe were mobilized, and by summer's end the world was drawn into the all-engulfing conflict of the First World War. During its first weeks, crowds across Europe pulsed with an eerie excitement and viewed the war as a crusade for the noblest goals, the so-called war to end all wars. The general sentiment was that the war would be over by Christmas, and no one on either side could have foreseen the apocalyptic scale of slaughter, devastation, and horror that ensued. More than 9 million combatants and 7 million civilians perished by the time the armistice was signed on 11 November 1918. An entire generation of European men was wiped out. It was one of the deadliest and costliest conflicts in history. It paved the way for major political changes, and it provided an experience, an object of reflection, and a mixture of powerful emotions that forced the generation of the fin-de-siècle European intellectuals to revise entirely their pre-war beliefs. This revision, in turn, inspired an outpouring of fiction, memoirs, and writing on ideology, culture, aesthetics, and the role of the intellectual in the reconstruction of Europe.

Post-1918 scholars have produced an equally plentiful, varied, and often contradictory body of critical works, keeping the tragic events of 1914–18 firmly present in the mind and memory of later generations. Until recently, however, Western scholars have focused exclusively on the works of male authors, such as Henri Barbusse, Siegfried Sassoon, Robert Graves, Wilfred Owen, and Erich Maria Remarque. Paul Fussell's *The Great War and Modern Memory* (1975), which remains the most frequently cited study on the literature of the First World War, exemplifies this exclusionary tendency. Fortunately, large-scale scholarly projects of recent decades have begun to retrieve and analyse the experiences of women, bringing attention to the neglected corpus of women's literary responses to one of the greatest catastrophes in modern history. Authoritative and noteworthy contributions, such as Sandra Gilbert's and Susan Gubar's *No Man's Land* (1988), Claire Tylee's *The Great War and Women's Consciousness* (1990), Sharon Ouditt's *Fighting Forces, Writing Women* (1994), and Jane Potter's *Boys in Khaki, Girls in Print* (2005), have filled the conspicuous void left by Fussell and others and moved the designation of war literature beyond the battlefield to include creative accounts by anyone – soldier or civilian, man or woman – who struggled to express the unthinkable horrors of war. Drawing on recent scholarship on literature of the First World War, this chapter argues that Kobylians'ka's war stories, a rare case of a Ukrainian woman writing about the First World War on the Eastern Front, deserve our attention as astute psychological profiles of Western Ukrainians struggling with multiple loyalties during the First World War and as valuable cultural documents that present an original perspective on the collective European experience of 1914–18.

Although Kobylians'ka and her work have received sustained critical attention, her literary response to the First World War remains barely discussed, let alone properly researched and contextualized. Early on, Soviet censorship found the pro-Austrian rhetoric and pronounced anti-Russian sentiments in some of Kobylians'ka's war stories unfit for the Soviet context and banned them from publication.[1] As a result, Kobylians'ka's war fiction has received little critical attention. On the few occasions when the stories have appeared in scholarly discussions, their ideological statements have typically been dismissed as mere opportunistic oratory (Tomashuk 1969a, 179–80; Mel'nychuk 2006, 6, 121) or as a critique of the uneducated peasant mind (Babyshkin 1963, 171–2). Past critics also tended to read the complete body of Kobylians'ka's writings of the First World War as a single artistic and ideological entity (Vasylenko 1928, 85; Babyshkin 1963, 171–4; Pavlyshyn 2008, 244), a "novel in novelettes" held together by its anti-war rhetoric (Mel'nychuk 2006, 109).[2] This unifying reading proves problematic once we examine the thematic, ideological, and stylistic particularities of Kobylians'ka's war stories, which fall into several distinct cycles separated by time and by the different claims they made on contemporary readers' attention. The stories that Soviet censors silenced are particularly revealing. Not only do they provide additional insight in what the war felt like to Kobylians'ka at its difference stages and how she got through it, but they also testify to the writer's continuous search for, and experimentation with, the rhetorical possibilities for expressing the unspeakable brutality of war, which she experienced first-hand during Russia's three occupations of Bukovyna between 1914 and 1917. They register a gradual evolution in Kobylians'ka's views on loyalty, patriotism, civic duty, and national identity, as well as her simultaneous transformation from a pro-Habsburg loyalist to a supporter of Ukraine's political independence. More importantly, a close reading of Kobylians'ka's works virtually unknown to readers and scholars of Ukrainian literature – "Lisova maty" ("The Forest Mother," 1915), "Shchyra liubov" ("Sincere Love," 1916), and "Vasylka" ("Vasylka," 1922) – alongside her popular texts, such as "Na zustrich doli" ("To Meet Their Fate," 1917), "Iuda" ("Judas," 1917), and "Lyst zasudzhenoho voiaka do svoiei zhinky" ("A Letter from a Convicted Soldier to His Wife," 1917), demonstrates that Kobylians'ka's war writings not only present a gripping record of the unforgettable experiences of outrage, fear, pain, and comedy in the war zones but also offer a way to reimagine the transformative experience of an unprecedented range of encounters, exchanges, and entanglements among peoples from different ethnic, social, and cultural backgrounds that took place during the First World War and had lasting cultural, social, and political effects.

First Literary Responses, 1914–15

When the First World War broke out, the fifty-one-year-old Kobylians'ka was suffering serious illness, poverty, and major depression. Her letter to Khrystia Alchevs'ka on 2 March 1913 presents the best-known testimony of her pre-war financial and emotional distress. In the letter, the writer confessed to her friend that she "could not be the same person that ... [she] once used to be," that "financial problems and the poor health of ... [her] sister" put a tremendous pressure on her, and that she could not write anything anymore because "the poet inside [her] ... folded his wings and was slowly dying" (V:518). She finished her letter by stating that she "was never happy" any longer (V:518).[3] Kobylians'ka's first war narratives, "The Forest Mother" and "Sincere Love," nevertheless display the same poignancy, critical depth, and ideological complexity as her earlier works. The most noteworthy aspect of Kobylians'ka's first war stories is their somewhat jingoistic pro-Habsburg rhetoric. Past critics have often read Kobylians'ka's Austrophilism as problematic and irrelevant to the Ukrainian national project of the day. As a result, a variety of apologetic narratives, each tailored to a specific ideological framework from socialist to neo-patriotic and revisionist, has arisen over the past century to justify it (Babyshkin 1963, 171–4; Tomashuk

1969a, 179–81; Mel'nychuk 2006, 121, Demchenko 2001, 174–8). The contemporary scholarship on the complex system of multiple loyalties held by Ukrainian subjects of the Habsburg Empire at the turn of the nineteenth century (Himka 1999, 3–12; Magocsi 2002, 73–82; Subtelny 1988, 307–35; Snyder 2008, 95–148), however, problematizes these apologies, suggesting a more nuanced reading of Kobylians'ka's pro-Habsburg sentiments.

As historians have shown, Galician and Bukovynian Ukrainians were among the most ardent of Austria-Hungary's many nationalities in their loyalty to the Habsburg Empire – from its beginning in 1772 until and even after the empire's dissolution in 1918. Ukrainian loyalty reflected a genuine appreciation of the religious, economic, and political gains Ukrainians achieved under Habsburg rule (Magocsi 2002, 73–82; Subtelny 1988, 307–35). For example, in 1774, Emperor Joseph II granted the Ukrainian Greek Catholic Church legal equality with the Roman Catholic Church, which led to positive changes in Ukrainian cultural and political life. In 1848, the Austrian government abolished serfdom and freed the Ukrainian peasantry, which substantially improved its economic situation. In addition, in 1861, Emperor Franz Joseph established a new Austrian parliament that gave Ukrainian secular leaders an opportunity to join the Austrian intellectual and political elite, which bolstered the growth of Ukrainian civil society. These reforms, along with the social and cultural changes they brought about, caused a significant percentage of the Western Ukrainian intelligentsia and peasantry to see Austria as "their legitimate homeland" and to regard their Habsburg rulers as "benevolent father figures" (Magocsi 2002, 73, 77). During the First World War, expressions of Ukrainian gratitude went beyond rhetoric alone: almost 250,000 Ukrainians fought bravely in various branches of the Austro-Hungarian imperial army between 1914 and 1918. It is also worth noting that, despite the repressive nature of Austro-Hungarian wartime rule in Galicia and Bukovyna, on the occasions when Austro-Hungarian troops retook provinces from the Russian army, many Western Ukrainians maintained loyalty to the Habsburg dynasty even after the empire's collapse – in hopes of its reincarnation (Magocsi 77–8; Snyder 2008, 95–148).[4] This historical context calls for a thorough reconsideration of Kobylians'ka's pro-Habsburg rhetoric in her early war stories.

The symbolic and stylistic particularities of "The Forest Mother" and "Sincere Love" suggest that Kobylians'ka viewed her *habsburgtreu* (loyal to the Habsburgs), or more precisely *kaisertreu* (loyal to the emperor), peasant characters with more sympathy and fascination than earlier scholars have argued (Babyshkin 1963, 172; Tomashuk 1969a,

179–81; Pavlyshyn 2008, 247). In "The Forest Mother," for example, Kobylians'ka used intricate stylistic devices to assert the exceptional insight and sense of belonging of her heroine, the old Hutsul Dokiia, who develops an attachment to the monarchy so deep that she is able, with dignity and even equanimity, to part with her only son, who has been called to fight in the war. Although Dokiia lacks a formal education and is detached from the political debates in Europe, she possesses an acute understanding of her own existence and clearly places it in the broader context of such historical events as the 1898 assassination of the Habsburg empress Elisabeth of Austria and the 1914 outbreak of the First World War. Following nineteenth-century models of psychological realism, Kobylians'ka intercut ethnographic depictions of Dokiia's primitive daily life with her internal dialogues. Thereby she created a vibrant picture of the heroine's cognitive and emotional life, which continually disrupts and thus subverts the overall doom-and-gloom tone of the story. Dokiia's own associations between the forest and her "whole country" (tsil[yi] kra[i]) (1927, 60) – that is, a broader community, perhaps as broad as the entire empire to which she belongs – which the old woman constructs while pondering her place in the world, complicate her devotion to the Habsburg crown: it frames the Austro-Hungarian Empire as an extended family formed of members who are heterogeneous yet intimately connected to one another. The "forest mother," the ancient pine tree in the nearby forest which Dokiia associates with the Empress Elisabeth, constitutes the central image in the chain of associations that establish a coherence among nature, the Habsburg family, and their imperial subjects.

Dokiia's personalized conception of the empire brings to mind important studies on group psychology of the time and hints at what we might compare to Sigmund Freud's libidinal explanation of group inner dynamics. Freud positioned libido, that is, the totality of "instincts, which have to do with all that may be comprised under the word of love," as the key psychological bond that cements a group together (Freud 1989b, 29). He placed eroticism as the nucleus of his concept of love, but he did not exclude other manifestations of love: self-love; love for family, friends, or humanity in general; and devotion to concrete objects and abstract ideas. Freud particularly emphasized the importance of a leader who poses as the ideal father figure in the psychology of the group. Libidinal ties and self-identification with the group's leader, Freud observed, bind individual members of any socially constructed group to each other (Freud 1989b, 46–68). In this light, Kobylians'ka's representation of Dokiia's sincere devotion to the Habsburg empress could be viewed as the writer's inquiry into the nature of the pro-Austrian loyalty of Western Ukrainians at the outbreak of the First World War.

"The Forest Mother" opens with a mystical paragraph that sets the story in a distant wonderland of Bukovyna populated by spirits, mermaids, and enchanted children of the Carpathian Mountains, whose wits are often bewitched by magic herbs (1927, 54). This introduction instantly transports the reader into the mysterious world in Mykhailo Kotsiubyns'kyi's renowned novel *Tini zabutykh predkiv* (*Shadows of Forgotten Ancestors*, 1911) and evokes the mood in Kobylians'ka's earlier "rustic" works that combines sincere admiration of the Hutsuls' authentic spirit with a sharp anti-populist criticism of their circumscribed world view and superstitious beliefs.[5] Admittedly, it is possible to read these intertextual references as Kobylians'ka's critique of Dokiia's simple mind, but the heroine's flashback to her enlightening experience with a visiting village teacher leaves little room for such an interpretation. Immediately after the story's introduction, the reader meets Dokiia, who, while gathering wood and contemplating the natural beauty of the pristine forest, confesses that "there used to be a time when she [Dokiia] did not notice and did not understand any of it" (1927, 56). Dokiia's reflection implies a profound cognitive transformation that took place in her past. The heroine credits the visiting village teacher with instructing her in how to interpret and relate to the surrounding world. She also credits him with encouraging her to think critically and reflect on philosophical questions such as "where does longing come from and where does it go?" (1927, 56). Later in the story, the reader learns that the teacher's allegorical parallels between the human condition and life in the forest form the foundation of Dokiia's personalized conception of the world, which illuminates the psychological mechanisms of her *Habsburgtreu* attitude, presenting it as a well-substantiated and long-term sentiment.

The most powerful representations of the heroine's pro-Habsburg loyalty appear in the two final scenes of the story, which feature Dokiia's emotional response to the 1898 assassination of Elisabeth of Austria and the 1914 outbreak of the war. In both cases, dialogue plays the key role in capturing Dokiia's internal world in its rawest state. The first exchange takes place between the old Hutsul woman and the local priest when the heroine first hears about the assassination of the empress. Deeply moved by the tragic news, Dokiia lights up the only candle she has in her household to commemorate the empress and, perhaps, to turn away a calamity that she believes is about to overcome her whole land (1927, 59). Three days later, she walks several miles to a nearby village and offers all of her life savings to the priest, asking him to say a mass for the repose of the empress's soul. Kobylians'ka's rhetorical choices for Dokiia's emotional request provide curious insight into the heroine's thought process:

> "I haven't seen [you] in a long time," said the priest.
>
> "That's true, father – it's been a long time. The work keeps me busy ... but now I left everything and came here, so it's not too late ..."
>
> "What is it that you need?" he asked when he failed to guess it from her facial expression. The old woman did not respond right away. It was obvious that she was hesitant. She looked as if she was confused or frightened.
>
> "Did something happen to Iurko? Did he get in another fight?"
>
> "Oh, no, Iura is very polite."
>
> "Do you need to pay taxes, or, perhaps, you've been summoned to court?"
>
> "No ... I am here, dear father ... because ... because ... if I've heard it right, our empress, the mother of our whole land, died."
>
> "She was assassinated! She was killed by a wretched, criminal hand, woman, and this crime is calling on heaven for vengeance! God is with us ... She was a noble and innocent woman. She never hurt a fly ... So what is it that you want? ..."
>
> The Hutsul woman looked at him in silence for a moment ... and said, "I am very poor, very poor, dear father. You know best how poor I am. But ... here ... here it is, father. I have been saving and putting away money for a long time, and now I have five kronen. Don't be angry, take it, father, take it ... I give it with my sincere love [vid shchyroho sertsia]."
>
> "Why? What is it for?" he asked with surprise.
>
> "Don't despise it ... I give it with my sincere love. I saved it for my funeral and hid [it] in my pantry. Even my own child didn't know about it. My only child ... Take it."
>
> "What is it for?" repeated the priest ...
>
> "This is for her, for the empress, to hold a service for her, for our mother! Oh, father! She was the mother of our whole country [tsiloho kraiu] and such a mother has been killed! Won't Jesus come down from heaven and avenge her? He will do so ..." The white-haired man looked at her, and it seemed that for the first time in his life he couldn't find the right words to reply. (1927, 61)

The fragmented nature of Dokiia's speech not only conveys her shock, disbelief, confusion, and profound agitation but also reveals her deep psychological connection to the assassinated empress. She sees the empress as an ideal mother, an abstraction of the fatherland, peace, and prosperity and symbolically links the loss of the empress to her own death and to the destruction of her whole country. By emphasizing that she is not the only one who treats the empress as a maternal figure, the heroine links her sorrow to the deep mourning of the entire Austro-Hungarian nation and thus asserts her membership in a broader community. The priest's admiration for her sincere offering and his support of her call for just vengeance continue the theme. His heartfelt sympathy and respect for the heroine's emotional state invite the reader to see Dokiia not so much as a poor, insignificant, and "lost in the deep woods" peasant (1927, 61), but as a compassionate and devoted community member who inspires empathy rather than scorn or reproach.

Dokiia's loyalty to the Habsburg crown is further complicated in the story's ending, where the heroine sees off her only son, Iurko, to the Austro-Hungarian Army. The scene evokes the biblical story of the binding of Isaac, reinforcing the reader's appreciation of the genuine patriotism of the old Hutsul woman. The abrupt shift from the 1898 episode with the priest to the 1914 scene with Dokiia's mobilized son brings the two fragments together, symbolically connecting the assassination of a Habsburg with the outbreak of the First World War. This connection, in turn, presents Dokiia's son as another sincere and conscious sacrifice that the heroine makes to the imperial family. Dokiia's last conversation with her son is terse but emotionally charged. As is suggested by the narrator's commentary, both characters understand the grim prospects of Iurko's military service, realizing that this conversation might be their last. Both, however, demonstrate exemplary self-control and accept their civic duty, as did millions of their compatriots, with dignity and determination.

Dokiia's successful resolution of the profoundly painful struggle between her maternal love and her loyalty to the Habsburgs proves especially striking when we compare the final scene of "The Forest Mother" to a similar episode in Kobylians'ka's post-war short story "Vovchykha" ("The She-Wolf," 1923). Whereas Zoia Zhmut, the self-absorbed antiheroine of the latter story, convulses in lamentations and begs her sons not to go to war, rejecting their duty to the emperor, Dokiia methodically packs her son's sack and sees him off with only a few words of encouragement and a modest request. Dokiia's last words – "Write to me where you are going to be!" (1927, 62) – reveal her eagerness to stay connected to her son, now an imperial solder, and, by extension, to follow the ongoing political crisis that has taken him away. The actions of the two heroines after their respective sons leave prove even more telling. While Zoia Zhmut loses her sense of reality and collapses unconscious to the ground, Dokiia kneels gracefully in prayer, asking the two holy mothers of her people, the Mother God and the deceased empress, to look after her son. On a symbolic level, Zoia's collapse dramatizes her sorrow and inability to control the lives of her sons. Dokiia's prayer, in contrast, frames the scene of Iurko's departure as a ritual of divine sacrifice, as the last trial of Dokiia's loyalty akin to God's test of Abraham's faith, which celebrates her sincere devotion to the Habsburgs. The motif of a divine test also allowed Kobylians'ka to universalize Dokiia's response to the outbreak of the war. Although Kobylians'ka's ironic point, which lies in the fact that personalized and sacrificial notions and feelings of devotion are what enables Dokiia to come to terms with the modern war, is apparent, the story's final scene foregrounds Dokiia's wholehearted aspirations, which would appear to have been the aspirations of the great majority of Habsburg subjects. Despite radical ethnic, religious, and class differences that separated them internally, these people united as a single nation in August 1914 in the belief that giving their lives to emperor and country was the only right and honourable thing to do (Botushans'kyi et al. 2009, 148–9; Cross 1983, 1–10).

Similar veneration and devotion permeate Kobylians'ka's second war narrative, tellingly called "Sincere Love." The story aims to denounce tsarist imperialist politics during Russia's 1914–15 invasion of Bukovyna through a juxtaposition of emotions displayed by Russian and Austrian soldiers towards their respective monarchs. On the one hand, Kobylians'ka's fictional Russian soldiers express fearful obedience to their despotic tsar, whom they perceived as "cradled in opaque mist" and as "no more than a legend that dwells far away behind the walls of guards and armies ... in isolated rooms filled with treasure, sorrow, and blood-stained decrees" (1916, 12). On the other hand, her Austrian soldiers admire their emperor with unmatched earnestness. The story's most powerful scene takes place when the narrator and his interlocutor, a wounded Russian officer, unintentionally witness an Austrian soldier, an ethnic Ukrainian, praying to a portrait of Franz Joseph. Following Kobylians'ka's damning description of the Russian tsar and his imperialist campaign in Bukovyna, the Austrian soldier's naive but sincere appeal to his emperor – "You raised us; we grew up with you; we do not need any foreign tsars. God save you and us!" – can be read as the expression of a genuine appreciation for the economic, political, and cultural achievements Ukrainians attained under Habsburg rule before the outbreak of the First World War (1916, 12). This somewhat comical episode provides perhaps Kobylians'ka's most vivid depiction of the pro-Austrian attitude she shared with the majority of Western Ukrainians, who in 1914 considered Austria their legitimate homeland and hoped to resolve their national problems within the Habsburg Empire (Magocsi 2002, 73, 77–8; Snyder 2008, 95–148). In a historical setting where one could simultaneously be a Ukrainian patriot and a loyal Habsburg subject, Kobylians'ka's intricate fusion of Austrophilism and anti-tsarist sentiments could be read as an expression of loyalty not only to Austria but also to the Ukrainophile national project, which hoped before the First World War to inspire fellow Ukrainians in the Russian Empire to join Western Ukrainians in the creation of a new, unified Ukrainian entity under the benevolent rule of the Habsburgs (Magocsi 2002, 81–2; Subtelny 1988, 339–44; Karpynets' et al. 2005, 39–52).

Fictionalized Accounts of Combat, 1915–1917

In her later war narratives, Kobylians'ka maintained pro-Austrian attitudes throughout the early 1920s but began questioning the value of multiple loyalties and hybrid identities once the war revealed their inherent contradictions.[6] In the stories of late 1915 – "To Meet Their Fate," "Judas," and "A Letter from a Convicted Soldier to His Wife" – Kobylians'ka brought her Bukovynian characters into contact with German-speaking Austrian authorities or ethnically Ukrainian soldiers of the invading Russian army. The resulting interactions allowed her to explore the Ukrainian national project and its possibilities under either Austrian or Russian rule. By focusing on the debilitating confusion and consequent inability of her Bukovynian characters to understand, let alone influence, events that radically altered their lives, Kobylians'ka questioned the success of Ukraine's national project under any imperial rule, articulating the need for Ukraine's political independence for the first time.

"To Meet Their Fate" is the first text in the 1915–17 cycle. Its entire narrative structure is made up of seven interspliced episodes, which comprise an on-the-spot report of the Russian offensive culminating in the capture of Chernivtsi during Russia's second invasion of Bukovyna. Kobylians'ka dramatized her account by depicting the main battle from the perspective of the small peasant girl Nastka, contrasting the innocence of her childhood with the utter savagery of war. In the opening section, for example, the story situates little Nastka in a lush, pastoral setting prolific with sunflowers, rue, birds, bees, butterflies, and fruit-bearing gardens – a setting that represents war's symbolic "other" and hints by antithesis at the indescribable horrors of war. Paul Fussell offers a comprehensive analysis of pastoral details and their use in works of British writers, letter writers, and poets, who most hauntingly memorialize the First World War. In his observations, Fussell remarks, "If the opposite of war is peace, the opposite of experiencing moments of war is proposing moments of pastoral" (2013, 251). As Fussell indicates further, "recourse to the pastoral" is an effective means of both "fully gauging the calamities of the Great War and imaginatively protecting oneself [and the reader] against them" (2013, 255). Both modes are at play in Kobylians'ka's "To Meet

Their Fate."[7] Nastka's daydreaming about future love, marriage, and motherhood, implied by the folk song she hums while rocking her handmade rag doll, further amplify the dramatic effect of the opening pastoral moment. The next episode disrupts Nastka's play with heavy fire from machine guns and artillery, which "splash blood," "scatter chunks of human flesh," and "bring [the] hell" of the industrialized war into Bukovyna's pastoral paradise (IV:383). Oleksandr Dovzhenko, a notorious admirer of Kobylians'ka's work, canonized Kobylians'ka's image of the barbaric devastation of the serene sunflower field by modern artillery in the opening sequence of his 1939 film *Shchors*, thus acknowledging its expressionist power to illustrate the otherwise inexpressible brutality of the First World War.

In the remainder of the story, Kobylians'ka intertwines Nastka's immediate reactions to the war with brief, impersonal reports on the Russian army's crossing of the Prut River. The most infamous report describes the cold-blooded execution of surrendering Cossacks, whom Kobylians'ka loosely described as "a unit of the Russian army, mostly Ukrainians" (iakyis' viddil rosiis'koho viis'ka, zdebil'shoho tamoshni ukraintsi) (IV:379):

> Russian troops, both cavalry and infantry, were crowded in the water trying to get to the opposite shore, where entrenched Austrian soldiers, who were waiting for them, would, most likely, greet them with bullets or artillery fire. Those were painful moments ... Russian soldiers were about to reach the fortified shore ... They were almost there ... Suddenly, something happened, and no one knows whether it happened spontaneously or on someone's order. The swimming soldiers threw their rifles into the water, and every one of those who approached the shore raised his arm to signal surrender. All those who were watching them gasped for air – what would happen next? They [the Russian soldiers] cried and begged, while fighting the waves ... Both shores were tensed with terror. But suddenly ... what was it? Hundreds of shots rang out from behind the swimmers' backs – a frightful cry of pain pierced the air ... Almost everyone who raised his arm lowered it ... The arms rose one last time for a moment, a brief moment. One here ... another there ... A young head rose here, and one more with a wild expression of despair there ... Was [that soldier] saying his last goodbye? Was he begging for mercy? Was he complaining? No one knew it ... On the opposite shore, Austrian soldiers, who were prepared for a fight only a moment ago ... stood as if struck by lightning. Russian troops were shooting their own soldiers in the back. (IV:379–80)

The dry description of a bloody reality increases the scene's emotional charge, encouraging readers to visualize its brutality as captured in the telling silence of the bewildered Austrian soldiers. As one recent scholar points out, silence and speechlessness are a recurring theme in literature of the First World War, indicating much greater loss and pain than are often invisible at the time. Simultaneously, the critic adds, silence and speechlessness accentuate the incapacity of conventional literary forms, and ultimately of language itself, to represent the life and death of the war (Stevenson 2013, 47–53).

The scene, in which Nastka turns up trapped in no-man's-land in the midst of a battle, proves even more revealing in this respect:

> When small Nastka ... came to a field, she heard the crack of machine guns. Scared and shaken to her core, she started to run, and heavy tears clouded her vision. "Mommy!" She screamed with horror, "Daddy!" She looked around and started to run faster, but the crack of machine guns did not cease. She ran unconsciously, and did not know anymore where she was ... It seemed as if she was suddenly blinded. The only thing she could think about was how to cross the field as quickly as possible. She only wished to get away from the crack of machine guns, which rang terrifyingly in her ears, and which, it seemed to her, would throw her to the ground. She did not think of what could happen then ... She ran without stopping. The farther she ran, the greater her terror grew. It seemed as if she suddenly lost her wits. Her eyes were filled with tears so much that she did not know where to go anymore. She stopped for a moment and looked helplessly forward. Where was she? Where was she going? Why was she running? Oh, that terrifying crack of machine guns! She screamed loudly from fear ... There were as many troops on the ground as leaves on the trees ... But dear God ... Something cracked, hissed, and wailed in the air. Something terrible happened, and the earth shook under her feet ... Oh! What was she compared to that thundering power? An insect, a maybug ... a nothing ... She ... [fell] to the ground unconscious. She did not know how long she was lying there and what happened to her. It was one of those cannon shots that bring hell on earth, splash blood, and scatter chunks of human flesh. She finally got up. She looked as if every drop of blood had rushed out of her face. Her gaze was almost insane. She pulled herself together and made a few steps. Her whole being nearly screamed, "What does it all mean?" ... She wanted to go home. She moaned, but could not utter a single word ... "Mommy!" she screamed. Suddenly she stopped and opened her eyes even wider. What was that ... on the *other* side? Troops? A great deal of them ... They clustered together, and something was going on among those people ... Something drew her in the direction of the troops ... She could now distinguish the colour of their uniforms. It was muddy green. They were not Austrian soldiers; they were

> the enemy ... This was the end of her. She was standing in front of her death. She could feel it ... it was death ... death ... "Mommy!" was the last thing she screamed. (IV:383–4)

By recording the little girl's impressions articulated through cries of anguish, despair, and incomprehension of the ongoing battle, Kobylians'ka mixes silence with disorder, constructing expressionist images of mass slaughter and its aftermath. The story's emphasis on shell shock is particularly telling. Although "To Meet the Fate" follows the story of a small girl and her experience of war, there is a clear symbolic link between the shell-shocked heroine and millions of soldiers, many barely eighteen years old, who often lost self-control after they had experienced shells raining on them. The symbolic implication of a small, shell-shocked victim thus allowed Kobylians'ka to eradicate the sharp division between the civilian world and the world of the troops, which Fussell calls "the *versus* habit" and which, according to the critis, permeates war narratives and is often a sign of simplification (Fussell 2013, 86–90). Thereby, she was able to underpin the universal dehumanizing and demeaning nature of war.

The intrinsic value of "To Meet Their Fate" lies not only in its immediacy but also in its commentary on the "particular absurdity" of Ukraine's position in the First World War. Mobilized to two different imperial armies, Ukrainian soldiers were often forced to kill each other while defending the geopolitical interests of either Austria or Russia – but not Ukraine.[8] Although Kobylians'ka made no direct statements, dramatic irony underlines the bitter nickname that Nastka gives the Ukrainian soldier in the Russian army who carries her from the battle. She instantly classifies her saviour as "the enemy" because of his Russian military uniform, and does not stop calling him so even after her parents welcome the Russian imperial soldier into their house as a fellow Ukrainian. The irony intensifies in the closing episode when the adult characters, the Russian soldier and Nastka's father, discuss the tragic circumstances of their encounter and the grim paradox of their situation in which, despite their personal affinity, common language, and shared culture, they remain enemies. Previous scholars have written extensively on Kobylians'ka's implicit criticism of the "fratricidal" character of the First World War for Ukrainian combatants, overlooking, however, the writer's comments on how the war facilitated the formation of national consciousness among Ukrainian peasants (Babyshkin 1963, 173; Tomashuk 1969a, 187; Mel'nychuk 2006, 120). Although the overall tone of the men's encounter is grim, the closing scene optimistically recognizes that, despite the annihilation of the world into which the Russian soldier and Nastka's father were born, the First World War brought the Ukrainian population of the two rivalling empires together, intensifying, as Kobylians'ka hoped in 1915, their shared sense of national identity and ethnic solidarity.

Curiously, "To Meet Their Fate" is the only case in Kobylians'ka's war narratives in which the writer depicts an encounter between a Western Ukrainian and a Russian Ukrainian in a positive light. All her subsequent accounts of similar scenarios brim with indignation at the harsh treatment by Russian troops, and Cossacks in particular, of Bukovynian civilians during Russian military control of the region, especially during the Austrian counteroffensive, which began in May 1915. There is a historical explanation of this radical change in the writer's attitude. During the first months of the second Russian occupation of Chernivtsi, Kobylians'ka was pleasantly surprised and even flattered by frequent visits from numerous Eastern Ukrainians, who came to Bukovyna with the Russian military (Vozniuk 2006, 360–1). "As Muslims to Mecca," recalled one of Kobylians'ka's friends, "flowed the Dnieper Ukrainians to pay their respect to the Bukovynian writer" in those days (Korduba 1928, 235–6). Naturally, such recognition gave Kobylians'ka hope for friendly interactions, if not ethnic solidarity, between local Ukrainians and Russian Ukrainians in the tsarist army. The newly established Russian civilian administration, however, began to terrorize Ukrainian cultural, educational, and religious institutions in the region (Botushans'kyi et al. 2009, 150–3; Bryndzan et al. 1956, 296–301; Magocsi 2002, 25; Subtelny 1988, 341–4), and, as Kobylians'ka's next story, "Judas," indicates, quickly undermined the writer's initial enthusiasm for encounters between Bukovynian and Russian Ukrainians.

The short story "Judas," written only three months after "To Meet Their Fate," registers Kobylians'ka's growing frustration with the Russian military and her decision to rekindle pro-Austrian patriotism among her countrymen. As the story's title implies, "Judas" addresses issues of loyalty, betrayal, and consequent remorse. Like "To Meet Their Fate," the story depicts a fatal encounter between a Bukovynian peasant and a squadron of Russian Cossacks. Although in "Judas" Kobylians'ka did not differentiate Russian soldiers by ethnicity, as she did in "To Meet Their Fate," their ability to communicate with the Bukovynian old man suggests that they are at least Russian speaking, if not Ukrainian speaking. The Cossacks torture the old peasant to extract intelligence that helps them eliminate a unit of Austrian scouts. When the old man learns that his only son was among the slain Austrians, he realizes the tragic consequences of his betrayal, and, like Judas Iscariot, hangs himself out of remorse. His last words before the suicide call his countrymen "to go from house to house and tell people about him, the Judas, and warn them against becoming [traitors] like him" (IV:403). The story's psychological force and didactic message were immediately appreciated: in 1917 alone, "Judas" was published three times.

Kobylians'ka's next story, "A Letter from a Convicted Soldier to His Wife," addresses the issue of multiple loyalties by placing a Bukovynian soldier named Vasyl' in a German-speaking environment. Stylized as Vasyl''s five-page letter to his wife, which the character writes after his German-speaking superiors presumably wrongfully accuse him of treason, the story is "unmatched in Ukrainian literature in its powerful depictions of human emotions," as one past critic observes (Tomashuk 1969a, 183). Kobylians'ka, however, did not focus on Vasyl''s internal turmoil per se, but used it to dramatize the significance of the war to those who experienced it first-hand, be it in the trenches, at military headquarters, or on the home front. For example, while explaining his death sentence, Vasyl' comments at length on his time on the Italian Front, depicting his life in the trenches as a strange combination of tedium and horror, of degradation and brutalization:

> [In war] a man does not think. He trembles amidst the cannon fire; he is deaf; he is amidst roaring and screaming; he has no control over himself. The only thing he wants is to push forward the power of iron ... farther and farther ... faster and faster ... He is not the same man he was at home ... He is ... he is ... a *nothing* ... [In war] something other than men is at work. [In war] *iron* works and a soldier is nothing, and a man as he was at home is nothing, and hundreds and thousands – all mean nothing. (IV:373–4)

Using simple syntax, parallel constructions, and repetitive negations, Kobylians'ka intensified here Vasyl''s morbid remarks on the dehumanizing experience of war, which, as the character points out, transforms soldiers into insensible automatons, mere extensions of the machinery of war. Through Vasyl''s commentary, Kobylians'ka joined the broader discussion of the terrifying and demeaning experiences of war, which permeated war literature of her time and stood in sharp and ironic contrast to the heroic images of war circulating before 1914 and in the mainstream propaganda pamphlets. Tommaso Marinetti's futurist glorification of war as "the world's only hygiene" (2006, 11–17) and his call to fuse man with machine (2006, 210) appear particularly absurd in this context. As Kobylians'ka's passage suggests, war did indeed merge men with steel and machines, but instead of creating hyper-masculine, powerful bodies, it produced pitiful "cogs in a great machine," which, as another commentator of the First World War describes, "sometimes rolled forward, no one knew where, sometimes rolled backward, no one knew why" (Toller [1934], 82).

The underlying drama of Vasyl″s combat experience, as well as Kobylians'ka's overall anti-heroic treatment of war or the moral issues it raises, is exacerbated by the soldier's recollections of family and loved ones, of household and wheat fields, of work and religious holidays. By juxtaposing two distinct periods in Vasyl″s life, Kobylians'ka constructs a powerful and universal anti-war statement, linking her personal observations to the general attitude of her contemporaries, most of whom, like Vasyl', divided their lives into a pre-war phase of innocence and laughter and a post-war period of hopelessness and loss.

Vasyl″s letter, which blends anecdotes about his military service with memories of a peaceful life and parting instructions for his wife, also offers a curious social commentary on the intense struggle on the home front, which, as the character foresees, forced women into new social roles after the war. In fact, the opening account of Vasyl″s nightmare of his wife's multiple suicide attempts suggests that the character is more concerned with the future of his family and, by extension, his people than with his own fast-approaching death. Despite the gruesome descriptions of war and its dehumanizing effects, that is, the story is primarily concerned with Ukraine's national revival after the war. Throughout his letter, Vasyl' methodically reiterates an appeal to his wife "not to lose her mind" when she hears about his death, something that happens to many soldiers and officers when they see "too much blood and too many severed heads and limbs in battles" (IV:371; similar appeals reappear in the closing episode, 427). After the war, Vasyl' explains, his wife will need all her wits to raise children, restore life in peacetime, and, most importantly, preserve the memory of modern history's most catastrophic disaster. Here the reader is reminded about Kobylians'ka's earlier views on the pivotal role played by women in the biological and cultural regeneration of a nation, the profound significance of which becomes particularly evident during the war.[9]

In "A Letter from a Convicted Soldier to His Wife," as in previous war stories, Kobylians'ka intertwined universal statements with commentary of national significance. Foremost, she embedded both in Vasyl″s reflections on the ineffectiveness of his mother tongue, Ukrainian, during the Austro-Hungarian court martial. Critics tend to read Vasyl″s execution as a criticism on Kobylians'ka's part of the Austro-Hungarian authorities and their unjust persecution of thousands of Ukrainian peasants and low-ranking soldiers, whom they typically considered Russian spies during the First World War (Babyshkin 1963, 171; Tomashuk 1969a, 181–2; Komyshanchenko 1963, 39–40; Mel'nychuk

2006, 116–17). Factual data, however, problematize this reading. Although the Austro-Hungarian court-martial systems are rated among the harshest military justice systems in the First World War, the total number of Austro-Hungarian soldiers executed for desertion, 430, seems relatively modest if we consider that the Austro-Hungarian Amy mobilized over 7 million men during the war. Furthermore, although the overall number of soldiers that Austro-Hungarian courts martial sent to the firing squad for desertion is higher than the numbers of similar cases in other belligerent countries, accused soldiers on all sides enjoyed few legal protections and their punishments were generally swift and often harsh regardless of their ethnicity. As historians have shown, the primary purpose of military justice during the First World War was to maintain discipline; achieving justice in individual cases was a secondary concern (Welsh 2015, 12–15; Hochschild 2011, 242). Several textual and intertextual details in Kobylians'ka's story also suggest that the previous critical assessment of Vasyl''s court-martial experience merits a revision. For example, Kobylians'ka's stories "Judas" and "Tuha" ("Anguish," 1932) claim that some Bukovynian Ukrainians deserved punishment for treason, cowardice, and desertion but were pardoned once they explained their motives and expressed sincere regret for their misconduct. These stories suggest that the Austrian government strove, and often succeeded, in remaining as fair and humane as before the war, when its judicial system was ranked among the most just in the world. Kobylians'ka promoted a similar idea in another story, "Voiennyi akord" ("A Chord of War," 1932), in which a former captain and a court-martial judge of the Austro-Hungarian imperial army, also an ethnic Ukrainian, confesses his remorse for the death sentences he endorsed during the war because he had neither the time nor the means to continue investigations. In this light, Vasyl' thus appears not so much a victim of the Austro-Hungarian military justice, which, as he himself admits, must be "inexorable and quick like a machine gun" during wartime (IV:374), but as a victim of the same social and political disintegration that undermined the Austrian government and toppled the Habsburg Empire. Vasyl''s inability to communicate with high-ranking officers in Ukrainian, in turn, also seems not as much a commentary on the injustices that Ukrainian soldiers suffered in the imperial army but as a much broader statement on the overall ineffectiveness of the power structure of the Habsburg Empire and its imperial army, where three-quarters of the officers were of German-speaking stock but only one enlisted man in four understood the language.

The fact that Vasyl''s unjust persecution forces him to re-evaluate his own role in the ongoing conflict and to ponder the overall contribution of Ukrainians to Austro-Hungarian society also merits recognition but has attracted no critical attention in the past.[10] As Vasyl' suggests in his confession, the war not only breaks but also transforms him. In addition to reforging his understanding of ethnic and national identity, the war redefines his views on loyalty and the motherland. Vasyl's new revelations reflect one of the major political demands of the time among Western Ukrainians, whose less conciliatory attitudes towards Austrian rule by the end of the war led them to the conclusion that the Ukrainian national project was ultimately incompatible with Austria's imperial interests.[11] Kobylians'ka continued her discussion on Ukraine's self-recognition that took place during the First World War in another short story of the same period, "Snyt'sia" ("A Dream," 1917). The story is structured as a surrealist dream sequence, a nightmare, which depicts a dialogue between two groups of people separated by a river: a group of combatants and a group of civilians, mostly women, children, and elders. The fragmented narrative structure of the dialogue, along with its highly expressionist language, conveys the disorientation of the war and the immense suffering it imposed on Western Ukrainians. While foregrounding brutalization and destruction, the story also suggests that, despite its pain, war allowed for the rediscovery of the virtues necessary for Ukrainian national life and promised to put them into practice anew. The last two fragments of the story comment on the nascent vision of the post-war world held by Western Ukrainians, both combatants and civilians. Neither group has a clear vision of the future; however, both groups express palingenetic hope for Ukraine's revival, as implied in the ultimate mission that the old men set for their mobilized offspring – "to leave *their* trace on *their own* land" – and the soldiers' commitment to return from the war and to carry out this mission (IV:411).

Post-war Revisions

After the war, Kobylians'ka continued to explore the notion of national self-recognition and rediscovery, embedding it in the historical and social context of the early 1920s. Her first post-war work on the subject, "Vasylka," came out in 1922. Its plot revolves around the war experiences of its title character, a Bukovynian peasant woman, and narrates the story of how during Russia's third occupation of Bukovyna she hid from the Russian troops a fugitive prisoner of war, a Ukrainian soldier in the Austro-Hungarian imperial army named Ivan Rotenchuk. Despite obvious ties to Kobylians'ka's earlier war narratives, "Vasylka" constitutes a qualitatively different text because it focuses on memory, recovery, and the transition to a new future. Stylistically, "Vasylka" also deviates from Kobylians'ka's previous war narratives. Although the story takes place during the Brusilov Offensive, the Russian Empire's greatest feat of arms during the First World War and one of the most lethal offensives in world history, it offers no direct descriptions of carnage, which characterize Kobylians'ka's 1915–17 stories.[12] Instead, it uses an elaborate and highly condensed allegory to evoke the apocalyptic nature of the First World War, displaced into an eerie dream, or better a nightmare, that Vasylka's husband, Maksym, sees seven years before the war breaks out:

> The night before his departure [for Canada] ... [Maksym dreams that] he walks as if in his own field, looking for its boundaries amid other landowners' fields, but cannot find them. His field and the fields of those other people are such a flat plain, which blends off in the distance with the sky so sincerely, that it makes you think: if you can get that far you'll touch heaven itself. But wait, not quite. Things never go the way man wants, but the way God Almighty wills. Maksym strains his eyes trying to distinguish the boundaries of his field, which he knows like his hands, plowed by years of work, but instead he catches a glimpse – and what does he see? From that far-off place where the earth and the sky usually meet as if greeting each other at daybreak, enormous billows of smoke are emerging quickly, one after another, and all of this is rolling directly onto the fields. Onto the fields, I say. Some slither like black vipers up into the sky, and others coil over the fields like snakes. What could it be? If it does not turn out for good, it will bring about something violent. And what do you know – here it comes. A white, elongated horse emerges from the smoke. The horse is without a saddle, its neck stretched for six hands. It is terribly emaciated. As if from a bullet wound, blood gushes from between its ribs. With its mouth wide open, the horse gallops feverishly, braying mournfully and menacingly. Billows of smoke rise behind it. The field is no longer a field, not a green wave of new sprouts, not God's freshly plowed land, but some kind of wasted plain, covered with dried lumps of turned-up soil, one larger than the other, and trenches of some sort. Is it a desert? What else can it be? (1927, 16; Ladygina trans., 125)

Maksym's dream foreshadows the upcoming brutal events by using images of plundered fields and a wounded horse that have come to epitomize the senseless destruction of the First World War. Later in the story, Kobylians'ka directly links Maksym's dream to the war by using similar images to announce the war's outbreak:

> Then the war broke out ... It broke out and shook the world ... The earth was ripped apart, turned over, and flooded with blood. That was when it really got going. Everything was covered with corpses. The voices of humans,

> animals, and cannon wailed, filling the air with their sound. Wounded soldiers wandered to and fro. The white, black, and brown ghosts of horses fell heavily to the ground ... At night ... black crows came flying in and hurriedly descended to the ground. (1927, 20; Ladygina trans. 129)

When taken together, these two episodes arguably offer Kobylians'ka's most aestheticized representation of the war, a "mad dream" that destroyed millions of human lives and turned Europe into a wasteland. Vasylka's brief but graphic commentary on Maksym's death in an explosion, which he was supervising while working on railroad construction in Canada, is also complicit with the mutilation and dismemberment of the battlefield:

> [When Vasylka] made an inquiry [about Maksym], a letter came [from Canada] saying that he had died. They wrote he had been blowing up some cliffs with dynamite for a railroad. He was working there, and one time he, his supervisor and a few other men were blown up in a blast. Only his hands, they wrote, were found. Of the others – a leg, a head, and some pieces of flesh, like in a war. That was all. (1927, 35; Ladygina trans. 143)

The direct comparison between Maksym's and his co-workers' torn-up bodies and the carnage of the modern warfare that took place during the First World War suggests that this episode serves as another displacement of the violent war experience before which the mind and the ability to articulate inevitably retreat. Like tropes of silence and incoherent speech, which figure in Kobylians'ka's 1915–17 stories, both allegorical episodes in "Vasylka" – Maksym's nightmare and the story of his death – render Western rationality and conventional forms of communication dysfunctional. At the same time, they also communicate a new tendency in Kobylians'ka's treatment of the war – an unremitting desire to come to terms with the traumatic experiences of the recent past and to transition to a new future free of fear, disillusionment, and regret.

To amplify the critical distance between the reader and the traumatic events of the war, and thus to facilitate a productive reassessment of the war and its aftermath, Kobylians'ka used elements of *skaz* and even comedy in "Vasylka." This is another stylistic choice that sets Kobylians'ka's 1922 story apart from her earlier war narratives. The comic element comes across particularly strong in the second part of the story structured as Vasylka's dialogic monologue. Chaotically recreated dialogue exchanges between the heroine and different Russian,

Austrian, and Bukovynian characters constitute much of this monologue. Using distinctive colloquialisms and, on occasion, forms taken from vernacular dialect, Kobylians'ka forged an alternative style that was purged of inflated language and conventional stereotypes to communicate Vasylka's individual war experience and to locate it in the broader historical context. The heroine's verbal inventiveness and resourceful manipulation of language not only demonstrate her ability to adapt but also highlight Kobylians'ka's own experimentation with narrative structures that explores the limits of language in expressing the unutterable trauma of war. Similarly, Vasylka's anecdotes about how she outsmarts Russian soldiers, local spies, and fellow villagers, as well as the overall naiveté and clumsiness of her *skaz* narration, have ultimately a double function. Vasylka's humour serves both as a defence mechanism that helps the heroine to make her war experience tolerable and as a means for Kobylians'ka to emphasize her heroine's profound emotional turmoil. In one of the most revealing examples of this double-edged humour, Vasylka recalls a startling tragicomedy she staged that combined seduction, self-pity, and flattery in the attempt to avoid execution after Russian troops find the Austrian fugitive soldier in her house:

> When the Muscovites took [Ivan], they told the villagers and me that we were facing *years in Siberia* ... Early next morning, I went to see [a local informer].
>
> "Would you be so kind as to appeal to those in power not to punish me and not to send me to Russia ..." I asked him.
>
> At this moment, the commander in charge of the search entered.
>
> "We captured *that* soldier at *this* woman's house," he said.
>
> "Why did you hide the Austrian?" he asked, turning toward me.
>
> "Gentlemen! For seven years, I have been living without a husband. It's been four since I last heard from him. I think he is already dead. And I love *this* man, and he loves me. He doesn't have a wife and we could have gotten married. And he also used to tell me, 'I wish the Muscovites stayed here longer because when our Austrians return they'll either shoot me or send me back into the trenches, and you wouldn't have me anyway. The Muscovites are very kind people. If they take me to Russia, it might be even better for me. They are kind people.'"
>
> But everything that I told them wasn't true. I had to be cunning, so that the Muscovites wouldn't get angry and wouldn't kill us.
>
> "She loves the Muscovites," the commandant continued. "Sure she loves them. But we were told that your Austrian officers left money for you to hide him, and that he is a spy – it's just that simple."

"Our officers didn't leave us any money, and I fed and housed this man out of love, and he didn't trick the Muscovites," I objected once again.

"So how much do you love him?" the commandant and the informer asked me then.

"Very much, gentlemen, as much as I love my own heart. Let me see him one last time."

At this point, both men burst out laughing.

"We know," the commandant said, "how love goes. I am sorry you haven't had a husband for seven years, but ... perhaps ... perhaps we can help you a little." (1927, 29–31; Ladygina trans. 138–9)

Here Vasylka openly admits her frustrated sex life while indirectly hinting that only the Russian troops can help her with this grievance, which makes the Russian officers giggle. The sharp juxtaposition between the humorous mode of narration and the formidable circumstances, however, also communicates the heroine's extreme distress. The overall flatness of Vasylka's story, and its focus on mere surface events, betrays tremendous internal pressures and invites readers to probe the heroine's immediacy of speech more deeply in order to reconstruct her inner thoughts and feelings.

Kobylians'ka's use of allegory, comedy, and *skaz,* which often entail cultural and social criticism, along with the turbulent historical context of the story's creation, suggests the possibility of embedded political commentary. For example, Vasylka's relationship with the fugitive Ivan and the interactions of the two Ukrainian characters with the Russian soldiers can be viewed as an allegorical reference to the unified effort of Ukrainophile forces to resist Russia's occupation during the First World War, as well as during Ukraine's struggle against the Bolsheviks in 1918–22. Curiously, the collective image of Russian soldiers is identified throughout the story with the popular ethnonym *Moskali* (the Muscovites), which acquired new ideological connotations in the early 1920s. During the nineteenth century, the word *Moskali* typically designated a soldier in the Russian imperial army and carried mild negative connotations.[13] After the Bolshevik Revolution, however, it became an ethnic slur and a derogatory epithet for Russian Bolsheviks and all pro-Moscow opponents of Ukraine's political independence.[14] Kobylians'ka's choice of the word *Moskali,* which appears nowhere in her earlier fiction, thus indicates a shift in the writer's attitude towards Russians. In 1915–17, Kobylians'ka rarely described Russian soldiers in exclusively negative terms and often justified their cruelty in combat or ameliorated it with their humanity. In 1922, however, she depicted Russians as a gang of simpletons, rapists, and thieves, highlighting their lack of loyalty and national pride.[15] As one Russian spy openly states in a conversation with Vasylka, Russian troops "would sell Russia for two kopecks" (1927, 31; Ladygina trans. 139). Kobylians'ka's pejorative representations of Russian troops, and by extension their government, suggest that in 1922, she, like many Western Ukrainian patriots, had no longer any illusions as to Ukraine's political future under the new Russian government.

In turn, the emasculated image of the fugitive Ukrainian soldier, Ivan Rotenchuk, who was fighting his war of attrition entrenched under Vasylka's bed, suggests that in 1922 Kobylians'ka also held a realistic view of the effectiveness of the Ukrainian army and the political institutions it represented. Her parodic commentary becomes most sardonic when Vasylka cross-dresses Ivan as a woman. Once the heroine costumes him in "her shirt and her skirt, makes him a head-dress out of her scarf, cloaks him in two sheepskin coats, and gives him her small boots," Ivan loses the last traces of his already fragile manhood and becomes the object, rather than the subject, of ongoing historical events (1927, 23; Ladygina trans. 132). His symbolic castration reaches its pinnacle shortly afterward, when two Russian soldiers attempt to rape him, mistaking him for a woman. We can easily view the representation of a Ukrainian soldier as a demoralized, somewhat cowardly, and helpless product of Ukraine's psychological unpreparedness for the First World War and, by implication, for the consequent struggle for national liberation as Kobylians'ka's contribution to the revanchist criticism of Ukraine's political weakness in the wake of the war.[16] Kobylians'ka revisited this theme in her last novel, *Apostol cherni* (*Apostle of the Rabble*, 1936), which will be discussed in the next chapter.

Like many other cultural and political commentators of the time, Kobylians'ka combined her critique of Ukraine's political ineffectiveness with her alternative vision of post-1918 Ukraine. She embedded it in the image of Vasylka. Kobylians'ka's 1922 conception of Ukraine's political future substantially differs from the flamboyant images of a new Ukraine that her radical nationalist compatriots forged in the mid-1920s. Dmytro Dontsov and Ievhen Malaniuk, leading intellectuals of the interwar Ukrainian nationalist movement, for example, glorified aggressive masculinity and military action. They used female characters only to castigate Ukraine's political immaturity in the hopes of bolstering Ukraine's interwar state-building efforts with a new warrior ethos. Kobylians'ka, in contrast, conveyed her understanding of Ukraine's current political situation through a robust and resourceful female character. In comparison either to the heroines violated by *Moskali* and canonized by the leading nineteenth-century Ukrainian poet Taras Shevchenko or to their shocking adaptations by Ievhen Malaniuk, who often depicts Ukraine as the whore of khans, tsars, and sultans, Kobylians'ka's post-war heroine has clearly positive symbolic connotations.[17]

Even the heroine's name, a derivative of the masculine Vasyl', suggests that Vasylka embodies the strong, proactive, and self-sufficient woman who the unfortunate hero of "A Letter from a Convicted Soldier to His Wife" implores his wife to be. The first part of "Vasylka" emphasizes the profound transformation in character that the heroine undergoes once Maksym goes to work in Canada, leaving her alone with two small children. Despite the difficulty of farm work, Vasylka quickly discovers that skill and diligence are as serviceable as strength, and that the traditionally gendered division of household tasks is mere convention. During her six years of independently running the household, Vasylka increases her livestock, buys new shares of land, and learns how to negotiate with bankers, market traders, and government officials. Simultaneously, she gradually transforms "from a slim, young, and girlish-looking woman" into "a serious, robust, and hard-working mistress of the house" (1927, 18–19; Ladygina trans. 128). Vasylka's mature image resembles another unusual peasant woman, in Kobylians'ka's 1897 short story "Uncultured." Like the 1897 heroine Paraska, Vasylka is self-sufficient, hard-working, full of energy, determined, clever, outspoken, and exceptionally resourceful in protecting her interests. The narrator acknowledges Vasylka's assertiveness and authority by describing her scrutinizing eyes and piercing gaze, which "demand respect" and "evoked discomfort" (1927, 4; Ladygina trans. 128), granting the heroine the symbolic agency of someone who looks and not someone who is looked at. Vasylka, however, is more than a mere post-war revision of Paraska. Although Vasylka, like Paraska, has no formal education, her systematic exposure to urban culture helps her to understand better her social, cultural, and historical context, and develop a strong sense of belonging to broader communities, both local and imperial. Consequently, while Paraska remains, owing to her childlike naiveté and blissful ignorance, the subject of a dreadful and aimless existence, tellingly captured in her nearly fatal night wandering through the woods in search of the magic devil's mill (II:323–55), Vasylka courageously stands up to the challenges of the First World War, demonstrating heroism so exceptional that it places her on an equal, if not superior, footing with her cultured contemporaries. Vasylka's physical, spiritual, and cognitive transformation suggests that Ukraine emerged from the First World War as a radically new entity with a fervent anti-Moscow sentiment, which, along with its pronounced Austrophilism, we can interpret as a clearly defined national goal: a Ukrainian state both independent of Russia and with a strong pro-European orientation.

Kobylians'ka, however, was far from being naively optimistic about Ukraine's political prospects after the war. The story's grim ending, full of drab domestic details, suggests that Kobylians'ka was bitterly aware that although Ukraine survived the war, its toll was staggering, with the country's people emotionally crippled and incapable of dissociating themselves from the tragic past. The only hope the writer left for Vasylka's post-war recovery, and, by extension, for Ukraine's political revival, lies in the character of Vasylka's teenage son Dmytryk and his determination to wipe away all tears from his mother's eyes – a vivid personification of the new post-war generation of Ukrainians and their commitment to the national cause. Dmytryk's aspiration to ease Vasylka's suffering suggests that in 1922, Kobylians'ka, like many of her contemporaries, realized that overcoming the full effects of the war would occupy not only the generation that survived it but also many future generations.

Kobylians'ka's 1923 story "Ziishov z rozumu" ("A Madman"), in which a fatally wounded Ukrainian officer prophesies Ukraine's political resurrection, promotes a similar message. Although the story of the young Ukrainian officer who is left to die by the side of the road because his wounds are beyond treatment has a pitiful and somewhat ironic ending, his final words, which a passerby interprets as an ominous delirium, imply the same transformation of ethnic and national awareness suggested in the 1917 short story "A Letter from a Convicted Soldier to His Wife":

> Until the very end, I faced the bullets thinking it was for *Ukraine* ... But now, I lie here, like that [dying] dog thrown in a waste pit ... There is no room for a Ukrainian [anywhere else] ... But where would it be ... This is a soldier's end ... But please let me know when *the one* [Ukraine] I was fighting for would revive ... I'm dying, but *it* [Ukraine] would not perish. (IV:417–18)

While lamenting over his personal tragedy, the dying officer also acknowledges here that despite, or perhaps precisely because of, its destructiveness and pervasive injustice, the war helped to crystalize among Western Ukrainians the previously inchoate national aspirations for political independence, a goal that defined post-war Ukrainian politics.

Conclusion

The catastrophic events of 1914–18 functioned for Kobylians'ka, as for many of her contemporaries across Europe and beyond, as the catalyst for a thorough revision of her pre-war beliefs. While focusing on the transformations in the Bukovynian character, Kobylians'ka's war stories redefine key universal notions of loyalty, duty, honour, political agency, and artistic expression. They thereby contribute to the reshaping of the traditional understanding of Europe's first shocking experience with modern mass warfare and the role of the individual in it. The clearly defined chronological shifts in Kobylians'ka's representations of the Bukovynian home front, along with her creative assessment of the Austro-Hungarian and Russian treatment of Western Ukrainians during different stages of the war, expose anew fatal political weaknesses in Europe's old imperial order. More importantly, they provide a better understanding of why Ukrainians, like other so-called non-historic ethnic groups without states of their own to protect their specific interests, began to pursue their national goals more aggressively as the war progressed.[18] The early cycle of Kobylians'ka's war stories shows that already in the nineteenth century representatives of marginalized ethnic and social groups, such as Bukovynian peasants, were able to identify with a larger community and forge a cosmopolitan Austro-Hungarian identity that superseded their local, ethnic, and national identities. Kobylians'ka's reflections on the Ukrainian case imply that this stratified, multilayered identification took place in response to a variety of economic, political, religious, and social gains that some under-represented ethnic groups achieved under Austrian rule prior to the First World War. The second cycle of Kobylians'ka's war stories, however, suggests that the identification with a larger community lasts so long as people remain confident in the fulfilment of their basic human, ethnic, and national rights. Once these rights are violated, Kobylians'ka's stories assert, marginalized ethnic groups tend to reorganize around small-scale alternatives that help them cope with a major global crisis such as the First World War. While some critics might view the shift in focus to the local as a sign of social retrogression, Kobylians'ka, alongside other defenders of the right of small nations to self-determination, viewed it as a positive development and envisioned national space as a venue to protect the right of non-historical nations without a state of their own, such as Ukraine, thereby protect heterogeneity and democratic world interests.

The variety of ways in which Kobylians'ka articulated her encounter with war testifies that she, like many other war commentators, quickly discovered the inadequacy of traditional literary conventions in capturing the unspeakable horrors of war and ventured to search for alternative rhetorical means of expression. Although Kobylians'ka's experimentation with language reveals many points of contact with other authors who wrote about the First World War, the stylistic idiosyncrasies of her prose, particularly her use of *skaz* and tragicomedy, as well as its specific thematic and ideological aspects, highlight a wide spectrum of reactions among the general European population, a spectrum whose plurality remains far from complete. Her representations of Bukovynian peasant women also illustrate that women's collective experiences of the First World War were not confined to that of Western European, middle-class women. They open a fresh perspective on women's intense struggle for survival in war zones and their unique role in preserving the memory of one of the greatest catastrophes in modern history. Therefore, Kobylians'ka's war writings deserve a place in the expanding canon of war literature, not only as legitimate studies of national attitudes, cultural awakening, and a redefinition of the Western Ukrainian self, but also as valuable cultural documents that help us to recreate and reimagine the collective experience of 1914–18 and force us to reconsider the enormous social, political, economic, and cultural repercussions of war.

Chapter Six

Between the Right and the Left

The First World War officially ended with the signing of the Treaty of Versailles and a series of additional agreements that assigned liabilities for reparations, imposed military restrictions, and redrew national borders in four continents. While some commentators celebrated this as "the most far-reaching and comprehensive settlement ever effected in any international dispute" (Lloyd George 1938, 17), years later many scholars came to agree with Alfred Milner, one of Britain's five signatories of the Treaty of Versailles, who prophetically called it "a Peace to end Peace" (qtd. in Hochschild 2011, 357–8). Although the Allies supported the newly emerged states in their right to national self-determination, and established the League of Nations to oversee the implementation of peace treaties and regulate potential future conflicts, the recklessly harsh terms that they imposed on Germany and the insufficient attention that they paid to Bolshevik Russia provided the essential conditions for the rise of the twentieth century's two greatest totalitarian regimes, Nazism and Stalinism, which eventually led to an even more brutal and costly war.

Like the Germans, the Ukrainians, who numbered almost 40 million and who had struggled to assert their national statehood in the aftermath of the First World War and the Bolshevik Revolution, found themselves among peoples who were mistreated by the Allies. In 1918, Ukraine was divided among four states: Central and Eastern Ukraine went under Bolshevik control, Galicia and Western Volhynia were incorporated into Poland, Transcarpathia became part of Czechoslovakia, and Bukovyna became part of Romania. The public disdain for being dictated to by the Allies rankled deeply across the political spectrum, eroding support for the moderate and pro-democratic aspirations that defined Ukraine's pre-war politics. In the atmosphere of political frustration, many prominent Ukrainians came to believe that liberalism, democracy, and a lack of will were to blame for Ukraine's political fiasco of 1917–20. A new generation of political activists began to emphasize authority, solidarity, discipline, and strong leadership as essential to the successful achievement of Ukraine's national goal – an independent and ethnically homogeneous Ukrainian state – promoting the radical shift from liberal and democratic discourse to an alternative model of national revival offered by Western fascism. As the disillusionment with Western democracies and dissatisfaction over Joseph Stalin's repressions in Soviet Ukraine grew, interwar fascism became increasingly appealing to independently minded Ukrainian patriots as perhaps the only remaining means of bolstering nationalism and thereby giving Ukraine a chance to consolidate its people in their fight against foreign colonization. By the mid-1930s, Ukrainian patriots in Western Ukraine and among Ukrainian émigrés were convinced that only radical means could help them change the existing political order and were prepared to battle all who stood in their path (Motyl 1980).

Kobylians'ka, one of the very few living canonical writers of the pre-war era, found herself in the midst of the post-war political debates and at the centre of public attention when diverse Ukrainian political camps began to compete for her ideological support in the 1920s. The grand celebrations of the fortieth anniversary of her creative career, known as the "all-Ukrainian jubilee of the writer" (zahal'noukrains'ke sviatkuvannia iuvileiu avtorky), which took place between November 1927 and June 1928, is a telling testimony to the profound role that the Ukrainian public assigned to Kobylians'ka and her works in the forging of a new modern Ukrainian identity and in the reunification of the Ukrainian people in the interwar period. Kobylians'ka's admirers and political opponents alike organized a series of jubilee concerts, commemorative lectures, and public readings of her latest works in all of the major cities in Soviet and Western Ukraine and in more than forty locations in Europe and North America. As one commentator rightly observed, it was the most grandiose jubilee of a living writer in Ukrainian history to that date (Kohut 1928, 102). The most dazzling celebrations took place in Chernivtsi and Kolomyia, both of which Kobylians'ka attended in person. For these occasions, poets wrote jubilee odes, musicians composed hymns (see figure 7), publishers released special issues of journals and editions of Kobylians'ka's collected works, scholars wrote critical essays, and hundreds of Ukrainian institutions and organizations of diverse political orientations – from the Union of Ukrainian Nationalist Youth, which shortly became the founding member of the Organization of the Ukrainian Nationalists (OUN), to the Communist Party of the Bolshevik Ukraine (CPBU) – expressed

ІПОЛІТ ОМЕЛЬСЬКИЙ

ПРИВІТ і СЕРЕНАДА

пісні на муж. хор

ПРИСВЯТА

Високодостойній Пані

ОЛЬЗІ КОБИЛЯНСЬКІЙ

укр. письменниця, Доктор honoris causa Укр. Вільного Універзітету в Празі, почесна членка товариств: „Жіноча Громада“ і „Український Народний Дім“ в Чернівцях, американських і инших заграничних інстітуцій і т. д.

з нагоди річниці 76-літних уродин
дня 27. листопада 1939.

Випуск V. Видане тов. „Буковинський Кобзарь“. Ціна 20 л.

Figure 7. Dedication pamphlet, Chernivtsi, 1939

ПРИВІТ.

Слова й музика
Іполіта Омельського.

2. Володарко тайн відвічних
царства гір і пралісів,
Весь народ Тебе шанує,
людства гордосте верхів.

3. Най живе краси жрекиня,
всвідомителька жінок,
Зірка рідного писменства,
слави народу вінок.

4. В цей святочний день врочистий
щирий наш прийми привіт,
Хай Бог зволить Ти прожити
мирно, щасно много літ!

СЕРЕНАДА.

Слова й музика
Іполіта Омельського.

2. Ой, та цвітка наша гордість,
Музи духова донька,
Це пера мистеця славна,
Рідная писателька.

3. Ти нам дала красні твори,
Повні ніжного чутя,
Мов ті перли, мов мережка, —
Чим захоплюєсь душа.

4. Жий, велика Ти Землячко,
Народу й собі на честь,
Твої успіхи і слава
Щира нам утіха й лесть.

ROMÂNIA
ŢINUTUL SUCEAVA

Cenzurat

No. 30383/39 — Cernăuţi, 12/XI 1939.
s. s. Tomorug.

Tipografia JEREMIE OPRIŞEANU, Cernăuţi, Piaţa Ghica Vodă 5

their veneration in telegrams and letters that came to Chernivtsi from around the world. Along with many other prominent Ukrainian intellectuals and politicians, Mykhailo Hrushevs'kyi, Mykola Zierov, Serhii Iefremov, Ahatanhel Kryms'kyi, Hryhorii Kosynka, Mykola Kulish, Ostap Vyshnia, Bohdan Lepkyi, Oleksandr Kolessa, Mykyta Shapoval, Dmytro Dontsov, and Mykola Skrypnyk sent their greetings to Kobylians'ka. Lev Kohut included most of these telegrams and letters in the jubilee almanac that he published in Chernivtsi in July 1928. While some of the congratulators exalted Kobylians'ka exclusively as the populist writer, "the author of *The Earth* and *On Sunday Morning She Gathered Herbs*" (Hrushevs'kyi, qtd. in Kohut 1928, 115), and some hoped that these populist trends in Kobylians'ka's earlier fiction would eventually lead to a more pro-Soviet positions in the writer's world view and that in the future she would "devote her work to the interests of the working class" (Skrypnyk, qtd. in Kohut 1928, 118), others hailed her as a committed modernizer of Ukrainian culture and equated the power of her words to the "thousands of bayonets" that bravely fought for Ukraine's independence in 1917–20 (Kohut 1928, 141). Regardless of their own political persuasions, admirers around the world unequivocally recognized Kobylians'ka as not only a leading writer of their time, "the Princess of Ukrainian literature" (Kohut 1928, 116, 145), but also as an important public figure and a living prophet, whose works exhibited a unique power to heal the wounds of the recent political failures and to consolidate Ukrainians around a new national ideal. In his letter, Hryhorii Kosynka, one of the most outstanding Ukrainian short-story writers of the 1920s, captures the new significance that Kobylians'ka and her works had acquired in the interwar period most eloquently:

> We celebrate your jubilee, this historical day for Ukrainian culture, in difficult and sombre times when our land [is divided between hostile powers] ... but I believe, beloved teacher, as deeply as your heroine Verkovychivna used to believe that "although [our enemies] might oppress us ... and take measures that ... [would] claim many of our lives, they would never be able to decimate us as a nation (*iak natsiiu*) ... I am confident that if even one hundredth of my people feel the way I feel, we won't perish!" (qtd. in Kohut 1928, 116)

Other congratulators, who were committed to the cause of Ukraine's independence, echoed Kosynka's rhetoric by wishing their "beloved teacher" from Bukovyna a long and productive life in hopes that her future works would continue to transcend all borders and unite

Ukrainians around the world "to their delight and the fear of their enemies" (*na radist' nam i na strakh voroham nashym*) (Kohut 1928, 141).

Although it might be an exaggeration to say that those who opposed Ukraine's independence saw Kobylians'ka and her influence on the Ukrainian people as a serious threat, they surely realized the important role she played in Ukrainian culture and took measures to neutralize her potential collaboration with Ukrainian nationalists. While the Romanian regime put Kobylians'ka under strict surveillance and banned all her works from publication, the Soviet authorities invested a lot of energy and resources to secure her ideological support. As Kobylians'ka's correspondence with Mykola Biliach, the chief editor of the Rukh (Movement) publishing house in Soviet Kharkiv, testifies, the Soviets provided Kobylians'ka with funds to purchase and renovate her first house in Chernivtsi; awarded her an honorary monthly pension of 150 Soviet rubles, which the writer received regularly for the rest of her life;[1] and released more than twenty different editions of her collected works alongside the first edition of her complete works in nine volumes that came out in Kharkiv in 1927–9.[2] Although Kobylians'ka accepted the much-needed financial support from the Soviet government and eagerly pursued every opportunity to disseminate her works "na Velykii Ukraini" (in Great Ukraine), she did not support the Soviet regime directly and continually emphasized in all her public speeches and official correspondence of the late 1920s and 1930s that "she never took any part in ... political life ... because she knew very little about politics, and only used her skills and energy to serve Ukrainian culture" (V:658). Kobylians'ka's close association with pro-Ukrainian periodicals and publishing houses in Western Ukraine, elsewhere in Europe, and North America,[3] and even more so the radical and openly pro-Ukrainian themes of her late fiction, suggest, however, that not only did she remain firm in her dedication to the Ukrainian nation-building project, but she also worked hard on positioning herself as a national writer. She also put a lot of effort into staying relevant in a political and cultural environment where radical nationalism constituted the main discourse and where strategies on how to overcome Ukraine's political failure to assert its independence in 1917–20 were at the centre of public discussions. Kobylians'ka's major work of the interwar period, *Apostol cherni* (*Apostle of the Rabble*, 1936) – a deliberately patriotic story of an esteemed Western Ukrainian officer in search of personal freedom and meaningful vocation on the eve of a major modern war in Europe – testifies that in the 1920s and the early 1930s Kobylians'ka refused to accept the existing political situation and continued to develop her discourse on

Ukraine's independence. The honorary doctoral degree (honoris causa) from the Ukrainian Free University in Prague, a university-in-exile, which Kobylians'ka received for her contribution to Ukraine's liberationist cause in 1931, shortly after the original publication of *Apostle of the Rabble* in the Prague-based journal *Nova Ukraina* (*A New Ukraine*), as well as the novel's immense popularity among Western Ukrainian readers in the late 1930s, provides even more telling insight into the depth of ideological significance that Kobylians'ka's works acquired in the interwar period for Ukrainians in Western Ukraine and Ukrainian émigrés elsewhere in Europe and North America.

Upon its publication in 1936, *Apostle of the Rabble* – a story that offers a panoramic view of the life of the Western Ukrainian intelligentsia by introducing, unlike any other of Kobylians'ka's works, many significant characters from different vocations of life and encompassing a timespan of some fifty years – was met with enthusiastic reviews and quickly became the major literary attraction in Western Ukraine. In 1936, the novel was even nominated for a prestigious literary award of the Ukrainian Catholic Union. The only reason *Apostle of the Rabble* did not win it, as the official award announcement stated, was because it could not compete for the award since its first part was already published in the 1920s. The award committee acknowledged, however, that Kobylians'ka's novel deserved the highest recognition.[4] Critics praised it for its authenticity, uplifting tone, and didactic nature. The original commentators did not use any specific terms in discussing the novel's ideological tenets; however, many of them described it as the most successful representation of the zeitgeist,[5] which in interwar Western Ukraine and among Ukrainian postwar émigrés was greatly shaped by radical nationalism and pro-fascist ideologies.[6] Not only did the novel address the unsettling anxieties of its original readers about the ongoing political and cultural transformations in Ukraine, but it also gave them, intentionally or not, hope and lucid formulas for how to mould "new, robust, and adamant fighters for the independence of Ukrainian people" (Vil'de 1937a, 19).

Consequently, it comes as no surprise that the Soviet authorities found the novel's overarching pro-nationalist rhetoric unfit for the Soviet context and banned it from publication. As a result, *Apostle of the Rabble* remained virtually unknown to readers and scholars of Ukrainian literature until its post-Soviet publication in 1994. While still largely undiscovered in the West, the novel received a fair amount of critical attention in Ukraine. For the most part, post-Soviet literary scholars assess the novel's patriotic messages favourably; some even find them to be "the quintessence of Kobylians'ka's reflections on Ukraine's historical development and the role of the intellectual in this process" (Krupa 1994, 7).[7] There are, however, a few commentators who either problematize such enthusiastic readings and argue that *Apostle of the Rabble* did not purport to be a political speech or a surrogate treatise on Ukrainian nationalism (Pavlyshyn 2014, 575–6) or continue to read *Apostle of the Rabble* within the critical framework established by Soviet scholars as a hodgepodge of "laborious and painful ideological and philosophical meanderings," if not a testimony of Kobylians'ka's creative and intellectual decline (Pohrebennyk 1968, 205–6 and 1983, 18; Tomashuk 1969a, 200; Vozniuk 2006, 193). The cited post-Soviet critics agree only on two points: they acknowledge that the question of Ukraine's national revival and political independence, whatever its clarity and goals might be, is central in *Apostle of the Rabble*, and that the novel's main character, Iuliian Tsezarevych, represents Kobylians'ka's revision of her earlier views on the relationship of intellectuals to society at large and their duties within it. Furthermore, while recognizing *Apostle of the Rabble* as an important reflection on the ideological debates that took place in Western Ukraine in the 1920s and the 1930s, most of the cited critics do not read it as a modernist text, a reading initiated by Mykhailo Rudnyts'kyi, one of the head editors of *Dilo* (*Task*) newspaper that published Kobylians'ka's novel in 1936 (1936, 239). In their assessment, some recent critics tend to follow conventional critical doctrines that have firmly distinguished between the modernism of the 1920s, typically associated with democratic ideals, pluralism, and formal experimentations, and the literature of the 1930s, associated with populism, traditionalism, and obsolete forms of literary realism. In Ukrainian literary scholarship, this polarized picture turned into a dogma that has been challenged only recently.[8]

Drawing on contemporary scholarship that has indicated the intimate kinship between modernism and fascism, the following analysis argues that *Apostle of the Rabble* not only offers valuable insight into the interwar discussions of national identity, nationalism, and its application for Western Ukrainians, but also represents an important development in Ukrainian modernism that highlights its variegated nature and points to profound contestations not only within the artistic movement but also within Ukrainian nationalism itself. The new reading of Kobylians'ka's last novel also contributes to the broader discussion about the relationship between Western intellectuals, women in particular, and the various aesthetic and ideological practices collected under the name of fascism. Erin Carlston's 1998 literary study *Thinking Fascism: Sapphic Modernism and Fascist Modernity* and Roger Griffin's theory of generic fascism and his work on the constitutive relationship between interwar fascism and modernism have proved most helpful in assessing Kobylians'ka's response to various fascist ideologies and movements of her time, whose nature and significance often seemed as unstable and vague in the 1920s and the 1930s as they do today.

Building on Max Weber's theory of "ideal type"[9] and George Mosse's cultural studies of fascism[10] and taking into account the numerous manifestations of fascist influence on European political, cultural, and intellectual life in the interwar period, Griffin observes that fascism is a unique, full-fledged ideology, which is foremost defined by its core myth of national rebirth. He consequently describes it as a revolutionary form of ultranationalism "bent on mobilizing all 'healthy' social and political energies to resist the onslaught of 'decadence' so as to achieve the goal of national rebirth, a project that involves the regeneration (palingenesis) of both the political culture and the social and ethical cultures underpinning it" (Griffin and Feldman 2004, 6). Griffin further indicates that fascism, as a generic phenomenon, is based on a primarily vitalist philosophy and syncretic ideology, that is, an ideology that synthesizes conflicting elements of right and left, conservative and revolutionary currents of thought. Alongside other scholars of fascism, Griffin identifies a set of secondary, but no less "ineliminable," characteristics of fascism, such as anti-liberalism, anti-communism, and anti-conservatism, alongside several common features of style and organization – extreme elitism, mass mobilization, the strong leadership principle, and normatization of military virtues (Griffin 1995, 4–8; Payne 1995, 7; Laqueur 1996, 13–21). Griffin thus views fascism as a product of the manifold modern aesthetic, philosophical, and political influences that aimed at overcoming what it saw as modernity's social, spiritual, and political crisis – its "disaggregation, fragmentation, and loss of transcendence with respect to premodern societies" (1993, 38–9; 2007, 10). Thereupon, Griffin argues that fascism should be viewed as one of the political and ideological responses to modernity:

> In its varied permutations fascism took it upon itself not just to change the state system, but to purge the civilization of decadence, and foster the emergence of a new breed of human beings which it defined in terms not of universal categories but essentially mythic national and racial ones. Its activists set about their tasks in the iconoclastic spirit of "creative destruction" legitimized not by divine will, reason, the laws of nature, or by socio-economic theory, but by the belief that history itself was at a turning point and could be launched on a new course through human intervention that would redeem a nation and rescue the West from the imminent collapse. (2007, 6)

Griffin's definition of generic fascism is invariably a heuristic construction and cannot encompass all aspects of fascism. It is, however, widely recognized as the most productive interpretive aid in approaching fascism as a general, trans-historical phenomenon, which has only been extended and modified, not replaced, over the past decade of scholarly reflections on fascism, its ideology, and its aesthetics. It certainly proves useful in discussing Ukrainian interwar radical nationalism, one of the most controversial and vibrant topics in contemporary Ukrainian historiography,[11] as well as works created by artists associated with the Organization of Ukrainian Nationalists (OUN) and Ukrainian interwar radical nation-building projects.[12]

Accordingly, Kobylians'ka's longing for national rebirth, alongside her emphasis on rapture and renewal, which define the thematic composition of *Apostle of the Rabble*, link her last work to interwar fascist aesthetics and thereby to the alternative modernist aesthetics forged by pro-fascist artists. The fusion of several opposing themes that will be discussed in detail in the remainder of this chapter further embeds *Apostle of the Rabble* in the interwar fascist philosophical and aesthetic paradigm. Some of these unconventional thematic fusions are the conservative view of man limited by nature and the more progressive belief in the possibility of creating a new victorious man; a profound interest in science, especially in terms of understanding human psyche, and a more anti-positivist inquiry into the unlimited possibilities of the will; the faith and service of Christianity and the heroism of classical thought; and finally the traditional understanding of family and property relations more typical of the right and altruistic commitment to communal good and social activism more typical of the left. Although it is hard to draw any definite conclusions about Kobylians'ka's reception of interwar fascism as an ideology without a thorough analysis of her personal archives of the 1930s, which remain unavailable to scholars,[13] attentive reading proves that *Apostle of the Rabble* deserves a re-examination as not only the most celebrated novel produced outside Soviet Ukraine in the 1930s and a critical record of the political radicalization of Western Ukrainians in the interwar period, but also an embodiment of an important development in European modernism.

Erin Carlston's work, which demonstrates that interwar non- and anti-fascist discourses share a vernacular with fascist discourses of the same period and argues that "fascism itself ... suppl[ied] the vocabulary and the methodology of even the most rigorously anti-fascist critics, such as Virginia Woolf's in *Three Guineas*" (5), provides a useful set of tools to assess the anti-fascist nature of Kobylians'ka's creative appropriation of various pro-fascist discourses of her time and to contextualize it into a broader discussion of the ways in which European modernists conceptualized fascism. Drawing on Carlston's model and keeping Griffin's theory of generic fascism in mind – both of which insist that fascist modernity was not a discontinuity in history and culture – the following study adopts a broad definition of fascism by conflating distinct national phenomena and emphasizing different and sometimes contrary aspects of fascist thought to suit its own purposes. It is important to note that this study does not purport to treat a particular national version of fascism, but rather sets out to examine Kobylians'ka's peculiar reception of various fascist discourses of her time, which could mean to her, variously and simultaneously, the Romanian Iron Guard or Italian Fascism, Dmytro Dontsov's political theories or the OUN's radical ideology, or something else, some still-evolving and amorphous concepts, images, and political practices, which she was trying to identify and define.

Nietzsche, Christ, and Caesar: Traces of Pro-Fascist Philosophies and Aesthetics in Kobylians'ka's 1936 *Zeitroman Apostle of the Rabble*

Although Kobylians'ka did not provide any dates in *Apostle of the Rabble* that could clearly demarcate the historical setting of her last novel, past critics univocally situate its main events within the decade preceding the First World War (Babyshkin 1956, 56; Pohrebennyk 1968, 205–6; Tomashuk 1969a, 200–10; Pavlyshyn 2008, 255 and 2014, 560). Considering that Kobylians'ka started working on the novel during the First World War and that some realities of the novel correspond to that period, this conclusion seems logical. Kobylians'ka, however, worked long and hard on her last novel – a little over twenty years – continually revising her manuscript and adjusting it to the ever-changing political and cultural climate in the interwar Western Ukrainian lands. In this regard, Kobylians'ka's deliberate avoidance of any time references and some glaring inconsistencies between the ethnic landscape of the historical pre-war Western Ukrainian lands within the Austro-Hungarian Empire that presumably offered the setting of the final 1936 version of the novel,[14] as well as the writer's effort to stay relevant to her historical time and place – the historical juncture when the threat of a second world war was very much in the air – deserve recognition. Situating the main events of the novel in the 1904–14 decade might lead to a temptation to read *Apostle of the Rabble* as a historical novel that represents ideologies and world views of that period and to interpret the story of its main character, Iuliian Tsezarevych, as the writer's critique of Ukrainian intellectual and political leaders who had a decade to prepare for the world-historical upheaval but failed to use the opportunity that it provided to establish an independent Ukrainian state in the aftermath of the First World War (Babyshkin 1956, 57; Pohrebennyk 1968, 205–6; Pavlyshyn 2014, 560). As this chapter will demonstrate, *Apostle of the Rabble* and its main character are considerably more complex and not only offer a deft reflection on the past and the present, but also present an empowering message for the future. For that reason, the following analysis will honour the author's avoidance of any historical demarcations.

Kobylians'ka started working on the novel in 1915, shortly after the outbreak of the First World War, and completed its first draft, initially titled *Tsezarevych,* in 1922, when Ukraine was forced to cope with its failure to assert its independence between 1917 and 1920 and the sense of unjust treatment at the hands of Western powers in the aftermath of the First World War. The original title, which is the last name of the novel's protagonist and is derived from the Ukrainian "tsezar" (Caesar), suggests that in the early 1920s, Kobylians'ka prioritized the Caesarian aspect in the character of her new hero, which at the time many Ukrainian politicians considered to be the most important quality for a successful national leader. In 1922, Kobylians'ka energetically wrote to a number of public and private organizations in the United States, Canada, and several European countries to arrange for her novel's publication. Although she received many warm letters and even several advance payments for her future novel, all her efforts came to nothing.[15] The manuscript did not make it either to North America or to Europe that year because, most likely, the Romanian authorities confiscated it. In 1922, as Kobylians'ka recalled much later, the Romanian secret police searched her study and "took everything that was on and in her desk: letters, literary notes, manuscripts, some short sketches, and one completed novel which [she was] especially sorry [to lose]" (qtd. in Panchuk 1976, 7). The Romanian policemen justified their actions by claiming that they had irrefutable evidence that proved Kobylians'ka's active participation in anti-Romanian conspiracies. As they put it, "The Kingdom of Rumania is for Rumanians, but you invent [stories about] Ukraine and thereby incite Ukrainians to revolt" (qtd. in Panchuk 1976, 8).[16] The Romanian authorities never returned Kobylians'ka's manuscripts and, as a result, little is known about the 1922 version of the novel. Kobylians'ka's initial selection of potential publishing institutions reveals, however, that at the time, she sought out pro-democratic organizations as potential venues for the publication of her new novel.

From 1926 onward, as Romanization policies directed at the Ukrainian population in Bukovyna grew particularly brutal and the OUN's radical ideology began to attract many young people in the region, Kobylians'ka, it seems, was much more flexible in her choice of potential publishers and reached out to organizations that belonged to rival political camps.[17] In 1926, for example, she contacted two L'viv journals, *Nova Khata* (*New Hut*) and *Svit* (*The World*), along with the Prague journal *Nova Ukraina* (*A New Ukraine*), all of which campaigned for Ukraine's political independence and the all-around free development of the Ukrainian people. Mykyta Shapoval, a prolific publicist and prominent leader of the Ukrainian Social-Revolutionaries in exile in Czechoslovakia who at the time was the head editor of *Nova Ukraina*, responded enthusiastically to Kobylians'ka's inquiry. He praised her work for its patriotic vigour and didactic nature, and arranged for its publication in his journal.[18] The publication, however, was interrupted because the journal ceased to exist in 1928. Around the same time, the Soviet Ukrainian authorities made a robust effort to secure Kobylians'ka's ideological support, and they also showed vivid interest in publishing her latest work. Once the Soviet critics read the manuscript, however, they were no longer keen on publishing a novel that openly propagated Ukraine's right for cultural and political self-determination and that called on its readers to stand up, with weapons in hand, against the enemies of Ukraine's independence.[19] Realizing that "her novel would not be published in Great Ukraine," as she put it in a letter written to Kyrylo Strudnyts'kyi on 9 January 1933 (*U pivstolitti zmahannia* 1993, 633), Kobylians'ka made further changes and sent her work to Mykhailo Rudnyts'kyi, a prominent literary critic and one of the head editors of *Dilo*, the most influential L'viv daily newspaper representing the moderate nationalism of the largest Ukrainian parliamentary party within Poland, the Ukrainian National Democratic Association (UNDO). Although Rudnyts'kyi criticized Kobylians'ka's work as "a novel with very weak observations and psychological material," and pointed out that technically it was "not at all modern"(1936, 239), he published it in *Dilo* after significant editorial redactions, many of which Kobylians'ka did not approve.[20] The convoluted publication history of the novel thus suggests that while in the 1920s Kobylians'ka was mainly preoccupied with selling her work and securing a much-needed income,[21] in the mid-1930s, when money was no longer an issue, she was able to focus on intellectual reasoning and critical revisions of her earlier elitist views.

Already in the early 1890s, Kobylians'ka took an active part in the cultural rebellion against the Enlightenment project generally known as "the revolt against positivism."[22] Inspired first by German Romantics and later by Nietzsche, she specifically looked to mythic energies rather than Enlightenment reason as the basis for the regeneration of Ukrainian society, firmly moving away from cultural pessimism towards palingenetic hope. Kobylians'ka's earlier works – particularly *The Princess, Over the Bridge*, and *After Situations* – decisively foreground the instinctual forces and capacity to be inspired to heroic action and self-sacrifice through the power of belief, myth, and symbol, such as the family, the nation, the leader, or the revival of culture. All of these features, which in the interwar period have come to be associated with fascism,[23] are present in *Apostle of the Rabble*. What is new and shows even more pronounced affinities with the philosophical premise of interwar fascism[24] is Kobylians'ka's fusion of Nietzsche's idea of the overman with elements of Christian and classical philosophy, which, as some scholars observe, was endowed with a unique power to heal the divisions of modern society.[25] The simplified dictum that the novel's title and the name of its protagonist offer a pointed allusion: Iuliian Tsezarevych, a name that phonetically is close to Julius Caesar – a new apostle of Ukraine's rabble. The same conceptual framework (the fusion of Nietzsche's philosophy, Christianity, and Caesarism) underpins the story of Iuliian's cognitive, ideological, and psychological transformation. Similar to Natalka Verkovychivna, the Nietzschean heroine of Kobylians'ka's 1896 novel *The Princess*, Iuliian undergoes a three-stage spiritual metamorphosis, gradually overcoming his self-doubt and cultural despair.[26] Iuliian's transformation, however, evolves not after Nietzsche's camel-lion-child scenario, but after its interwar modification – seafarer-priest-warrior. As with many heroes of the typical interwar pro-fascist coming-of-age novels, Kobylians'ka's character, a young lad of noble descent infused with Nietzschean will, undergoes a series of trials during which he sacrifices his personal interests for the sake of the communal good, and from which he emerges as the new man destined to transform his nation.[27]

Using the basic formula of the interwar hero-narratives, Kobylians'ka introduces Iuliian Tsezarevych as a good-looking, well-disciplined, and well-educated seventeen-year-old of unusual physical strength and with a healthy dose of ambition. In the opening scenes, which depict Iuliian's childhood, Kobylians'ka accentuates the hero's racial purity and targeted cultural education, presenting the two as equally defining agencies in the formation of Iuliian's national identity.[28] Born into a family of Ukrainian patriots whose ancestors were highly esteemed military officers or Orthodox priests, and raised deliberately "for Ukraine" and its future (*Apostle of the Rabble* 1994, 10),[29] Iuliian is exceptionally firm in his national self-identification and often dreams of becoming "a fighter for Ukraine" and its national independence (AR 21). At this stage, the young man models his self-image as a future political leader after "great men of Greek and Roman times" and prominent figures of the French Revolution and French Republic (AR 21). The latter are of particular interest because Iuliian compares French revolutionary leaders of the 1790s to the Ukrainian intelligentsia of his time, recognizing the urgent need for resolute and authoritative leadership in interwar Ukraine. These remarks could not but appeal to Kobylians'ka's original readers, whose concern with reorienting Ukrainian politics and reorganizing the chaotic crowd of the people into a disciplined mass movement was similar to those of French revolutionaries and those of supporters of interwar fascism who also admired the French Revolution and its attempt to integrate masses into national politics (Mosse 1999, 69–93).[30]

Iuliian's reflections on strong political rule are articulated in a dream he has that features Gaius Julius Caesar. The dream contains several allegories with cogent political statements. The image of Gaius Julius Caesar, who guides Iuliian in the world of his unconscious, emulates the charismatic strongman and his rule by force, projecting Caesarism as the form of political rule the young hero admires the most. Caesar's instructions to Iuliian build up the pro-military undertone. For example, we can read Caesar's advice to stay away from a plow as a displaced repudiation of the populist gentle politics of cultivating the masses, popular among the pro-democratic Ukrainian camps before the First World War.[31] A bow and quiver of arrows, which in the dream Iuliian receives from Caesar, evoke, in turn, the political strength of Homer's epic hero Odysseus, and could be interpreted as another affirmation of anti-democratic politics. Caesar's closing oration about blood sacrifice, which, as the Roman hero contends, Ukrainian soil must receive "to bear any fruits [because] life arises and dies in blood, and [because] life is what is needed for the salvation of [Iuliian's land]," also celebrates violence, aggressive masculinity, and military prominence in politics (AR 20). Moreover, it alludes to the popular "blood and soil" current of German fascism that promoted the idea of breeding a new German aristocracy out of a rural population unspoiled by urbanization and industrial capitalism.[32] As one recent critic points out, similar issues of breeding new "Ukrainian ironmen" (krytsevi ukraintsi)comprise a recurring theme in *Apostle of the Rabble* (Mel'nychuk 2006, 159–61). While foregrounding the young man's fascination with modern Caesarism, Iuliian's dream also offers an ambitious narrative forecast. As a narrative digression, it presents a displaced temporal prolepsis that projects a narrative direction for the hero's subsequent spiritual and intellectual journey. By positioning Iuliian as the chosen hero who aspires to save his Ukraine from political ruin and cultural decline, the dream sets up readers' expectations, making them wonder whether the character is truly fit for the quest. Curiously, although it is the novel's central question, Kobylians'ka does not answer it directly, inviting her readers to pass final judgment over Iuliian's aptitudes on their own. In this light, *Apostle of the Rabbles* follows the tradition of *Entwicklungsroman* – a novel dealing with the development of a character from childhood to maturity – not typical of modernism, as one of Kobylians'ka's early critics observes,[33] but popular with the interwar pro-fascist writers and their potential audiences – the educated bourgeoisie. Artur Dinter's novel *Die Sünde wider das Blut* (*The Sin against the Blood*, 1917) and Hans Grimm's novel *Volk ohne Raum* (*People without Room*, 1926) are among the most representative examples here. As one recent study indicates, the mainstream readers in Soviet Ukraine of the 1920s shared similar conservative tastes for transparent plot constructions, intrigue, and traditional forms of cultural expression, often classified as "populist," or even "nationalist" (Shkandrij 2016, 167–8).

Kobylians'ka identifies Iuliian as an exceptional and heroic youth in one of the opening scenes where the young hero steps in front of the stampeding horses to save from injury or imminent death three people – a local Ukrainian priest named Father Zakharii, his fifteen-year-old daughter, Eva, and a coachman. The writer, however, refrains from idealizing her protagonist. In fact, throughout the first two-thirds of the novel, which combine elements of domestic novel, country house fiction, family saga, and adolescent *Bildungsroman*, Kobylians'ka underscores Iuliian's youthful indecisiveness, self-doubt, and lack of self-control, projecting him not as an ideal but rather as a realistic character, human and down to earth. Contrary to the claims of some critics who read Iuliian as one of a long series of Kobylians'ka's male characters whose ambitions or promise far outweigh their achievement (Babyshkin 1963, 176; Pavlyshyn 2015 559–60), the writer does not dwell on Iuliian's character flaws per se and shows little interest in passing any moralistic judgment about her hero.[34] Instead, she frames Iuliian's weaknesses as triggers of his spiritual and cognitive transformations, thereby evoking Nietzsche's ideas of self-discovery, spiritual evolution, and wilful overcoming.[35] Iuliian's youthful uncertainty about the forms of activity that would benefit his nation, for example, becomes the main reason for the hero's year-long mind-altering trip across Europe. Not only does Iuliian, now a Nietzschean seafarer,[36] perfect his German, English, French, and Russian languages during his journey, he also makes astounding cultural discoveries, which inspire him to revisit his earlier frustration with the low status of Ukrainian culture in the European context – or what one critic views as his "national inferiority complex" (Pavlyshyn 2008, 254–5 and 2014, 265). Consequently, he also channels his psychic energies towards a critical examination of Ukraine's diverse social groups and their potential to break free from "the enchanted circle" of their recent political frustrations and reorganize themselves into a coherent movement around a new national idea (AR 128). Iuliian's youthful indecisiveness thus sets off the first cycle of his cognitive and spiritual transformation, definitely a positive rather than an embarrassing process, from which the hero emerges with firm convictions and clear goals for the future.

Kobylians'ka presents Iuliian's newly acquired fortitude and self-confidence in a series of dynamic conversations with Father Zakharii, ironically named after the biblical prophet Zachariah who promised salvation to his people and is identified as "an ideal priest" (AR 46), and who could be viewed as a pre-war populist exemplar of the "apostle of the rabble" (AR 16).[37] To accentuate the vigour of Iuliian's new political visions, which continue to revolve around the same pro-militant and elitist themes that permeate his youthful convictions, Kobylians'ka juxtaposes them to Father Zakharii's meek, pro-democratic beliefs. As the old priest's initial comments about his parishioners reveal, his political stance has a doctrinaire and somewhat ludicrous nature. While recognizing the rabble, that is, the peasantry, as an uncultured, coarse, and primitive mass, Father Zakharii paradoxically believes in the people's potential to grow into a strong political force and projects them as "the ideal matter from which Ukrainian nation would arise" (AR 50). Accordingly, he promotes the populist politics of cultivating the rabble by teaching them what Nietzsche would describe as values associated with the ascetic ideal – how to "love and respect one another, keep together, love their land, and fight against even the slightest lie" (AR 46). Nietzsche developed his concept of the ascetic ideal in the third treatise of his *On the Genealogy of Morality* (1887), capturing its essence quite nicely with a simple slogan – "poverty, humility, chastity" (1998, 76). As Nietzsche indicated, the ascetic priest uses the ascetic ideal on the weak as a way of controlling and disarming their self-destructive resentment and a way of treating the symptoms, but not the causes, of their suffering and nihilism. During this process, Nietzsche observed, the ascetic ideal takes on the characteristics of the morality of good and evil. Among its most celebrated tenets, the German philosopher listed the valuation of freedom from suffering, the love of one's neighbour, and self-abnegation for the sake of the group (1998, 67–118). Although Iuliian reveres Father Zakharii's dedication and self-sacrifice, the young man openly questions the futility of those "seeds of [knowledge] that [Father Zakharii] plants" among his parishioners, thereby questioning the old priest's irrational claims that they "would sprout on their own one day" (AR 51). Leading their conversation into a Socratic argument with a series of provocative questions, Iuliian not only asserts himself as an insightful thinker and an outstanding orator but also forces the old priest, and even more so the reader, to re-examine critically Father Zakharii's circumscribed political views.

By observing how the very people who "blindly follow Father Zakharii in the important matters" often cheat their priest in the daily affairs, Iuliian exposes the ineffectiveness of the priest's nation-building methods and sharply criticizes the implied populist dogmas (AR 46). The young man takes his critique of populist politics even further in his commentary on Father Zakharii's ultimate political mission "to nurture a dozen of those who would effectively represent their culture" (AR 46), in which Iuliian, like many of Kobylians'ka's earlier intellectual heroes, claims that much broader measures must be taken to lead Ukrainian "mediocrity" to greatness (AR 49). While condemning the narrow-mindedness of the populist political agenda and the general political apathy of the Ukrainian intelligentsia, Iuliian emphasizes a need for a highly cultured and strong-willed intellectual elite that would be able to organize and lead the Ukrainian masses to a better political future. By the end of their conversation, Father Zakharii wholeheartedly agrees with the young man, acknowledging "with some internal satisfaction" that Iuliian's gift of persuasion could make him "an outstanding preacher" one day (AR 50). In this scene, the young hero thus emerges as a new type of character – not an irresolute and self-doubting youth, but an insightful and strong-willed man who demonstrates the very qualities of the new victorious hero that many interwar radical ideologues, pro-fascists including, promoted passionately.

The novel, however, makes it clear that, despite a profound character change, Iuliian is not quite ready to become an effective leader of his people at this stage of his life. The young man admits that he is still "too proud," "too unyielding," and does not love the people with that Christian love that "washes neighbours' feet and serves them sincerely" (AR 50–1). Father Zakharii also observes that Iuliian is still too young and lacks experience. But it is Iuliian's lack of self-control that delays his rise to social and political prominence. As implied, the hero inherits this character trait from his paternal grandfather, also named Iuliian Tsezarevych, a captain in the army, who committed suicide after losing his family fortune at cards. Kobylians'ka used Iuliian's inability to control his passions as a trigger for another life-altering experience, in the same way as she did earlier with his youthful indecisiveness about what course of action to take in order to contribute best to Ukraine's nation-building efforts. Hence, Iuliian's spontaneous fornication with Father Zakharii's only daughter, Eva, becomes the watershed event that not only shapes the remainder of Iuliian's life but also sets off the second cycle of the hero's cognitive and spiritual transformation, re-emphasizing the importance of perpetual self-perfection and total purification.

The story of Iuliian's and Eva's sexual encounter deserves particular attention because it not only illuminates the widespread condition of sexual repression, which the writer experiences along with many of her bourgeois readers, but also introduces the Christian aspect of the novel's underlying philosophical synthesis, linking elements of the classical and Christian traditions with Nietzsche's concept of the man of vigour and self-help.[38] Alongside other textual devices, Kobylians'ka uses the characters' names, Eva and Iuliian, to bridge symbolically the faith and service of Christianity with the heroism of classical thought. Although there is no explicit description of the characters' sexual intercourse – perhaps due to Rudnyts'kyi's editorial redactions – intricate allusions that saturate the scenes leading to and immediately following the insinuated act leave little doubt as to its occurrence. The abundant references to the biblical story of original sin and Adam and Eve's discovery of bodily pleasures stand out the most. Besides the seductress's symbolic name and the name of the place of the lovers' rendezvous, a pristine forest described as "paradise," the appearance of a venomous snake along with a ripe apple minutes before the implied act also alludes to the biblical story. While accentuating the sexual nature of Iuliian's and Eva's encounter, biblical references also suggest that the two young people are innocent in their act because they, as descendants of the first man and woman, are destined to do so. Consequently, Iuliian's implied innocence invites the reader to focus not as much on his sexual transgression but on how he deals with the new and difficult situation that arises in its aftermath.

In contrast to the biblical hero, Iuliian neither hides his sin nor blames it on others but confesses it to Father Zakharii and claims full responsibility. To atone for what he perceives to be his moral crime against Eva's family, Iuliian asks for Eva's hand in marriage and gives his word to become a priest, as Father Zakharii has always wanted him to do. Although the confession scene introduces themes of ancestral sin, fall from grace, remorse, repentance, and perhaps even redemption – they are reinforced by the symbolic name of Father Zacharii's estate, Pokutivka, derived from the Ukrainian word "spokuta" (penance, atonement, redemption) – the raging storm that takes place during Iuliian's audience with Father Zakharii suggests that the young man's deviation from accepted social and sexual norms might have severe consequences, thereby making Iuliian's engagement to Eva a dangerous enterprise, if not a dead end. The grim subject matter of Franz Schubert's lied "Das Erlkönig" ("The Erlking"), which Eva and Iuliian sing together after their spontaneous fornication, suggests similarly ominous connotations. The lied's lyrics, one of Goethe's best-known poems of the same title, tells a story of a dying boy, who dreams in his last moments of being abducted from his father by a dark spirit. On the one hand, the poem's theme of abduction resonates with how Iuliian feels about his misconduct against the Zakharii family – he believes that his sexual encounter with Eva, although mutual, is a theft of a daughter from her father: "I enticed his only daughter without his permission, without any right to do so ... I think that no judge would judge me as severely as my own conscience judges me" (AR 156–7). On the other hand, prolific biblical allusions that lead to Eva's and Iuliian's intercourse, as well as what happens next in their story, invite us to read Eva as the temptress, as Goethe's dark spirit, who incites Iuliian against his better judgment to transgress prevalent social norms of conduct, thus abducting the young man from his family and his earlier goals and luring him into what could be read as a pernicious bond.

Indeed, the story of Iuliian's relationship with Eva, a passionate and overly sensual woman of hybrid Polish-Ukrainian ethnic heritage, is a story of the hero's spiritual decline and destructive self-abnegation. The only positive aspect of Iuliian's commitment to Eva and her family is a discovery of Christian love towards the people, which the young hero lacked during his student years. Iuliian's budding love for the people and his resolution to serve them first emerge in his conversation with Eva upon her return from elsewhere in Europe, where she studies medicine for a year. When Eva makes pungent remarks about what she perceives as the horrendous cultural primitivism of the Ukrainian peasantry, Iuliian urges her not to distance herself from the peasants but to look closely into their huts because, as he argues, each of them constitutes "a small universe" that offers the only possible entry into the broader Ukrainian community (AR 161). Developing his idea about the duty of every educated person "to serve his or her people" (AR 160), Iuliian urges Eva to follow the example of all the foreign students they met in Switzerland, who came to study there only to "return to their native hives and work on their land for their own people" (AR 160). His closing statement undermines, however, his grand vision of service and passionate rhetoric on self-sacrifice in the cause of others: "Every one of us [educated Ukrainians] must have a sense of duty to serve one another and our people. When each of us sincerely brings even a brick or two to our circumscribed world, we would be able to construct ever better foundations for our new generation and our new state" (AR 160–1) These words, which echo Father Zakharii's limited populist ideal for the individual's contribution to the Ukrainian cause, signify Iuliian's ideological digression into the very narrow thinking that he had rejected earlier as inadequate for Ukraine's current political needs. Eva, who at this point represents the new type of progressive, critically thinking Ukrainian woman, is the first to read Iuliian's claims as a sign of his extreme self-abnegation. In accordance with her new views, she urges her fiancé to abandon the priesthood – an occupation for which Iuliian believes his personality to be a poor fit – and calls on him to pursue a vocation that would suit his character and intellectual aptitude, and through which, consequently, he would be able to contribute better to the development of his nation. When Iuliian, being a man of his word, refuses to break his promise to Father Zakharii and follow his own interest in public service, Eva steps up to rescue Iuliian from the doomed commitment and calls off their engagement. Iuliian's argument with Eva captures the tension between the hero's ideal to serve the higher national cause and his duties to family – an ideal that was characteristic of many pro-fascist ideologies. The young man's breakup with Eva also follows a common pro-fascist aesthetic pattern: it projects the hero's deliverance from a treacherous seductress as the final external stimulus to purge himself of his youthful hesitations and embrace the cause of something far greater than himself and his local community (Mosse 1999, 50). In Iuliian's case, this greater purpose is the cause of Ukraine's cultural greatness and political statehood.

Liberated from obligations towards the Zakharii family, Iuliian rejoins the military, entering the final stage of his spiritual and intellectual metamorphosis, which transforms him into a new type of hero – an "apostle of the sword" (AR 213). His new heroic image is clearly modelled not on the popular image of the medieval bishop who used to advance, sword in hand, against his enemies, but rather on Nietzsche's controversial image of "the Roman Caesar with Christ's soul." In his notes published posthumously as *The Will to Power* (1901–6), Nietzsche applied this image to convey his thoughts on what it means to be a powerful and effective leader:

> Education in those rulers' virtues that master even one's benevolence and pity: the great cultivator's virtues ("forgiving one's enemy" is child's play by comparison), the affect of creator must be elevated – no longer to work on marble – the exceptional situation and powerful position of those beings (compared with any prince hitherto): the Roman Caesar with Christ's soul. (1968, 513)

The main message here articulates Nietzsche's thoughts on the requisite education in the virtues proper for a creator of the higher order, an ideal ruler. On the one hand, these virtues include, but also exceed, those associated with Christianity. As Nietzsche put it, compared to the virtues of ideal rulers, the Christian virtues of pity and benevolence – that is, the ascetic ideal of loving one's neighbour and forgiving one's enemy – are mere child's play. Nietzsche wanted his ideal humans to overcome and transform Christian love into what he calls elsewhere a gift-giving virtue (1978, 58) – a virtue of giving not out of pity but out of personal abundance and overflow.[39] On the other hand, the above passage highlights that the virtues of ideal rulers exceed qualities that are typically associated with powerful leaders who, as Nietzsche implied, are prone to impose their authority on others in order to aggrandize themselves and who are often motivated by greed, resentment, and vengeance, whose will to power consumes them, and who, consequently, do not know the value of the self-overcoming and gift-giving virtue of a creator. Tyranny over others is not part of Nietzsche's vision. As one scholar indicates, what Nietzsche celebrated in Caesar is not the military or political success, "but the embodiment of the passionate man who controls his passions: the man who, in the face of universal disintegration and licentiousness, knowing the decadence as part of his own soul, performs his unique deed of self-integration, self-creation and self-mastery" (Kaufmann 2013, 316). Accordingly, Nietzsche's fusion of Caesar and Christ combines love for humanity with cruel self-discipline, identifying the ideal ruler as a bearer of a worldly creed that commends the perfection of men.[40] While Nietzsche used image of "the Roman Caesar with Christ's soul" to outline an ideal ruler as an agent of a practical program of enlightenment, in popular modern political theory this image was often interpreted as a fusion of Christian ideals of service and self-surrender with modern ideals of force and virility.[41] Considering that Kobylians'ka's character openly promotes militant politics at this point of her life, it is fair to suggest that Kobylians'ka's version of "the Roman Caesar with Christ's soul" is closer to those of her contemporaries than to Nietzsche's.

One of Iuliian's later conversations with Eva is instrumental for understanding the ideological premise that underpins Kobylians'ka's image of the "apostle of the sword." In this conversation, Iuliian justifies chauvinism as "a means of resistance in the struggle for independence and as a response to the chauvinism of the enemy" (AR 163). Later in the story, while reflecting on his new role as an officer, the hero develops his claim by quoting Helmuth Karl von Moltke, a prominent

German field marshal and one of the greatest military strategists of the late nineteenth century:

> He is now a warrior, and he often recalls the words of his professors and military instructors, who used to say that there have always been wars and there will always be wars, and that he, as an individual, would either win them or fall defeated. Yes, he is a warrior – "an apostle of the sword." He remembers one passage from Moltke that has been forever engraved in his heart: "Military service is a big burden, which brings to mind the worst periods of ancient slavery. Without this burden, however, European society would fall prey to diverse barbaric elements ... The moral influence of the military regime on the people's character has, therefore, such immense value that one can hardly exaggerate it." He thinks about the history of different nations, their rebellions, and the history of Ukraine. His heart fills with sorrow when he thinks that he does not have a country of his own [independent Ukraine], and that he cannot be proud of it like other nations are proud of their countries. He would like [to] serve his country, but first he needs to accumulate strength, both physical and intellectual. (AR 213)

Iuliian's references to the popular discussions on the prominence of the military in modern politics endorse struggle and justify violence as a necessary and even an ethical act that cannot be expelled from history. As Iuliian implies, the military not only protects communities from external enemies but also plays a key role in organizing the people with a common cause into a disciplined formation with hierarchical command structures. His military analogy likewise positions a virile man – the hero Iuliian eventually becomes – as the principal driving force of history and one of the main symbols of the nation's strength, harmony, and progress. In this light, Kobylians'ka's image of a new man stands in sharp contrast to her dramatic descriptions of the dehumanizing experiences of war in her cycle of short stories about the First World War. The contrast, however, suggests that, although it is unlikely that Kobylians'ka, as an eyewitness of some of the most brutal battles of the First World War, would promote aggressive military action, she had a clear understanding of the political situation in interwar Europe. Thus, she consciously chose, along with many prominent Ukrainian political and cultural leaders of the time, to advocate authority, organization, and strong military leadership as necessary measures to avoid the mass slaughter of Ukrainians in a new total war, which by 1936 was easy to foresee.[42]

Kobylians'ka's pronounced emphasis on virile and dynamic masculinity, with its promise to bring order and a cure to an ailing Ukrainian society, is amplified through the representations of female characters, which the writer projected not necessarily as inferior to men but as politically passive in their roles as mothers, wives, and caregivers. Iuliian's first fiancée, Eva Zakharii, and his eventual wife, Dora Val'de, whose images embody two different ideals of the New Ukrainian Woman, modern and radically conservative, are the most interesting examples. Although Eva and Dora have fundamentally different personalities, they share some common characteristics, which link them to Kobylians'ka's earlier progressive heroines – Olena Liaufler, Natalka Verkovychivna, Zonia Yakhnenko, and Mania Obryns'ka. Both Eva and Dora are intelligent women who meet adversity with strong wills and independent minds and who bravely struggle against the conservative nineteenth-century vision of women as weak, inactive, and unthinking. While the degree and nature of the heroines' social revolt substantially differ, both Eva and Dora eventually mute their protests into a liberal compromise and fulfil their destinies at home and in small-scale community work. The same applies to the secondary female characters of the novel – the three Tsezarevych sisters. Zonia, the oldest sister, while establishing herself as a tradeswoman, balances her professional life with her marriage and family obligations. Maria, the middle sister, finds personal fulfilment exclusively in marriage and motherhood. Oksana, the youngest and the most proactive of the three sisters, studies to be a school teacher, becomes, like Zonia, financially independent, and works together with Dora on several social welfare initiatives to provide impoverished local children with warm clothing and footwear. None of these women, however, participate in the discussions of feminism or national questions or partake in any broad nation-building projects. As one recent critic observes, the work that Dora and the Tsezarevych women perform "is not dissimilar to that undertaken by the organization Zhinocha Hromada (Woman's Community) in Bukovyna or the Union of Ukrainian Women in Galicia" (Pavlyshyn 2014, 572), which in the early twentieth century, according to another scholar, were mostly focused on small-scale "pragmatic activity" (Bohachevsky-Chomiak 1988, 158).

Maksym Tsezarevych, the father of Iuliian, Zonia, Maria, and Olena, conveys the novel's vision of an ideal woman in his reflection on the future social roles of his three daughters. In a conversation with his wife, the old watchmaker compares women to "mechanical wheels, which surround and, following the laws of mechanics, rotate around the engine [that is, a man] as satellites" (AR 6). While promoting men as "engines," and thus the main driving force of history, Maksym's futuristic allegory also projects women as vital supporting historical actors whose responsibility is to secure the home front and thus assist men in their political struggles. Iuliian's views on feminism, which he shares with Eva at some point, evoke similar ideas:

> You want to know what I honestly think about "emancipation"? A man is a man, and a woman is a woman ... I hate this question because it can potentially divide the society and lead to extremes. Let women study, let them work, but do not let them destroy the so-called hearth and home, or replace it with restaurants and other places of entertainment. (AR 136–7)

Iuliian's position on the woman question in this passage brings to mind Kobylians'ka's 1894 public statement on feminism, as well as her 1927 reassessment of what a new, interwar Ukrainian woman should be, in which she advocates somewhat modernized yet traditional roles for women within the family and their immediate communities as intelligent mothers, supportive spouses, and compassionate caregivers, endorsing to a degree a sexual division of labour.[43] Hence, while working hard on creating the new Ukrainian man, an unprecedented image in Kobylians'ka's previous works, the writer makes no attempt in her last novel to reinvent the Ukrainian woman. Rather, her familiar conventions remain intact and resonate with typical interwar pro-fascist claims that "for a man, military service is the most profound and valuable form of participation in the State – for the woman it is motherhood" (Strasser 1995).[44] It is fair to suggest that Kobylians'ka's clear differentiation between the new Ukrainian man and the New Ukrainian Woman, unprecedented in pre-1914 fiction, might be rooted in the writer's first-hand experience of the First World War. At the same time, it presented the Western Ukrainian and émigré public with a certain open-endedness, which offered a fresh vision of an intellectual elite but co-opted a traditional reality. The writer's treatment of the woman question, promised, on the one hand, an alternative spiritual revolution and addressed those needs that, at the time, seemed essential to the preservation of Ukrainian civil society. On the other hand, it also underpinned a philosophical synthesis that shows strong affinity with the pro-fascist views on women and their social roles – a synthesis that might be partially credited for the novel's tremendous success in the late 1930s.

While discussing *Apostle of the Rabble*'s emphasis on the value of masculine vigour and military violence, it is important to point out that in 1936, Kobylians'ka remained firm in her repudiation of xenophobia. Although Kobylians'ka used theories of heredity and evolution while constructing her 1936 hero as a superior being and identified Poles as morally inferior foes of Ukraine's national revival, tellingly representing them as tricksters and drunkards, she never positioned the Ukraine's problem in exclusively Polish terms. More importantly, she advocated peaceful methods of conflict resolution, as Iuliian's marriage with his Polish-Ukrainian bride, Dora Val'de, implies. The closing lines of the novel make it explicit that Kobylians'ka firmly believed that military action could be used only as a means of protection in the face of foreign aggression. They also attest that in the mid-1930s, the writer viewed the main threat to Ukraine's national revival not from external forces but in the lack of an organized Ukrainian civil society and strong political leadership. As Iuliian prophetically observes at the end of the novel, Ukraine could be an independent state unless Ukrainians "themselves ruin" their chances (AR 243). Ukrainian-Polish, and for that matter Ukrainian-Romanian, Ukrainian-German, Ukrainian-Jewish, or Ukrainian-Russian, relations, therefore, were secondary to what Kobylians'ka perceived as the crisis of Ukraine's interwar politics. This approach sets her reception of pro-fascist ideologies sharply apart from those forms that espoused doctrines of inherent collective superiority for their nations and led to the systematic inhumanity and destructiveness of the Second World War.

At the end of the novel, Iuliian Tsezarevych thus emerges as a radically new type – a disciplined, intelligent, and virile man who embodies a potential nucleus for an alternative revolution around which a new Ukraine can henceforth order itself. Naturally, Kobylians'ka's contemporaries read her 1936 hero as a promise of a new ideal and a model for emulation. In many ways, Iuliian replicates Kobylians'ka's earlier intellectual heroines in his strong will, determination, Nietzschean striving for self-perfection, and, most importantly, dedication to Ukraine's cultural and political progress. The novel's pronounced emphasis on masculine vigour and political militarism, however, sets Kobylians'ka's "apostle of the sword" apart from her earlier versions of ideal intellectual leaders – most of them are women – and embeds her interwar hero in the ideological framework of the popular pro-fascist philosophical cluster of Nietzsche's thought, Christianity, and Caesarism. Although it might be questionable whether Kobylians'ka saw Iuliian as an ideal,[45] she clearly presented him as an exceptional individual and a symbol of a new mode of thinking and feeling necessary to secure Ukraine's political survival in the turbulent 1930s and thus guarantee "the fulfilment of old Herder's words, who prophesied for Ukraine the role of new Greece" in the renewal of Europe (AR 243).[46]

As attested by the initial reviews, Kobylians'ka's contemporaries saw Iuliian as a realistic character who is able to come to terms with his shortcomings, tame his passions, and overcome his self-doubt and cultural pessimism – a character symbolic of what other individuals could become. For that reason, one commentator defined *Apostle of the Rabble* as one of the most relevant works of its time and celebrated its author as a true "apostle of ideas," who "not simply kept up with life, but was often far ahead of it" (Vil'de 1937b, 14). This warm reception of the novel thus testifies that Kobylians'ka knew exactly what her interwar readership in Western Ukraine and among Ukrainian émigrés in the rest of Europe and North America wanted and gave them a compelling hero – a robust and resolute warrior whose image continues to appeal to many contemporary Ukrainians in the wake of recent economic, political, social, and moral crises. Lyudmyla Pochyniuk presents the latest enthusiastic reception of Iuliian Tsezarevych most eloquently by pointing out that "the type of nationally self-aware, socially active, creative personality delineated by O. Kobylians'ka serves – through its moral purity and dignity, elevated spirituality and intellectualism, patriotism and community mindedness – as a high ideal for today's generation of Ukrainian people" (2005, 171; also qtd. in Pavlyshyn 2014, 559).[47]

Conclusion

Apostle of the Rabble confronted interwar Western Ukrainians with their essential selves as they discussed, accepted, and even welcomed radical nationalist ideologies of their time. It was Kobylians'ka's final reflection on the political situation in interwar Ukraine and its prospects of statehood in the future. Some of the novel's arguments resonate with the writer's earlier views on the national question: the critique of Ukrainian culture as underdeveloped in comparison with the cultures of other European countries such as Poland or Germany; the propagation of social modernization; and the recognition of national sentiment as a powerful social force (Pavlyshyn 2014, 574). The novel's longing for national rejuvenation and a new Ukrainian man, which gives form to its latent mythic core, is also familiar from Kobylians'ka's earlier writings. What is new is the novel's emphasis on masculine virility and military virtues, its emphatic attention to the construction of national identity, particularly the role of heredity and purity of blood in this process, and its philosophical fusion of classical vitalism, Christian idealism, and Nietzsche's revolt against the rationalism of modern culture and morality. These three features establish clear philosophical affinities between Kobylians'ka's last novel and various pro-fascist discourses of the same period, which were widespread in Eastern Europe and which many Western Ukrainian and Ukrainian émigrés accepted as the only alternative way to reverse Ukraine's national defeat of the period 1917–20. The novel's key aesthetic and thematic foci further link it to interwar pro-fascist discourses. Its neoclassicist celebration of the beautiful male body modelled on the harmonious form of the Greek sculpture, its endorsement of aggressive masculinity, its continuous tension between ideal manliness and family life, its sharp distinction between friend and foe, along with its general tendency to reconcile traditional values with progress and with the radical spiritual-psychological transformation of its hero, represent the very aesthetic trends that lie at the heart of the alternative modernists aesthetics forged by interwar fascism (Griffin 2007, 288). At the same time, the novel's setting within the broader European context of interwar ideological debates demonstrates that Kobylians'ka's dialogue with selected myths and aesthetic ideals of interwar fascism were certainly triggered by her deliberate effort to embody, crystalize, and articulate the mood of national palingenesis that reflected the popular attitudes of Western Ukrainians and Ukrainian émigrés and defined the mainstream political and artistic discourse across Europe in the 1930s. In this light, *Apostle of the Rabble* could be viewed as a representative work of its time with multiple philosophical and aesthetic links to the alternative modernism developed by pro-fascist artists who set out to purge civilization of cultural pessimism by creating a new man defined by mythic national categories.

The novel's contextualization in its cultural and political milieu also demonstrates that Kobylians'ka's reception of fascism stemmed from thorough intellectual reasoning that excludes blind acceptance of all pro-fascist ideological doctrines and gives no ground for labelling her a fascist in the pejorative sense of the word. Rather, as a writer notorious for synthesizing diverse and often incompatible ideas into creative commentaries regarding Ukraine's cultural, social, and political revival, Kobylians'ka borrowed from interwar fascism only those themes and tropes that she believed to be applicable to Ukraine's political struggle against foreign aggression and that would resonate with her prospective audience of the 1930s, while also sometimes departing sharply from fascist rhetoric in some manner. Accordingly, her interpretation of interwar pro-fascist ideologies radically differs from those of the OUN ideologists. On the one hand, Kobylians'ka accepted several pro-fascist mythical and ideological structures that shaped the *Weltanschauung* of interwar Ukrainian radical nationalists: the palingenetic myth, strong-willed leadership, and normatization of military virtues. But on the other hand, she foregrounded the self-defence goal of Ukrainian interwar national mobilization and firmly repudiated xenophobia. This peculiar ideological stance, which could be well defined using Peter Suger's ironic but symbolically powerful concept as "anti-fascist fascism,"[48] indicates that Kobylians'ka's reception of interwar fascism was the product of political idealism, desire for national renewal, and a general longing for a new and better age, not the offspring of sectional class interests, racism, or nihilism. Consequently, Kobylians'ka's individual case, along with the original success of her 1936 novel, proves that the interwar discussion of fascism in Ukraine cannot be reduced either to the fiery political writings of Dmytro Dontsov or to the destructive activities of the OUN during the Second World War, but should be treated as a considerably more complex and ambiguous phenomenon than some of the resonant and frequently quoted passages from the works of the OUN ideologues might suggest. More importantly, Kobylians'ka's reception of fascism puts her in conversation with those non-fascist and openly anti-fascist European intellectuals who engaged with beliefs, themes, and images commonly found in texts by writers identified with fascism to discern from them a set of new rhetorical tools for a more effective rebuttal of the ideology it represented.

Kobylians'ka's peculiar reception of interwar fascism and the appeal of her 1936 novel for contemporary readers also invite us to look for the continuities that link Ukrainian interwar radical nationalism to the contemporary far-right political movements, not so much with regard to radical ethno-nationalism, aggressive xenophobia, or anti-Semitism, but in political idealism and a strong desire to overcome economic and political crises. As some recent political scientists observe, the majority of post-Soviet nationalists often "interpret ... ultra-nationalism in national-liberationist rather than racist or xenophobic terms," and fervently take up the cause of "liberating Ukraine from the Kremlin's hegemony" (Shekhovtsov and Umland 2014, 62) – a stance which resonates with the ideological views and political goals of Kobylians'ka's "apostle of the sword." In this light, although Kobylians'ka's 1936 novel might be weaker artistically than her earlier works, it deserves a re-examination both as an intricate psychological profile of Western Ukrainians as they struggled to overcome their political defeats of 1917–20 and as a means to penetrate radical nationalist self-understanding and grasp the reasons why so many apparently civilized and cultured people can tolerate, accept, and even welcome radical ideologies whose potentially brutal realizations stand in absolute contrast to accepted standards of political, social, and individual morality.

Afterword

In 1933, in the twilight of her creative career, Kobylians'ka described her work as apolitical and strictly regional, claiming that she "never took any part in ... political life" because she "knew little about politics," and that she devoted "all her skills and energy" to "serve Ukrainian culture" exclusively (V:658). Yet a close examination of the intersection among aesthetics, philosophy, and ideology in Kobylians'ka's fictional and non-fictional writings, alongside the contextualization of her works in fin-de-siècle and interwar European intellectual history, shows that Kobylians'ka dramatically underestimated in the above quote the depth of her own engagement with the political, social, artistic, and philosophical contexts of her tumultuous times. Furthermore, it proves that Kobylians'ka's decision to downplay political aspects of her prose was deliberate and prudent. It allowed her to retain a substantial degree of intellectual freedom and engendered opportunities to disseminate her works not only in Western Ukraine but also in the rest of Europe, North America, and the Soviet Union. Kobylians'ka's 1933 rejection of any political affiliation likewise proved beneficial in the Soviet context because it allowed a group of dedicated scholars to legitimize her as belonging to the pantheon of Ukrainian writers of the Soviet people and to initiate an extensive research into her life and works. With the fall of the Soviet Union, the benefits of Kobylians'ka's claim of non-partisan regionalism expired, and it is time we recognize her as a vitally important voice in modern thought – a voice that not only represented and dominated Ukrainian intellectual discourse of the early twentieth century but also articulated the struggle of the fin-de-siècle and interwar generations of European intellectuals to overcome the multiple tensions and contradictions of their time.

Kobylians'ka wrote in an original and groundbreaking style, moving Ukrainian literature in a new direction; she also introduced progressive

Western ideas into contemporary Ukrainian intellectual debates and succeeded in forging a new Ukrainian identity, empowered and confident in its inherent cultural and political potential. Kobylians'ka, however, merits recognition not only for her national service but also for her rigorous contributions to broader discussions of aesthetic, philosophical, social, and ideological models generated by fin-de-siècle and interwar European intellectuals. Her daring experimentation with synthesizing diverse and often opposing currents of philosophical and political thought – feminism, populism, social Darwinism, Nietzsche's elitism, Marxism, nationalism, Christian thought, and fascism, among others – is the most significant feature that defines her intellectual heritage and also links her personal plight to the struggle of European fin-de-siècle and interwar intellectuals seeking to navigate the multiple cultural, social, and political projects of their times. Among the most important conceptual syntheses that embed Kobylians'ka's works into this larger context are a conservative view of humans bound by nature with a more progressive belief in the possibility of creating a new human being; a firm commitment to understanding human nature by means of science with an exploration of the unlimited possibilities of the will; Nietzsche's elitism with nineteenth-century Russian radicalism and its dictum of the intellectual's duty to the people; the faith and service of Christianity with the heroism of classical thought; and, finally, a bourgeois understanding of private property relations with grassroots social activism.

Kobylians'ka's 1894 image of the New Ukrainian Woman and her 1936 image of the new Ukrainian man, which frame the evolution of her creative commentaries on Ukraine's liberationist effort chronologically, convey the syncretic nature of her daring conceptual experimentations with distinctive eloquence. In the late 1880s, Kobylians'ka emerged on the Ukrainian literary stage as an original and creative thinker who shrewdly muted her radical revolt against traditional patriarchal dogmas into a sophisticated liberal compromise. While agreeing with the leading European and Ukrainian theoreticians of feminism on the importance of higher education for women, she, like many Russian and German nineteenth-century anti-socialist realist writers, rejected the socialist ideological framework of feminism by dismissing its ideal of a self-sufficient emancipationist. Kobylians'ka was particularly critical of its concept of "free love" and its class-based notion of equality. Instead, she propagated intellectual and moral self-improvement as the only way to achieve women's liberation and advocated somewhat modernized yet traditional roles for women within the family as conscientious mothers and supportive spouses. In the mid-1890s,

Kobylians'ka infused her discussion of feminism with Nietzsche's thought and nineteenth-century Russian radicalism, notably its dictum on the intellectual's duty to his or her society. Her new heroine type, a Ukrainian overwoman who not only offered Ukrainian women a new ideal for emulation but also reconfigured the traditional models of national martyrdom by forging an innovative myth of Ukraine's cultural and political revival, tellingly captures its principal conceptual tenets. More importantly, contrary to the prominent fin-de-siècle symbols of Ukraine's struggle for liberation, this type suggested that a successful future could be created not by drawing strength from the ancestral past or the values of the Ukrainian peasant community but by carrying out a regenerative cultural revolution and fostering a united and highly educated national elite. In the interwar period, when Ukraine was aspiring to overcome its dramatic political fiascos of the early 1920s, Kobylians'ka adjusted her model to the interwar climate of moral nihilism by accepting a measure of militarist rhetoric and embracing a heroic tone. As with her earlier works, she succeeded in assuring her Ukrainian readers of their distinctive qualities and in inspiring them for radical yet thoughtful action by giving them a new symbol of Ukraine's liberation – this time, a robust and resolute warrior with a strong political will whose image continues to appeal to many contemporary Ukrainians in the wake of new post-Soviet economic, political, social, and moral crises.

Kobylians'ka shared not only theoretical daring and artistic audacity with the fin-de-siècle and interwar generations of European intellectuals but also their profound uncertainty towards the multitude of social and political movements that sprang up in Europe in the early twentieth century, when old and new attitudes interacted with unmatched fecundity. As her continuous push to rethink and reassert her views in response to rapidly changing cultural, social, and political circumstances suggests, Kobylians'ka could not surmount the unsettling ambivalence of European intellectuals of her time towards liberalism, whose celebration of equality she criticized but could not renounce. Neither could she overcome their obsession with radical change and revolution, whose necessity she asserted but whose brutality she eventually despised, nor their sense of a cultural and political apocalypse, which she both welcomed and repudiated. Most importantly, however, she found their continuous oscillation between the individual and the masses, between the I and the we, impossible to escape.

Kobylians'ka's inability to define the relationship between the individual and the masses, or more precisely to delineate the role of the individual and that of the masses in Ukraine's social and political progress, is felt perhaps most sharply in her representations of Ukrainian peasants. Yielding to persistent pressure from the Ukrainian populist camp in the late 1890s to pay more attention to peasant themes, Kobylians'ka crafted a series of "rustic" works in which she exposed the populists' uncritical glorification of the Ukrainian village community and the natural person, the Ukrainian villager. Instead of dwelling on the material conditions and ethnographic peculiarities of everyday peasant life, which was a common practice in the nineteenth-century Ukrainian populist tradition, she depicted the emotional and cognitive lives of her peasant characters, projecting them as natural beings, pristine in their culture but often chaotic and ruthless in their behaviour. While depicting her peasant characters as unfit for any social or political struggle, Kobylians'ka nevertheless drew attention to their downtrodden social position. She also acknowledged on many occasions their spiritual authenticity and unconventional insight into broader geopolitical issues. Kobylians'ka found peasant characters and their speech patterns particularly effective in conveying the dramatic experiences of the First World War and in transmitting her views on the multiple identities of Western Ukrainians and their disintegration in times of major global conflict during which Ukraine was disregarded as a "non-historical" nation, and in the aftermath of which the Ukrainian question was altogether neglected by global powers.

Although Kobylians'ka continuously revised the conceptual underpinnings of her works, proceeding from feminism and social Darwinism to Nietzsche's elitism and anti-populism, to political militarism and radical nationalism, she remained uncompromising on a cluster of key principles. Her dedication to Ukraine's cultural and political palingenesis, her celebration of Western culture, and her firm repudiation of ethnocentrism, xenophobia, and any other type of heterophobia remained immune to all changes in her cultural, social, and political environment. While growing up in the multicultural setting of Austrian Bukovyna, where diverse cultures and ideologies continually overlapped, connected, and clashed along borders that were both physical and psychological, Kobylians'ka developed an understanding of a Ukrainian nation that was both irredentist and inclusive at the same time. Throughout her creative career, she saw the denationalization of the Ukrainian intellectual elite as one of the main threats to Ukraine's national project, and deemed anything and anyone who jeopardized the well-rounded education and solidification of the Ukrainian elite as a villain. As a result, Kobylians'ka often portrayed Poles, Romanians, Russians, and occasionally Jews as morally inferior foes to Ukraine's national revival. She, however, never positioned the Ukraine's problem in exclusively Polish, Romanian, Russian, or Jewish terms. What is more, she saw the main threat to Ukraine's nation-building project not in the external source but in the lack of organized Ukrainian civil society and strong political leadership. That is why she is justly famous for giving her readers both appealing images of the new Ukrainian women and men and for scandalizing the Ukrainian public with ominous depictions of ruthless, self-centred, and often feeble-minded Ukrainian peasants and no less brutal and coarse Ukrainian denationalized provincial intelligentsia. Her best-known novel, *The Earth*, and her less critically acclaimed novel *Niobe* offer, respectively, the most powerful representations of the two types of spiritually and morally corrupted Ukrainians that the writer despised the most.

While Kobylians'ka's post-1914 fiction has generally been viewed as less interesting artistically than her earlier works, a close examination shows that her writings of the later period actually made important contributions to European modernism. New readings of Kobylians'ka's war narratives, many of which have remained barely known over the past century, demonstrate that Kobylians'ka's post-1914 works display the same rhetorical vigour and stylistic complexity as her earlier writings. Like many other modernist war commentators in Europe, Kobylians'ka crafted a series of alternative literary means of expression that allowed her to capture the unspeakable horror of war with profound acuteness and rhetorical power. Ample intertextual allusions, unconventional allegories, sharp juxtapositions, symbolic use of silence, elements of *skaz,* irony, and a mixture of gruesome naturalism with elements of black humour and tragicomedy highlight a wide spectrum of ways in which Kobylians'ka articulated her encounter with war. A broader discussion of conceptual affinities between interwar pro-fascist aesthetics and modernism also shows that Kobylians'ka's last novel, *Apostle of the Rabble,* with its palingenetic myth, its affirmation of strong political rule, its fascination with masculine vigour, and its general tendency to reconcile traditional values with progress, is a product of the manifold modernist aesthetic.

Despites its innovative approach and new perspective on Kobylians'ka's life and work, the present study does not exhaust the topic. There is still much work that needs to be done, particularly in regard to Kobylians'ka's post-1914 writings. For example, biographical accounts of Kobylians'ka's life and work in the post-1914 period have too many gaps. Missing data can surely be found, but it will require diligent and persistent research in places beyond the obvious range of sources. There is also a need for further exploration of Kobylians'ka's contributions to First World War literature and Ukrainian nationalist literature produced outside the Soviet Union in the 1930s, where the foci should be less on the peculiarities of her prose and more on the patterns and features that link varied writers of these genres to other interwar European intellectuals who engaged, directly or indirectly, with radical ideologies of their time. Another area for further work lies in studies of Kobylians'ka's many fictional and non-fictional writings that have not been included in this book: Kobylians'ka's critical essays and memoirs, another dozen little-known stories, and her private correspondence of the 1920s and the 1930s, which remains closed to scholars. It is my hope that this book will encourage new research into Kobylians'ka's life and work with a clear sense of the foundational role of her commitment to fin-de-siècle and interwar European intellectual debates and to Ukraine's liberation efforts, with an understanding of her idiosyncratic methods and the ever-conflicted and ever-changing nature of her intellectual self, but without the ideological bias that characterized so much of the writing about her in the past. I also hope that this book will lead to new translations of Kobylians'ka's works into English, which will not only enrich world culture with new euphonies but also open a valuable perspective on the common European experience at some of the most defining moments in modern European history.

Notes

Introduction

1 Pavlychko's "Retseptsiia Ol'hy Kobylians'koi i konflikt kul'tury zblyz'ka" ("Reception of Ol'ha Kobylians'ka and the Conflict of Culture" in Pavlychko 2009, 68–77), Hundorova's *Femina melancholica. Stat' i kul'tura v gendernii utopii Ol'hy Kobylians'koi* (*Femina Melancholica: Gender and Culture in the Gender Utopia of Ol'ha Kobylians'ka*, 2002), Mel'nychuk's *Na vechirn'omu pruzi: Ol'ha Kobylians'ka v ostannii period tvorchisti, vid 1914 roku* (*On the Evening Prut: Ol'ha Kobylians'ka's Post-1914 Fiction*, 2006), and Pavlyshyn's *Ol'ha Kobylians'ka: Prochytannia* (*Ol'ha Kobylians'ka: A Reading*, 2008) are the most prominent examples here.

1. The Art of Feminist Compromise

1 This and all subsequent translations of the Ukrainian- and German-language originals, including all Kobylians'ka's fictional and non-fictional writings, are mine unless otherwise indicated as in the case with Roma Franko's translations of Kobylians'ka's selected short stories and her first novel, *A Human Being*, collected in the six-volume series *Women's Voices in Ukrainian Literature* (Winnipeg: Language Lanterns Publication, 1998–2000), edited by Sonia Morris.
2 Today, the town of Kobylians'ka's birth is called Gura-Humorului and is located in Romania.
3 Roman and Arabic numerals refer to volume and page number of Komyshanchenko's historical-critical edition *Ol'ha Kobylians'ka: Tvory v piaty tomakh* (Kyiv: Derzhavne vydavnytstvo khudozhn'oi literatury, 1962–3).
4 Potthast's 1926 dissertation, which remains a solid introduction to Marlitt's life and work, is the most telling example of typical interpretations of

Marlitt's works as trivial and of meagre aesthetic value. Some of the key scholarly investigations of the 1970s were also quick to condemn Marlitt's work as reactionary (Schulte-Sasse and Werner 1977), or as regressive, narcissistic daydreams (Kienzle 1975). Only in the 1990s did scholars begin to look into the more progressive aspects of Marlitt's fiction. See Arens 1994, Coupe 1996, and Kontje 1998.

5 Horbatsch, for example, argues that through Marlitt's fiction, Kobylians'ka discovered classical models of domestic fiction, such as Charlotte Brontë's *Jane Eyre* of 1847 (1984, 207–15). Similarly, Hundorova defines Marlitt's style of writing as "a style of feminine kitsch" and points to its traces in Kobylians'ka's early works (2008, 146).

6 See Horbatsch 1984, 207–15; Hundorova 2008, 146; and Pavlyshyn 2008, 27.

7 For a brief analysis of the intellectual discussions during social gatherings at the Ozarkevych family, see Bohachevsky-Chomiak 1988, 72–3.

8 For a detailed discussion of this reference, see pages 42–4 of this study.

9 By "Western Ukraine" I refer here to former Austro-Hungarian territories with a dominant Ukrainian population – namely, Galicia, Transcarpathia, and Bukovyna – which were annexed by the Soviet Union after 1939 and later became an integral part of independent Ukraine.

10 See *Slova zvorushenoho sertsia* 1982, 68, 199, 217, 284 and V:215 and 447; V:313 and 470; and V:170, 215, 216, 241, 308, and 524, respectfully.

11 For a detailed discussion of aesthetic elitism and its dissemination in Western Europe at the turn of the twentieth century, see Mosse, "Theories of the Elite," in Mosse 1988, 297–312.

12 For further discussion of Dobroliubov's influence on feminist discourse in the late nineteenth century, see Stites 1978, 34–5.

13 In her autobiography, Kobryns'ka points out that she was introduced to Dobroliubov's work, along with works by Belinsky, Chernyshevsky, and Pisarev, through one of her brothers after he moved to L'viv in the mid-1870s and made friends with Ivan Franko, one of the most adamant champions of the Russian radical thought of the 1860s in Western Ukraine (1958, 375). Kobryns'ka must surely have been among the first Ukrainian intellectuals who introduced Kobylians'ka to Dobroliubov's thought.

14 In a letter written to Makovei on 7 December 1898, Kobylians'ka confessed that she cried bitterly when she learned that Terlets'kyi had mocked her story with a sarcastic comment: "Panienki nie mają zajęcia i piszą za parawanem romansiki" (the young lady has nothing better to do, but to write love stories behind the screen). V:375–6.

15 For a detailed discussion of Kobylians'ka's early publication efforts, see *Slova zvorushenoho sertsia* 1982, 111, 112, 114, 117, 124, and 125.

16 Kobryns'ka made similar speculations in her letter to Kobylians'ka on 23 March 1887, quoted in Tomashuk 1963, 246.
17 For a comprehensive discussion of Kobryns'ka's socialist feminism, see Bohachevsky-Chomiak 1988, 71–85.
18 Kobylians'ka's critique of socialism is elaborated and nuanced in the subsequent chapters of this study.
19 Ivan Franko develops his criticism of Kobylians'ka's tribute to Marlitt in his 1905 letter to Vatroslav Jagic. See Franko 1976–86, 50:281.
20 For further discussion on Kobryns'ka's role in editing *The First Garland*, see Denysiuk and Kryl' 1980.
21 For a detailed analysis of the two conspectuses, see Pavlyshyn 2008, 61–4.
22 While elaborating on the heroine's awakening sexuality and her attempts to repress it, Hundorova, for example, interprets Olena's emotional outburst as a hysterical breakdown triggered by the psychological trauma of slipping into a physical reality that annihilates her dreams. See Hundorova 2002, 101–2. Levchenko, who describes *A Human Being* as "an original psychological experiment with a woman-narcissist" who attempts to function in a system of masculine values, nonetheless also reads Olena's story as a promising enterprise that eventually degenerates into the heroine's self-negation. See Levchenko 2008, 71. Similarly, Aheieva claims that, in spite of Olena's initial heroic rebellion against patriarchal dogma, she ultimately fails because she forces herself into a financially sound marriage with a person who does not share her intellectual aspirations. See Aheieva 2008, 213–14. Likewise, Marko Pavlyshyn, while approaching Kobylians'ka's works anew and deconstructing many of the popular Marxists myths surrounding them, shares the general consensus on the symbolic meaning of the story's conclusion. Despite his thorough discussion of Kobylians'ka's interest in evolutionary theory and his analysis of a Darwinian polemic in *A Human Being*, Pavlyshyn adds his voice to the chorus of those critics who read Olena's struggle as futile. He concludes that, regardless of her high consciousness, the heroine is unable to cope with her unfortunate circumstances and is forced to marry for money. See Pavlyshyn 2008, 65.
23 See Bakhtin, "Discourse in the Novel," in Bakhtin 2008, 392–3.
24 See, for example, Kobylians'ka's record of her private conversations with Okunevs'ka about the "physical life of men and women" in her diary entry recorded on 26 June 1886. See *Slova zvorushenoho sertsia* 1982, 126–7.
25 See pages 19–21 of this study.
26 For a well-informed account of Kobylians'ka's relationship with Makovei, see Pavlyshyn 2008, 171–228. Also see Vozniuk 2006, 80–5.
27 See, for example, Hundorova 2002, 101–2; Levchenko 2008, 71; Aheieva 2008, 213–14; Pavlyshyn 2008, 65.

2. New Woman, New Myth

1 For a detailed discussion of Iulian Bachyns'kyi's idea of Ukrainian statehood, which he elaborated in his 1985 pamphlet Ukraina irredanta, see Rudnytsky 1987, 391.

2 Komyshanchenko's and Babyshkin's assessments are the most representative examples of the derogatory Soviet reviews of Kobylians'ka's dialogue with "the decadent bourgeois philosopher" Nietzsche. See Komyshanchenko 1962, 1:18, and Babyshkin 1963, 12.

3 For relevant passages in *Thus Spoke Zarathustra*, see Nietzsche 1978, 286–96 and 12–14, respectively.

4 For relevant passages in *Historical Letters*, see Lavrov 1967, 114–15.

5 Max Nordau's virulent critique of Nietzsche's philosophy and its influence on art, as presented in his 1892 book *Entartung* (*Degeneration*), is perhaps the most striking example of the original negative reception of Nietzsche in Europe.

6 See, for example, Landsberg 1902, 97–9; Reiner n.d., 68; Stöcker 1906, 65–74.

7 Two recent Ukrainian scholars of Kobylians'ka and her work, Lubkivs'ka and Kyryliuk, discern several other Nietzschean motifs in *A Human Being*, including the "great longing." See Lubkivs'ka 1995, and Kyryliuk 2003, 29.

8 For relevant passages in *Thus Spoke Zarathustra*, see Nietzsche 1978, 12, 199, and 287. For a detailed discussion of the story's publication history and an insightful analysis of its Nietzschean themes, also see Pavlyshyn 2008, 92–108.

9 For a well-researched survey of Kobylians'ka's references to Nietzsche, his works, and his most famous metaphors (the herd, self-overcoming, the laughing lion, the higher people, the great noon, the overman) in her correspondence, see Pavlyshyn 2008, 82–91. Also see ibid., 85–7, for a discussion of Kobylians'ka's tribute to Brandes's and Kaatz's interpretations of Nietzsche's philosophy. Pavlyshyn claims that Kobylians'ka's reception of Nietzsche shows some traces of Brandes's interpretations, particularly in regards to Nietzsche's ruthless criticism of Christian morality and somewhat dogmatic and even fantastical nature of his concept of the overman (ibid., 85). As to Kobylians'ka's reading of Kaatz's *The Worldview of Friedrich Nietzsche*, Pavlyshyn also makes several curious observations. While analysing her correspondence with Makovei, Pavlyshyn establishes that Kobylians'ka paid particular attention to the second volume of Kaatz's attempt at systematizing Nietzsche's world view, especially to the sections on politics and nationality, advising her friend to skip sections

on women because of their "overly generalized nature," as she put it (V:297–8). Pavlyshyn finds it odd that Kobylians'ka was more interested in Kaatz's assessment of Nietzsche's views on politics than on women issues and speculates that Kobylians'ka simply "did not want to share her Nietzsche even with someone as close to her as Makovei." The following discussion in this chapter, however, demonstrates that Kobylians'ka's reception of both Brandes's and Kaatz's works is much more complex and that she might have had other, more programmatic reasons for her use of their works.

10 For an in-depth discussion of Nietzsche's reception among Ukrainian intellectuals at the turn of the twentieth century, see Pavlychko 1999, 127–32.

11 Babyshkin's tribute to Lutsiv's thesis on Kobylians'ka's borrowings from Nietzsche is the most representative example from the Soviet literary criticism. See Babyshkin 1963, 11–12. Among post-Soviet adaptations of Lutsiv's thesis, Lubkivs'ka's work stands out the most. See Lubkivs'ka 1995, 146.

12 See, for example, Hundorova 2002.

13 See, for example, Pavlyshyn 2008, 142, and Kyryliuk 2003, 29.

14 While Hundorova acknowledges Kobylians'ka's references to Ukraine's national revival in *The Princess*, she reads them as no more than a "romantic pathos of national regeneration." See Hundorova 2002, 152. Pavlyshyn complicates Hundorova's reading but also views Kobylians'ka's promise of Ukraine's social and political regeneration as merely a "tale" or a "fantasy." More importantly, Pavlyshyn argues that Kobylians'ka developed her position on the nation question "naperekir Nitsshe" (in contradiction to Nietzsche), that is, arguing against what he defines as Nietzsche's apolitical concept of the overman. See Pavlyshyn 2008, 139–42.

15 A well-documented record of Kobylians'ka's correspondence with chief editors of several Austrian and Prussian publication houses and periodicals, such as *An der Schönen Blauen Donau* (*By the Beautiful Blue Danube*), *Wiener Mode* (*Viennese Fashion*), *Freie Deutsche Bühne* (*Free German Stage*), and *Die Neue Zeit* (*The New Times*), is preserved at Chernivtsi State O. Iu. Kobylians'ka Literary and Memorial House-Museum. For further discussion of this correspondence, see Tomashuk 1969, 19–20, and Pavlyshyn 2008, 39–41.

16 In 1891, when Kobylians'ka sent her manuscript to Mykhailo Pavlyk, the novel was titled *Lorelei* after the German folkloric feminine water spirit. Several years later, in a letter written on 7 November 1894 to Vasyl' Lukych, who was at the time the head editor of the L'viv-based bimonthly

periodical *Zoria* (*The Dawn*), Kobylians'ka referred to her novel using another title – *Bez podii* (*Without Events*). In 1895, shortly before sending the final version of her text for publication in the Chernivtsi-based periodical *Bukovyna*, she renamed it for the last time *The Princess*. For further discussion on the history of the novel's title, see Babyshkin's commentary in 1:575–6.

17 See, for example, Kobylians'ka's less than flattering commentaries on Nataliia Kobryns'ka, her feminist circle, and its activities that Kobylians'ka shared with Mykhailo Pavlyk in a letter written on 11 November 189; V:257.

18 Polonized half-Gypsy Vasyl' Oriadyn in *The Princess* (1896), Anna Iakhnovych's Jewish daughter-in-law in *Niobe* (1905), the half-Gypsy Hryts' in *She Gathered Herbs on Sunday Morning* (1909), Germanized Iohanes Shvarts in *After Situations* (1913), Polonized Zoia Zhmut in "She-Wolf" (1923), and Polonized Eva Zakharii in *Apostle of the Rabble* (1926–8) offer the most obvious examples.

19 For further discussion of how Kobylians'ka used various ethnic markers in her prose, see Pavlyshyn 2008, 234–5.

20 In a letter written to Makovei on 16 March 1898, Kobylians'ka reported that Russian censors banned her work from publication because of its subversive subject matter. See V:333.

21 Although there are no known records proving that Kobylians'ka read Chernyshevsky's *What Is to Be Done?*, Pisarev's volume from Kobylians'ka's personal library that includes his essay "Posmotrim!" ("We Will See!" 1865), testifies that Kobylians'ka was well aware of Chernyshevsky's work and its main contributions to the Russian radical thought of the late nineteenth century, which were also broadly discussed by Ukrainian intellectuals in Western Ukraine of her time. See chapter 1, pages 19–21, of this study.

22 The relevant passage in *Human, All Too Human* comes from aphorism 292, where Nietzsche calls on his reader to embrace him- or herself as his or her own goal, an object of exploration and a source of experience:

> And so onwards along the path of wisdom, with a hearty tread, a hearty confidence! However you may be, be your own source of experience! Throw off your discontent about your nature; forgive yourself your own self ... You have it in your power to merge everything you have lived through – attempts, false starts, errors, delusions, passions, your love and your hope – into your goal, with nothing left over: you are to become an inevitable chain of culture-rings, and on the basis of this inevitability, to deduce the inevitable course of culture in general. (1996, 134–5)

In the aphorism 270 of his *The Gay Science*, Nietzsche phrases the motto "to be one's own goal" slightly differently – "You shall become the person you are." In the footnote to this aphorism, Michael Kaufman points out Nietzsche derived this motto from Pindar and later gave his *Ecce Homo* the subtitle "How One Becomes What One Is." See Nietzsche 1974, 219, and 1992.

23 See note 6 of this chapter.

24 Taras Shevchenko's poems "Prychynna" ("The Bewitched Girl," 1837), "Topolia" ("The Poplar," 1839), "Utoplena" ("The Drowned Girl," 1841), and "Kateryna" ("Kateryna," 1843) provide the most obvious examples.

25 Lesia Ukrainka's great dramatic works, especially *Kassandra* (*Cassandra*, 1907) and *Boiarynia* (*The Boyar's Wife*, 1910), present the most compelling examples of the new heroine type.

26 The German text of the comment reads as follows: "Man darf nie vergessen, dass Nietzsche als Mensch der Zukunft in 'Zarathustra' eine Gestalt gewollt hat, die nicht aus unserer Welt ist, und zu der deshalb noch niemand eigentlich innere Beziehung haben kann." All emphases are Kobylians'ka's. The original visiting card is preserved in the Kyiv Institute of Literature, F14, N1021.

27 For further discussion of the active and reactive in Nietzsche, see Deleuze 1983, 39–72.

28 The sea and the seafarer are some of the most recurrent metaphors in Nietzsche's *Thus Spoke Zarathustra*. When Zarathustra reaches the Blessed Islands, he calls the sea an embodiment of the overman and later defines the seafarers as "bold searchers and researchers" driven by a desire to embark on "dangerous seas" and thereby to discover the implied terra incognita of a still unimaginable human future (1978, 85, 155). For further references to "seafaring" and "laughing waves" in *Thus Spoke Zarathustra*, also see ibid., 96, 152–6, and 228–30. On Zarathustra's discussion of the "great noon," see ibid., 79, 172, 178, 191, 198, 215, 221, 286, and 327.

29 This entire passage is also omitted in Komyshanchenko's 1962 edition of *The Princess*. See I:326.

30 For further discussion of Lavrov's philosophical arguments, see Scanlan, "Piotr Lavrov: An Intellectual Biography." For Lavrov's original text, see his "Fourth Letter: The Coast of Progress," in Lavrov 1967, 129–40.

31 See chapter 1, pages 19–21, of this study.

32 For further discussion of Nietzsche's concepts of the gift-giving virtue, see White 2016, 348–64.

33 Notably, this section is omitted in Komyshanchenko's 1962 edition of Kobylians'ka's works. See I:358.

34 For a detailed discussion of Nietzsche's concept of *ressentiment*, see pages 71–2 of this chapter.
35 This whole conversation is also missing in Komyshanchenko's 1962 edition of Kobylians'ka's works. See I:270.
36 For further discussion on Russian intelligentsia of the nineteenth century and the role of literature in their social and political activism, see Berlin 1978, 129.
37 See, for example, Kryms'kyi 1963, 36–8, or Hrushevs'kyi 1898.
38 For a detailed discussion of Dobroliubov's and Turgenev's interpretations of Insarov's role in Russian literature, see Mathewson 2000, 56–7.
39 While reviewing Kobylians'ka's last novel, *Apostle of the Rabble*, Vil'de, a prominent Western Ukrainian social activist, compared its educative, patriotic rhetoric to a similarly powerful message in Kobylians'ka's earlier text, *The Princess*, which, according to Vil'de, "shaped entire generations of [Ukrainian] women and taught them to assert their character in public life." See Vil'de 1937b, 19. Mykola Shapoval, a prolific publicist and prominent leader of the Ukrainian Social-Revolutionaries in exile in Czechoslovakia, expressed similar views on the didactic power of Kobylians'ka's second novel. He even claimed that it was Kobylians'ka's novel, *The Princess*, and its call on Ukrainian intellectuals to make self-education and self-assertion their primary goal ("buty sobi tsileiu") that turned him into a revolutionary. See his letter to Kobylians'ka of 24 November 1927, in Kohut 1928, 250.
40 Gellner argues that nationalism is a sociological condition and a likely result of modernization. His theories focus on political and cultural aspects of modernization. In particular, he examines the unifying and homogenizing roles of the educational systems and high culture. As he observes, "high culture or great tradition" consolidates a people by imposing a particular "style of conduct and communication," "a norm which should be, but alas is not, satisfied in real life, and the rules of which are usually codified by a set of respected norm-giving specialists within society." See Gellner 1983, 92.
41 See, for example, Grabowicz's assessment of *Krytyka*, a leading Ukrainian intellectual magazine since 1997, and its role in shaping the nucleus of Ukraine's intellectual life, where he points out that "the creation of new [intellectual] standards and ... a new [intellectual] discourse" is the key feature of *Krytyka*'s nation-building objective, which he finds "extremely necessary" for *Krytyka*'s intellectual model. Grabowicz also claims that the revival of the Humanities in Ukraine and the reorganization of the Ukrainian Academy of Sciences must be state priorities if Ukraine to succeed in its ongoing state-building efforts (2017, 2–6).

3. The Populist Trial

1 In 1883, Ostap Terlets'kyi was the first to call Kobylians'ka "simply an exotic flower" in Ukrainian literature, who was out of sync with Ukrainian reality (qtd. in Kobylians'ka's letter to Oleksandr Barvins'kyi written on 17 December 1909; V:609). Fifteen years later, once Kobylians'ka was already an established writer, Vasyl' Shchurat, a well-known populist literary scholar of the time, expressed a similar opinion. In his review of Kobylians'ka's 1898 long story "Valse mélancolique" – in which the writer explored the relationship between three independent women who reject patriarchal mores and share a home together, living only for art – he claimed that Kobylians'ka's text did not reflect Ukrainian life and made an impression of an "exotic" text written by a "foreign author" (opovidannia zagranychnoi avtorky), who wrote about things that were foreign to Ukrainian readers (qtd. in Turbats'ky 1963, 41). While responding to Shchurat, Lev Turbats'kyi, the head editor of the daily populist newspaper *Bukovyna* published in Chernivtsi, agreed that Kobylians'ka's "Valse mélancolique" was indeed a "work of European culture," atypical for Ukrainian literature (1963, 42). In a letter to Makovei written on 5 April 1898, Kobylians'ka's also mentioned that Turbats'kyi, nevertheless, made an unpleasant remark in a private conversation, pointing out that she made on him an impression of a German and not a Ukrainian writer (V:338). The most fervent critique of Kobylians'ka's perceived non-Ukrainianness was Iefremov's polemical article "In Search of the New Beauty" of 1902. For a detailed discussion of Iefremov's article and Kobylians'ka's response to it, see chapter 4, pages 119–22, of this study.

2 Franko was among the first to review Kobylians'ka's peasant novel positively as an "important document that captured the world view of [Ukrainian] people" and to recognize its publication as "a defining moment in Ukrainian literature" (1976–86, 50:282). Similarly, Iefremov, despite his criticism of Kobylians'ka's modernist aesthetics, acknowledged her "fundamental knowledge of peasant life" (1993, 101). Even modernist critics in their discussions of *The Earth* often recognized its truthful depictions of peasant life, interpreting them as the key traits of Kobylians'ka's "true realism" (Khotkevych 1963a, 146). From the 1930s onward, Soviet critics often framed *The Earth* as a pinnacle in the evolution of Kobylians'ka's high realism and the dominant populist fictional model, which propagated an espousal of the peasant language and the peasant way of life. Tomashuk's account is perhaps the most representative here. See Tomashuk 1969a, 84–5.

3 Hutsuls are a dominant ethnic group living in the Ukrainian part of the Carpathian Mountains. At the turn of the nineteenth century, Hutsuls were largely peasants.

4 In the 1850s and 1860s, the *khlopomany* movement was founded by a group of young populist descendants from the Polonized nobility who actively engaged in educational and cultural work among peasants in Galicia and right-bank Ukraine. The *khlopomany* enlightenment project had a great influence on the Ukraine national revival movement and was popular through the 1880s. Starting from the early 1890s, however, the new generation of radical progressive intellectuals criticized the *khlopomany* movement and decried its methods as inadequate and shortsighted. For further discussion of the history and significance of the movement, see Subtelny 1988, 279–307.

5 The most representative examples are Stefanyk's "Novyna" ("News," 1899) and "Kaminnyi khrest" ("The Stone Cross," 1900) and Kotsiubyns'kyi's *Tini zabutykh predkiv* (*Shadows of Forgotten Ancestors*, 1911).

6 For a well-documented discussion of the close relations between the Kobylians'kyi and the Zhyzhyian families, see Vozniuk 2006, 33–5. As the diary of Kobylians'ka's younger brother, Volodymyr, indicates, Vozniuk points out, the two families were close as early as 1882, twelve years before Mykhailo's mysterious murder and almost two decades before the publication of *The Earth*. El'pedefor Panchuk also highlights in his memoirs that Kobylians'ka spent a lot of time interviewing the Zhyzhyian family and other peasants from Dymka while working on her novel and developed an intimate relationship with all of them that lasted long after the publication of *The Earth*. See Panchuk 1963, 396–7.

7 In a letter to Makovei written on 7 December 1898, Kobylians'ka pointed out that Franko was not quite satisfied with her creative works and suggested to her that she adopt the realist fictional model, that is, to focus on the themes of the peasant life (V:376). In his 1898 review of *The Princess*, Hrushevs'kyi also indicated that although Kobylians'ka created a compelling narrative with masterful psychological insights, she barely paid any attention to the local sociocultural setting of the story and offered no description of Ukrainian Bukovyna and its broad social strata. Hrushevs'kyi used this point to support his argument about the novel's circumscribed discussion of the Ukrainian national question, implying that to address issues of Ukrainian national revival, it is not sufficient to focus on the life of Ukrainian intelligentsia alone (1898, 178–9).

8 For an insightful reflection on the fin-de-siècle discussion of "the peasant mind" and its potential for Ukraine's political transformation, see Ivan Franko's remarks about Herbert Spencer's formula of "the simple peasant mind" and its reception among Ukrainian political activists in his 1900 essay "Beyond the Limits of the Possible." Franko 1996.

9 Babyshkin 1963 and Tomashuk 1969a are the most representative of the genre.

10 Pohrebennyk's 1983 Marxist reading of *The Earth*, which frames Kobylians'ka's novel as an effective depiction of "the characteristic processes of the capitalist reality of the time, connected to the proletarianization of peasantry," is perhaps the most telling example in this category. See Pohrebennyk's introductory overview "Ol'ha Kobylians'ka" in *Olha Kobylians'ka: Tvory v dvokh tomakh*, 13.

11 For further discussion of Zola's positive depictions of the countryside in the Rougon-Macquart novels, see Berg and Martin 1992, 124.

12 The most revealing account of Kobylians'ka's disdain for the countryside lifestyle is presented in a letter to Pavlyk written in April 1891, in which Kobylians'ka complained about her dull and monotonous life in Dymka. As Kobylians'ka put it, her daily toil in Dymka "progressively stupefied" her (KLMHM N67).

13 For a well-researched discussion of Kobylians'ka's approach to the determinist theory of human behaviour and how it was interpreted in Soviet criticism, see Pavlyshyn 2008, 158–60.

14 In an unpublished letter to Makovei written on 2 August 1900, Kobylians'ka indicated that she quoted Jonas Lie, one of the Four Greats of nineteenth-century Norwegian literature, in her epigraph to *The Earth* (IL F14, N198).

15 For Nietzsche's discussion of "the herd" and "herd morality" in *The Gay Science*, see aphorisms 1, 116, 117, 174, 296, 328, 352, and 354 in 1974, 73, 174–5, 202, 238, 258–60, and 295, respectively. For his discussion of the "higher people" in *Thus Spoke Zarathustra*, see the "On the Higher Man" essay in 1978, 286–96.

16 For further discussion of *ressentiment*, see chapter 2, pages 71–2, of this study.

17 In 1905–6, Kobylians'ka worked intensely on the second part of *The Earth*, which, according to her unfinished manuscript, was intended to focus on Sava's and Rakhira's family life after they inherited a meagre plot of land from Ivonika and Mariika. While Rakhira grows to be a hard-working and shrewd household manager and a devoted mother, Sava's character completely degenerates as he takes to the bottle (II:407–72). Past critics offered many speculations as to why Kobylians'ka never finished the

second part of her peasant novel – poor health and the decline of her talent among them. Yet Panchuk's suggestion that the writer simply did not find it productive to continue with a story seems to be most convincing (qtd. in Babyshkin 1956, 40).

18 For a detailed discussion of the lack of textual evidence in *The Earth* that would incriminate Sava, see Pavlyshyn 2008, 143–69.

4. Hidden Modernism

1 Griffin's concept of generic fascism, defined as a genus of political ideology whose mythic core in its various permutations is a palingenetic form of populist ultra-nationalism, provides a model for the proposed treatment of fascist themes in Kobylians'ka's prose of the 1910s, 1920s and 1930s, which is addressed in chapter 6. For further references on Griffin's theory of generic fascism, see Griffin 1995, 1–4.

2 Kobylians'ka started to work on her long story "Valse mélancolique" in 1894. At the time, she was finalizing her first major novel *The Princess*, and it is little surprise that the two works share the same fundamental principles that, at the time, defined Kobylians'ka's views on the woman question. While advocating for women's right to education, work, and financial independence and openly speaking about female sexuality, both texts reclaim the value of matrimony, presenting well-matched marriage and conscientious motherhood as an important and gratifying pursuit for the New Woman, thereby moulding their radical protest against the patriarchal subjection of women into a liberal compromise. In "Valse mélancolique," which presented the Ukrainian audience with three types of the New Ukrainian Woman whose actions challenged the conventional bourgeois order of the day, Kobylians'ka's intellectual model of what could be defined as radically conservative feminism (see chapter 1 of this study for broader discussion of this model) is embedded in the life story of Marta, the only victorious heroine, who achieves self-fulfilment in both professional sphere and family life. Notably, the other two heroines, Hanna the artist and Sofiia the musician, who are described as significantly more talented and modern than Marta, fail to achieve professional accomplishment and personal happiness because they lack the very resourcefulness, determination, and willpower needed to overcome external societal obstacles and internal psychological turmoil, which Kobylians'ka celebrates in Marta and Natalka Verkovychivna, the main heroine in *The Princess*. Both Hanna and Sofiia could be seen as precursors of Aglaia-Felicitas Fedorenko, the tragic heroine in Kobylians'ka's 1913 novel *After Situations*. For further discussion of the latter novel and its significance, see chapter 4 of this study, pages 152–60.

When "Valse mélancolique" was first published in 1898 in the L'viv-based *Literary and Scientific Herald*, its daring subject matter triggered a bitter controversy. Some critics claimed that the story did not reflect Ukrainian life and thus was an "exotic" text written by a "foreign author" (see chapter 3 of this study, note 1); others celebrated it as a radically new text in Ukrainian literature and even viewed it as a founding work of Ukrainian modernism (see, for example, Turbats'ky 1963, 41–3). Many post-Soviet critics support the latter assessment of Kobyalins'ka's story and its significance in Ukrainian literature. See, for example, Pavlychko 1999, 83. Because "Valse mélancolique" has recently received a lot of critical attention (Aheieva 2008, 197–246; Hundorova 2002, 138–50; and Pavlychko 1999, 81–3) and because almost every existing study of Kobylians'ka's works establishes unequivocal affinities between the story's heroines and the heroines in Kobylians'ka's major novels about Ukrainian intelligentsia that are discussed in length in this study – *A Human Being, The Princess, Over the Bridge*, and *After Situations* – a close reading of the story is omitted from this study. For the most elaborate discussion and visually appealing diagram that establishes parallels between the heroines in *A Human Being, The Princess*, "Valse mélancolique," *Over the Bridge*, and *After Situations*, see Izotov 1928, 89–91.

3 For further discussion, see Krupa 2004.

4 For a comprehensive and well-informed discussion of the symbolic connotations in Shevchenko's individual-family-society continuum, see Grabowicz 1982, 63–76.

5 In her commentary on the main ideas in Kobylians'ka's "The Thoughts of an Old Man," Krupa mostly focuses on Kobylians'ka's propagation of Christian love, claiming that Kobylians'ka saw it as unattainable "without the love for native people." See Krupa 2004, 23.

6 For further references on Nietzsche's views on marriage, see Nietzsche 1978, 69–71.

7 For a detailed and well-documented discussion of Kobylians'ka's and Makovei's relationship, see Pavlyshyn 2008, 171–227.

8 In his critique of bourgeois culture, Marx defined religion as an expression of material realities and economic injustice, and viewed it as a tool by which oppressors make people feel better about the distress they experience due to poverty and exploitation. This interpretation constitutes the premise of his famous comment that religion is the "opium of the people." In Kobylians'ka's *Niobe*, Ostap's remark on the illusory and oppressive nature of religion is a direct allusion to Marx. For further reference on Marx's analysis of religion, see his essay *Introduction to a Contribution to the Critique of Hegel's Philosophy of Right* in Tucker 1978, 52–4.

9 At the turn of the twentieth century, the word "people" (*narod*) was used specifically to refer to the common people, mostly peasantry in the Ukrainian context, while the word "nation" (*natsiia*) was used as a broader concept and encompassed all social strata of a people.

10 See chapter 1, note 26, of this study.

11 Commentaries by Mochul's'kyi, Babyshkin, Tomashuk, Komyshanchenko, Chopyk, Hundorova, and Levchenko are most representative examples here.

12 In the original Ukrainian text, Kobylians'ka used the word *muzhyk*, meaning "a common man" or "a peasant," which is, in turn, the key concept in nineteenth-century populist discourse. Kobylians'ka, however, occasionally used the word *muzhyk* as an antonym to Nietzsche's idea of the overman, which semantically is closer to Nietzsche's "plebe" or "herd man." Although Kobylians'ka maintained some populist connotations in her use of *muzhyk*, in the given context "plebe" would be a more effective translation than "peasant."

13 For Marx's theory of alienation, see his chapter "Estranged Labor" in his *Economic and Philosophical Manuscripts of 1844* in Tucker 1978, 70–81.

14 Ievgenii Bazarov, a challenger of Russian Orthodox conservatism and Western liberalism, is the main character in Kobylians'ka's favourite novel by Turgenev, *Fathers and Sons* (1862). In her earlier works, Kobylians'ka often alluded to Bazarov as a yardstick against which her readers should measure the leading male characters in her own works. Olena Liaufler's first fiancé, Stefan Liievych, is the best example of this.

15 For further references on the history of the Russophile movement in Western Ukraine, which is also known as Moskvophilism, see Subtelny 1988, 317–22, 329, 334; Magocsi 2002, 88; and Motyl 1980, 6–7.

16 For further discussion on Nietzscheanism and its popularity in Eastern Europe, particularly in Russia, see Rosenthal 1986, 3–48. See also Rosenthal 2002, 1–25.

17 In the third part of the novel, Shvarts is persistently labelled as a "demon" (*demon*). See V:105, 107, 109, 126, 130, 136, 138, 141, and 143.

5. War and Fiction

1 Kobylians'ka's two war stories with the strongest pro-Austrian undertones, "The Forest Mother" and "Vasylka," were last published in 1929 in the second volume of the first Soviet edition of Kobylians'ka's collected works in nine volumes (1927–9), edited by Ivan Lyzanivs'kyi.

2 Lesyn was the first to read Kobylians'ka's war prose as a unified anti-war cycle in his 1958 article "Antyvoienni tvory Ol'hy Kobylians'koi" (Lesyn 1958). Babyshkin, Tomashuk, and Pohrebennyk, the leading Soviet

scholars of Kobylians'ka's works, supported Lesyn's interpretation, thereby influencing subsequent post-Soviet scholars of Kobylians'ka's late fiction. See Babyshkin 1963, Tomashuk 1969a, and Pohrebennyk 1983.

3 For further discussion of Kobylians'ka's financial and emotional state on the eve of the First World War, see Vozniuk 2006, 147–53.

4 When the advancing Russian army broke through Austrian defences and occupied much of Eastern Galicia and Bukovyna in the first months of the war, the setback had terrible repercussions for local Ukrainians. They were often accused of treason and were either executed without trial or sent by the thousands to concentration camps. While looking for excuses for their defeats, Austrian and Hungarian commanders likewise accused Western Ukrainians of treason. This led to almost constant terrorizing of the Ukrainian population in Galicia and Bukovyna by both warring parties. For further discussion of Austro-Hungarian wartime repressions in Galicia and Bukovyna, see Botushans'kyi et al. 2009, 150–3; Bryndzan et al. 1956, 296–301; Karpynets' et al. 2005, 60–7; and Subtelny 1988, 341.

5 Kobylians'ka's short stories "Nature" (1895) and Uncultured" (1897), alongside her two novels, *The Earth* (1902) and *On Sunday Morning She Gathered Herbs* (1909), are the best examples here.

6 See note 4 to this chapter.

7 For further discussion of the use of pastoral in fiction and memoirs about the First World War, see Fussell 2013, 251–92.

8 During the First World War, there were about 3.5 million Ukrainian soldiers fighting in the Russian army and about 250,000 in the Austrian forces. For more information, see Subtelny 1988, 340.

9 For a detailed discussion on Kobylians'ka's views on women's roles in the biological and cultural regeneration of a nation, see chapter 1, pages 27–9, of this study.

10 See, for example, discussions offered in Babyshkin 1963, 171; Tomashuk 1969a, 181–2; Komyshanchenko 1963, 39–40; Mel'nychuk 2006, 116–17; and Pavlyshyn 2008, 244–5.

11 Ievhen Petrushevych (1863–1940) was one of the first prominent Western Ukrainian politicians to insist on Ukraine's autonomy and demand Galicia's separation from the Austrian Empire, long before its official dissolution. For further discussion, see Motyl 1980, 26.

12 For a comprehensive discussion of the Brusilov Offensive and its role in the First World War, see Afflerbach 2014.

13 See, for example, Hrinchenko's definition in his *Slovar' ukrainskogo iazyka*, 4 vols. (Kyiv: Druk aktsiinoho tovarystvava Korchaka-Novyts'koho, 1907–9), 2:447.

14 The Manifesto of the Organization of Ukrainian Nationalists (OUN), written in December 1940, which describes the USSR as "the Muscovite prison of nations," conveys the new ideological connotation that "Muscovite" and "Muscovy" acquired in the Ukrainian cultural paradigm after the Bolshevik Revolution. See excerpts in Lindheim and Luckyj 1996, 291, 294. Similar connotations permeate Ievhen Onats'kyj's encyclopedia entry "Moskali," one of the most extensive and passionate encyclopedic entries on the subject to date. See Onats'kyj 1959, vol. K, 1041–3.

15 Kobylians'ka's first pejorative description of Russian troops appeared in her letter to Stefaniia Sadovs'ka written on 11 January 1918, where she spitefully called Russian soldiers "prokliati chorty-vorohy" (cursed, demonic enemy). See V:629.

16 For a comprehensive discussion on the nationalist critics of Ukraine's interwar political weakness, see Shkandrij 2001, 243–9.

17 From the mid-nineteenth century onward, Ukrainian writers often employed images of docile and violated women to symbolize their oppressed nation. In the Ukrainian cultural paradigm, this tradition derived from folk songs and became canonized in Shevchenko's poetry, where Ukraine is often represented through images of orphans, lovelorn girls, or simply poor folks suffering at the hands of the well-off evildoers. See Grabowicz 1982, 61. For a sample of Ievhen Malaniuk's allegorical representations of Ukraine, see "Z chornoi Ellady" and "Lezhysh, rozpusto, na rozputti" in his collection of poems *Zemna Madonna* (1991, 99, 104–5).

18 Miroslav Hroch, a leading historian of nationalism in Eastern Europe, delineates the non-historical, or non-dominant, ethnic groups as nations, which, as opposed to nation states, lacked their own nobility, possessed no state, and had scarce or interrupted literary traditions in their own languages. See Hroch 2000, xiii.

6. Between the Right and the Left

1 Besides Kobylians'ka's correspondence with Biliach, there are several other important documents that prove that she began to receive a pension of 150 Soviet roubles from the Soviet government. Mykola Skrypnyk, the people's commissar of education in Soviet Ukraine, first announced that Kobylians'ka would receive a pension in a congratulatory telegram of November 1927. Two months later, in a letter written to the Taras Shevchenko Scientific Society in L'viv on 6 February 1928, Kobylians'ka publicly acknowledged that she had begun to receive monthly payments from the Soviet government. As she put it, "On 19 January 1928, the Council of People's Commissars of the Ukrainian Socialist Soviet Republic issued a resolution to award me a monthly pension in the amount of 150

roubles starting from 1 January, 1928" (KLMHM F13, N297). In 1928, 150 Soviet roubles equalled about $75. For a detailed discussion of the financial support that Kobylians'ka received from the Soviet Union, see Vozniuk 2006, 198–9.

2 Readers in Soviet Ukraine first encountered several of Kobylians'ka's works through the *Khrestomatiia novoi ukrains'koi literatury* (*Reader of the New Ukrainian Literature*, 1923), which was republished five times by 1927. In 1925, the first edition of Kobylians'ka's collected works, *Noveli* (*Stories*), with an introduction by Bohdan Iakubovs'kyi, came out in Kyiv. More than twenty other editions of Kobylians'ka's collected works came out in Soviet Ukraine between 1925 and 1931. The collected works in nine volumes, which came out from 1927 to 1929 in Kharkiv, is the largest publication of Kobylians'ka's collected works to date. See Kushch 1960.

3 On 21 January 1928, Biliach wrote to Kobylians'ka that her recent publications in the openly anti-Soviet periodicals, the L'viv-based *Literary and Scientific Herald* and the Prague-based journal *Nova Ukraina* (*A New Ukraine*), as well as the anti-Soviet proclamations that some of her admirers delivered during the celebration of her fortieth jubilee in Western Ukraine and across Europe, led to "minor misconceptions" and gave a negative "aftertaste" to Soviet readers. Later in the same letter, Biliach unequivocally stated that Kobylians'ka must cut all ties with "enemies of the [Soviet] regime," threatening that otherwise she might lose the financial support of the Soviets. See KLMHM F35, N1845.

4 For the full text of the award announcement, see the jury's announcement in *Dzvony* (*The Bells*) 1–2 (1937): 63.

5 See Mel'nychuk's overview of the initial reception of *Apostle of the Rabble* in her *Ol'ha Kobylians'ka v ostannii period tvorchosti*. Mel'nychuk 2006, 155.

6 In both political and academic spheres, Ukrainian interwar radical nationalism is mainly associated with the writings of Dmytro Dontsov (1883–1973), the principal ideologue of Ukrainian militant nationalism. Influenced by Nietzsche, Bergson, Sorel, and Italian Fascism, Dontsov propagated a version of radical nationalism – "the nationalism of the deed" (*chynnyi natsionalism*), as he named it – which exalted the ethnic nation as a supreme form of human organization entitled to independent statehood. Because Dontsov, like many radical ideologues in Western Europe, saw politics as a Darwinian struggle of nations for survival, he welcomed conflict and argued that the new Ukrainian state could only be created by "the fire of fanatical commitment," "the iron force of enthusiasm," "social voluntarism," and "the organization of a new violence." Respectively, he saw the future Ukrainian state as ethnically homogeneous and run by a nationalist organization with a supreme *vozhd'* (leader) at its head. See

Dontsov 2006, 260–8. While largely disagreeing on what constitutes a typical fascist movement, contemporary scholars recognize the profound ideological, conceptual, and aesthetic affinities between Western fascism and Ukrainian nationalism of the 1920s–1940s. For further discussion, see note 10 of this chapter.

7 Many post-Soviet scholars of Kobylians'ka's interwar works share Krupa's views. See, for example, Demchenko 2001, Khymyn 1994, Matusiak 1999, Mel'nychuk 2006, Mykosianchyk 2004, Pochyniuk 2005, Slon'ovs'ka 2000.

8 See, for example, Shkandrij's 2015 study of the seven writers associated with the OUN, *Ukrainian Nationalism: Politics Ideology, Literature, 1929–1956*.

9 See Weber 1949, 90–103.

10 For the most complete collection of his essays on the subject, see Mosse 1999.

11 Until recently, Ukrainian interwar radical nationalism was an obscure topic, little discussed among Ukrainian scholars and specialists on Eastern European affairs. But after far-right nationalist movements re-emerged in post-Soviet Ukraine, the history of Ukrainian interwar nationalism and its links to fascism has become the most debated subject in contemporary Ukrainian historiography. Zenon Kohut's and John-Paul Himka's polemic is the best example. In 2010, *Krytyka*, a Kyiv-based intellectual journal, published the Ukrainian translations of their arguments under the title *Dyskusiia: Bandera iak problema* (*Discussions: Bandera as a Problem*). See Himka et al. 2010, 10–12. Shortly thereafter, the collection also came out in book form titled *Strasti za Banderoiu* (*Passions after Bandera*).

Kohut's and Himka's debate clearly demonstrated that Griffin's theoretical framework, whose emergence coincided with the post-Soviet informational revolution, brought on a series of important revisions of Dontsov's interwar theories and their application by the OUN, a conspiratorial, terrorist movement founded in Vienna in 1929 by the Ukrainian Military Organization, the Union of Ukrainian Fascists, and several other radical nationalist groups that led Ukraine's liberationist struggle in the 1930s and 1940s. Andrew Wilson was among the first to argue that interwar Ukrainian nationalism was a variety of fascism, more specifically, "a voluntaristic form of fascism" (1996, 112). Following his lead, Himka, Kost' Bondarenko, Anton Shekhovtsov, and other researchers re-examined the influence of Western fascism on the OUN's ideology and the involvement of Ukrainian nationalists in mass murders of Poles and Jews during the Second World War, which were deliberately downplayed in previous criticism. See, for example, John Armstrong 1955 or Motyl 1980. Himka's assessment of the OUN's activities during the Second World War is an effective illustration of why increasingly more post-Soviet scholars problematize Armstrong's paradigm of integral nationalism, which attempts to differentiate Ukrainian nationalism from Western fascism without providing any coherent explanation of the title term (Armstrong 1955):

> OUN was a typical fascist organization as shown by many of its features: its leadership principal (*Führerprinzip*), its aspiration to ban all other political parties and movements, its fascist-style slogan (*Slava Ukraini! Heroiam slava!* [Glory to Ukraine! Glory to heroes!]), its red and black flag, its raised-arm salute, its xenophobia and anti-Semitism, its cult of violence, its admiration of Hitler, Mussolini, and other leaders of fascist Europe. What is not fascist here? (Himka 2010, 87)

Despite the extensive evidence, the new studies on the OUN's link to fascism leave many champions of the OUN heritage unconvinced. Oleksandr Zaitsev's latest study on Ukrainian interwar nationalism, *Ukrains'kyi integralnyi natsionalism (1920–ti – 1930–ti roky): Narysy intelektual'noi istorii* (*Ukrainian Integral Nationalism of the 1920s–1930s: An Essay on Intellectual History*, 2013) demonstrates that Armstrong's paradigm is not likely to disappear from the scholarly discussion in the near future. At the same time, Zaitsev's work shows that although contemporary scholars might disagree on what constitutes a typical fascist movement, they no longer deny the profound ideological, conceptual, and aesthetic affinities between Western fascism and Ukrainian radical nationalism of the 1920s–1940s.

12 In his *Ukrainian Nationalist: Politics, Ideologies, Literature, 1929–1956*, Shkandrij uses Griffin's theory of generic fascism to set up a conceptual framework for his discussion of the seven Ukrainian writers associated with the OUN. See Shkandrij 2015, 12.

13 Oleh Panchuk, the writer's grandson, holds Kobylians'ka's personal archive of the 1930s privately and keeps it closed to scholars and the public.

14 At the turn of the twentieth century, Bukovyna was the most heterogeneous of the Austro-Hungarian provinces, populated by Romanians, Ukrainians, Jews, Germans, Poles, and Hungarians. In 1910, a new Austrian constitution and an experimental franchise law gave limited personal autonomy to the six nationalities, guaranteeing their national self-determination to prevent any potential ethnic tensions in the region. As one critic rightfully points out, however, Kobylians'ka's 1936 novel deals with the nationality question exclusively "on the basis of Ukrainian and Polish evidence," without making any effort to recreate the polyethnic landscape of historic Austria-Hungary (Pavlyshyn 2014, 566–7). The novel also has no references to the ethnic structure of power and privilege in Austria-Hungary: there are neither Hungarian nor Romanian characters in the story, and the only Germans it depicts come across as

positive characters. This disregard of the ethnic composition of historic Austria-Hungary presents an additional reason not to situate the main events of the novel in the decade preceding the First World War.

15 In April 1922, the Ukrainian National Association of America was first to send Kobylians'ka 12,000 Romanian lei, which at the time was worth about 70 dollars. Over the summer of 1922, Kobylians'ka received another substantial sum of 21,000 Romanian lei, approximately 125 dollars, from Canada. During 1923, she received additional contributions from her admirers in Canada and Western Europe. In January 1924, the Women's Union of Detroit sent her 75 dollars. For further references, see Vozniuk 2006, 177–82.

16 The exact date of the search is unclear. Using Kobylians'ka's letter written on 17 April 1926 to the editorial board of the Kolomyia monthly *Zhinocha dolia* as his evidence, Tomashuk asserts that it took place in 1924. See Tomashuk 1969a, 2. Kobylians'ka's biographer Vozniuk, however, offers a more convincing argument based on a close investigation of further archival materials. He claims that the search could not have taken place any later than September 1922. See Vozniuk 2006, 168–70.

17 For further discussion of the interwar Romanization campaign in Bukovyna, see Subtelny 1988, 446–8.

18 See, for example, Shopoval's letter to Kobylians'ka written on 24 November 1927, in Kohut 1928, 249–52.

19 For further discussion of Kobylians'ka's relationship with the Soviet authorities, see Vozniuk's analysis of Kobylians'ka's correspondence with Biliach in Vozniuk 2006, 201–21.

20 Simovych extensively comments on Kobylians'ka's frustration with Rudnyts'kyi's draconian editorial changes in his memoir. See Simovych 1942, 5. Kysilievs'ka offers similar remarks in her essay "Pislia nedavn'oi hostyny na Bukovyni." See Kysilievs'ka 1937, 11.

21 In an open letter to the Ukrainians in America written on 5 February 1924 and published in the daily Ukrainian newspaper *Svoboda* in New York on 6 March 1924, Kobylians'ka described the miserable conditions of her daily life with characteristic artistry to underscore the timeliness and urgency of the new initiative by Canadian Ukrainians, who had founded the non-profit organization Tovarystvo Pomochi Pys'mennykam (Society of Helping Writers) to provide financial support for Ukrainian writers. Kobylians'ka's suggestive description of her primitive living quarters merits quoting at length:

> My dear brothers and sister across the ocean! The snow and wind rage violently outside, and the cold makes its way through the cracks in the windows and doors into my room, located in the attic of an apartment

> building. My room is filled with piercing cold ... I sit all bundled up at my desk and from time to time look anxiously through the window while writing: what would happen by morning when already in the afternoon the blizzard swirls up so intensely. To keep the draft away, I covered the balcony door, the only exit in my room, with shabby, moth-eaten scarfs and old, motley, patched-up curtains. I also stuffed [the door cracks] with the old fur; it's so worn out that only a few spots can still remind you that it once used to [be] a fox. All wrapped in rags, the door looks like an old beggar. I cannot go downstairs to get some fresh air because I am partially paralysed. Moreover, I would not want to run into my landlady or some of her children there. She would surely assault me with her harsh words: "How much longer are you going to occupy the room? If it's not for you, I'd have a [paying] renter. I lose profit because of you ..." But there is little I can do about it. There are barely any other available rentals [in town] ... That's why the poor put up timidly with the injustice and harshness of their landlords. And it doesn't matter whether he is a gentleman, a craftsman, a worker, or an artist ... My fingers got a bit stiff and red while writing in the cold room, but it's all right. It's not the first time. The point is that while dwelling on the prose [of my daily life] ... I haven't mentioned what I was supposed to talk about at the very beginning: namely, about the new society to provide financial aid to Ukrainian writers founded in Toronto, Canada – so far away from our old world. (KLMHM N807; also qtd. in Vozniuk 2006, 174–5)

For further discussion on Kobylians'ka's financial hardships in the early 1920s, see Panchuk 1976, 78–82, and Vozniuk 2006, 171–82.

22 A phrase popularized by Hughes 1958.

23 See, for example, Griffin's and Payne's respective classifications, in Griffin 1995, 6; and Payne 1995, 8.

24 Eatwell offers the most articulate assessment of the Nietzschean, Caesarian, and Christian philosophical undertones in fascist ideology. See Eatwell 1992.

25 See, for example, Spengler's discussion of Caesarism in Spengler 1933, 142–5, 164–5, and Mosley's discussion on Christ, Nietzsche, and Caesar in fascist ideology in Mosely 1935. In his discussion of interwar Ukrainian radical nationalism and its literature, Shkandrij points out that interwar Galicians and émigré Ukrainians commented widely on the Roman world and its virtues, which provided interwar radical intellectuals with "the ideal of a stable and powerful state, as well as the ideal of strong bodies and minds." See Shkandrij 2015, 163–71.

26 Shapoval was perhaps the first to point out the conceptual link between Kobylians'ka's fist intellectual heroine in *The Princess* (1896) and her 1928

vision of a new interwar Ukrainian hero. See his letter to Kobylians'ka written on 24 November 1927, quoted in Kohut 1928, 249–52.

27 For further discussion of the new fascist hero of the 1920s and 1930s, see Mosse 1999, 32–3 and 110–11.

28 Pavlyshyn problematizes Kobylians'ka's discussion of national identity and its formation and argues that in *Apostle of the Rabble* nationality is neither genetically nor culturally acquired but is subject to choice, which, in turn, depends on a variety of irrational forces, love being the most intangible of all (2014, 566). Pavlyshyn grounds his argument in the analysis of the two heroines, Eva Zakharii and Dora Val'de, two cousins whose ethnic heritage is identical and who have similar exposure to Polish and Ukrainian culture, but end up with "mutually exclusive national identities." See Pavlyshyn 2008, 257–8, and 2014, 564–7. This reading, however, disregards the fact that both heroines make situational decisions as to their official national identity only within the framework put in place by their genealogy and cultural upbringing – neither choses to identify as French or Korean, for example. Neither also completely renounces her hybrid Polish-Ukrainian ethnic ancestry. Pavlyshyn's reading also overlooks the fact that national self-identification is never an issue with Kobylians'ka's characters of pure ethnic heritage and targeted cultural upbringing, be they Ukrainians, Poles, Germans, or Armenians. The extended Tsezarevych family, all Ukrainians, and the patriarch of the Al'bins'kyi family, Alfons Al'bins'kyi, a Pole, are the most telling examples in this regard.

29 All translations of *Apostle of the Rabble* are mine. This and all following citations refer to the 1994 Ukrainian edition, *Apostol cherni* (L'viv: Kameniar; hereafter AR).

30 Dontsov often evoked the French Revolution, its leaders, and their political ardour as relevant examples for emulation in Ukraine's interwar political struggle. See, for example, Dontsov 1996, 263, 267. Considering that Kobylians'ka was a subscriber and published extensively in the *Literaturno-naukovyi visnyk* before the First World War and maintained contact with its editors in the interwar period, it is fair to suggest that she read the journal in the interwar period and thus was familiar with the writings of Dontsov, the journal's editor-in-chief during 1922–32 period, whose works appeared in every issue during his tenure. For further discussion of Kobylians'ka's relationship with *Literature and Science Herald* in the interwar period, see Pavlyshyn 2014, 567.

31 For a detailed discussion on the emergence, views, and activities of Ukrainophiles (*khlopomany*) and Ukrainian populists (*narodovtsi*), see Subtelny 1988, 281–6, 319–25. See also Lindheim's and Luckyj's introduction to *Towards an Intellectual History of Ukraine*, where the two scholars emphasize the fundamental distinction between Russian populists, who focused on radical social action and terrorism, and

Ukrainian populists, who stressed national enlightenment and the soft politics of cultivating the masses. Lindheim and Luckyj 1996, 20–7.

32 The "Blood and Soil" slogan was popularized by Richard Walther Darre (1895–1953), who used his knowledge in animal breeding to articulate his scheme for reviving German nobility. Although Darre's ideas were hopelessly utopian, his slogan made a significant contribution to the rationale for the systematic destructions carried out by the Third Reich. For a sampling of his writing, see Darre 1995.

33 Rudnyts'kyi, the head editors of *Dilo*, an influential Galician newspaper of national-democratic orientation in which *Apostle of the Rabble* was first published, criticized Kobylians'ka's work as "a novel with very weak observations and psychological material" and pointed out that "technically it was not modern at all." See Rudnyts'kyi 1936, 234.

34 In his discussion of *Apostle of the Rabble*, Pavlyshyn argues that Kobylians'ka "condemns" (*zasudzhuie*) Iuliian Tsezarevych's limited contribution to the national cause by exposing his "national inferiority complex," his "uncertainty about the course of his [patriotic] action," and his "skepticism about women's potential to contribute [to] the nation-building process." Pavlyshyn 2008, 254–5, and 2014, 559–60.

35 For a discussion on Nietzsche's ideas of self-overcoming, see chapter 2, page 69, of this study.

36 The sea and the seafarer are some of the most recurrent metaphors in Nietzsche's *Thus Spoke Zarathustra*. For a detailed discussion, see chapter 2, note 28, of this study. In her first novel, *The Princess*, Kobylians'ka used the seafarer metaphor to describe Doctor Marko as a "higher person" and to highlight his central role in Natalka Verkhovychivna's intellectual evolution. See chapter 2, pages 82–3, of this study.

37 Zachariah is the eleventh of the Twelve Minor Prophets in the Old Testament. Traditionally, he is viewed as the author of the Book of Zachariah who prophesied the coming glory of Jerusalem and promised salvation to his people (Zach. 8:7). Zachariah's confidence in the glory of his people clearly contradicts Father Zakharii's sceptical attitude to the possibilities of cultural transformation of his parishioners.

38 For a discussion on Christianity and fascism, particularly its Italian version, see Mosse 1999, 73–4 and 130–3.

39 For further discussion on Nietzsche's views on gift-giving virtues, see chapter 2, pages 78–9, of this study.

40 For the further discussion on Nietzsche's image of "the Roman Caesar with Christ's soul," see Desmond 1999; Kaufman 2013, 316; or Thiele 1990, 169.

41 For some relevant examples, see note 25 of this chapter.

42 For further discussion on the justification of war and celebration of violence as some of the defining features of a new interwar collective

mythology generated by Galician and émigré Ukrainian radical nationalists, see Shkandrij 2015, 157–71.

43 See, for example, Smal'-Stots'kyi's 1927 assessments of Kobylians'ka's peculiar feminism, which he supported with a telling quote from one of Kobylians'ka's personal letters, where she states that "to create a state ... we [Ukrainians] also need women, who ... can substitute fathers, if needed ... and who would pursue only one goal – not themselves and their demanding I, but their children." Quoted in Kohut 1928, 277–88. For further discussion, see chapter 1, pages 28–9, in this study.

44 Similar positions permeate the official German National Socialist policy on women as outlined in Paula Siber's 1933 programmatic essay "The Woman Question and Its National Socialist Solution." For an abstract of Siber's text, see Griffin 1995, 136–7.

45 Although the majority of the post-Soviet critics exalt Iuliian Tsezarevych as a new ideal type of Ukrainian intellectual leader (see note 47 of this chapter), Pavlyshyn detects with precision several character flaws – "inactivity," "confusion about courses of personal action likely to benefit the national weal," "debilitating inferiority complex," and "conservative attitudes to women" – rightfully arguing that "the Tsezarevych model" invites a great degree of criticism. See Pavlyshyn 2014, 559–60.

46 Kobylians'ka quoted here Johann Gottfried Herder, an eighteenth-century German philosopher who challenged the universalists' views of the Enlightenment by stressing the uniqueness of different cultures, and whose concepts of "Volk" and an "Aryan race" eventually formed the basis of Nazi racial views. After a trip to Eastern Europe, Herder stated in his *Journal meiner Reise im Jahr 1769* that Ukraine had the potential to become a new Greece and lead Europe to its cultural regeneration. The exact passage in Herder reads: "Ukraine will become a new Greece: the delightful skies enjoyed by this people, its cheerful demeanour, its musical nature, its fertile land, etc. will awaken one day. From many uncivilized small tribes, such as the Greeks once used to be, a cultured nation will emerge: its borders will stretch from the Black Sea, and from there into the world." See Herder 1997, vol. 9–2, 67–8.

47 For similar views, also see Khymyn 1994, Krupa 1994, Matusiak 1999, Mel'nychuk 2006, Mykosianchyk 2004, Pochyniuk 2005, and Slon'ovs'ka 2000.

48 In his conclusion to a scholarly volume on Eastern European interwar fascism, Peter Suger emphasizes the almost ridiculous contradictions by definition of the paradoxical Eastern European social and political phenomena, which he defines as "fascism with reservations," often bordering on "anti-fascist fascism." See Suger 1971, 155.

Works Cited

Primary Sources

Archival Sources

Archives and Manuscripts Collection at T.H. Shevchenko Institute of Literature of the National Academy of Science of Ukraine (IL)
Kobryns'ka, Nataliia. Letter to Ol'ha Kobylians'ka. 17 February 1894. F14, N756.
Kobylians'ka, Ol'ha. "Etwas über die darwinistische Theorie." F14, N1017.
– Letter to Osyp Makovei. 17 December 1898. F14, N166.
– Letter to Osyp Makovei. 2 August 1900. F14, N198.
– "Schiksal oder Wille." F14, N181.
– "Vision." F14, N1812.
Kobylians'kii, Yulian. Visiting Card. F14, N1021
Okunevs'ka, Sofiia. Letter to Ol'ha Kobylians'ka. 7 June 1882. F14, N787.
– Letter to Ol'ha Kobylians'ka. 5 June 1894. F14, N811.

Archives and Manuscripts Collection at Chernivtsi State O. Iu. Kobylians'ka Literary and Memorial House-Museum (KLMHM)

Biliach, Mykola. Letter to Ol'ha Kobylians'ka. 16 May 1927. N1850–1850.
– Letter to Ol'ha Kobylians'ka. 12 September 1927. N1855–1855.
– Letter to Ol'ha Kobylians'ka. 21 January 1928. F35, N1845.
– Letter to Ol'ha Kobylians'ka. 29 January 1928. N1875–1875.
Kobylians'ka, Ol'ha. A fourteen-page outline of Serhii Podolyns'kyi's 1881 article "Hromadianstvo i teoriia Darvina." N1992–1992.
– Letter to the Ukrainians in Canada. 21 August 1922. N1979–1979.
– Letter to Kyrylo Strudnyts'kyi. 3 June 1928. F13, N303.
– Letter to Mykhailo Pavlyk. April 1891. N67.

– Letter to the Balyts'kyi Family. 15 February 1936. F18.
– Letter to the T.H. Shevchenko Scientific Society in L'viv. 6 February 1928. F13, N297.
– Letter to the Ukrainians in America. 6 March 1924. N807.
– The first twenty pages of the original German-language manuscript of *Tsarivna*. N1681–1681.

Okunevs'kyi-Morachevs'kyi, Iuliian. Letter to Ol'ha Kobylians'ka. 13 March 1926. N1784–1784.

Pisarev, Dmitrii. 1904. *Polnoe sobranie sochinenii v shesti tomakh.* Vol. 5. Saint Petersburg: Tipografiia U.N. Erlikh. N308.

[189?] List of Ol'ha Kobylians'ka's personal books. N2009–2003.

1909 List of Ol'ha Kobylians'ka's personal books. N2008–2002.

Other Editions and Selected Publications

Ale Hospod' movchyt'... i inshi opovidannia. 1927. Edited by Ostap Hrytsai. Chernivtsi: Vesna.

Apostol cherni. 1994a. L'viv: Kameniar.

Apostol cherni. 1994b. Ternopil': Zbruch.

"Bytva." 1923. Edited by Vasyl' Vernyvolia. Kyiv-Leipzig: Ukrains'ka nakladnia.

Kleinrussische Novellen. 1901. Edited by Georg Adam. Minden in Westfalen: Bruns Verlag.

Noveli. 1925. Edited by B. Iakubs'kyi. Kyiv: Knyhospilka.

Ol'ha Kobylians'ka: Tvory v deviaty tomakh. 1927–9. Edited by Ivan Lyzanivs'kyi. Kharkiv: Rukh.

Slova zvorushenoho sertsia: Shchodennyky, avtobiohrafii, lysty, statti ta spohady. 1982. Edited by Fedir Pohrebennyk. Kyiv: Khudozhnie vydavnytstvo "Dnipro."

Tvory v dvokh tomakh. 1983. Edited by Fedir Pohrebennyk. Kyiv: Derzhavne vydavnytstvo khudozhn'oi literatury.

ORIGINAL PUBLICATIONS

"Shchyra liubov." 1916. *Viis'kovyi lystok Shtryfliera: Pil'na chasopys'* 17 (Vienna): 12–13.

Tsarivna. 1896. Chernivtsi: Bukovyna.

"Tuha." 1932. *Novi shliakhy* 6–7:237–43.

"Voiennyi akord." 1932. *Novi shliakhy* 3:234–40.

ENGLISH TRANSLATIONS

A Human Being. 2000a. Translated by Roma Franko. In *Women's Voices in Ukrainian Literature: For a Crust of Bread.* Edited by Sonia Morris. Winnipeg: Language Lanterns Publication, 160–219.

Selected Prose Fiction. 1999. Translated by Roma Franko. *Women's Voices in Ukrainian Literature: But ... The Lord Is Silent*. Edited by Sonia Morris. Winnipeg: Language Lanterns Publication, 2–326.

"To Meet Their Fate." 2000b. Translated by Roma Franko. In *Women's Voices in Ukrainian Literature: Warm the Children, O Sun*. Edited by Sonia Morris. Winnipeg: Language Lanterns Publication, 271–85.

"Vasylka." Translated by Yuliya Ladygina. *Ukrainian Literature: A Journal of Translation* 4 (2014): 125–44. http://sites.utoronto.ca/elul/Ukr_Lit/Vol04/. 31 May 2017.

Secondary Sources

English and German

Afflerbach, Holger. 2014. "The Eastern Front." In *The Cambridge History of the First World War*. Vol. 1. Edited by Jay Winter. Cambridge: Cambridge University Press. 256–64.

Anderson, Benedict. 2006. *Imagined Communities: Reflections on the Origin and Spread of Nationalism*. London: Verso.

Arens, Hans. 1994. *E. Marlitt: Eine kritische Würdigung*. Trier: Wissenschaftlicher Verlag.

Armstrong, John. 1955. *Ukrainian Nationalism, 1939–1945*. New York: Columbia University Press.

– 1982. *Nations before Nationalism*. Chapel Hill: University of North Carolina Press.

– 1990. *Ukrainian Nationalism*. Englewood, NJ: Ukrainian Academic Press.

Bakhtin, Mikhail. 2008. *The Dialogic Imagination*. Edited by Michael Holquist. Translated by Caryl Emerson and Michael Holquist. Austin: University of Texas Press.

– 2009. *Problems of Dostoevsky's Poetics*. Edited and translated by Caryl Emerson. Minneapolis: University of Minnesota Press.

Belgum, Kirsten. 2002. "E. Marlitt's Narratives of Virtual Desire." Kontje 2002, 259–82.

Berg, William, and Laurey Martin. 1992. *Emile Zola Revisited*. New York: Twayne.

Berlin, Isaiah. 1978. *Russian Thinkers*. New York: Penguin Books.

– 2000. "The Role of the Intelligentsia." In *The Power of Ideas*. Edited by Henry Hardy. Princeton, NJ: Princeton University Press. 103–11.

Bohachevsky-Chomiak, Martha. 1988. *Feminists despite Themselves: Women in Ukrainian Community Life, 1884–1939*. Edmonton: Canadian Institute of Ukrainian Studies, University of Alberta.

Brandes, George. 1900. *Menschen und Werke: Essays*. Frankfurt am Mein: Literarische Anstalt.

Calhoun, Craig. 2007. *Nations Matter: Culture, History, and the Cosmopolitan Dream*. London: Routledge.

Carlston, Erin. 1998. *Thinking Fascism: Sapphic Modernism and Fascist Modernity*. Stanford, CA: Stanford University Press.

Chernyshevsky, Nikolai. 1989. *What Is to Be Done?* Translated by Michael Katz. Ithaca, NY: Cornell University Press.

Childs, Peter. 2008. *Modernism*. New York: Routledge.

Clowes, Edith. 1981. "A Philosophy 'For All and None': The Early Reception of Friedrich Nietzsche's Philosophy in Russian Literature." PhD diss., Yale University.

Cornwall, Mark. 1990. *The Last Years of Austro-Hungary: A Multinational Experiment in Early Twentieth Century Europe*. Exeter, UK: University of Exeter Press.

Coupe, W.A. 1996. "Eugenie Marlitt: In Defense of a Writer of Kitsch." *German Life and Letters* 49, no. 1:42–58. https://onlinelibrary.wiley.com/doi/10.1111/j.1468-0483.1996.tb01663.x.

Cross, Tim, ed. 1983. Introduction. In *An International Anthology of Writers, Poets, and Playwrights: The Lost Voices of World War I*. Iowa City: University of Iowa Press. 1–14.

Čyževs'kyj, Dmytro. 1997. *A History of Ukrainian Literature*. New York: Ukrainian Academic Press.

Darre, Richard Walther. 1995. "Blood and Soil." Griffin 1995, 125–7.

Darwin, Charles. 1968. *The Origins of Species by Means of Natural Selection*. Harmondsworth, UK: Penguin Books.

Deleuze, Gilles. 1983. *Nietzsche and Philosophy*. Translated by Hugh Tomlinson. New York: Columbia University Press.

Desmond, W. 1999. "Caesar with the Soul of Christ: Nietzsche's Highest Impossibility." *Tijdschrift voor Filosofie* vol. 61, no. 1:27–61.

Dinter, Artur. 1920. *Die Sünde wider das Blut*. Leipzig: Matthes und Thost Verlag.

Dobroliubov, Nikolai. 1948a. "A Ray of Light in the Realm of Darkness." In *Selected Philosophical Essays*. Translated by J. Fineberg. Moscow: Foreign Language Publishing House. 543–628.

– 1948b. "When Will the Real Day Come?" In *Selected Philosophical Essays*. Translated by J. Fineberg. Moscow: Foreign Language Publishing House. 388–438.

Dontsov, Dmytro. 1996. "Nationalism." Lindheim and Luckyj 1996, 260–8.

Drahomanov, Mykhailo. 1996. "Draft Constitution for the Ukrainian Society in the Free Union." Lindheim and Luckyj 1996, 171–83.

Eatwell, Roger. 1992. "Toward a New Model of Generic Fascism." *Journal of Theoretical Politics*, vol. 4, no. 2:161–94. https://doi.org/10.1177/0951692892004002003.

Foucault, Michel. 1977. *Language, Counter-Memory, Practice: Selected Essays and Interviews*. Ithaca, NY: Cornell University Press.

Franko, Ivan. 1996. "Beyond the Limits of the Possible." Lindheim and Luckyj 1996, 193–200.

Freud, Sigmund. 1965. *The Interpretations of Dreams*. New York: Avon Books.

– 1989a. *Civilization and Its Discontents*. New York: Norton and Company.

– 1989b. *Group Psychology and the Analysis of the Ego*. New York: Norton and Company.

– 2000. *Three Essays on Theory of Sexuality*. New York: Basic Books.

Fussell, Paul. 2013. *The Great War and Modern Memory*. 3rd ed. Oxford: Oxford University Press.

Gellner, Ernest. 1983. *Nations and Nationalism*. Oxford: Blackwell.

Gentile, Emilio. 2003. *The Struggle for Modernity: Nationalism, Futurism, and Fascism*. Westport, CT: Praeger.

– 2006. *Politics as Religion*. Princeton, NJ: Princeton University Press.

Grabowicz, George. 1982. *The Poet as Mythmaker: A Study of Symbolic Meaning in Taras Ševčenko*. Cambridge, MA: Distributed by Harvard University Press for the Harvard Ukrainian Research Institute.

Greenfeld, Liah. 1992. *Nationalism: Five Roads to Modernity*. Cambridge, MA: Harvard University Press.

Griffin, Roger. 1993. *The Nature of Fascism*. London: Routledge.

– ed. 1995. *Fascism*. Oxford and New York: Oxford University Press.

– 2007. *Modernism and Fascism: The Sense of the Beginning under Mussolini and Hitler*. Houndmills, Basingstoke, UK: Palgrave Macmillan.

– 2008. "Modernity, Modernism, and Fascism. A 'Mazeway Resynthesis.'" *Modernism/Modernity*, 15, no. 1: 9–24. https://doi.org/10.1353/mod.2008.0011.

Griffin, Roger, and Matthew Feldman, ed. 2004. *Fascism: Critical Concepts in Political Science*, vol.1. London: Routledge.

Grimm, Hans. 1926. *Volk ohne Raum*. Munich: Langen Verlag.

Guibernau, Montserrat, and John Hutchinson, eds. 2001. *Understanding Nationalism*. Cambridge: Polity Press.

Hanebrink, Paul. 2008. "The Sickness of the Empire." In *The Austro-Hungarian Dual Monarchy 1867–1918*. Edited by Szusza Gaspar. London: New Holland Publishers UK Ltd. 176–207.

Herder, Johann Gottfried. 1997. *Werke in zehn Bänden*. Frankfurt am Main: Deutscher Klassiker Verlag.

Himka, John Paul. 1999. *Religion and Nationality in Western Ukraine: The Greek Catholic Church and the Ruthenian National Movement in Galicia, 1867–1900*. Montreal: McGill-Queen's University Press.

– 2009. *Ukrainians, Jews and the Holocaust: Divergent Memories*. Saskatoon, SK: Heritage Press.

– 2010. "The Organization of Ukrainian Nationalists and the Ukrainian Insurgent Army: Unwelcome Elements of an Identity Project." *Ab Imperio* 4:83–101. https://doi.org/10.1353/imp.2010.0101.

Himka, John Paul, et al.. *Dyskusiia: Bandera iak problema*. http://krytyka.com/ua/articles/dyskusiya-bandera-yak-problema. 19 July 2015.

Hochschild, Adam. 2011. *To End All Wars: A Story of Loyalty and Rebellion, 1914–1918*. Boston: Mariner Books and Houghton Mifflin Harcourt.

Horbatsch, Anna-Halja. 1984. "Ol'ha Kobylians'ka und Eugenie Marlitt (John)." *Jahrbuch der Ukrainekunde*. Munich: Ukrainische freie Universität. 207–15.

Hroch, Miroslav. 2000. *Social Preconditions of National Revival in Europe: A Comparative Analysis of the Social Composition of Patriotic Groups among the Smaller European Nations*. New York: Columbia University Press.

Hrushevsky, Mykhailo. 1996. "A Free Ukraine." Lindheim and Luckyj 1996, 227–38.

Hughes, Stuart. 1958. *Consciousness and Society: The Reorientation of the European Social Thought 1890–1930*. London: McGibbon and Kee.

Hutchinson, John. 2001. "Nations and Culture." *Understanding Nationalism*. Edited by Montserrat Guibernau and John Hutchinson. Cambridge: Polity Press. 74–96.

Hutchinson, John, and Anthony Smith, eds. 1994. *Nationalism*. London: Oxford University Press.

Ionescu, Ghita. 1969. "Eastern Europe." In *Populism: Its Meaning and National Characteristics*. Edited by Ernest Gellner and Ghita Ionescu. London: Macmillan. 97–121.

Kaatz, Hugo. 1892–3. *Die Weltanschauung Friedrich Nietzsches*. Dresden: C. Pierson.

Kann, Robert. 1950. *The Multinational Empire: Nationalism and National Reform in the Habsburg Monarchy 1848–1918*. New York: Columbia University Press.

Kaufmann, Walter. 2013. *Nietzsche: Philosopher, Psychologist, Antichrist*. Princeton, NJ: Princeton University Press.

Kienzle, Michael. 1975. *Der Erfolgsroman: Zur Kritik seiner poetischen Ökonomie bei Gustav Freytag und Eugenie Marlitt*. Stuttgart: Metzler.

Kohn, Hans. 1944. *The Idea of Nationalism: A Study in Its Origins and Background*. New York: Macmillan.

Kontje, Todd. 1998. *Women, the Novel, and the German Nation, 1771–1871: Domestic Fiction in the Fatherland*. Cambridge: Cambridge University Press.

– ed. 2002. *A Companion to German Realism, 1848–1900*. New York: Camden House.

Kostomarov, Mykhailo. 1996. "Two Russian Nationalities." Lindheim and Luckyj 1996, 124–32.

Ladygina, Yuliya. 2013. *Narrating the Self in the Mass Age: Ol'ha Kobylians'ka in the European Fin de Siècle and Its Aftermath, 1886–1936*. PhD diss., University of California, San Diego.

– 2015. "Beyond the Trenches: Ol'ha Kobylians'ka's Literary Response to the First World War." *East/West Journal of Ukrainian Studies* vol. 2, no. 2:111–35. https://doi.org/10.21226/t2s888.
Landsberg, Hans. 1902. *Friedrich Nietzsche und die deutsche Literatur*. Leipzig: H. Seemann.
Laqueur, Walter, ed. 1976. *Fascism: A Reader's Guide; Analysis, Interpretations, Bibliography*. Berkley: University of California Press.
– 1996. *Fascism: Past, Present, Future*. London: Oxford University Press.
Lavrov, Petr. 1967. *Historical Letters*. Edited and translated by James Scanlan. Berkley: University of California Press.
Lindheim, Ralph, and George Luckyj, eds. 1996. *Towards an Intellectual History of Ukraine: An Anthology of Ukrainian Thought from 1710 to 1995*. Toronto: University of Toronto Press.
Lloyd George, David. 1938. *The Truth about the Peace Treaties*. Vol. 1. London: Victor Gollancz.
Luckyj, George, ed. 1956. *Literary Politics in the Soviet Ukraine, 1917–1934*. New York: Columbia University Press.
Magocsi, Paul Robert. 1978. *The Shaping of a National Identity: Subcarpathian Rus', 1848–1848*. Cambridge, MA: Harvard University Press.
– 2002. *The Roots of Ukrainian Nationalism: Galicia as Ukraine's Piedmont*. Toronto: University of Toronto Press.
– 2007. *Ukraine: An Illustrated History*. Seattle: University of Washington Press.
– 2010. *A History of Ukraine: The Land and Its People*. 2nd ed. Toronto: Toronto University Press.
Marinetti, Fillipo Tommaso. 2006. *Critical Writings*. Translated by Doug Thompson. Edited by Günter Berghaus. New York: Farrar, Straus and Giroux.
Marlitt, Eugenie. [1888a]. *Das Geheimnis der alten Mamsell*. Leipzig: Keil.
– [1888b]. *Die zweite Frau*. Leipzig: Keil.
– [1888c]. *Goldelse*. Leipzig: Keil.
Marx, Karl. 1976. *Introduction to a Contribution to Critique of Hegel's Philosophy of Right. Collected Works of Karl Marx and Friedrich Engels*. Vol. 3. New York: International Publishing Company. 3–10.
– 1998. *The Communist Manifesto*. London: Verso.
Mason, John. 1985. *The Dissolution of the Austro-Hungarian Empire 1867–1918*. London: Longman.
Mathewson, Rufus. 2000. *The Positive Hero in Russian Literature*. Evanston, IL: Northwestern University Press.
McAdams, Dan. 2001. "The Psychology of Life Stories." *Review of General Psychology* 5, no. 2:100–22. https://doi.org/10.1037//1089–2680.5.2.100.
Mikhnovsky, Mykhailo. 1996. "An Independent Ukraine." Lindheim and Luckyj 1996, 201–15.

Mill, John. 1997. *The Subjection of Women: Selected Works*. Edited by Alan Rayn. London: Norton and Company.

Morson, Gary. 1995. "Prosaic Bakhtin: Landmarks, Anti-Intelligentsialism, and the Russian Countertradition." In *Bakhtin in Context: Across the Disciplines*. Edited by Amy Mandelker. Evanston, IL: Northwestern University Press. 33–78.

Mosley, Oswald. 1935. "The Philosophy of Fascism." *Fascist Quarterly* 1:35–46.

Mosse, George. 1966. "Introduction: The Genesis of Fascism." *Journal of Contemporary History* 1, no. 1:14–26. https://doi.org/10.1177/002200946600100103.

– 1988. *The Culture of Western Europe: The Nineteenth and Twentieth Centuries*. Boulder, CO: Westview Press.

– 1999. *The Fascist Revolution: Toward a General Theory of Fascism*. New York: Howard Fertig.

Motyl, Alexander. 1980. *The Turn to the Right: The Ideological Origins and Development of Ukrainian Nationalism, 1919–1929*. New York: Columbia University Press.

– 2013. "On Nationalism and Fascism." *World Affairs*. http://www.worldaffairsjournal.org/blog/alexander-j-motyl/nationalism-and-fascism-part-1. 31 July 2015.

Nietzsche, Friedrich. [1930]. *Also Sprach Zarathustra. Ein Buch für Alle und Keinen*. New York: Frederick Ungar Publishing Co.

– 1967. *The Birth of Tragedy and the Case of Wagner*. Translated by Walter Kaufmann. New York: Vintage Books.

– 1968. *The Will to Power*. Translated by Walter Kaufmann. New York: Vintage Books.

– 1974. *The Gay Science*. Translated by Walter Kaufmann. New York: Vintage Books.

– 1978. *Thus Spoke Zarathustra: A Book for All and No One*. Translated by Walter Kaufmann. New York: Penguin Books.

– 1992. *Ecce Homo: How One Becomes What One Is*. Translated by Reginald John Hollingdale. New York: Penguin Books.

– 1996. *Human, All Too Human*. Translated by Reginald John Hollingdale. Cambridge: Cambridge University Press.

– 1998. *On the Genealogy of Morality*. Translated by Alan Swensen. Indianapolis, IN: Hackett Publishing.

– 2003a. *Beyond Good and Evil: Prelude to a Philosophy of the Future*. Translated by Reginald John Hollingdale. New York: Penguin Books.

– 2003b. *Twilights of the Idles, or, How to Philosophize with a Hammer*. Translated by Reginald John Hollingdale. New York: Penguin Books.

Nordau, Max. 1892. *Entartung*. Berlin: Duncker.

Paperno, Irina. 1988. *Chernyshevsky and the Age of Realism: A Study in the Semiotics of Behavior*. Stanford, CA: Stanford University Press.

Pavlyshyn, Marko. 2015. "The Intellectuals, the People, and the Nation: Ol'ha Kobylians'ka's *Apostol cherni*." *Harvard Ukrainian Studies*. 32–3:557–78.

Payne, Stanley. 1995. *A History of Fascism, 1914–1945*. Madison: University of Wisconsin Press.

Pippin, Robert. 2015. "Introduction." In *Thus Spoke Zarathustra: A Book for All and None*, by Friedrich Nietzsche. Edited by Adrian Del Caro and Robert Pippin. Translated by Adrian Del Caro. 4th ed. Cambridge: Cambridge University Press. viii–xxxv.

Pisarev, Dmitrii. 1958. "Bees." In *Selected Philosophical, Social, and Political Essays*. Moscow: Foreign Languages Publishing House, 115–39.

Plokhy, Serhij. 2005. *Unmaking Imperial Russia: Mykhailo Hrushevsky and the Writing of Ukrainian History*. Toronto: University of Toronto Press.

Potthast, Bertha. 1926. *Eugenie Marlitt: Ein Beitrag zur Geschichte des deutchen Frauenromans*. PhD diss., University of Cologne.

Reiner, Julius. n.d. *Friedrich Nietzsche. Leben und Werken*. Berlin: Hermann Seemann Nachfolger Verlagsgesellschaft. 68.

Rosenthal, Bernice. 1986. *Nietzsche in Russia*. Princeton, NJ: Princeton University Press.

– 1994. *Nietzsche and Soviet Culture: Ally and Adversary*. Cambridge: Cambridge University Press.

– 2002. *New Myth, New World: From Nietzsche to Stalinism*. University Park: Pennsylvania State University Press.

Rudnytsky, Ivan. 1987. *Essays in Modern Ukrainian History*. Edmonton: Canadian Institute of Ukrainian Studies.

Scanlan, James. 1967. "Peter Lavrov. An Intellectual Biography." In *Historical Letters* by Petr Lavrov. Edited and translated by James Scanlan. Berkeley: University of California Press

Schulte-Sasse, Jochen, and Renate Werner. 1977. "E. Marlitt's "Im Hause des Kommerzienrates": Analyse eines Trivialromans in paradigmatischer Absicgt." In *Im Hause des Kommerzienrate* by Eugenie Marlitt. Munich: Fink. 389–434.

Shekhovtsov, Anton. 2007. "By Cross and Sword: 'Clerical Fascism' in Interwar Western Ukraine." *Totalitarian Movements and Political Religions* 8, no. 2:271–85. https://doi.org/10.1080/14690760701321171.

Shekhovtsov, Anton, and Andreas Umland. 2014. "Ukraine's Radical Right." *Journal of Democracy* 25, no. 3:58–63. https://doi.org/10.1353/jod.2014.0051.

Shkandrij, Myroslav. 2001. *Russian and Ukraine: Literature and the Discourse of Empire from Napoleonic to Postcolonial Times*. Montreal: McGill-Queen's University Press.

– 2015. *Ukrainian Nationalism Politics, Ideology, and Literature, 1929–1956*. New Haven, CT: Yale University Press.

– 2016. "The Ukrainian Reading Public in the 1920s: Real, Implied, and Ideal." *Canadian Slavonic Review* 58, no. 2:160–83. https://doi.org/10.1080/00085006.2016.1152681.

Siber, Paula. 1995. "The Woman Question and Its National Socialist Solution." Griffin 1995, 136–7.

Sielke, Sabine. 2002. *Reading Rape: The Rhetoric of Sexual Violence in American Literature and Culture, 1790–1990*. Princeton, NJ: Princeton University Press.

Skrypnyk, Mykola. 1996. *Speeches*. Lindheim and Luckyj 1996, 278–83.

Smith, Anthony. 1991. *National Identity*. Las Vegas: University of Nevada Press.

Snyder, Timothy. 2003. *The Reconstruction of Nations: Poland, Ukraine, Lithuania, Belarus, 1569–1999*. New Haven, CT: Yale University Press.

– 2008. *The Red Prince: The Secret Lives of a Habsburg Archduke*. New York: Basic Books.

Spengler, Oswald. 1933. *Jahre der Entscheidung*. Munich: Beck.

Stevenson, Randall. 2013. *Literature and the Great War, 1914–1918*. Oxford: Oxford University Press.

Stites, Richard. 1978. *The Woman's Liberation Movement in Russia: Feminism, Nihilism, and Bolshevism, 1860–1930*. Princeton, NJ: Princeton University Press.

Stöcker, Helene. 1906. *Die Liebe und die Frauen*. Minden, Germany: Bruns Verlag.

Strasser, Gregor. 1995. "Motherhood and Warriorhood as the Key to a National Socialism." Griffin 1995, 123–4.

Subtelny, Orest. 1988. *Ukraine: A History*. Toronto: University of Toronto Press.

Suger, Peter, ed. 1971. *Native Fascism in the Successor States, 1918–1945*. Santa Barbara, CA: Clio Press.

Szporluk, Roman. 1988. *Communism and Nationalism: Karl Marx versus Friedrich List*. New York: Oxford University Press.

Tarnawsky, Maxim. 2001. Forward. "The Duality of Ol'ha Kobylians'ka." In *On Sunday Morning She Gathered Herbs* by Ol'ha Kobylians'ka. Translated by Mary Skrypnyk. Edmonton: Canadian Institute of Ukrainian Studies Press. v–xi.

– 2002. "Mykhailo Rudnytsky – Literary Critic." *Journal of Ukrainian Studies* vol. 27, nos. 1–2: 161–72. https://cius-archives.ca/items/show/1171.

Taylor, Brandon, and Wilfried van der Will, eds. 1990. *The Nazification of Art: Art, Design, Architecture, and Film in the Third Reich*. Winchester, UK: Winchester School of Art and the Winchester Press.

Thiele, Leslie Paul. 1990. *Friedrich Nietzsche and the Politics of the Soul: A Study of Heroic Individualism*. Princeton, NJ: Princeton University Press.

Toller, Ernst. 1934. *I Was a German*. Translated by Edward Crankshaw. London: John Lane and the Bodley Head Ltd.

Tucker, Robert, ed. 1978. *The Marx-Engels Reader*, 2nd ed. New York: Norton and Company.

Turgenev, Ivan. 2009. *Fathers and Children*. Translated by Michael Katz. New York: Norton and Company.

Vynnychenko, Volodymyr. 1996. "The Rebirth of a Nation." Lindheim and Luckyj 1996, 248–50.
Weber, Max. 1949. *Max Weber on the Methodology of the Social Sciences*. Edited and translated by Henry Finch and Edward Shils. Glencoe, IL: Free Press.
Welsh, Steven. "Military Justice." *International Encyclopedia of the First World War*. http://encyclopedia.1914–1918–online.net/pdf/1914–1918–Online-military_justice-2014–10–08.pdf. 22 July 2015.
White, Richard. 2016. "Nietzsche on Generosity and the Gift-Giving Virtue." *British Journal for the History of Philosophy* 24, no. 2:348–64. https://doi.org/10.1080/09608788.2015.1088820.
Wilkie, Claudia. 1987. "Eugenie Marlitt vor 100 Jahren gestorben." *Neue Deutsche Hefte* 34:331–47.
Wilson, Andrew. 1996. "Ukraine: Between Eurasia and the West." In *Europe and Ethnicity: The First World War and Contemporary Ethnic Conflict*. Edited by Seamus Dunn and Thomas Grant Fraser. London: Routledge. 110–37.
– 1997. *Ukrainian Nationalism in the 1990s: A Minority Faith*. Cambridge: Cambridge University Press.
– 2000. *The Ukrainians: Unexpected Nation*. New Haven, CT: Yale University Press.
Yekelchyk, Serhy. 2007. *Ukraine: Birth of a Modern Nation*. Oxford: Oxford University Press.
Yuval-Davis, Nira. 2001. "Nationalism, Feminism, and Gender Relations." In *Understanding Nationalism*. Edited by Montserrat Guibernau and John Hutchinson. Cambridge: Polity Press. 120–41.
Zola, Emile. 1980. *The Earth*. Translated by Douglas Parmée. New York: Penguin Books.

Ukrainian, Russian, and Polish

Aheieva, Vira, ed. 2004. *Genderna perspektyva*. Kyiv: Fakt.
– 2008. *Zhinochyi prostir*. Kyiv: Fakt.
Alchevs'ka, Khrystia. 1963. "Iz statti 'Maistry slova (krytychnyi shkits)'." Pohrebennyk 1963, 152–6.
– 1990. *Tvory*. Edited by L. Hruzyns'ka. Kyiv: Khudozhne vydavnytstvo "Dnipro."
Amar, Tarik Cyril, Ihor Balynskiy, and Iaroslav Hrytsak, eds. 2010. *Strasti za Banderoiu*. Kyiv: Grani-T.
– "Announcements." 1937. *Dzvony* 1–2:63.
Babyshkin, Oleh. 1952. *Ol'ha Kobylians'ka: Literaturno-krytychnyi narys*. Kyiv: Derzhavne literaturne vydannia Ukrainy.
– 1956. "Tvorchist' Ol'hy Kobylians'koi." In *Ol'ha Kobylians'ka: Tvory v tr'okh tomakh*. Kyiv: Derzhavne vydannia khudozhn'oi literatury. 5–63.

– 1963. *Ol'ha Kobylians'ka: Narys pro zhyttia i tvorchist'*. L'viv: Knyzhkovo-zhurnal'ne vydavnytstvo.

Bilets'kyi, Leonid. 1951. *Try Syl'vetky: Marko Vovchok, Lesia Ukrainka, Ol'ha Kobylians'ka*. Vinnipeg: Soiuz Ukrainok Kanady.

Bobyns'kyi, Vasyl'. 1927. "Iuvilei Ol'hy Kobylians'koi." *Vikna* 2:10.

Bondarenko, Kost'. 1997. "Fashyzm v Ukraini. Do istorii problemy." *Ukrains'kyi variant* 2:74–82.

Botushans'kyi, Vasyl', Svitlana Bilenkova, and Oleksandr Dobrozhans'kyi, eds. 2009. *Chernivtsi: Istoriia i suchasnist'*. Chernivtsi: Zelena Bukovyna.

Bryndzan, Taras, Denys Kvitkovs'kyi, and Vasyl' Zhukovs'kyi, eds. 1956. *Bukovyna: Ii mynule i suchasne*. Paris: Zelena Bukovyna. 296–301.

Burdeha, Ol'ha. 2004. "Ol'ha Kobylians'ka v otsintsi Serhiia Iefremova." *Naukovyi visnyk chernivets'koho universytetu* 216–17:144–8.

Cheredaryk, Mykola. 1983. "Malovidomi biohrafichni materialy pro Ol'hu Kobylians'ku ta ii ridnykh." *Obrii*. Bucharest: Kryterion. 186–96.

Chernyshevsky [Chernyshevskii], Nikolai. 1985. *Chto delat'?* Moscow: Khudozhestvennaia literatura.

Chopyk, Roman. 1998. *Perestupnyi vik: Ukrains'ke pys'menstvo na zlami XIX–XX stolitt'*. L'viv: Lileia-NV.

Demchenko, Iryna. 1999. ""Apostol cherni" O. Kobylians'koi iak tvir pro ukrains'koho sviashchennyka." *Naukovyi visnyk chernivets'koho universytetu* 58–9:97–100.

– 2001. *Osoblyvosti poetyky Ol'hy Kobylians'koi*. Kyiv: "Tvim–inter."

Denysiuk, Ivan. 1999. "Dvi erotychni novely O. Kobylians'koi." *Naukovyi visnyk chernivets'koho universytetu* 58–9:35–7.

Denysiuk, Ivan, and Kateryna Kryl'. 1980. "Pobornytsia progresu." In *Nataliia Kobryns'ka: Vybrani tvory*. Edited by Ivan Denysiuk and Kateryna Kryl'. Kyiv: Khudozhnie vydavnytstvo "Dnipro." 5–20.

Dontsov, Dmytro. 2006. *Nationalism*. Vinnytsia: DP DKF.

Doroshko, Lidiia. 2004. "Tsilisna kontseptsiia liudyny u povisti O. Kobylians'koi 'Zemlia'." *Naukovyi visnyk chernivets'koho universytetu* 216–17:68–72.

Dostoievskii, Fiodor. 1972–90. *Polnoie sobranie sochinenii v tridtsati tomakh*. Leningrad: Nauka.

Drobot, Ivan. 2002. *Bukovyns'ki ukraintsi v borot'bi za sobornu derzhavnist'*. Kyiv: Vydavnytstvo natsional'noho pedahohichnoho universytetu imeni M. P. Drahomanova.

Dziuba, Ivan. 1986. "Chytaiuchy Kobylians'ku (kil'ka zistavlen'). *Ukrains'ka mova i literatura v shkoli* 2:20–7.

Franko, Ivan. 1963. "Iz statti 'Z ostannikh desiatylit' XIX v." Pohrebennyk 1963, 84–6.

– 1976–86. *Zibrannia tvoriv u piatydesiaty tomakh*. Kyiv: Naukova dumka.

Furtak, Maria. 1962. "Ol'ha Kobylians'ka." *Nova khata* 7, no. 8:1–3.
Fylypovych, Pavlo. 1928. "Ol'ha Kobylians'ka v literaturnomu otochenni." *Zhyttia i revoliutsiia* (February): 105–20.
– 1971. "Spustoshena idyliia ("Zemlia" Ol'hy Kobylians'koi)." *Literatura: Statti, rozvidky, ohliady*. New York: Ukrains'ka Vil'na Akademiia Nauk v SShA.
Grabowicz, George. 2017. "Model' "Krytyky"." *Krytyka* 11, no. 12:2–6.
Holota, Olena. 2004. "Aspekty styl'ovoi sporidnenosti poezii v prozi O. Kobylians'koi i I. Turhenieva." *Naukovyi visnyk chernivets'koho universytetu* 216–17:130–3.
Horbaliuk, Oleh. 2004. "Ol'ha Kobylians'ka v inteprytatsii Stepana Smal'-Stots'koho." *Naukovyi visnyk chernivets'koho universytetu* 216–17:140–3.
Khotkevych, Hnat. 1963a. "Klika pry chasopysi *Kievskaia starina* i ii vidnoshennia do Ol'hy Kobylians'koi." Pohrebennyk 1963, 91–2.
– 1963b. ""Zemlia": Povist' Ol'hy Kobylians'koi (krytychna otsinka)." Pohrebennyk 1963, 104–47.
Hrinchenko, Borys ed. 1907–9. *Slovar' ukrainskogo iazyka*. Kyiv: Druk aktsiinoho tovarystva Korchaka-Novyts'koho.
Hrushevs'kyi, Mykhailo. 1898. "'Tsarivna,' opovidaniie Ol'hy Kobylians'koi." *Literaturno-naukovyi visnyk* 1 (3 February): 174–9.
Hrynevycheva, Katria. 1928. "Ol'ha Kobylians'ka." *Literaturno-naukovyi visnyk* 95:41–2.
Hrytsai, Ostap. 1927. Introduction. "Ol'ha Kobylians'ka iak pys'mennytsia." In *Ale Hospod' movchyt' ... i inshi opovidannia* by Ol'ha Kobylians'ka. Edited by Ostap Hrytsai. Chernivtsi: Vesna.
Hrytsak, Iaroslav. 2004. *Strasti za natsionalizmom. Istorychni esei*. Kyiv: Krytyka.
Hundorova, Tamara. 1997. "Kobylians'ka – Dovzhenko: Navkolo 'Zemli,' abo riznytsia analohii." *Slovo i chas* 11–12:57–68.
– 2002. *Femina melancholica. Stat' i kul'tura v gendernii utopii Ol'hy Kobylians'koi*. Kyiv: Krytyka.
– 2008. *Kitch i literatura*; Kyiv: Fact.
Huzar, Zenon. 1978. *Vyvchennia tvorchosti Ol'hy Kobylians'koi: Posibnyk dlia vchytyliv*. Kyiv: Radians'ka shkola.
Iaremchuk, Andrii. 2000. "'Apostol cherni' – khto vin?" *Chas* no. 19:11.
Iefremov, Serhii. 1993. "V poiskax novoi krasoty." *Iefremov Serhii: Literaturno-krytychni statti*. Kyiv: Khudozhnie vydavnytstvo "Dnipro." 48–121.
Ievdokymenko, Volodymyr. 1968. *Krytyka ideinykh osnov ukrains'koho burzhuaznoho natsionalismu*. Kyiv: Naukova dumka.
Ievshan, Mykola. 1995. "Ol'ha Kobylians'ka." *Krytyka, literaturoznavstvo, estetyka*. Kyiv: Osnovy. 199–205.
Iuriichuk, Mykola. 1999. "O. Kobylians'ka v otsintsi hazety 'Bukovyna.'" *Naukovyi visnyk chernivets'koho universytetu* 58–9:25–30.

Izotov, Ivan, 1928. "Do kharakterystyky tvorchosti O. Kobylians'koi." *Chervonyi shliakh* no. 2:80–92.

Karpynets', Ivan, Feodosii Steblii, Bohdan Iakumovych, eds. 2005. *Halychyna: Viis'kova istoriia, 1914–1918*. Lviv: Vydavnychyi dim "Panorama."

Kasianenko, Tamara. 1999. "Ol'ha Kobylians'ka v Kolomyi." *Naukovyi visnyk chernivets'koho universytetu* 58–9:152–5.

Khymyn, Olesia. 1994. *Ol'ha Kobylians'ka i natsional'ne pytannia*. Zhydachiv, Ukraine.

Kobryns'ka, Nataliia. 1958. *Vybrani tvory*. Edited by O.N. Moroz. Kyiv: Derzhavne vydavnytstvo khudozhn'oi literatury.

Kobryns'ka, Nataliia, and Olena Pchilka. 1984. *Pershyi vinok*. New York: Ukrainian Women's League of America.

Kohut, Lev, ed. 1928. *Ol'ha Kobylians'ka: Al'manakh u pamiatky ii sorokolitn'oi pys'mennyts'koi diial'nosti (1887–1927)*. Chernivtsi: Nakladom Iuvyleinoho komitetu v Chernivtsiakh.

Kohut, Zenon, and John-Paul Himka. 2010. *Dyskusiia: Bandera iak problema. Krytyka 3–4*: 10–12.

Komyshanchenko, Maksym. 1962. Introduction. In *Ol'ha Kobylians'ka: Tvory v piaty tomakh*. Vol. 1. Edited by Maksym Komyshanchenko. Kyiv: Derzhavne vydavnytstvo khudozhn'oi literatury. 5–42.

– 1963. *Ol'ha Kobylians'ka: Do storichchia z dnia narodzhennia*. Kyiv: Tovarystvo dlia poshyrennia politychnykh i naukovykh znan' Ukrains'koi RSR.

Kopach, Oleksandra. 1972. *Movostyl' Ol'hy Kobylians'koi*. Toronto: T.H. Shevchenko Scientific Society.

Korduba, Ievhen. 1928. "Moi spomyny." Kohut 1928, 233–6.

Kosach, Mykhailo. 1963. "Pyshit' iak dusha velyt'." Pohrebennyk 1963, 88–9.

Kosach-Kryvyniuk, Ol'ha. 1970. *Lesia Ukrainka: Chronolohia zhyttia i tvorchosti*. New York: Vydavnycha spilka "Homin Ukrainy."

Koval'chuk, Olesia. 1993. "Pys'mennyts'ka pozytsiia v povisti Kobylians'koi 'Zamlia.'" *Ukrains'ka mova ta literatura v shkoli* 2:16–19.

Kovalets', Lidiia. 2004. "Dity v khudozhn'omu sviti Ol'hy Kobylians'koi." *Naukovyi visnyk chernivets'koho universytetu* 216–17:43–7.

Koval's'kyi, Viktor. 2008. "Pro zlochyn i karu v ukrains'kii prozi." *Zlochyn i kara v ukrains'kii prozi*. Kyiv: Iurinkom Inter.

Krupa, Maria. 1994. Forward. In *Apostol cherni* by Ol'ha Kobylians'ka. L'viv: Kameniar. 5–29.

– 1998. *Movleneva struktura obrazu avtora v tvorchosti Ol'hy Kobylians'koi*. Kyiv: Ridna mova.

– 2004. "Tretii 'Zapovit' ukrains'koi literatury i kompozytsiino-movlenevi zasoby ioho deklaratsii u liryko-filosofs'kii noveli Ol'hy Kobylians'koi 'Dumy staryka'." *Naukovyi visnyk chernivets'koho universytetu* 216–17:21–3.

Kryms'kyi, Ahatanhel. 1963. "*Tsarivna* – opovidannia Ol'hy Kobylians'koi." Pohrebennyk 1963, 36–8.

Kudriavtsev, Mykhailo. 2004. "Povist' Ol'hy Kobylians'koi *Zemlia* u konteksti literatury pro zlochyn i karu." *Naukovyi visnyk chernivets'koho universytetu* 216–17:21–3.
Kushch, O.P. 1960. *Ol'ha Kobylians'ka: Bibliografichnyi pokazhchyk*. Kyiv: Vydavnytstvo AN URSR.
Kyryliuk, Ievhen. 1965. "Velych Kobylians'koi." *Ukrains'ke literaturoznavstvo* no. 6:41–53.
Kyryliuk, Svitlana. 2003. *Kobylians'ka i svitova literatura*. Chernivtsi: Ruta.
– 2004. "Modyfikatsiinyi rakurs faustivs'koho motyvu v povisti O. Kobylians'koi 'Za sytuatsiiamy.'" *Naukovyi visnyk chernivets'koho universytetu* 216–17:77–82.
Kysilievs'ka, Olena. 1937. "Pislia nedavn'oi hostyny na Bukovyni." *Zhinocha dolia* no. 7:11.
– 1938. "V vidvidynakh Ol'hy Kobylians'koi." *Zhinocha dolia* no. 20:6.
Laslo, Magdalena. 1963. "Tema emansypatsii zhinky u tvorchosti O. Kobylians'koi." Pohrebennyk 1963, 324–39.
Lebedova, Vira. 1963. "Zhinochi typy v nainovishii ukrains'kii literaturi." Pohrebennyk 1963, 324–40.
Leshchenko, Myroslava. 1973. *Ol'ha Kobylians'ka*. Kyiv: Khudozhnie vydavnytstvo "Dnipro."
Lesyn, Vasyl'. 1958. "Antyvoienni tvory Ol'hy Kobylians'koi." Lesyn et al. 1958, 87–98.
– 1963. "Ol'ha Kobylians'ka i Vasyl' Stefanyk." *Ol'ha Kobylians'ka: Do 100–richcha z dnia narodzhennia*. Edited by H.I. Sinchenko. Vinnytsia: Knyzhkovo-hazetne vydavnytstvo, 152–86.
Lesyn, Vasyl', Ivan Slyn'ko, and Ivan Cherednychenko, eds. 1958. *Ol'ha Kobylians'ka: statti i materialy*. Chernivtsi: Chernivets'kyi derzhavnyi universytet.
Levchenko, Halyna. 2008. *Zacharovana kazka zhyttia Ol'hy Kobylians'koi*. Kyiv: Knyha.
Lubkivs'ka, Oksana. 1995. "Modeli vyiavu nitssheans'koi filosofii v ukrains'kii literaturi." *Suchasnist'* no. 4:144–7.
Lutsiv, Luka. 1930. "Dvoie mriinykiv (O. Kobylians'ka i E. Iakobson)." L'viv: Z drukarni A. Salievycha.
– 1963. *Ol'ha Kobylians'ka: V 100–richchia ii narodyn*. New York: Vydannia "Svoboda."
– [1975]. "O. Kobylians'ka i F. Nitsshe." In *Literatura i zhyttia: Literaturni otsinky* by Luka Lutsiv. New York: Vydannia "Svoboda." 151–78.
Luts'kyi, Iurii, ed. 1994. *Ostap Luts'kyi i suchasnyky: Lysty do O. Kobylians'koi i I. Franka ta inshi zabuti storinky*. New York: Vydannia Ukrains'koi Vil'noi Akademii Nauk u SShA.
Makovei, Osyp. 1925. "Avtobiohrafiia." *Literaturno-naukovyi visnyk* 88, no. 11:231–40.

– 1954. Forward. *Tsarivna*. Saddle River, NJ: Surma.
– 1963. "Ol'ha Kobylians'ka." Pohrebennyk 1963, 44–67.
– 1990. Forward. In *Tvory v dvokh tomakh*. Edited by O. Myshanych. Kyiv: Khudozhnie vydavnytstvo "Dnipro."
Malaniuk, Ievhen. 1991. *Zemna Madonna: Vybrane*. Bratislava: Slovats'ke pedahohichne vydannia.
Matusiak, Liudmyla. 1999. "Roman 'Apostol cherni' v konteksti tvorchoi spadshchyny O. Kobylians'koi." *Naukovyi visnyk chernivets'koho universytetu* 58–9:89–93.
Mel'nychuk, Iaroslava. 2004. "Mistse tvoriv Ol'hy Kobylians'koi 1920–1930kh rokiv u khudozhnii spadshchyni pys'mennytsi." *Naukovyi visnyk chernivets'koho universytetu* 216–17:90–3.
– 2006. *Na vechirn'omu pruzi: Ol'ha Kobylians'ka v ostannii period tvorchosti, vid 1914 roku*. Chernivtsi: Bukrek.
Mochuls'kyi, Mykhailo. 1963. "Ol'ha Kobylians'ka: 'Cherez kladku.'" Pohrebennyk 1963, 164–72.
Mykhailyn, Ihor. 2007. "Zhinochyi proekt v ukrains'kii literaturi." In *Ukrains'ka zhinocha proza: Marko Vovchok, Nataliia Kobryns'ka, Ol'ha Kobylians'ka*. Edited by N.D. Kusaikina. Kharkiv: Prapor.
Mykosianchyk, Iuliia. 2004. "Problema vykhovannia v romani O. Kobylians'koi 'Apostol cherni.'" *Naukovyi visnyk chernivets'koho universytetu* 216–17:101–4.
"Natsional'nyi svitohliad Ol'hy Kobylians'koi." 1937. *Zhinoch dolia* no. 22:2.
"Nova povist' Ol'hy Kobyliansk'koi." 1936. *Svit molodi* no. 10:15.
Oleksiuk, Myroslav. 1970. *Borot'ba filosofs'kyh techii na zakhidnoukrains'kykh zemliah u 20–30kh rokakh XX stolittia*. L'viv: Vydavnytstvo l'vivs'koho universytetu.
Onats'kyj, Ievhen. 1928. "Lysty z Italii, 1." *Rozbudova Natsii* vol. 1, no. 3:93–6.
– ed. 1959. *Ukrains'ka mala entsyklopediia*. Buenos Aires: Administratsiia UAPC v Arhentyni.
Panchuk, El'pedefor. 1963. "Frahmenty iz spohadiv pro Ol'hu Kobylians'ku." Pohrebennyk 1963, 381–401.
– 1970. "Lysty Ol'hy Kobylians'koi do Avhusty Kokhanovs'koi." *Ukrains'ke literaturoznavstvo* 10:129–47.
– 1976. *Hirs'ka orlytsia: Spohad*. Uzhhorod: Karpaty.
Pavlenko, M, ed. 1923. *Khrestomatiia novoi ukrains'koi literatury*. Kharkiv: Rukh.
Pavlychko, Solomiia. 1999. *Dyskurs modernizmu v ukrains'kii literaturi*. Kyiv: Lybid'.
– 2000. *Natsionalism, seksual'nist', orientalism: Skladnyi svit Ahatanhela Kryms'koho*. Kyiv: Osnova.
– 2002. *Feminism*. Kyiv: Osnova.
– 2009. *Teoria literatury*. Kyiv: Osnovy.

Pavlyshyn, Marko. 2008. *Ol'ha Kobylians'ka: Prochytannia*. Kyiv: Akta.
Pihuliak, Ivan. 1922. "Khronolohichnyi pokazhchyk pysan' Ol'hy Kobylians'koi (1894–1922)." *Promin'* no. 2:41–2.
Pisarev, Dmitrii. 1955. "Bazarov." In *Sochineniia v chetyr'okh tomakh*. Vol. 2. Moscow: Gosudarstvennoe izdatel'stvo khudozhestvennoi literatury, 7–50.
– 1955. "Realisty." In *Sochineniia v chetyr'okh tomakh* . Vol. 3. Moscow: Gosudarstvennoe izdatel'stvo khudozhestvennoi literatury.
Pochyniuk, Liudmyla. 2005. *Ol'ha Kobylians'ka: Znaioma postat' u novomu rakursi*. Kamianets'-Podil's'kyi: Ministerstvo osvity i nauky Ukrainy, Kamianets'-Podil's'kyi derzhavnyi universytet.
Pohrebennyk, Fedir, ed. 1963. *Ol'ha Kobylians'ka v krytytsi ta spohadakh*. Kyiv: Derzhavne vydavnytstvo khudozhn'oi literatury.
– 1968. "Ol'ha Kobylians'ka." In *Istoriia ukrains'koi literatury u vos'my tomakh*. Vol. 5. Kyiv: Naukova dumka. 177–206.
– 1982. "Ol'ha Kobylians'ka pro sebe." In *Slova zvorushenoho sertsia: Shchodennyky, avtobiohrafii, lysty, statti ta spohady*. Edited by Fedir Pohrebennyk. Kyiv: Khudozhnie vydavnytstvo "Dnipro." 5–14.
– 1983. Forward. "Ol'ha Kobylians'ka." In *Ol'ha Kobylians'ka: Tvory v dvokh tomakh*. Kyiv: Khudozhnie vydavnytstvo "Dnipro." 5–20.
– 1999. "Ostap Luts'kyi pro Ol'hu Kobylians'ku." *Ukrains'ka mova ta literatura v shkoli* nos. 21–4:6.
Pohrebennyk, Iaroslava. 2005. *Nimets'komovnyi kontekst tvorchosti Ol'hy Kobylians'koi*. Chernivtsi: Ruta.
Popyk, Serhii. 1999. *Ukraintsi v Avstrii 1914–1918: Avstriis'ka polityka v ukrains'komu pytanni periodu Velykoi viiny*. Chernivtsi: Zoloti litavry.
Rudnyts'kyi, Mykhailo. 1936. "Ol'ha Kobylians'ka." In *Vid Myrnoho do Khvyl'ovoho*. L'viv: Naukove vydavnytstvo spilky "Dilo." 228–37.
Rymarenko, Iurii. 1974. *Burzhuaznyi natsionalism ta ioho 'teoriia' natsii*. Kyiv: Naukova dumka.
Shapoval, Mykyta. 1928. "Dorohyi druzhe, Ol'ho Iulianivno!" Kohut 249–52.
Shekhovtsov, Anton. 2015. "K voprosu ob ukrainskom natsional'no-vyzvol'nom fashizme (kratkie razmyshleniia nad stat'ioi Aleksandra Zaitseva)." http://anton-shekhovtsov.blogspot.com/2012/03/blog-post_14.html. 31 July 2015.
Shevchenko, Taras. 1985. *Tvory v piaty tomakh*. Kyiv: Khudozhnie vydavnytstvo "Dnipro."
– 2008. *Kobzar*. Donets'k: BAO.
Simovych, Vasyl'. 1942. "Budni i heroi Ol'hy Kobylians'koi." *Nashi dni* no. 6:5.
Slon'ovs'ka, Ol'ha. 2000. "Kramalni problemy povisti 'Apostol cherni' Ol'hy Kobylinas'koi." *Dyvoslovo* no. 11:32–5.
Smal'-Stots'kyi, Stepan. 1928. "Dorohyi zemliaku!" Kohut 1928, 277–88.

Sosnovs'kyi, Mykhailo. 1974. *Dmytro Dontsov: Politychnyi portret*. New York: Trident International.

Sriblians'kyi, Mykola. 1922. "Ol'ha Kobylians'ka (Z nahody 35–littia literaturnoi tvorchosti)." *Nova Ukraina* no. 1:29–31.

Stefanyk, Vasyl'. 2007. *Kaminnyi khrest*. Kyiv: Shkola.

Szota, Wiesław. 1973. *Droga do nikad. Dzialalnosc Organizacji Ukrainskich Nacjonalistow i jej Likwidacja w Polsce*. Warsaw: Wydawnictvo Ministerstwa Obrony Narodowej.

Tarnawski, Maxim. 2004. "Feminizm, modernizm i ukrains'ke zhinotstvo." In *Genderna perspektyva*. Edited by Vera Aheieva. Kyiv: Fakt, 204–17.

Tomashuk, Nykyfor. 1958. "Literaturno-estetychni pohliady O. Iu. Kobylians'koi rann'oho periodu." Lesyn et al. 1958, 43–70.

– 1959. *Rannee tvorchestvo Ol'gi Kobylianskoi, 1880–1900*. Chernovtsi: Chernivets'kyi derzhavnyi universytet.

– 1963. "Povist' O. Kobylians'koi 'Liudyna.'" Pohrebennyk 1963, 246–68.

– 1969a. *Ol'ha Kobylians'ka: Zhyttia i tvorchist'*. Kyiv: Khudozhnie vydavnytstvo "Dnipro."

– 1969b. "Roman O. Kobylians'koi 'Apostol cherni.'" *Pytannia maisternosti* no. 1:65–84.

Torzecki, Ryszard. 1972. *Kwestia ukrainska w polityce III Rzeszy, 1933–1945*. Warsaw: Książka i Wiedza.

Turbats'kyi Lev. 1963. Excerpt from "Literaturni zamitky." Pohrebennyk 1963, 41–3.

Turgenev, Ivan. 1988. *Sochineniia v triokh tomakh*. Moscow: Khudozhestvennaia literatura.

Turnerova, Tereza. 1963. "Pro ukrains'kykh zhinok." Pohrebennyk 1963, 298–300.

U pivstolitnikh zmahanniakh: Vybrani lysty do Kyryla Strudnyts'koho (1891–1941). 1993. Edited by Arkheohrafichna komisiia Akademii nauk Ukrainy. Kyiv: Naukova dumka.

Ukrainka, Lesia. 1963a. "Hirs'ka verkhovyna." Pohrebennyk 1963, 69–70.

– 1963b. "Iaki typy, iaki peizazhi." Pohrebennyk 1963, 75–6.

– 1963c. "Malorusskie pisateli na Bukovine." Pohrebennyk 1963, 76–83.

– 1963d. "Pravdyvyi literaturnyi talant." Pohrebennyk 1963, 30–1.

– 1963e. "Shmatok zhyttia." Pohrebennyk 1963, 162–3.

– 1975–9. *Zibrannia tvoriv u dvanadtsiaty tomakh*. Kyiv: Naukova dumka.

Ustyianovych, Ol'ha. 1928. "Spomyn." Kohut 211–14.

Vasylenko, V. 1928. "V zavorozhenim kruzi." *Krytyka: Zhurnal marksys'koi krytyky ta bibliografii* no. 1:68–85.

Verhanovs'ka, Olena. 1928. "Deshcho pro Ol'hu Kobylians'ku." *Literaturno-naukovyi visnyk* 95:43–51.

Vernyvolia, Vasyl'. 1923. Introduction. In "Bytva" by Ol'ha Kobylians'ka. Kyiv-Leipzig: Ukrains'ka nakladnia.
Vil'de, Iryna. 1937a. "Eva, Dora, i tetia Olia. 'Apostol cherni' O. Kobylians'koi." *Svit molodi* no. 2 :13–14.
– 1937b. "Novi knyzhky z-pid zhinochoho pera." *Zhinocha dolia* nos. 1–2:19.
Vozniuk, Volodymyr. 1983. *Pro Ol'hu Kobylians'ku: Novi materialy. Rozdumy. Znakhidky*. Kyiv: Khudozhnie vydavnytstvo "Dnipro."
– 1996. "Tsvit paporoti: Literaturno-hromads'ki ta osobysti vzaemyny Ol'hy Kobylians'koi ta Lesi Ukrainky." *Bukovyns'kyi zhurnal* nos. 1–2:53–82.
– 2004. "Do pytannia pro neuchast' O. Kobylians'koi v al'manasi 'Pershyi vinok.'" *Naukovyi visnyk chernivets'koho universytetu* 216–17:59–62.
– 2006. *Bukovyns'ki Adresy Ol'hy Kobylians'koi*. Chernivtsi: Knyhy XXI.
– 2012. *Ol'ha Kobylians'ka*. Kharkiv: Folio.
Vrublevs'ka, Valeriia. 2007. *Sharitka z Runhy*. Kyiv: Akadamiia.
Zabuzhko, Oksana. 2006. *Filosofiia ukrains'koi idei ta ievropeis'kyi kontekst: Frankivs'kyi period*. 2nd ed. Kyiv: Fakt.
– 2007. *Notre Dame d'Ukraine: Ukrainka v konflikti mifolohii*. Kyiv: Fakt.
Zeitsev, Oleksandr. 2012. "Ukrains'kyi natsionalizm ta italiis'kyi fashizm (1922–1939)." *Ukraina Moderna* (11 January 2012). http://bandera.lviv.ua/?p=1569. 1 August 2015.
– 2013. *Ukrainskyi integralnyi natsionalism (1920ti–1930ti roky): Narysy intelektual'noi istorii*. Kyiv: Krytyka.
Zhyzhchenko, Larysa. 2004. "Problema iak fakrot zhanrotvorennia v romani 'Apostol cherni.'" *Naukovyi visnyk chernivets'koho universytetu* 216–17:94–100.

Index

www.ingramcontent.com/pod-product-compliance
Lightning Source LLC
LaVergne TN
LVHW090153080826
844660LV00013B/788/J
* 9 7 8 1 4 4 2 6 3 0 7 7 2 *